Lecture Notes in Computer Science 10176

Commenced Publication in 1973
Founding and Former Series Editors:
Gerhard Goos, Juris Hartmanis, and Jan van Leeuwen

Editorial Board

More information about this series at http://www.springer.com/series/7411

Mohamed Ali Kaafar · Steve Uhlig
Johanna Amann (Eds.)

Passive and Active Measurement

18th International Conference, PAM 2017
Sydney, NSW, Australia, March 30–31, 2017
Proceedings

 Springer

Editors
Mohamed Ali Kaafar
CSIRO
Sydney, NSW
Australia

Johanna Amann
International Computer Science Institute
Berkeley, CA
USA

Steve Uhlig
Queen Mary University of London
London
UK

ISSN 0302-9743   ISSN 1611-3349   (electronic)
Lecture Notes in Computer Science
ISBN 978-3-319-54327-7   ISBN 978-3-319-54328-4   (eBook)
DOI 10.1007/978-3-319-54328-4

Library of Congress Control Number: 2017933285

LNCS Sublibrary: SL5 – Computer Communication Networks and Telecommunications

Printed on acid-free paper

This Springer imprint is published by Springer Nature
The registered company is Springer International Publishing AG
The registered company address is: Gewerbestrasse 11, 6330 Cham, Switzerland

Preface

The 18th edition of the Passive and Active Measurement conference (PAM) took place in Sydney, Australia, during March 30–31, 2017. The technical program included papers on a wide range of topics in Internet measurements, including performance and troubleshooting, the Web and applications, IPv6, security, and wireless.

PAM brings together both the network research and operations communities to discuss novel network measurement and analysis techniques, with a particular focus on early-stage research. PAM has traditionally focused on research and practical applications of specific network measurements. However, over the past few years, PAM has broadened its scope to encompass measurements of networked applications and systems, content distribution networks, online social networks, overlay networks, and more. Indeed, measurement technology is needed at all layers of the stack, e.g., for power profiling of hardware components, at the MAC/network/transport layers, as well as up the stack for application profiling and even to collect user feedback. Measurement technologies are being designed for the digital home, residential access networks, wireless and mobile access, enterprise, ISP, and data-center networks. PAM encourages a broad range of submissions across all these topics. We aim at understanding the role that measurement techniques can play in networked environments and applications, across different layers, and how they can serve as building blocks for broader measurement needs. This year PAM received 87 submissions originating from most continents, including North America, South America, Europe, Asia, the Pacific, and the Middle East, with authors from both academia and industry. The program was the result of a thorough review process, followed by a two-week-long discussion phase. In the first phase of the review process, papers were assigned to Technical Program Committee (TPC) members for review. The TPC consisted of 34 recognized researchers, with expertise covering the topics of interest to PAM, and were drawn mostly from academic and research institutes but also industry. Special attention was paid this year to the TPC member selection, so as to include a mix of early career and more established researchers, as well as to ensure diversity in the institutions and countries represented. The TPC worked diligently, writing many thoughtful, fair, and thorough reviews. Most papers received three reviews by the end of this stage. Also, throughout the review process, special attention was paid to conflicts (declared by the authors or not), to guarantee impartial reviewing. Indeed, more than half of the submitted papers had TPC conflicts. Papers in conflict with TPC members were marked as conflict in the conference management system and were reviewed only by non-conflicting TPC members.

At the end of the reviewing phase, marking the beginning of the discussion phase, each paper was then assigned a discussion lead among its assigned reviewers. The discussion leads were responsible for leading and moderating the discussion. By the end of the discussion phase, a consensual decision had been made by the reviewers. This led to 20 papers being accepted out of the 87 submitted. Some of the accepted papers were assigned a shepherd to ensure that the authors addressed the reviewers comments adequately.

The final program is the result of hard work of many individuals. We thank all the authors who submitted their work to PAM. We appreciate the effort that goes into producing a quality research paper and hope that authors received useful feedback on their submissions. As program chair, I would like to extend a big thank you to our hardworking TPC members for volunteering their time and expertise with passion.

Before closing this preface, our most sincere thanks also go to our local volunteers who devoted their time and effort to make the conference possible. We would also like to thank Prashanthi Jayawardhane and the local organization chairs, Wei Bao and Jonathan Chan, for their diligence and care in reviewing logistics and organizational details. We are also grateful to Ralph Holz, who was the finance chair, Johanna Amann as the publication chair, and Kanchana Thilakarathna, who served as the publicity chair.

We hope you enjoyed the proceedings.

March 2017   Dali Kaafar
                                                                 Steve Uhlig

Organization

General Chair

Mohamed Ali (Dali) Kaafar   Data61-CSIRO, Australia

Program Chair

Steve Uhlig   Queen Mary University of London, UK

Finance Chair

Ralph Holz   University of Sydney, Australia

Local Arrangements Chairs

Wei Bao   University of Sydney, Australia
Jonathan Chan   Data61-CSIRO, Australia

Web Chair

Guillaume Jourjon   Data61-CSIRO, Australia

Publicity Chair

Kanchana Thilakarathna   Data61-CSIRO, Australia

Publication Chair

Johanna Amann   ICSI, USA

Submission Chair

Timm Boettger   Queen Mary University of London, UK

Steering Committee

Fabio Ricciato   University of Salento, Italy
George Riley   Georgia Institute of Technology, USA
Ian Graham   Endace, New Zealand
Neil Spring   University of Maryland, USA
Nevil Brownlee   The University of Auckland, New Zealand
Nina Taft   Google, USA

Matthew Roughan	University of Adelaide, Australia
Rocky K.C. Chang	The Hong Kong Polytechnic University, Hong Kong, SAR China
Yong Liu	New York University, USA
Xenofontas Dimitropoulos	University of Crete, Greece
Mohamed Ali (Dali) Kaafar	Data61-CSIRO, Australia

Program Committee

Mark Allman	ICSI, USA
Gianni Antichi	University of Cambridge, UK
Fabian Bustamante	Northwestern University, USA
Alberto Dainotti	CAIDA, UC San Diego, USA
Xenofontas Dimitropoulos	FORTH and ETH Zurich, Switzerland
Amogh Dhamdhere	CAIDA/UC San Diego, USA
Benoit Donnet	University of Liege, Belgium
Anja Feldmann	TU Berlin, Germany
Kensuke Fukuda	National Institute of Informatics, Japan
Monia Ghobadi	Microsoft research, USA
Sergey Gorinsky	IMDEA, Spain
Ralph Holz	University of Sydney, Australia
Te-Yuan Huang	Netflix, USA
Thomas Karagiannakis	MSR, UK
Myungjin Lee	University of Edinburgh, UK
Youngseok Lee	Chungnam National University, Korea
Simon Leinen	SWITCH, Switzerland
Yong Li	Tsinghua University, China
Marco Mellia	Politecnico di Torino, Italy
Alan Mislove	Northeastern University, USA
Andrew Moore	University of Cambridge, UK
Cristel Pelsser	University of Strasbourg, France
Maria Papadopouli	FORTH, University of Crete
Costin Raiciu	Universitatea Politehnica din București, Romania
Michael Rabinovich	Case Western Reserve University, USA
Cigdem Sengul	Nominet, UK
Justine Sherry	UC Berkeley, USA
Georgios Smaragdakis	MIT/TU Berlin, Germany
Rade Stanojevic	Telefonica, Spain
Kanchana Thilakarathna	Data 61, Australia
Guillaume Urvoy-Keller	University of Nice, France
Narseo Vallina-Rodriguez	IMDEA Networks/ICSI, Spain
Gaogang Xie	ICT, CAS, China

Sponsoring Institutions

Data61-CSIRO, Australia
Akamai, USA
University of New South Wales, Australia
University of Sydney, Australia

Contents

Performance

Latency

Characterization and Troubleshooting

Wireless

IPv6

Understanding the Share of IPv6 Traffic in a Dual-Stack ISP

Enric Pujol[1,2(✉)], Philipp Richter[2], and Anja Feldmann[2]

[1] BENOCS GmbH, Berlin, Germany
[2] TU Berlin, Berlin, Germany
enric@inet.tu-berlin.de

Abstract. After almost two decades of IPv6 development and conse-
quent efforts to promote its adoption, the current global share of IPv6
traffic still remains low. Urged by the need to understand the reasons
that slow down this transition, the research community has devoted much
effort to characterize IPv6 adoption, i.e., *if* ISPs and content providers
enable IPv6 connectivity. However, little is known about *how much* the
available IPv6 connectivity is actually used and precisely which factors
determine whether data is exchanged over IPv4 or IPv6. To tackle this
question, we leverage a relevant vantage point: a dual-stack residential
broadband network. We study interactions between applications, devices,
equipment and services, and illustrate how these interactions ultimately
determine the IPv6 traffic share. Lastly, we elaborate on the potential
scenarios that dual-stack ISPs and content providers may confront during the Internet's transition to IPv6.

1 Introduction

The initial and ubiquitously deployed version 4 of the Internet Protocol has a
fundamental resource scarcity problem: it reached the limit of available, globally
unique, IP address space. As of today, IPv4 address scarcity has become a global
issue, forcing some ISPs to NAT large chunks of their customers [43] or even to
buy blocks of remaining free IPv4 address space on address markets [41]. IPv6,
which offers a vastly larger address space was intended to replace IPv4 long
before scarcity of IPv4 address blocks commenced. However, despite initiatives
by Internet governing bodies to promote IPv6 deployment [5], the transition to
IPv6 has been slow and challenging in production environments [7,16]. As of
today, there is no clear consensus about when IPv6 will really "hit the breaking
point", i.e., when IPv6 will become the preferred interconnectivity option on
the Internet. The research and operations communities have put substantial
effort into measuring and tracking IPv6 deployment with the goal of assessing
this transition (e.g., [19]). However, current statistics show a disparity between
two adoption metrics: *connectivity* and *traffic share*. For example, while Google
reports optimistic *connectivity* adoption rates as high as 16% for end hosts [4]
as of January 2017, the IPv6 *traffic share* at major Internet eXchange Points
(IXPs) still ranges between 1–2% [2]. The comparably low share of IPv6 traffic is

© Springer International Publishing AG 2017
M.A. Kaafar et al. (Eds.): PAM 2017, LNCS 10176, pp. 3–16, 2017.
DOI: 10.1007/978-3-319-54328-4_1

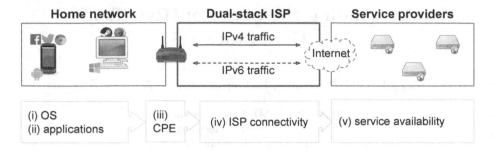

Fig. 1. IPv6 traffic in dual-stack networks. Barriers are present at home networks (operating systems, applications and CPEs), ISPs (offered DSL connectivity), and at service providers.

not only one of the main reasons for disappointment regarding the pace of IPv6 adoption, but has also fueled a different interconnection structure among ISPs. The provider hierarchy in the IPv6 Internet shows vastly different properties compared to that of IPv4 [23], i.e., the one ISP offering free IPv6 tunnels has the largest customer cone in the IPv6 Internet, whereas Tier-1 ISPs with worldwide backbones are less prominent in this hierarchy.

We argue that increasing IPv6 traffic shares will eventually provide the incentives for ISPs to provision proper IPv6 infrastructure, establish genuine interconnectivity, and finally make IPv6 the first-class citizen on the Internet. However, to exchange data over IPv6, all components on the path from a source to a destination need to fully support IPv6 (see Fig. 1). This includes *(i)* end-user devices and operating systems supporting IPv6, *(ii)* applications making proper use of the available connectivity options (see [49]), *(iii)* customer premises hardware (CPEs) supporting and providing IPv6 to the home network [3,48], *(iv)* the ISP assigning IPv6 to the subscribers CPEs [20], and finally *(v)* content providers enabling their services over IPv6 [34]. Moreover, even if all of the above conditions apply, i.e., all components *support* IPv6, a second dimension of the problem is whether IPv6 will be preferred over IPv4, as modern applications employ a technique named *"happy eyeballs"* to *choose* between IPv4 and IPv6 according to the current network conditions [51].

Determined to investigate the reasons that refrain the increase of IPv6 traffic on the Internet, we study this problem from the perspective of 12.9 K subscribers of a dual-stack ISP. This vantage point gives us a unique opportunity to analyze the interactions between applications, devices, equipment and services, and how they eventually influence the share of IPv6 traffic. Our main findings can be summarized as follows:

(i) Even though this ISP supports IPv6 connectivity, a large number of subscribers can not *use* IPv6. While in some few cases the ISP does not provide IPv6 connectivity to its subscribers, more often the CPE limits IPv6 connectivity.

(ii) Consequently, IPv6-ready services exchange a significant amount of traffic over IPv4. IPv4-only speaking devices and fallback mechanisms further increase the share of IPv4 traffic for these services. We observe, on the other hand, a strong *intent* for IPv6 traffic that IPv4-only services are not yet ready to correspond to.

(iii) Due to dual-stack applications' preference for IPv6, dual-stack networks could face a rapid and substantial increase of the IPv6 traffic share if only a few major service providers enable IPv6 for high-traffic domains.

The rest of this manuscript is organized as follows: Section 2 summarizes related work. We describe our methodology in Sect. 3 and introduce our dataset in Sect. 4. Section 5 presents our findings. We discuss implications and limitations of our work in Sect. 6, and conclude with Sect. 7.

2 Related Work

The research community has called for data that can help tracking the evolution of IPv6 [17]. Some works have reported the IPv6 traffic share at multiple vantage points in the Internet. In 2008, most IPv6 traffic at a tier-1 ISP in the US was DNS and ICMP [29]. While initiatives such as the "World IPv6 day" in 2011 ignited the increase of IPv6 traffic at various vantage points [46], by 2013 the share of IPv6 traffic at European IXPs or at 260 network providers was still below 1% [19,42]. Nonetheless, every year IPv6 traffic experiences a many-fold increase [19]. This development has encouraged studies on dual-stack networking performance [11,16,38,40], active measurements of the Internet's IPv6 infrastructure [13,32] and analyses of the AS-level topology [21,23]. Moreover, a large body of literature has focused on measuring IPv6 adoption among ISPs and service providers [18,19,21,23,28,29]. Some works seek to understand the root causes that slow down IPv6 adoption and find a slower pace of adoption at the edge compared to core networks [21], or poor IPv6 quality in the early days of this transition [37]. As of today, the IPv6 control and data planes are—when applicable—*almost* on par with IPv4 [31], while both control planes show signs of convergence [23]. In parallel to the research community, standardization bodies have invested decades to address IPv6-related aspects. Relevant to our work are fallback mechanisms for dual-stack applications [51] (*happy eyeballs*) and their implementations (see e.g., [6,26,27,47]). We complement this body of work with a passive measurement study at a dual-stack ISP to shed light on why some data exchanges occur over IPv4 instead of IPv6.

3 Methodology

The focus of our study is the traffic at a residential broadband network of a dual-stack ISP. As shown in Fig. 1, IPv4 and IPv6 traffic coexist at such a vantage point. Whether IPv4 or IPv6 is used depends on a large variety of factors mentioned earlier in Sect. 1. Hence, a dual-stack ISP presents a unique opportunity to study the interactions of this ecosystem and its influence on the share of IPv6 traffic. To this end, we first need to discover the connectivity options of the two engaged parties, i.e., the subscribers (the client side) and the service providers (the server side). With this information in hand we can proceed to study which traffic is exchanged over which protocol, and why.

3.1   Measuring IPv6 Connectivity

Connectivity of subscribers ("client side"). Broadband network providers typically rely on Remote Authentication Dial-In User Service (RADIUS [44]) to assign IP addresses to subscribers. With this protocol, CPEs obtain IP addresses, usually a single IPv4 address that multiplexes devices (NAT). This protocol specification also supports the delegation of IPv6 addresses to subscribers [8,20, 45]. If the CPE receives an IPv6 prefix assignment, we say that the subscriber obtains IPv6 connectivity from the ISP. Traffic statistics later tell us whether the subscriber's devices make actual use of this assigned IPv6 prefix.

Since not all devices within home networks support IPv6, the raw traffic statistics are necessary but not sufficient to infer if a device within a subscriber's premise can use IPv6. We use AAAA DNS requests as an indicator for the presence of IPv6-speaking devices. Most dual-stack applications follow the *happy-eyeballs* proposed standard (see [51]), and issue A as well as AAAA DNS requests. If the requested service is available over IPv6, the device attempts to connect simultaneously to two addresses contained in the DNS resource records (RRs); one being IPv6 and the other IPv4. An application that adheres to the example implementation then establishes two TCP connections and uses the one that completed the handshake faster. Some implementations introduce a preference towards IPv6. For example, Apple devices issue an IPv6 connection immediately after a successful AAAA request if the A response did not arrive already, or if historical RTT data suggests a difference > 25 ms [47]. Given that most DNS clients issue AAAA requests first [36], some dual-stack devices do not always attempt a connection over both IPv4 and IPv6 although they issue requests for both RRs.

One important fact regarding IPv6-speaking devices is that many resolver libraries avoid suppressing AAAA requests if there is no global IPv6 connectivity, but just link-local, i.e., within the home network. The rationale is that doing so can lead to undesired situations [1]. Thus, we can use this information to further identify CPEs that offer link-local IPv6 connectivity even if the ISP does not provide IPv6 connectivity to them.

Connectivity of services ("server side"). In this paper we use the term service to refer to content and functionality that is available on the Internet via a *Fully-Qualified Domain Name* (FQDN). For example, at www.google.com we can find a search service as well as plain content. If the network infrastructure that hosts a service supports IPv6, a service provider willing to make its services available over IPv6 just needs to update the corresponding DNS AAAA and PTR resource records (RRs) [34]. Henceforth, we can analyze DNS traffic to infer if a service is IPv6-ready by looking for non-empty AAAA responses in our traces. However, as we may not be able to observe all AAAA RRs (e.g., if the clients are not IPv6 enabled), we complement passive data with active measurements, i.e., we actively request AAAA records for FQDNs found in our trace.[1]

3.2 From IPv6 Connectivity to IPv6 Usage

Now that we are aware of the *connectivity* options of subscribers and services (IPv4 and/or IPv6), we proceed to study the exchanged traffic. To accomplish this, we first need to annotate each flow in our trace with the respective subscriber and service.

Matching flows to names. One of the building blocks for our methodology is the ability to associate the DNS requests issued by an IP address to the network flows it generates, i.e., reproduce the mapping between FQDNs and server IPs for each subscriber. This problem has been already explored (see, e.g., [12,35,39]), and we extend it to include the connectivity information. It is important to notice that for dual-stack networks the IP addresses of the flows and those of the DNS traffic are not necessarily the same. Therefore, we cannot directly use the source IP of a DNS request as a *rendezvous*. Instead, we keep track of the IPv4 and IPv6 addresses assigned to each subscriber. Another caveat (as reported in related work) is that we need to update this mapping according to the TTL values of the DNS response RRs. We are aware that related studies have reported violations of the TTL field by clients [14,35]. For example, Callahan et al. [14] observe that 13% of the TCP connections use expired records and attribute it to security features present in modern Web browsers. In this work we opt for a conservative approach and strictly use the TTL expiration values. In addition, we do not consider negatively cached responses, e.g., a service without a AAAA RR. Our rationale is that although negative answers should, in principle, be cached according to the SOA record [10], some resolvers do not respect this [30]. The immediate consequence is that at times we will not observe a AAAA request for services without AAAA RR and may mis-attribute it to a device that does not support IPv6.

Annotating flows. We next annotate each flow with the following information: *(i)* whether the ISP has delegated an IPv6 prefix to the subscriber's CPE, *(ii)* the FQDN associated with the flow, where possible, and *(iii)* if the subscriber issued an A and/or a AAAA DNS request. After collecting the trace we extend this annotation with the following information: *(iv)* if the subscriber makes use of its assigned IPv6 prefix at all, and with *(v)* the connectivity options for the FQDN i.e., whether the service is available over IPv4 and/or IPv6.

4 Dataset

The dataset used throughout this study covers all IP traffic generated by 12.9 K DSL subscribers of a residential broadband network during a period of

---

[1] We conducted these additional measurements shortly after the data collection.

Table 1. Total traffic over IPv4/IPv6 and TCP/UDP.

Trace	#bytes	#flows
TCP$_{v4}$	80.5%	53.1%
TCP$_{v6}$	10.7%	4.7%
UDP$_{v4}$	7.4%	18.2%
UDP$_{v6}$	1.1%	21.7%
total	64.5T	356.2M

Table 2. Traffic contribution partitioned by the state of IPv4/IPv6 connectivity of subscribers and service providers.

Service Side	Subscriber Side			total
	IPv4-only	*IPv6-inactive*	*IPv6-active*	
IPv4-only	5.4%	20.1%	22.4%	47.9%
IPv6-ready	3.2%	9.2%	15.4%	27.8%
IPv6-only	0.0%	0.0%	< 0.1%	< 0.1%
Unknown	3.4%	8.8%	12.1%	24.2%
total	11.9%	38.1%	49.8%	100%

45 h in winter 15/16. We implemented a custom tool built on top of the *libtrace* library [9] to produce two streams of data from raw network data. The first stream consists of packet summaries, including packet size, SRC and DST IP addresses, and port numbers. For TCP packets, we also save TCP flags, SEQ, and ACK numbers. The second stream consists of full-sized packets of DNS traffic (UDP port 53). We then process our packet summaries to obtain flow-level statistics. Namely, we aggregate the packet summaries into the 5 tuple and expire inactive flows after 3600s. For TCP flows we also compute the time difference between the SYN packet and the SYN ACK packet to estimate TCP handshake times.[2] Given the location of our monitor within the aggregation network, these "handshakes" only capture the wide-area delays (backbone RTTs) and do not include delays introduced by the access- and home network (see [33] for details on the technique). Finally, we remark that the dataset was collected, processed, and analyzed at an isolated and secured segment infrastructure of the ISP. The toolset operates in an automated fashion and anonymizes line ids and addresses before writing the annotated flows to the disk. Table 1 summarizes the dataset collected for this study.

DNS transactions. We processed 141.9M DNS transactions, where we denote a transaction as an A or a AAAA request with a valid response. 69.6% of these entries are of type A and 30.4% of type AAAA. Out of these DNS transactions, 0.6% and 36.0% of the A and -respectively- AAAA requests could not be resolved (empty response). The high ratio of unresolved AAAA requests is the result of content that is indeed requested for IPv6, but still not accessible over IPv6 (see Sect. 2). 39% of the A requests were sent over IPv6, and 28% of the AAAA requests over IPv4.

Flow-level statistics. Table 1 shows a breakdown of the contribution of TCP and UDP traffic, dissected by IP version. Unsurprisingly, TCP$_{v4}$ dominates in terms of traffic volume. However, the share of IP$_{v6}$ is substantial (11.9%) especially when compared to older measurement studies at other vantage points [19,46]. Web traffic sums up to 86.6% of the trace volume (13.5%

---

[2] We exclude flows with retransmissions of packets with the SYN flag set.

over IPv6).[3] We find that QUIC contributes 2.8% of the overall trace volume (39.5% over IPv6). Considering the relative UDP contributions over IPv4 and IPv6, we see that the share of UDP_{v6} flows is well above the UDP_{v4} share. A closer look reveals that this bias is introduced by DNS traffic: DNS accounts for 71.0% of all UDP flows and 75.3% of DNS flows are sent over IPv6.

Classification coverage. We are able to associate up to 76.1% of the traffic to services using the flow-classification approach described in Sect. 3.2. While our coverage statistics are consistent with the base results reported in [35], we remark that ours are lower than related methods because our method *(i)* does not use a warm-up period to account for already cached DNS RRs, *(ii)* relies on each subscriber's own DNS traffic, and *(iii)* adheres to the TTL values included in DNS responses.

5   A Dual-Stack ISP Perspective on IPv6 Traffic

5.1   The Subscribers' Side

We find three classes of DSLs among the 12.9 K subscriber lines of this vantage point: *(i) IPv4-only*: lines that do not get IPv6 connectivity from the ISP (17.3%), *(ii) IPv6-inactive*: lines provisioned with IPv6 connectivity but no IPv6 traffic (29.9%), and *(iii) IPv6-active:* lines with IPv6 connectivity as well as IPv6 traffic (52.9%).

IPv4-only **subscribers.** This set of lines corresponds to subscribers for which the ISP has still not activated IPv6 connectivity (e.g., old contracts). They contribute 12.0% to the overall trace volume. 26.6% of their traffic is exchanged with services that are available over IPv6. We notice that some devices issue AAAA DNS requests, most likely because some CPEs create a link-local IPv6 network. In fact, for 11.6% of the traffic related to IPv6 services we observe a AAAA request. This first observation is relevant for *IPv6-adoption* studies, as it indicates that in some cases DNS traffic may not well reflect the actual connectivity. This shows that many devices are already prepared to use IPv6 connectivity, waiting for the ISP to take proper action.

IPv6-inactive **subscribers.** For 36.1% of the DSLs we do not observe any IPv6 traffic, even though the ISP assigned IPv6 prefixes to the CPEs. One explanation is that the CPE has not been configured to enable IPv6 on the home network (see e.g., [22,24,50]). Thus, the ISP provides IPv6 connectivity, but the end-devices only have internal IPv4 addresses (e.g., RFC1918), assigned from the CPE. Consequently, we find that only 1.7% of the traffic from these subscribers can be associated with a AAAA request, likely because most devices suppress AAAA requests in the absence of a link-local IPv6 address. Other, less likely, explanations are that none of the devices present at premises during the trace collection support IPv6 (e.g., Windows XP), or the subscribers do not contact

---

[3] TCP traffic on ports 80 and 8080 (HTTP), 443 (HTTPS), and UDP traffic on port 443 (QUIC).

services available over IPv6. The latter is unlikely, as 24.1% of the traffic in this subscriber class is exchanged with IPv6-ready services.

***IPv6-active* subscribers.** Subscribers in this category actively use the provided IPv6 connectivity. The share of IPv6 traffic for these subscribers is almost twice as high (21.5%) when compared to the overall trace (11.9%). When only considering traffic exchanged between IPv6-active subscribers and services that are indeed available over IPv6, the ratio is even higher (69.6%). Yet, that leaves us with 30% of the traffic exchanged between two IPv6-enabled hosts being carried over IPv4. This can be caused either by end-user devices not requesting content over IPv6 (no AAAA RR) or end-user devices choosing IPv4 over IPv6 because of their happy eyeball implementation. Indeed, when only considering traffic for which the client requested both IPv4 and IPv6 (A and AAAA), the share of IPv6 in this category raises up to 85.1%. This is an important observation for service providers and operators, as it implies that enabling IPv6 can increase the share of IPv6 traffic from/in dual-stack networks rapidly.

5.2   The Service Providers' Side

We next shift our focus from subscribers to services (FQDNs). Similar to the previous section, we define three categories. We say that a service is *IPv4-only* if it only has a valid non-empty A RR. *IPv6-only* services are those which only have a valid non-empty AAAA RR. A service that is *IPv6-ready* has valid and non-empty A and AAAA RRs. We report in Table 2 how these three categories of services contribute to the total traffic and intersect them with the three subscriber categories.

***IPv4-only* services (only A RR).** As expected, this set of services dominates the share of traffic (47.9%). However, for 36.2% of this traffic we observe a preceding AAAA request from the subscriber requesting the content, which implies that this traffic has the potential to be served over IPv6 if the corresponding service providers enable IPv6.

***IPv6-only* services (only AAAA RR).** We find around 500 services that *appear to be* available only over IPv6, accounting for less than 0.1% of the traffic. Manual inspection reveals that most of them are mere connectivity checkers. Some service providers add strings to host names, which may appear as an IPv6-only service (e.g., both *host.domain.org* and *hostv6.domain.org* have a AAAA RR, but only the former has an A RR).

***IPv6-ready* services (A and AAAA RRs).** These services generate a significant amount of traffic (27.8%). However, as many subscribers from this dual-stack network cannot use IPv6, the actual share of IPv6 traffic within this class of services is only 38.6%.

5.3   IP Traffic: Barriers and Intent for IPv6

As shown in Table 2, the upper bounds for IPv6 traffic share when looking at services and subscribers independently is roughly 2 and respectively 4 times

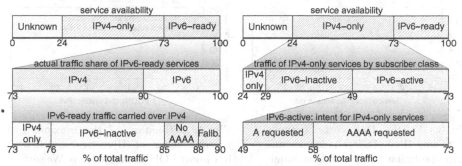

(a) **IPv6 barriers.** Top: service availability. (b) **IPv6 intent.** Top: service availability. Center: IP version that carries *IPv6-ready* content. Bottom: Reason why traffic is carried over IPv4 instead of IPv6.
ter: Breakdown of *IPv4-only* traffic by subscribers' type. Bottom: traffic from *IPv6-active* subscribers to *IPv4-only* services.

Fig. 2. Barriers and intent for IPv6 traffic in a dual-stack ISP.

the actual IPv6 traffic share. At the same time, not all traffic in the cross-product of *IPv6-active* subscribers and *IPv6-ready* services is carried over IPv6. We next proceed to study the root causes that lead to this lower-than-possible IPv6 share. To this end, we use the term *IPv6 barriers* to reason about traffic to and from IPv6-ready services, which is carried over IPv4 instead of IPv6. Correspondingly, we use the term *IPv6 intent* to reason about traffic to and from IPv4-only services, of which some portion could be carried over IPv6, as requested by the subscribers.

IPv6 barriers. Figure 2(a) illustrates why traffic related to *IPv6-ready* services is exchanged over IPv4. On the top of the figure we show a bar summarizing all traffic in the trace according to the service availability. As previously stated, 27.8% of the traffic relates to services available over IPv6. Nevertheless, the majority of it (61.4%) is actually exchanged over IPv4 (see middle bar). In the bottom bar we illustrate why data is exchanged over IPv4 instead of IPv6. Most of this traffic (70.5%) is carried over IPv4 because the subscribers do not use IPv6 connectivity at all (*IPv4-only* and *IPv6-inactive*). We make two observations for the remainder of this traffic (which is generated by *IPv6-active* subscribers). The majority of it has no associated AAAA request, which can primarily be attributed to end-devices that do not support IPv6: they do not issue AAAA requests. For another 40% of the IPv4 traffic from *IPv6-active* subscribers to *IPv6-ready* services we observe a AAAA request. These are likely flows generated by devices that fall back to IPv4 as a result of the *happy-eyeballs* algorithm.

IPv6 intent. Figure 2(b) illustrates what fraction of the traffic of *IPv4-only* services (top bar) could be carried over IPv6. While the bar in the middle depicts how much of this traffic they exchange with each subscriber category, the bottom bar shows the traffic characteristics for the *IPv6-active* subscribers. In particular, we observe that end-user devices in the *IPv6-active* group issue AAAA requests

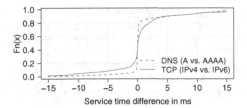
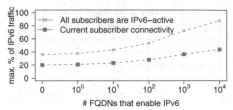

Fig. 3. ECDF: Differences between IPv6 and IPv4 TCP handshake and DNS resolution times per host name. Positive values indicate longer transactions for IPv6 and AAAA RRs.

Fig. 4. Estimation of the maximum *possible* share of IPv6 traffic when IPv4-only FQDNs enable IPv6. We sort FQDNs by their contribution in terms of bytes.

for 62.5% of this traffic. Thus, there is a strong intent for IPv6 traffic that cannot yet be satisfied by the service side. In fact, our measurement likely even underestimates this value because we do not take into account negatively-cached AAAA RRs (see Sect. 3.2).

Happy eyeballs. Given that part of the traffic carried over IPv4, which could be carried over IPv6, can be attributed to (un-)happy eyeballs, we now study two metrics concerning dual-stack applications and devices, i.e., the RTT estimates and the DNS resolution times (see [47]). Our RTT estimate corresponds to the backbone RTTs (Sect. refsec:dataset). For the DNS resolution time (A vs. AAAA), we only consider transactions with non-empty responses and for which we find just one request and one response in the same UDP flow. We aggregate these per host name and compute the median only for those host names with at least 10 samples. Generally, dual-stack services offer similar conditions, i.e., around 80% of the values are within a range of 10 ms. Under such conditions, happy-eyeball implementations likely select IPv6, as indicated by our earlier results. This observation is important for service providers transitioning to IPv6, as it implies that after enabling IPv6 they can expect a significant increase of IPv6 traffic if they already exchange high volumes of data with dual-stack consumer networks. We note that the final *choice* of connectivity is subject to how different implementations adapt to network conditions [6,26,27].

5.4 Case Studies

We next describe two case studies: a large search provider and a large CDN. Our case studies illustrate two opposite facets of the transition to IPv6. These providers contribute together to 35.7% of the overall and 73.1% of the IPv6 traffic. They both operate various Autonomous Systems (ASNs) as well as caches inside ISPs. To identify their traffic, we rely on the origin ASN as derived from the IP addresses in the flows. To identify traffic from caches, we obtain a list of the Fully Qualified Domain Names (FQDNs) associated with IP addresses managed by these ASNs.

A large search provider. Our first case study is a service provider that actively supports and promotes IPv6. 37.6% of its traffic is IPv6, and it alone contributes 69.9% of all IPv6 traffic in the trace. After annotating 91.8% of the traffic with FQDNs, we corroborate that almost all content –not all traffic relates to search services– requested by users at this vantage point is available over IPv6 (98.7%). *IPv4-only* and *IPv6-inactive* subscribers generate 74.1% of the IPv4 traffic while the share of IPv6 traffic for the *IPv6-active* subscribers is 70.5%. This observation suggests that for this provider the connectivity of the subscribers is the main obstacle for the increase in IPv6 traffic.

A large CDN. We are able to annotate 84.7% of the CDN traffic with FQDNs. Only 2.5% of the traffic is carried over IPv6, and only 3.3% of the CDN traffic relates to *IPv6-ready* services. This implies that here the bottleneck for IPv6 is the server side, since only 2.1% of the content requested with a AAAA is actually exchanged over IPv6.

Transition to IPv6. Service providers willing to transition to IPv6 need to update the corresponding DNS RRs. To illustrate the potential impact of this process on the share of IPv6 traffic, we next concentrate on *IPv4-only* services. We present in Fig. 4 an upper bound for the share of IPv6 traffic when the top traffic-contributing FQDNs enable IPv6. We produce two estimates. The first one assumes that there are no changes in the subscribers connectivity. The second one assumes that all subscribers become *IPv6-active*. Note, we do not take into consideration 24.2% of the bytes in the trace as we cannot associate them with a service. Enabling IPv6 connectivity for all subscribers immediately doubles the upper bound for the IPv6 traffic share (almost 40%). However, to reach IPv6 traffic shares close to 90%, more than 10 K FQDNs need to enable IPv6 connectivity. That said, and as shown earlier in this paper, *IPv4-only* devices and *happy-eyeballs* fallbacks to IPv4 can reduce this share.

6   Discussion

We are well-aware that our vantage point is not representative of the Internet as a whole. While this particular ISP promotes IPv6 connectivity, others opt to deploy Carrier Grade NATs to combat IPv4 address scarcity. Yet, we argue that our observations most likely apply to other dual-stack ISPs as well (e.g., [25]). Hence, these observations can aid ISPs and service providers by providing guidance on how to provision for IPv6 as well as insights on traffic dynamics during the transition phase. For example, *IPv4-only* service providers could exchange up to 30% of their traffic over IPv6 if they enable IPv6. By contrast, although 53% of the IPv4 traffic to *IPv6-ready* services involves subscribers whose CPEs most likely do not provide IPv6 connectivity to their home network, *happy eyeballs* usually *chooses* IPv6 over IPv4 (85%). We posit that IPv6 traffic shares will likely be subject to sudden increments when CPE devices enable IPv6 support in the home network. Virtual CPEs [15] could make it easier for operators to transition their subscribers to IPv6 and troubleshoot IPv6-related problems.

Hence, avenues for future work include a closer investigation of issues specific to devices and applications as well as a characterization of *happy-eyeballs* fallbacks to IPv4.

7   Conclusion

The Internet's transition to IPv6 is a tremendous operational effort. The research community supports this effort by providing measurements of *IPv6 adoption* across the Internet. In this work, we push the envelope further and study a lesser-known aspect: *IPv6 usage*. We reveal obstacles hampering IPv6 traffic in dual-stack ISPs, including CPE devices not supporting IPv6, applications falling back to IPv4, and a broad lack of IPv6 support among service providers. In spite of such obstacles, we report a pronounced increase, intent, and potential for growth regarding IPv6. We expect that increasing IPv6 traffic shares will eventually make IPv6 the first-class citizen of the Internet.

Acknowledgments. This work was partially supported by Leibniz Prize project funds of DFG - German Research Foundation (FKZ FE 570/4-1).

References

1. Current implementation of AI ADDRCONFIG considered harmful. https://goo.gl/prXWfz
2. Amsterdam Internet Exchange IPv6 Traffic (2016). https://goo.gl/ajS6PC
3. ARIN IPv6 Wiki: Broadband CPE (2016). https://goo.gl/Wydr3Q
4. IPv6 - Google (2016). https://goo.gl/Tl4cUZ
5. World IPv6 Launch (2016). https://goo.gl/hOoXNo
6. Aben, E.: Hampering Eyeballs - Observations on Two "Happy Eyeballs" Implementations. https://goo.gl/qUW6s
7. Aben, E., Trenaman, N., Kiessling, A., Wilhelm, R.: Lost Starts - Why Operators Switch off IPv6 (2016). NANOG 66
8. Aboba, B., Zorn, G., Mitton, D.: RADIUS and IPv6. RFC 3162 (2001)
9. Alcock, S., Lorier, P., Nelson, R.: Libtrace: a packet capture and analysis library. ACM CCR **42**(2), 42–48 (2012)
10. Andrews, M.: Negative Caching of DNS Queries (DNS NCACHE). RFC 2308 (1998)
11. Bajpai, V., Schönwälder, J.: IPv4 versus IPv6 - Who connects faster? In: IFIP Networking (2015)
12. Bermudez, I.N., Mellia, M., Munafò, M., Keralapura, R., Nucci, A.: DNS to the rescue: discerning content and services in a tangled web. In: ACM IMC (2012)
13. Beverly, R., Luckie, M., Mosley, L., Claffy, K.: Measuring and characterizing IPv6 router availability. In: Mirkovic, J., Liu, Y. (eds.) PAM 2015. LNCS, vol. 8995, pp. 123–135. Springer, Heidelberg (2015). doi:10.1007/978-3-319-15509-8_10
14. Callahan, T., Allman, M., Rabinovich, M.: On modern DNS behavior and properties. ACM CCR **43**(3), 7–13 (2013)
15. Cantó, R., López, R.A., Folgueira, J.L., López, D.R., Elizondo, A.J., Gamero, R.: Virtualization of residential customer premise equipment. Lessons learned in Brazil vCPE trial. Inf. Technol. **57**(5), 285–294 (2015)

16. Cho, K., Luckie, M., Huffaker, B.: Identifying IPv6 network problems in the dual-stack world. In: ACM SIGCOMM Network Troubleshooting Workshop (2004)
17. Claffy, K.: Tracking IPv6 evolution: data we have and data we need. ACM CCR **41**(3), 43–48 (2011)
18. Colitti, L., Gunderson, S.H., Kline, E., Refice, T.: Evaluating IPv6 adoption in the internet. In: Krishnamurthy, A., Plattner, B. (eds.) PAM 2010. LNCS, vol. 6032, pp. 141–150. Springer, Heidelberg (2010). doi:10.1007/978-3-642-12334-4_15
19. Czyz, J., Allman, M., Zhang, J., Iekel-Johnson, S., Osterweil, E., Bailey, M.: Measuring IPv6 adoption. In: ACM SIGCOMM (2014)
20. Dec, W., Sarikaya, B., Zorn, G., Miles, D., Lourdelet, B.: RADIUS Attributes for IPv6 Access Networks. RFC 6911 (2013)
21. Dhamdhere, A., Luckie, M., Huffaker, B., Claffy, K., Elmokashfi, A., Aben, E.: Measuring the deployment of IPv6: topology. Routing and performance. In: ACM IMC (2012)
22. Drake, K.: You have IPv6. Turn it on (2016). https://goo.gl/maSZRM
23. Giotsas, V., Luckie, M., Huffaker, B., Claffy, K.: IPv6 AS Relationships, Clique, and Congruence. In: PAM (2015)
24. Gysi, M.: Residential IPv6 at Swisscom, an Overview (2012). https://goo.gl/QO2SZF
25. Gysi, M.: Status of Swisscom's IPv6 activities, outlook and opportunities. In: Swiss IPv6 Council IPv6 Business Conference (2016)
26. Huston, G.: Bemused Eyeballs (2012). https://labs.apnic.net/?p=188
27. Huston, G.: Revisiting Apple and IPv6 (2015). https://goo.gl/qjKdv5
28. Karir, M., Huston, G., Michaelson, G., Bailey, M.: Understanding IPv6 populations in the wild. In: Roughan, M., Chang, R. (eds.) PAM 2013. LNCS, vol. 7799, pp. 256–259. Springer, Heidelberg (2013). doi:10.1007/978-3-642-36516-4_27
29. Karpilovsky, E., Gerber, A., Pei, D., Rexford, J., Shaikh, A.: Quantifying the extent of IPv6 deployment. In: Moon, S.B., Teixeira, R., Uhlig, S. (eds.) PAM 2009. LNCS, vol. 5448, pp. 13–22. Springer, Heidelberg (2009). doi:10.1007/978-3-642-00975-4_2
30. Lagerholm, S., Roselli, J.: Negative caching of DNS records. Technical report, Microsoft (2015)
31. Livadariu, I., Elmokashfi, A., Dhamdhere, A.: Characterizing IPv6 control and data plane stability. In: IEEE INFOCOM (2016)
32. Luckie, M., Beverly, R., Brinkmeyer, W., Claffy,K.: Speedtrap: internet-scale IPv6 alias resolution. In: ACM IMC (2013)
33. Maier, G., Feldmann, A., Paxson, V., Allman, M.: On dominant characteristics of residential broadband internet traffic. In: ACM IMC (2009)
34. McConachie, A.: How To Make Your Website Available Over IPv6 (2014). https://goo.gl/Vs2IuO
35. Mori, T., Inoue, T., Shimoda, A., Sato, K., Ishibashi, K., Goto, S.: SFMap: inferring services over encrypted web flows using dynamical domain name graphs. In: TMA (2015)
36. Morishita, Y., Jinmei, T.: Common Misbehavior Against DNS Queries for IPv6 Addresses. RFC 4074 (2005)
37. Nikkhah, M., Guérin, R.: Migrating the Internet to IPv6: An Exploration of the When and Why. IEEE ToN (2015)
38. Nikkhah, M., Guérin, R., Lee, Y., Woundy, R.: Assessing IPv6 through web access a measurement study and its findings. In: ACM CoNEXT (2011)
39. Plonka, D., Barford, P.: Context-aware clustering of DNS query traffic. In: ACM IMC (2008)

40. Plonka, D., Barford, P.: Assessing performance of internet services on IPv6. In: IEEE ISSC (2013)
41. Richter, P., Allman, M., Bush, R., Paxson, V.: A primer on IPv4 scarcity. ACM CCR **45**(2), 21–31 (2015)
42. Richter, P., Chatzis, N., Smaragdakis, G., Feldmann, A., Willinger, W.: Distilling the internet's application mix from packet-sampled traffic. In: PAM (2015)
43. Richter, P., Wohlfart, F., Vallina-Rodriguez, N., Allman, M., Bush, R., Feldmann, A., Kreibich, C., Weaver, N., Paxson, V.: A multi-perspective analysis of carrier-grade NAT deployment. In: ACM IMC (2016)
44. Rigney, C., Willens, S., Rubens, A., Simpson, W.: Remote Authentication Dial In User Service (RADIUS). RFC 2865 (2000)
45. Salowey, J., Droms, R.: RADIUS Delegated-IPv6-Prefix Attribute. RFC 4818 (2007)
46. Sarrar, N., Maier, G., Ager, B., Sommer, R., Uhlig, S.: Investigating IPv6 traffic. In: Taft, N., Ricciato, F. (eds.) PAM 2012. LNCS, vol. 7192, pp. 11–20. Springer, Heidelberg (2012). doi:10.1007/978-3-642-28537-0_2
47. Schinazi, D.: Apple and IPv6 - Happy Eyeballs (2015). https://goo.gl/XBP9g4
48. Singh, H., Beebee, W., Donley, C., Stark, B.: Basic Requirements for IPv6 Customer Edge Routers. RFC 7084 (2013)
49. Thaler, D., Draves, R., Matsumoto, A., Chown, T.: Default Address Selection for Internet Protocol Version 6 (IPv6). RFC 6724 (2012)
50. Tikan, T.: IPv6 Deployment in Estonia (2015). https://goo.gl/vTQUpH
51. Wing, D., Yourtchenko, A., Eyeballs, H.: Success with Dual-Stack Hosts. RFC 6555 (2012)

On the Potential of IPv6 Open Resolvers for DDoS Attacks

Luuk Hendriks[1]([✉]), Ricardo de Oliveira Schmidt[1], Roland van Rijswijk-Deij[2], and Aiko Pras[1]

[1] Faculty of Electrical Engineering, Mathematics and Computer Science, University of Twente, Enschede, The Netherlands
{luuk.hendriks,r.schmidt,a.pras}@utwente.nl
[2] SURFnet BV, Utrecht, The Netherlands
roland.vanrijswijk@surfnet.nl

Abstract. Distributed Denial of Service (DDoS) attacks have become a daily problem in today's Internet. These attacks aim at overwhelming online services or network infrastrucure. Some DDoS attacks explore open services to perform reflected and amplified attacks; and the DNS is one of the most (mis)used systems by attackers.

This problem can be further aggravated in the near future by the increasing number of IPv6-enabled services in the Internet. Given that the deployment of IPv6-enabled services is increasing, it becomes important to find vulnerable IPv6 open services that could be (mis)used by attackers, and prevent that misuse. However, unlike with IPv4, simply scanning the IPv6 address space to find these open services is impractical.

In this paper we present an active measurement approach to enumerate a relevant list of open resolvers on IPv6 in the wild that could be potentially exploited in a DDoS attack. Based on the assumption that IPv6 open resolvers can be found via IPv4 ones, we show that IPv6-based amplified DDoS attacks are a significantly potential threat in the Internet: the analyzed resolvers, of which 72% are assumingly infrastructural servers, showed a median amplification factor of 50.

1   Introduction

One of the most prevalent and noticeable types of attacks in our Internet today is the Distributed Denial of Service (DDoS) attack. Based on reports from Akamai [2] and Arbor Networks [3], we see an increase in both number and size of these attacks. The attacks come in many forms, with the DNS-based variant being one of the most observed. This type of attack is possible because of DNS open resolvers in the Internet, which accept DNS queries from any source. By spoofing the source IP of a DNS request with the target's address, an attacker is able to deceive an open resolver, which ultimately answers directly to the target, constituting a reflected DDoS (DRDoS) attack. Furthermore, as the DNS response can be many times larger than the request, there is a form of amplification in the attack. These phenomena combined result in a type of threat that

© Springer International Publishing AG 2017
M.A. Kaafar et al. (Eds.): PAM 2017, LNCS 10176, pp. 17–29, 2017.
DOI: 10.1007/978-3-319-54328-4_2

is effective and hard to mitigate, with direct consequences for both operators and end-users, *e.g.* significant decrease in quality of experience. It is therefore important for operators to be aware of open resolvers in their own networks, to fix them and prevent others from mis-using them in such an attack. Finding these open resolvers on IPv4 is feasible, and has been subject of multiple studies [13,14]. Tools and services [1,7] to find these open resolvers have existed for years. As these approaches rely on scanning the entire address space, they are not applicable in the IPv6 Internet. With this work, we present an approach to find open resolvers with IPv6 connectivity, and analyze their potential for attacks.

We assume that a certain share of open resolvers on IPv4 have a form of IPv6 connectivity, and are also resolving openly over IPv6. Besides dual-stacked hosts, running resolver software responding on both protocol versions, we expect to find *infrastructural DNS resolvers*: machines deployed by network operators to handle DNS resolution for their customers, but which are not directly used by the customers. Instead, a forwarding resolver in front of the actual resolving infrastructure is taking DNS questions and sends the answers to these customers, while the infrastructural resolvers perform the actual resolving. This infrastructural part should not be accessible for customers inside the network, let alone from connections outside of that network. Our hypothesis is that operators forget to ACL/firewall the IPv6 part of their resolving infrastructure, effectively enabling misuse. As tooling and services to find open resolvers lack support to find resolvers with IPv6-connectivity, most operators will be unaware of open resolvers in their networks. In order to find open resolvers with IPv6 connectivity, we present an active measurement approach (Sect. 3) based on querying a zone where the authoritative nameserver is only reachable over IPv6. With the results from that, we conduct additional experiments to analyze whether these are indeed infrastructural DNS resolvers.

Contributions: We present a novel methodology to find open resolvers on IPv6, and validate it by performing measurements using the complete IPv4 address space. Consequently, we show that finding open resolvers on IPv6 using our approach is feasible. Our analysis shows roughly 70% of the found resolvers are infrastructural, thus likely to have good connectivity and high bandwidth. Furthermore, we show that queries generate large answers over the found IPv6 paths, with amplification factors of over 100 for the top 5%. These findings emphasize the need for awareness, wherefore we will approach anti-abuse projects to share our code with for adoption. We believe incorporating the code in well-known, existing efforts will have the most effective impact. For ethical reasons, we do not publish our code: it will be shared with fellow researchers and interested anti-abuse projects on a request basis.

First, we will sketch out (Sect. 2) possible DNS resolver setups, and explain why our approach can determine their possible IPv6 connectivity. Our methodology (Sect. 3) describes the measurement setup (Sect. 3.2), the steps to obtain open resolvers on IPv6 (Sect. 3.3), measurements to identify infrastructural resolvers (Sect. 3.4), and an analysis of possible amplification (Sect. 3.5).

Then, we discuss (Sect. 5) our approach and findings, and list related work (Sect. 6). Lastly, we conclude (Sect. 7) that open resolvers on IPv6 have, although relatively low in number, a large potential for severe DDoS attacks.

2   Background

2.1   Using DNS to Traverse from IPv4 to IPv6

The approach in this work is based on normal behavior of the Domain Name System (DNS), in terms of resolving hostnames: a client sends a query to a resolver, which collects the required information at one or more authoritative nameservers. The resolver constructs the answer and sends it back to the client. The only trick is a special configuration of certain nameservers, making them only reachable over either IPv4 or IPv6, but not both. It is important to emphasize that we are dealing with two different forms of 'IPv4' and 'IPv6': the process involves Resource Record (RRs) for both, *i.e.* A and AAAA records, but we are interested in the protocol that is actually used for transport.

Using `example.v6only.ourdomain.net` as an example, where the `v6only` zone is delegated to a nameserver only reachable over IPv6, the following steps take place in the resolving process:

1. The client asks the resolver, over IPv4, for the A record of the domain.
2. The resolver contacts the `.` (root) and `net.` server, to find out where the authoritative nameserver of `ourdomain.net` is.
3. The resolver contacts the nameserver of `ourdomain.net`, asking for the NS record of the `v6only.` subdomain, in order to find out who to ask for anything under that subdomain. The NS record contains `ns6.ourdomain.net`, for which only an AAAA record exists.
4. The resolver tries to contact that nameserver on the IPv6 address from the AAAA record: only in case the resolver has IPv6 connectivity, traffic arrives at the nameserver.

Thus, while initially contacting the resolver over IPv4, eventually packets over IPv6 will arrive on the authoritative side—if and only if the resolver has any form of IPv6 connectivity. This way, **by using DNS on the application layer, we traverse from IPv4 to IPv6 on the network layer.**

2.2   Possible Resolving Setups

In practice, the aforementioned resolver is not necessarily a single entity. Multiple machines can form a resolving infrastructure, including *e.g.* load-balancers, without any ostensible difference for the end-user.

In our search for resolvers with forms of IPv6 connectivity, we generalize and consider two scenarios, as depicted in Fig. 1. The simple form Fig. 1a features a single host for the resolving, which is thus dual-stacked and both IPv4 and IPv6 connections are instantiated by that host itself. Examples of this scenario

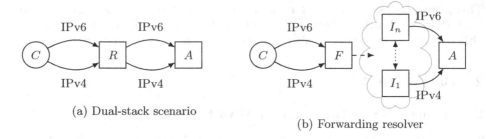

(a) Dual-stack scenario

(b) Forwarding resolver

Fig. 1. Generalized scenarios of DNS resolving setups. C: client, R: resolver, F: forwarding resolver, I_i: infra, A: auth. nameserver.

are (badly configured) Customer Premises Equipment (CPE) handling queries on their WAN-side, or a Virtual Private Server (VPS) running resolver software. In case of Fig. 1b, the resolver used by clients is not performing full resolving itself, but rather forwards queries to one or more upstream resolvers. In this case, IPv4 and IPv6 connections towards authoritative nameservers are not necessarily originating from one and the same machine.

3   Methodology

3.1   Finding IPv4 Open Resolvers

The first step in our approach is to enumerate open resolvers on IPv4 available in the Internet, which will later be tested for IPv6-connectivity (Sect. 3.2).

To find open resolvers in the Internet, we scan the routable IPv4 address space. In this scan we simply send out DNS queries to every IPv4 address and wait for incoming responses. However, the fact that a response is received does not necessarily mean that the replying open resolver can be somehow misused; that is, we distinguish responses where DNS resolution is not explicitly refused. To do so, we look into the returned RCODE[1], where RCODE 5 when the server refuses to answer: those are filtered out and not further acted upon. To maximize our results, we are liberal with other RCODEs. Our scans are based on zmap [7] and its DNS module, with an adaption to accept responses from unexpected ports, again to maximize results.

As we expect to find $e.g.$ CPEs subject to time (DHCP-leases, IPv6 address lifetimes), we perform our measurements directly after finding an open resolver on IPv4: this, combined with the aforementioned liberal selection criteria, makes existing available lists of open resolvers unfit for our research. We go into more ethical considerations of our measurements in Sect. 5.1.

---

[1] http://www.iana.org/assignments/dns-parameters/dns-parameters.xhtml#dns-parameters-6.

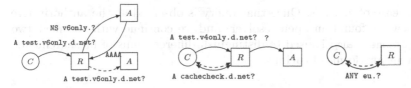

(a) Determine IPv6 con-   (b) Test for forwarding   (c) IPv4/IPv6 response
nectivity (Sect.3.3).   and shared caches (Sect.3.4). size comparison (Sect.3.5).

Fig. 2. Visualization of methodology steps, per phase. C: client, R: resolver (abstracted, see Fig. 1), A: authoritative. Solid lines depict IPv4 transport; dashed lines IPv6 transport.

Table 1. Configuration of DNS zone for all measurements.

v6only.ourdomain.net	NS	ns6.ourdomain.net.
ns6.ourdomain.net	AAAA	2001:db8::53
dns6ver.ourdomain.net	AAAA	2001:db8::53
v4only.ourdomain.net	NS	ns4.ourdomain.net.
ns4.ourdomain.net	A	123.123.123.123
dns4ver.ourdomain.net	A	123.123.123.123
cachecheck.ourdomain.net	A	123.123.123.123

3.2   Measurement Setup

With a list of open resolvers on IPv4 at hand, we start the actual measurements, divided in three steps (Fig. 2). In the following subsections, we detail the three phases, which all involve specifically configured resource records in the DNS. An overview of this configuration is given in Table 1. It is important to understand that there are two different uses of IPv4 and IPv6 in our approach. The DNS protocol specifies Resource Records of type A and AAAA designated to IPv4 and IPv6, respectively. Our interest is, however, in the IP protocol-version used for transport.

3.3   Determining IPv6 Connectivity

First, we determine whether the open resolver (found in Sect. 3.1) has any form of IPv6 connectivity (Fig. 2a). Every open resolver is queried over IPv4 for a specific qname under a zone for which the nameserver has only an AAAA-record, thus no A-record: $ipv4.$timestamp.**v6only**.ourdomain.net. If we observe the query arriving at the authoritative side, we can extract the initially queried resolver from the qname (*i.e.* $ipv4), and we know it has some form of IPv6-connectivity. To verify whether the IPv6 address we have thus uncovered is itself an open resolver, we send it a verification query: $ipv4.$timestamp.**dns6ver**.ourdomain.net. The initial $ipv4 is still included for ease of analysis. Once that query is observed at the authoritative side, we know we found an open resolver, and we continue with the next two steps. The $timestamp is used to distinguish different runs of measurements, and to prevent any forms of caching.

3.4 Distinguishing Dual-Stack and Infrastructural Setups

Now that we have pairs of IPv4 and IPv6 addresses belonging to a resolving entity, we perform additional queries (Fig. 2b) to gain insight in how this resolving entity is set up, distinguishing the two scenarios depicted in Fig. 1. Firstly, the IPv4 address is queried again, but now for a zone that is only reachable over IPv4: **$ipv4**.$timestamp.**v4only**.ourdomain.net. Upon the query incoming at the authoritative side, comparing the connecting IPv4 address and the initially queried address (*i.e.* $ipv4) tells us whether we are dealing with a single machine, or whether forwarding or distribution has occurred. Secondly, we test for a shared cache between the IPv4 and IPv6 addresses. For each pair of IPv4 and IPv6 addresses, both addresses are queried for the same qname, based on a hash of both addresses and the measurement timestamp: h($ipv4$ipv6$timestamp).cachecheck.ourdomain.net. This query is performed twice over IPv4, and twice over IPv6. All the four queries are 5 s apart. Based on the TTL values in the answers, we can determine whether the resolver is actually caching on any or both of the protocols, and whether that cache is shared.

3.5 Comparison of Response Sizes for IPv4 and IPv6

Finally, as shown in Fig. 2c, the response sizes of pairs of IPv4 and IPv6 addresses are compared. We aim at large responses, so queries are DNSSEC-enabled and ask for the ANY-record [16]. We do not use TCP fallback. Queries of this form for com. and eu. are sent to both the addresses. We capture the incoming packets with their full payload in order to find explanations for differences in response sizes.

Processing on the Authoritative Side. If a queried IPv4 open resolver has a form of IPv6 connectivity (or delegates the resolving to a host that has IPv6 capabilities), the constructed query ends up on the host with the IPv6-address configured in the AAAA record. From incoming queries, we extract the information listed in Table 2.

4 Results

4.1 What Share of the Resolvers Generate IPv6 Traffic?

Our measurement yielded 1038 *unique* IPv6 addresses, verified to be openly resolving. This number is distilled from 78698 unique pairs of IPv4 and IPv6

Table 2. Information extracted from incoming queries.

v6	IPv6 source address of query that reached our nameserver
qname	Queried name
qtype	Query type (should be A)
orig_ts	Timestamp extracted from qname
orig_v4	IPv4 address of the server initially queried, extracted from qname
asn4	ASN of orig_v4
asn6	ASN of v6

Table 3. Overview of measurement results

IPv6 connectivity	1.49M unique pairs		
Open on both IPv6/IPv4	78698 (5.3%) unique pairs		
of which unique IPv6	1038 addresses	745	(72%) infrastructural
		922	(89%) caching
of which unique IPv4	72784 addresses	258	(0.4%) infrastructural
		7486	(10%) caching
		55582	(76%) mismatches

addresses—of which both IPv4 and IPv6 addresses were openly resolving. In these pairs were 72784 unique IPv4 addresses, of which (based on the queries for the v4only zones) 76% did not match with the address contacting our authoritative nameserver. Upon verifying whether these *mismatches* were openly resolving, we found 258 IPv4 addresses to do so. These are what we call *infrastructural resolvers* (Sect. 2.2): 745 (72%) of the 1038 IPv6 addresses were associated with these. An overview of these numbers is given in Table 3.

In total, we found more than 1.49M unique pairs of IPv4 and IPv6 addresses to *generate* a form of IPv6 traffic, *i.e.* we observed incoming packets from the IPv6 address after sending a query to the IPv4 address. The verification query (dns6ver) reduced this to the aforementioned 78698 address-pairs (5.3%).

4.2   Caching Characteristics

Comparing the Time-to-live (TTL) values in answers for the cachecheck queries showed that for the 1038 unique IPv6 resolvers, 922 (89%) did cache answers. For pairs of IPv4 and IPv6 addresses that both cache, nearly 60% do not share their cache, as can be seen in Fig. 3a: for each pair, the TTL of the cachecheck answer over IPv4 is subtracted from the TTL of the answer over IPv6. As these queries were sent 10 s apart, the peak at −10 in the plot implicates 40% shared caches. The long tail can be explained by resolvers overwriting the actual TTL with their own minimal values, *e.g.* 600 s, on IPv4, while the IPv6 resolver respected the value configured in our zone, *i.e.* 60 s. (Note that the

40% is a conservative number as infrastructures can comprise multiple upstream resolvers, thus requiring multiple queries to detect shared caches.)

4.3 Amplification Factor

Looking into the achievable amplification factor, we measured the response sizes of the answers to our ANY queries. The distribution, Fig. 3b, shows the responses over IPv6 feature significant amplification. The median amplification factor is 50, whereas the top 5% is amplified more than 100 times.

Comparing the response sizes over IPv6 with those over IPv4 requires consideration, as the found IPv6 addresses belong to machines that are often different from the initial IPv4 open resolvers. While this does not allow us to draw general conclusions on the network layer protocols, it does provide insight on how much one with malicious intents can gain (in terms of amplification) when the transition from IPv4 to the IPv6 resolver is made. We compared the response sizes to the ANY queries for each *pair* of IPv4/IPv6 addresses, and show the difference in bytes in Fig. 3c. The dashed horizontal lines emphasize where the difference in response size is exactly 0 bytes, *i.e.* the response sizes are equal over both IPv4 and IPv6. The figure shows that, for the analyzed pairs, 90% of the answers over IPv6 are equal or bigger in size than the answers coming from the IPv4 address.

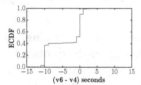
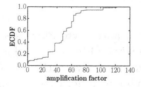
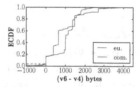

(a) TTL difference for servers caching on both IPv4 and IPv6.

(b) Distribution of amplification factor over IPv6.

(c) Difference between response sizes for pairs of v4/v6 resolvers for ANY.

Fig. 3. Analysis of caching, amplification and response size characteristics.

4.4 Distribution of Open Resolvers per Network

We looked further into which networks[2] the open resolvers reside in. Counting the number of unique IPv6 addresses acting as open resolvers per Autonomous system (AS), we find the top 10 to account for more than half of all the IPv6 open resolvers: the other half is spread over 216 different networks. Figure 4 lists these top 10 networks, showing their share of the total number of found open resolvers. The AS with most unique resolvers (accounting for almost 9% of the total) is a South-Korea based Internet service provider(ISP). Number 2 is the backbone of a mobile operator in Germany. The top 3 is completed by

---

[2] IP to ASN resolving done using *pyasn* with CAIDA RouteViews data. Network names and country codes obtained from Team Cymru.

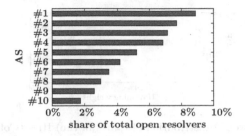

Fig. 4. Top networks with most unique open resolvers (IPv6). The 10 networks in this graph account for 51% of all open resolvers.

a French hosting company. The remainder of the top 10 consists of a mix of service providers and hosting companies, with the notable exceptions 6 and 7: there we find a public DNS resolver service from the US, and an organization famous for providing IPv6 tunnel solutions, also from the US. Geographically, there is not a definitive domination by any continent, although without 6 and 7, we are mainly left with networks from Western Europe and Asia. Aggregation on country indeed shows mainly countries from those continents (Table 4).

Table 4. Top 10 countries with most unique open resolvers (IPv6), accounting for 78% of all.

Country	Unique	% of total
Germany	186	17.9%
United States	150	14.5%
South Korea	104	10.0%
France	99	9.5%
Taiwan	78	7.5%
Mexico	72	6.9%
China	53	5.1%
Thailand	25	2.4%
Hong Kong	22	2.1%
Sweden	22	2.1%

4.5   Interface Identifier Analysis

From all unique IPv6 addresses found to be openly resolving, more than half are assumed to be configured by a human, strengthening the likeliness of these being infrastructural resolvers. For this, we look at the Interface Identifier (IID), the last 64 bits of the IPv6 address. Out of the 1038 addresses, 622 had non-zero bits only in their last hextet: all other of the 64 last bits of the address were 0. Of those, 570 (*i.e.* 55% of all) feature only decimal characters—no hexadecimals—in

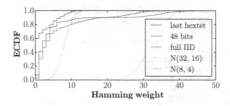

Fig. 5. Hamming weight distribution of (parts of the) IIDs (Color figure online)

Table 5. Characteristics of IID of resolver addresses

Total IPv6 addresses	1038	
Hex in IID	225	
of which SLAAC (`ff:fe`)		83
All 0 but last hextet	622	
of which decimal hextet		570

their "natural" notation. The addresses with hexadecimals were for 37% identifiable as Stateless Address Auto-Configuration (SLAAC) addresses. These numbers are further detailed in Table 5. The distribution of the hamming weights of the IIDs is far below a normal distribution. As shown in Fig. 5, where based on the central limit theorem a mean of 32 is to be expected for the last 64 bits (blue dotted line), we find only 10% of the addresses (solid red line) to feature that hamming weight. The solid blue and green lines depict the distribution of respectively the last hextet, and the 48 bits before that last hextet. For reference, the normal distribution of the last hextet is also plotted (pink dotted line).

5 Discussion

5.1 Ethical Considerations

Presenting a methodology that can be misused for malicious intents might raise ethical concerns. It is however comprised of technologies and configurations that are not new themselves, and have been available to anyone for a long time. Furthermore, we emphasize that the traversal from IPv4 to IPv6 using DNS will only reveal IPv6-connected resolvers, but does not enable direct use over IPv4, significantly reducing the opportunity to misuse found hosts.

Furthermore, in our measurements, we queried for the domain of the university (*i.e.* utwente.nl), to hint at the benign intent of our doings.

5.2 Pitfalls in Scanning/Great Firewall of China

Using zmap, the default query is A for google.com. Using this yielded ∼ 220M "open resolvers", which is not in line with literature. Using A, utwente.nl yields a far lower number. Initial analysis of this difference points us to a large share of IP addresses from Chinese networks. Those IP addresses acted as open resolvers in the sense that they seemingly returned answers on our DNS questions. However, they only do so for specific qnames, like google.com, while for utwente.nl no response was sent. Furthermore, when querying a subset of these IP addresses by hand, we observed responses to be incorrect—random to a certain degree. When querying for AAAA records, the responses contain invalid IPv6 addresses or (again, random) IPv4 addresses. Based on the large number of these fake resolvers, and their location, we reckon to have hit a network-level, government-managed entity.

5.3   Response Size Difference

The difference in response sizes has multiple explanations. Analysis of the full packet capture of the answers on our ANY queries shows 1.3× more answers over IPv6 than over IPv4. Of the answers over IPv4, 60% is *malformed*: more than 99% of these malformed answers are exactly 512 bytes in size, hinting at truncation of packets, possibly by middleboxes. On the contrary, no malformed answers were observed over IPv6. Looking at valid answers, we find 71% to be empty (*i.e.* ANCOUNT 0) over IPv4, versus 6% over IPv6; this likely indicates different configuration on the application level.

6   Related Work

To the best of our knowledge, we are the first to systematically investigate the potential of IPv6 open resolvers in the context of DDoS. However, complementary to our work, there are many studies that addressed the DDoS problem in multiple ways. In 2014, Welzel *et al.* [17] found more than 60% of targets of botnet-driven DDoS attacks to be impacted significantly. More recently, Moura *et al.* [9] assessed the impact of DDoS attacks against the Root DNS in Nov. and Dec. 2015, showing how the distribution of the root system allowed for resilience. Other works focused on individual aspects of DDoS, such as the amplification factor. In 2014, Rossow [12] found that 14 UDP-based protocols are succeptible to bandwidth amplification with a factor up to 4670; and later in 2015, Kührer *et al.* [10] collaborated in a large scale campaign to reduce the number of vulnerable NTP servers by more than 92%. Also in 2014, Czyz *et al.* [6] showed that there were 2.2M potential NTP amplifiers in the Internet, some replying to probes with several gigabytes of data; and van Rijswijk-Deij *et al.* [16] showed that DNSSEC-signed domains can result in very high amplification factors with responses 59× larger (and 179× in some cases). In 2015, MacFarland *et al.* [11] addressed the potential of amplification by authoritative DNS nameservers, showing that very few nameservers are responsible for the highest amplification factors.

On another angle, many studies have also addressed IPv6 measurements. Beverly *et al.* [5] present an active approach to identify shared IPv4 and IPv6 infrastructures in the Internet. Using a controlled authoritative nameserver,

Berger *et al.* [4] studied the relation between IPv4 and IPv6 DNS resolvers. A similar approach was used by Schomp *et al.* [13] to study the behavior of DNS servers in terms of caching and handling of TTL.

Finally, concerning IPv6 scanning, Ullrich *et al.* [15] proposed an active approach on the assumption that addresses are systematically assigned; they were able to identify a large number of active IPv6 addresses, although likely far from a realistic address census. Gasser *et al.* [8] proposed a hybrid active/passive approach by creating a hitlist, at the time containing 150M unique IPv6 addresses.

7   Conclusions

In this paper, we prove finding open resolvers with IPv6 connectvity is feasible. We leverage the fact that we can scan the entire IPv4 address space, and combine that with the traversal of IPv4 to IPv6 using the higher layer DNS protocol. With this approach, we prove that one can find both dual-stacked resolvers, as well as open resolvers that are part of a resolving infrastructure.

Comparing open resolvers on the infrastructure side, we see roughly three times more IPv6 resolvers than on IPv4, suggesting improper configuration is indeed more often the case for IPv6 resolvers than for their IPv4 counterparts. And while being open on IPv6 is likely to be a form of improper configuration on the network layer (firewall/ACL), the differences in response sizes are likely also caused by configuration errors on the application layer, *i.e.* missing parameters in the resolver software specifically for IPv6. Operators do have to pay attention to multiple layers to solve this problem adequately.

From the perspective of misuse, thus comparing the found IPv6 resolvers to the far larger number of IPv4 (forwarding) resolvers, there nonetheless is reason to be concerned: one may assume infrastructural resolvers to be connected via at least 1 G, or even 10 G links. This, combined with the larger response sizes, makes for very potent attack sources. A significant share of the found resolvers cache responses, making them more effective as they do not have to query authoritative nameservers that may implement Request Rate Limiting (RRL) on their part.

By sharing our measurement code with projects that enumerate open resolvers on IPv4, we attempt to create awareness for operators, and an accessible way for them to prevent their infrastructure from being misused in attacks.

References

1. Open Resolver Project (2016). http://openresolverproject.org
2. State of the Internet/Security. Technical report, Akamai, Q2 (2016). https://content.akamai.com/PG6852-q2-2016-soti-security.html
3. WISR. Technical report, Arbor Networks (2016). https://www.arbornetworks.com/insight-into-the-global-threat-landscape
4. Berger, A., Weaver, N., Beverly, R., Campbell, L.: Internet nameserver IPv4 and IPv6 address relationships. In: ACM IMC (2013)
5. Beverly, R., Berger, A., Siblings, S.: Identifying shared IPv4/IPv6 infrastructure via active fingerprinting. In: PAM (2015)

6. Czyz, J., Kallitsis, M., Gharaibeh, M., Papadopoulos, C., Bailey, M., Karir, M.: The rise and decline of NTP DDoS attacks. In: ACM IMC (2014)
7. Durumeric, Z., Wustrow, E., Halderman, J.A.: ZMap: fast internet-wide scanning and its security applications. In: USENIX Security (2013)
8. Gasser, O., Scheitle, Q., Gebhard, S., Carle, G.: Scanning the IPv6 internet: towards a comprehensive hitlist. In: IFIP TMA (2016)
9. Moura, G.C.M., Schmidt, R.O., Heidemann, J., Vries, W.B., Müller, M., Wan, L., Hesselman, C.: Anycast vs. DDoS: evaluating the November 2015 root DNS event. In: ACM IMC (2016)
10. Kührer, M., Hupperich, T., Rossow, C., Holz, T.: Exit from Hell? Reducing the impact of amplification DDoS attacks. In: USENIX Security (2014)
11. MacFarland, D.C., Shue, C.A., Kalafut, A.J.: Characterizing optimal DNS amplification attacks and effective mitigation. In: Mirkovic, J., Liu, Y. (eds.) PAM 2015. LNCS, vol. 8995, pp. 15–27. Springer, Heidelberg (2015). doi:10.1007/978-3-319-15509-8_2
12. Rossow, C., Hell, A.: Revisiting network protocols for DDoS abuse. In: NDSS (2014)
13. Schomp, K., Callahan, T., Rabinovich, M., Allman, M.: On measuring the client-side DNS infrastructure. In: ACM IMC (2013)
14. Takano, Y., Ando, R., Takahashi, T., Uda, S., Inoue, T.: A measurement study of open resolvers and DNS server version. In: Internet Conference (IEICE) (2013)
15. Ullrich, J., Kieseberg, P., Krombholz, K., Weippl, E.: On reconnaissance with IPv6: a pattern-based scanning approach. In: IEEE ARES (2015)
16. van Rijswijk-Deij, R., Sperotto, A., Pras, A.: DNSSEC and its potential for DDoS attacks - a comprehensive measurement study. In: ACM IMC (2014)
17. Welzel, A., Rossow, C., Bos, H.: On measuring the impact of DDoS Botnets. In: ACM EUROSEC (2014)

Something from Nothing (There): Collecting Global IPv6 Datasets from DNS

Tobias Fiebig[1(✉)], Kevin Borgolte[2], Shuang Hao[2], Christopher Kruegel[2], and Giovanni Vigna[2]

[1] TU Berlin, Berlin, Germany
tobias@inet.tu-berlin.de
[2] UC Santa Barbara, Santa Barbara, CA, USA

Abstract. Current large-scale IPv6 studies mostly rely on non-public datasets, as most public datasets are domain specific. For instance, traceroute-based datasets are biased toward network equipment. In this paper, we present a new methodology to collect IPv6 address datasets that does not require access to restricted network vantage points. We collect a new dataset spanning more than 5.8 million IPv6 addresses by exploiting DNS' denial of existence semantics (NXDOMAIN). This paper documents our efforts in obtaining new datasets of allocated IPv6 addresses, so others can avoid the obstacles we encountered.

1 Introduction

The adoption of IPv6 has been steadily increasing in recent years [4]. Unsurprisingly, simultaneously, the research question of efficiently identifying allocated IPv6 addresses has received more and more attention from the scientific community. However, unfortunately for the common researcher, these studies have—so far—been dominated by the analysis of large, restricted, and proprietary datasets. For instance, the well-known content delivery network (CDN) dataset used for most contemporary IPv6 analyses [8,15], Internet exchange point (IXP) datasets, which were used regularly by some other research groups [3,9], or, slightly less restrictive, the Farsight DNS recursor dataset [21]. Although public datasets do exist, they are traceroute-based datasets from various sources, including the RIPE Atlas project [17], which are limited due to their nature: they are biased towards addresses of networking equipment, and, in turn, bear their own set of problems for meaningful analyses.

Correspondingly, in this paper, we aim to tackle the problem of obtaining a dataset of allocated IPv6 addresses for the common researcher: We present a new methodology that can be employed by every researcher with network access. With this methodology we were able to collect more than 5.8 million unique IPv6 addresses The underlying concept is the enumeration of IPv6 reverse zones (PTR) leveraging the semantics of DNS' denial of existence records (NXDOMAIN). Although the general concept has been discussed in RFC 7707 [10], we

© Springer International Publishing AG 2017
M.A. Kaafar et al. (Eds.): PAM 2017, LNCS 10176, pp. 30–43, 2017.
DOI: 10.1007/978-3-319-54328-4_3

identified and overcame various challenges that prevented the use of this technique on a global scale. Therefore, we document how we can leverage the semantics of NXDOMAIN on a global scale to collect allocated IPv6 addresses for a new IPv6 dataset. Our detailed algorithmic documentation allows researchers everywhere to implement this technique, reproduce our results, and collect similar datasets for their own research.

In this paper, we make the following contributions:

- We present a novel methodology to enumerate allocated IPv6 addresses *without* requiring access to a specific vantage point, e.g., a CDN, IXP, or large transit provider.
- We focus on the reproducibility of our techniques and tools, to provide researchers with the opportunity to collect similar datasets for their own research.
- We report on a first set of global measurements using our technique, in which we gather a larger and more diverse dataset that provides new insights into IPv6 addressing.
- We present a case-study that demonstrates how our technique allows insights into operators' networks that could not be accomplished with previous techniques.

2   Previous Work

Active probing for network connected systems is probably one of the oldest techniques on the Internet. However, tools that can enumerate the full IPv4 space are relatively new. The first complete toolchain that allowed researchers to scan the whole IPv4 space was presented by Durumeric in 2013 [6] with ZMap. The problem of scanning the whole IPv4 address space is mostly considered solved since then. Especially the security scene heavily relies on these measures [19]. The address space for IPv6 is 128bit, which is significantly larger than the 32bit of IPv4. Hence, a simple brute-force approach as presented for IPv4 is—so far— not feasible. Indeed, most current research efforts in the networking community are concerned with evaluating large datasets to provide descriptive information on utilized IPv6 addresses [10].

Plonka and Berger provide a first assessment of active IPv6 addresses in their 2015 study using a large CDN's access statistics as dataset [15]. Subsequently, in their 2016 work Foremski et al. propose a technique to generate possibly utilized IPv6 addresses from initial seed datasets for later active probing [8]. Gasser et al. attempt a similar endeavor, using—among various other previously mentioned datasources—a large Internet Exchange Point (IXP) as vantage point [9]. However, prior work has the drawback that the used vantage points are not publicly accessible.

Measurement-studies using public data sources have been recently published by Czyz et al. [4,5]. They combine various public data sources, like the Alexa Top 1 million and the Farsight DNS recursor dataset [21]. In addition, they resolve all IPv4 reverse pointers and attempt to resolve the returned FQDNs for their IPv6 addresses.

Algorithm 1. Algorithm iterating over ip6.arpa., based on RFC7707 [10].

```
// Base-Case: max.ip6.arpa.len = 128/4 * 2 + len("ip6.arpa.");
Function enumerate(base, records={ }, max.ip6.arpa.len)
    for i in 0..f do
        newbase ← i+"."+base;
        qryresult ← getptr(newbase);
        if qryresult != NXDOMAIN then
            if len(newbase) == max.ip6.arpa.len then
                | add(records, newbase);
            else
                └ enumerate(newbase,records,max.ip6.arpa.len);
```

---

3   DNS Enumeration Techniques

Complimentary to prior approaches, van Dijk enumerates IPv6 reverse records by utilizing the specific semantics of denial of existence records (NXDOMAIN) [2, 10]: When correctly implementing RFC1034 [12], as clarified in RFC8020 [2], the Name Error response code (NXDOMAIN in practice) has the semantic of *there is nothing **here** or anywhere **thereunder** in the name tree*. Making this notion explicit in RFC8020 [2] is a relatively recent development. Combined with the IPv6 PTR DNS tree, where each sub-zone has 16 (0-f, one for each IPv6 nibble) children up to a depth of 32 levels, provides the possibility to exploit standard-compliant nameservers to enumerate the zone.

Specifically: Starting at the root (or any other known subtree), a request for each of the possible child nodes is performed. If the authoritative server returns NXDOMAIN, the entire possible subtree can be ignored, as it indicates that no entries below the queried node exist. Algorithm 1 shows the corresponding algorithmic description. Figure 1 provides a simplified visualization, e.g., if a queries for *0-e.ip6.arpa.* return NXDOMAIN, but *f.ip6.arpa.* returns NOERROR, we can ignore these subtrees, and continue at *f.ip6.arpa.*, finally finding *f.0.f.ip6.arpa.* as the only existing record.

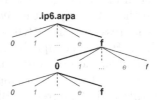

Fig. 1. Enumerating **f.0.f.-ip6.arpa.**, existing nodes are highlighted in bold.

4   Methodology and Algorithmic Implementation

The approach outlined in Sect. 3 has been used on small scales in the past: Foremski et al. [8] used it to collect a sample of 30,000 records from selected networks for their study. In this section, we analyze the challenges of a global application of the technique and describe how we can overcome these limitations.

Non RFC8020-compliant Systems: The current technique requires that RFC8020 [2] is correctly implemented, i.e., that the nameserver behaves standard-compliant. However, following RFC7707 [10], this is not the case for all authoritative DNS nameserver software found in the wild [2]. Specifically, if higher level servers (from a DNS tree point of view) are not enumerable by any of the presented techniques, then this can mask the enumerable zones below them. For example, if a regional network registry, like APNIC or, RIPE would use a DNS server that cannot be exploited to enumerate the zone, then all networks for which they delegate the reverse zones would become *invisible* to our methodology.

To approach this challenge, we seed the algorithm with potentially valid bases, i.e., known to exist *ip6.arpa.* zones. Our implementation obtains the most recent Routeviews [20], and the latest RIPE Routing Information Service (RIS) [18] Border Gateway Protocol (BGP) tables as a source. Particularly important to allow the approach to be easily reproducible: both are public BGP view datasets, available to any researcher.

Based on the data, we create a collapsed list of prefixes. Following prior work, we consider the generated list a valid view on the Global Routing Table (GRT) [22]. For each of the collapsed prefixes we calculate the corresponding ip6.arpa. DNS record. The resulting list is then used as the input seed for our algorithm. Alternative public seed datasets are the Alexa Top 1,000,000 [4,5] or traceroute datasets [8] (which, as aforementioned, are biased by nature; thus, special care must be taken for traceroute datasets). If available, other non-public datasets like the Farsight DNS recursor dataset [21] could also be used.

Complimentary approaches to collect ip6.arpa. addresses or subtrees from systems that implement RFC8020 incorrectly are those with which one can obtain (significant parts of) a DNS zone. For example, by employing insufficiently protected domain transfers (AXFRs), which are a prominent misconfiguration of authoritative nameservers [1].

Breadth-First vs. Depth-First Enumeration: For our data collection, we employ Algorithm 1. Unfortunately, the algorithm leverages depth-first search to explore the IPv6 reverse DNS tree. This search strategy becomes problematic if any of the earlier subtrees is either rather full (non-sparse) or if the authoritative nameservers are relatively slow to respond to our queries. Slow responses are particularly problematic: they allow an "early" subtree to delay the address collection process significantly.

Substituting depth-first search with breadth-first search is non-trivial unfortunately. Therefore, we integrate features of breadth-first search into the depth-first algorithm (Algorithm 1), which requires a multi-step approach: Starting from the seed set, we first use Algorithm 1 to enumerate valid ip6.arpa. zones below the records up to a corresponding prefix-length of 32 bits. If we encounter input-records that are more specific than 32 bits, we add the input record and the input record's 32-bit prefix to the result set. Once this step has completed for all input records, we conduct the same process on the result set, but with a maximum prefix-length of 48 bits, followed by one more iteration for 64-bit

---

Algorithm 2. Algorithm cooking down the initial seed records.

Function *cook_down (records)*
 for prefix.len in 32,48,64 **do**
  records.new ← { };
  cur.ip6.arpa.len ← *prefix.len*/4 ∗ 2 + *len*("*ip6.arpa.*");
  for base in records **do**
   // See Sect. 4 Dynamically-generated Zones/Prefix
   Exclusion/Opt-Out for details;
   if checks(base) == False **then**
    └ **pass**
   else if len(base) ≥ cur.ip6.arpa.len **then**
    add(*records.new, base*);
    crop.base = croptolength(base,cur.ip6.arpa.len);
    add(*records.new, crop.base*);
   else
    └ *add*(*records.new, enumerate*(*base, cur.ip6.arpa.len*));

---

prefixes. We opted to use 64 bits as the smallest aggregation step because it is the commonly suggested smallest allocation size and designated network size for user networks [11]. Algorithm 2 provides a brief description of the cook_down algorithm. The last step uses Algorithm 1 on these /64 networks with a target prefix size of 128 bits, effectively enumerating full ip6.arpa. zones up to their leaf nodes. To not overload a single authoritative server, the ip6.arpa. record sets are sorted by the least significant nibble of the corresponding IPv6 address first before they are further enumerated. Sorting them by the least significant nibble spreads zones with the same most significant nibbles as broadly as possible.

Combined with the observed low overall traffic that our modified technique generates, we can prevent generating unreasonably high load on single authoritative nameserver. Our approach, contrary to prior work, does not generate high load on the authoritative nameservers before moving on to the next one. Otherwise it would launch a denial of service attack against the nameserver. If our approach is more widely adopted by researchers, future work should investigate how distributed load patterns can be prevented, i.e., thousands of researchers querying the same nameserver simultaneously (see Sect. 4).

Detecting Dynamically-generated Zones: Dynamically generating the reverse IP address zone, i.e., creating a PTR record just-in-time when it is requested, has been popular in the IPv4 world for some time [16]. Unsurprisingly, utilizing dynamically generated IPv6 reverse zones has become even more common over time as well. Especially access networks tend to utilize dynamically-generated reverse records. While this provides a significant ease-of-use to the network operators, our algorithm will try to fully enumerate the respective subtrees. For a single dynamically-generated /64 network it leads to 2^{64} records to explore, which is clearly impractical. Therefore, we introduce a heuristic to detect if a zone is dynamically-generated, so that we can take appropriate action. To detect dynamically-generated reverse zones, we can rely on the semantic properties of reverse zones. The first heuristic that we use is the repeatability of returned FQDNs. Techniques for dynamically-generated reverse zones usually aim at providing either the same or similar fully-qualified domain names (FQDNs) for the reverse PTR records. For the former detection is trivial. In the latter case, one often finds the IPv6 address encoded in the returned FQDN. In turn, two or more subsequent records in an dynamically generated reverse zone file should only differ by a few characters. Therefore, a viable solution to evaluate if a zone is dynamically-generated is the Damerau-Levenshtein distance (DLD) [7].

Unfortunately, we encountered various cases where such a simplistic view is insufficient in practice. For instance, zones may also be dynamically-generated to facilitate covert channels via DNS tunneling [14]. In that case, the returned FQDNs appear random. Similarly in other cases, the IPv6 address is hashed, and then incorporated into the reverse record. In those cases the change between two records can be as high as the full hash-length of the utilized hash digest. We devised another heuristic based on the assumption that if a zone is dynamically-generated, then all records in the zone should be present. Following prior work by Plonka et al. and Foremski et al. [8,15], we determined that certain records are unlikely to exist in one zone all together, specifically, all possible terminal records of a base that utilize only one character repeatedly. For example, for the base *0.0.0.0.0.0.0.0.0.0.0.0.0.0.8.e.f.ip6.arpa* such a record would be *f.f.f.f.f.f.f. f.f.f.f.f.f.f.f.f.0.0.0.0.0.0.0.0.0.0.0.0.0.0.8.e.f.ip6.arpa*. Therefore, we build and query all sixteen possible records from the character set 0..f. Due to these records being highly unlikely [8], and the use of packet-loss sensitive UDP throughout DNS, we require only three records to resolve within a one second timeout to classify a zone as dynamically-generated. We omit the heuristic's algorithmic description for brevity, as the implementation is straight forward.

Prefix Exclusion: Naturally, in addition to excluding dynamically-generated zones, a network operator may ask to be excluded from her networks being scanned. During our evaluation, multiple network operators requested being excluded from our scans. Furthermore, we blacklisted two network operators that did use dynamically-generated zones, but for which our heuristic did not trigger, either due to rate-limiting of our requests on their side, or bad connectivity toward their infrastructure. Similarly, our algorithm missed a case for a US based university which used /96 network access allocations, which we did not detect as dynamically-generated due to the preselected step-sizes for Algorithm 2. In total, we blacklisted five ISPs' networks and one university network.

Ethical Considerations and Opt-Out Standard: To encourage best practice, for our experiments and evaluation, the outbound throughput was always limited to a maximum of 10 MBit/s in total and specifically to 2MBit/s for any single target system at a time following our least-significant byte sorting for ip6.arpa zones. Although the load we incurred was negligible for the vast majority of authoritative nameservers, we acknowledge that the load this methodology may put onto authoritative servers may become severe, particularly if more

---

Algorithm 3. Call-order in final script.

$seeds \leftarrow$ get_seeds();
$enum.records \leftarrow$ cook_down(seeds);
$final.result \leftarrow \{ \}$;
for base in enum.records **do**
  // See Sect. 4 Dynamically-generated Zones/Prefix Exclusion/Opt-Out for
  details;
  if checks(base) == False **then**
    | **return** $\{ \}$;
  $tmp.results \leftarrow$ enumerate(base, 128);
  $final.result \leftarrow final.result + tmp.results$;

---

researchers utilize the same approach simultaneously or do not limit their outbound throughput. Hence, we suggest to adopt and communicate the practice of first checking for the existence of a PTR record in the form of *4.4.4.f.4.e.5-.4.5.3.4.3.4.1.4.e. ... .ip6.arpa.*. The respective IPv6 record encodes the ASCII representation of DONTSCAN for /64 networks. For networks larger than /64, we suggest to repeat the string. We do not use a non-PTR conform record, as this would exclude users utilizing, e.g., restrictive DNS zone administration software possibly sanitizing input. We will carry this proposal toward the relevant industry bodies, to provide operators a simple method to opt out of scans.

CNAMEs: Our investigation also found cases of seemingly empty terminals in the DNS tree, i.e., records of 32 nibble length without an associated PTR resource record that do not return NXDOMAIN. Upon removal of these records, and by focusing on non-empty terminals in these address bases, we still obtain valid results. In addition to cases where the terminals are fully empty, CNAME records [13] may exist instead of PTR records, which is why it is necessary to resolve CNAME records if a PTR record does not exist.

Parallelization: Combining the previously presented algorithms, we can enumerate the IPv6 PTR space (see Algorithm 3). Due to our algorithm's nature, parallelization is ideally introduced in the *for* loop starting at line 5 of Algorithm 2 and the *for* loop at line 4 in Algorithm 3. Technically, it would also be possible to introduce parallelization in the first *for* loop of Algorithm 1. However, then parallelization might be performed over a single authoritative server. This would put a high load on that system. By parallelizing our approach through Algorithms 2 and 3 parallel queries are made for different IPv6 networks, thus most likely to different authoritative servers.

5   Evaluation

We evaluate our methodology on a single machine running Scientific Linux 6.7 with the following hardware specification: four Intel Xeon E7-4870 CPUs

Table 1. Overview of the results of our evaluation.

Experiment	Runtime					Records Found				Addresses		Queries	Dynamic Zones			Blacklisted	
	/32	/48	/64	Full	Total	Seed	/32	/48	/64	Total	Unique		/32	/48	/64	/32	/48
ip6.arpa.	120	130	429	3,244	3,932	/	3.5k	52.5k	1M	1.6M	335k	62M	615	15k	223k	0	1.5k
GRT_SEED$_{80}$	7	232	1,040	2,956	4,235	72k	73k	856k	582k	5.3M	2.8M	221.3M	1.5k	716k	80.5k	713	63
GRT_SEED$_{400}$	7	144	404	775	1,330	72k	73k	834k	1.4M	2.2M	33k	190.7M	1.5k	690k	796k	715	65
Unique Sum						73k	75k	895k	2,2M	5.8M			1.5k	732k	1M	715	1.6k

(2.4 GHz each) for a total of 80 logical cores, 512 GB of main memory, and 2TB of hard-disk capacity. We installed a local recursive DNS resolver (Unbound 1.5.1) against which we perform all DNS queries. Connection-tracking has been disabled for all DNS related packets on this machine, as well as other upstream-routers for DNS traffic from this machine. An overview of our results can be found in Table 1.

Enumerating .ip6.arpa.: In our first evaluation scenario, we enumerate addresses using the PTR zone root node of .ip6.arpa. as the initial input only, which will serve as basic ground-truth. The respective dataset corresponds to the first column of Table 1: ip6.arpa. The enumeration was completed within 65.6 h, of which most time was spent enumerating pre-identified /64s networks. As such, the impact of dynamic-generation is evident from this experiment: 615 /32 prefixes are ignored due to dynamically-generated PTR records, with an additional 15 k /48 prefixes and more than 223 k /64 networks subsequently. This experiment yields a total of 1.6 million allocated IPv6 addresses.

GRT_SEED$_{80}$: Seeded Enumeration (80 Threads): For our second experiment, we used the current IPv6 GRT as a seed and ran our algorithm with 80 threads in parallel. The respective dataset is identified as GRT_SEED$_{80}$ in Table 1. The GRT is compiled following our description in Sect. 4. In contrast to simply enumerating the ip6.arpa. zone, pre-aggregating to /32 prefixes takes significantly less time. The reduced time is primarily due to the seeds in the GRT having a certain prefix length already, mostly /32 prefixes. The same can be observed when comparing the seed set among aggregated /32 prefixes. Interestingly, the dataset only increases by around 1,000 prefixes in that aggregation step, mostly due to longer prefixes being cropped. However, in the next step, we do find a significantly larger number of prefixes than those contained in the seed set. Unfortunately, the next aggregation step demonstrates that a significant amount of them are in fact dynamically-generated client allocations. Nonetheless, at more than 5.4 million unique allocated IPv6 address collected, leveraging the GRT seed to improve collection exceeds the initial dataset by far (1.6 million to 5.4 million). It is important to note, however, that we discovered 335,670 records that are unique to the ip6.arpa. dataset. These originate from currently unannounced prefixes. The ip6.arpa. root-node should hence be included into every seed-set. However, depending on the purpose of the data collection, identified yet unrouted addresses should be marked in the collected data set.

(a) Enum. to /48   (b) Enum. to /64   (c) Enum. to /128

Fig. 2. Executed DNS queries vs. obtained records for GRT_SEED$_{80}$.

GRT_SEED$_{400}$: Seeded Enumeration (400 Threads): Unfortunately, a full run with 80 parallel threads takes nearly three full days to complete. Therefore, a higher time resolution is desirable. Due to low CPU load on the measurement machine we investigated the impact of running at a higher parallelization degree, using 400 threads to exploit parallelization more while waiting for input/output. We refer to this dataset as GRT_SEED$_{400}$, which was collected in less than a day. In comparison to collecting with less parallel threads, we do not see a significant impact at the first aggregation level toward /32s prefixes (which we expected) due to the generally low number of them that must be enumerated here.

At the same time, we see a far higher number of obtained prefixes, primarily /64 prefixes. However, when examining the number of detected dynamically-generated and blacklisted prefixes closer, we do see that a number of dynamically-generated prefixes are not being detected correctly, which we discovered is due to packet loss. This is highlighted by the number of prefixes in GRT_SEED$_{400}$ for each aggregation level, which are considered dynamically-generated in a less specific aggregation level of GRT_SEED$_{80}$. Indeed, for 92.94 % of dynamically-generated /64 in GRT_SEED$_{400}$, they have a /48 prefix already considered dynamically-generated in GRT_SEED$_{80}$.

Although the results between GRT_SEED$_{80}$ and GRT_SEED$_{400}$ differ significantly, CPU utilization for GRT_SEED$_{400}$ was not significantly higher. The core reason for this behavior is that our technique is not CPU bound. Instead, the number of maximum sockets and in-system latency during packet handling have a significantly higher impact on the result. Hence, instead of running the experiment on a single host, researchers should opt to parallelize our technique over multiple hosts.

Queries per Zone and Records Found: The number of queries sent to each /32, /48 and /64 prefixes respectively versus the number of more specific ip6.arpa. records obtained per input prefix is contrasted in Fig. 2(a)-(c). An interesting insight of our evaluation is that most zones at each aggregation level contain only a limited set of records. Furthermore, we discover that the number of records found versus the number of executed queries is most densely populated in the area of less than 10 records per zone. Additionally, we see a clear lower-bound for the number of required queries. Specifically, the lower bound consists of the 16 queries needed to establish if a zone is dynamically-generated, plus the minimum number of queries necessary to find a single record. Correspondingly, for the de-aggregation to /64, an additional 64 queries are required. To go from an aggregation level of /64 to a single terminal record, at least 256 queries are necessary.

Clear upper and lower bounds for the quotient of executed queries and obtained records are also visible. In fact, these bound become increasingly clear while the aggregation level becomes more specific and follows an exponential pattern, hinting at an overall underlying heavy-tailed distribution. Furthermore, the two extremes appear to accumulate data-points, which is evident from Fig. 2(c). The upper bound thereby corresponds to zones with very distributed entries, i.e., zones that require a lot of different paths in the PTR tree to be explored, e.g., zones auto-populating via configuration management that adds records for hosts with stateless address auto-configuration (SLAAC). On the other hand, the lower bound relates to well-structured zones, i.e., for which the operators assign addresses in an easily enumerable way, e.g., sequentially starting at *PREFIX::1*.

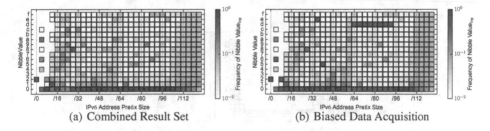

(a) Combined Result Set   (b) Biased Data Acquisition

Fig. 3. Probability mass function for each 4bit position in obtained datasets following Foremski et al. [8]. Figure 3(a) visualizes our combined dataset, with 5,766,133 unique IPv6 addresses. Figure 3(b) depicts an artifact from a measurement error in an earlier study.

Address Allocation: We utilized the visualization technique introduced by Foremski et al. [8] to analyze our dataset. To do so, we created the set of all unique IPv6 address records we obtained over all measurements. The respective results are depicted in Fig. 3: the least significant nibbles are relatively evenly distributed, which aligns with our observation that zones are either very random or in some form sequential.

Fortunately, the technique by Foremski et al. [8] also allows us to validate our dataset. Specifically, Fig. 3(b) has been created over an earlier dataset that we collected where an unexpected summation of the value d in IPv6 addresses between the 64_{th} and 96_{th} bit appears. A closer investigation revealed that this artifact was caused by a US-based educational institution that uses their *PREFIX:dddd:dddd::/96* allocation for their DHCPv6 Wi-Fi access networks. As aforementioned, this dynamically-generated network was not detected due to the step-sizes in Algorithm 2, which is why we excluded it manually, see Sect. 4. Further work should evaluate 4 nibble wide steps, as proposed earlier in this paper.

6   Case-Study

Following, we present how findings of our technique can be used to obtain in-depth insights into practical issues. We provide a brief analysis of the IPv6 efforts in the internal infrastructure of a large SaaS (Software-as-a-Service) cloud platform operator. For our investigation, we selected the prefixes of this operator based on its IPv6 announcements collected via bgp.he.net. To obtain further ground-truth, we also collected the PTR records for all IPv4 prefixes announced by the operator's autonomous system (AS) from bgp.he.net. We took two measurements, T_1 and T_2, two weeks apart in September 2016. Figure 4 shows an overview of the allocation policy of the operator. Specifically, the operator uses three /32 prefixes, with one being used per region she operates in (see Fig. 4(a)). In each region, the operator splits her prefix via the 40_{th} to 44_{th} bit of addresses. IPv6 networks used by network-edge equipment for interconnectivity links between different regions are distinguished by an 8 at the 48_{th} to 51_{st} bit, instead of 0, which is used by all other prefixes.

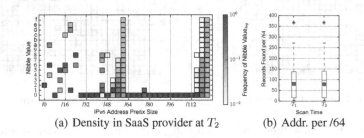

(a) Density in SaaS provider at T_2 (b) Addr. per /64

Fig. 4. Overview of address allocation in the SaaS cloud provider's network.

Another interesting part of the addressing policy are the /48 networks the SaaS provider allocates. Here, we can see that networks are linearly assigned, starting with *PREFIX:0000-::-/48*, thus creating pools of /64s for various purposes. Furthermore, with /48s being linearly assigned, we discover that prefixes with higher indexes have not yet been assigned. The same assignment policy holds for hosts in /64s networks, as indicated by the distribution over the three least significant nibbles used in addresses.

A third aspect of the operator's assignment policy is documented in Fig. 4(b). Specifically, the boxplots show the number of hosts per /64 prefix in the operators networks. For both measurements, we only observe two /64 prefixes with significantly more than 250 hosts. A closer investigation of these networks reveals that they are related to internal backbone and firewalling services spanning multiple Points-of-Presence, following the PTR naming schemes of the obtained records. Apart from this change, we do see a slight increase in the number of hosts per network in the median, but not the mean. An interesting side-note is that the IPv6 PTR records appear manually allocated by the operator's network staff.

We do arrive at this conclusion because we encountered various records with typographical errors in them.

Comparing of the datasets with the corresponding IPv4 PTR sets, we note that the diversity of records is far higher in the IPv4 set. There, various second-level domains can be found mixed together, which we did not encounter for the IPv6 set. Various naming schemes for infrastructure hosts are also present. For example, we discover that the customer-facing domain of the operator is being used for infrastructure services. However, it has apparently been disbanded with the growth of the organization, as we also discover infrastructure specific second-level domains. For the IPv6 set we only observe one infrastructure domain. In general, naming is far more consistent for IPv6. Our conjecture is that the operator made an effort in keeping a consistent state when finally rolling out IPv6, while IPv4 is suffering from legacy setups introduced during the company's growth. The last striking observation is that the PTR records returned for IPv4 and IPv6 reverse pointers do not resolve to valid A and AAAA records themselves. A direct consequence is that, for this network operator, the technique proposed by Czyz et al. [5] is not applicable. We conjecture that the operator chose this setup because she does not require forward lookups, yet wants traceroutes and other reverse-lookup related tools, especially distributed logging, to show the FQDNs.

7 Conclusion

We introduce a novel methodology to collect a large IPv6 dataset from exclusively public data sources. Our initial evaluation of the methodology demonstrates its practical applicability. Requiring no access to a specific network vantage point, we were able to collect more than 5.8 million allocated IPv6 addresses, of which 5.4 million addresses were found in just three days by issuing 221 million DNS queries. Specifically, our technique discovered one allocated IPv6 address per only 41 DNS queries on average. With the obtained dataset, we were able to provide an in-depth look into the data-centers of a large cloud provider. By comparing our results with the corresponding IPv4 reverse entries, we demonstrate that our technique can discover systems which would have been missed by previous proposals for collecting IPv6 addresses [5]. In summary, our technique is an important tool for tracking the ongoing deployment of IPv6 on the Internet. We provide our toolchain to researchers as free software at: https://gitlab. inet.tu-berlin.de/ptr6scan/toolchain.

We note that our technique can also be applied to E.164 records (Telephone Numbers in DNS), but leave this for future work. Furthermore, future work should utilize this technique over a period of time in order to obtain a progressing view on IPv6 deployment on the Internet. To increase coverage, additional seeds and other address collection techniques should be integrated. This extension of our work should be combined with security scanning as it is already done for IPv4 [19]. Following the findings of Czyz et al. [5], such projects are direly needed to increase overall security on the Internet.

Acknowledgements. We thank the anonymous reviewers for their helpful feedback and suggestions, and Peter van Dijk for suggesting this research path to us. This material is based on research supported or sponsored by the Office of Naval Research (ONR) under Award No. N00014-15-1-2948, the Space and Naval Warfare Systems Command (SPAWAR) under Award No. N66001-13-2-4039, the National Science Foundation (NSF) under Award No. CNS-1408632, the Defense Advanced Research Projects Agency (DARPA) under agreement number FA8750-15-2-0084, a Security, Privacy and Anti-Abuse award from Google, SBA Research, the Bundesministerium für Bildung und Forschung (BMBF) under Award No. KIS1DSD032 (Project Enzevalos), a Leibniz Price project by the German Research Foundation (DFG) under Award No. FKZ FE 570/4-1. The U.S. Government is authorized to reproduce and distribute reprints for Governmental purposes notwithstanding any copyright notation thereon. The opinions, views, and conclusions contained herein are those of the author(s) and should not be interpreted as necessarily representing the official policies or endorsements, either expressed or implied, of ONR, SPAWAR, NSF, DARPA, the U.S. Government, Google, SBA Research, BMBF, or DFG.

References

1. Atkins, D., Austein, R.: Threat Analysis of the Domain Name System (DNS). RFC3833
2. Bortzmeyer, S., Huque, S.: NXDOMAIN: There Really is Nothing Underneath. RFC8020
3. Chatzis, N., Smaragdakis, G., Böttger, J., Krenc, T., Feldmann, A.: On the benefits of using a large ixp as an internet vantage point. In: Proceedings of the ACM Internet Measurement Conference, pp. 333–346 (2013)
4. Czyz, J., Allman, M., Zhang, J., Iekel-Johnson, S., Osterweil, E., Bailey, M.: Measuring IPv6 adoption. Proc. ACM SIGCOMM **44**(4), 87–98 (2014)
5. Czyz, J., Luckie, M., Allman, M., Bailey, M.: Don't forget to lock the back door! a characterization of ipv6 network security policy. In: Proceedings of the Symposium on Network and Distributed System Security (NDSS), vol. 389 (2016)
6. Durumeric, Z., Wustrow, E., Halderman, J.A.: ZMap: fast internet-wide scanning and its security applications. In: Proceedings of the USENIX Security Symposium, pp. 605–620 (2013)
7. Fiebig, T., Danisevskis, J., Piekarska, M.: A metric for the evaluation and comparison of keylogger performance. In: Proceedings of the USENIX Security Workshop on Cyber Security Experimentation and Test (CSET) (2014)
8. Foremski, P., Plonka, D., Berger, A.: Entropy/IP: uncovering structure in IPv6 addresses. In: Proceedings of the ACM Internet Measurement Conference (2016)
9. Gasser, O., Scheitle, Q., Gebhard, S., Carle, G.: Scanning the IPv6 internet: towards a comprehensive hitlist (2016)
10. Gont, F., Chown, T.: Network Reconnaissance in IPv6 Networks. RFC7707
11. Hinden, R., Deering, S.: IP Version 6 Addressing Architecture. RFC4291
12. Mockapetris, P.: Domain names - concepts and facilities. RFC1034
13. Mockapetris, P.: Domain names - implementation and specification. RFC1035
14. Nussbaum, L., Neyron, P., Richard, O.: On robust covert channels inside DNS. In: Proceedings of the International Information Security Conference (IFIP), pp. 51–62 (2009)

15. Plonka, D., Berger, A.: Temporal and spatial classification of active IPv6 addresses. In: Proceedings of the ACM Internet Measurement Conference, pp. 509–522. ACM (2015)
16. Richter, P., Smaragdakis, G., Plonka, D., Berger, A.: Beyond counting: new perspectives on the active IPv4 address space. In: Proceedings of the ACM Internet Measurement Conference (2016)
17. Ripe NCC: RIPE atlas. http://atlas.ripe.net
18. Ripe NCC: RIPE Routing Information Service (RIS). https://www.ripe.net/analyse/internetmeasurements/routing-information-service-ris
19. ShadowServer Foundation: The scannings will continue until the internet improves (2014). http://blog.shadowserver.org/2014/03/28/the-scannings-will-continue-until-the-internet-improves/
20. University of Oregon: Route Views Project. http://bgplay.routeviews.org
21. Vixie, P.A.: It's time for an internet-wide recommitment to measurement: and here's how we should do it. In: Proceedings of the International Workshop on Traffic Measurements for Cybersecurity (2016)
22. Zhang, B., Liu, R., Massey, D., Zhang, L.: Collecting the internet as-level topology. ACM Comput. Commun. Rev. **35**(1), 53–61 (2005)

Web and Applications

The Web, the Users, and the MOS: Influence of HTTP/2 on User Experience

Enrico Bocchi[1(✉)], Luca De Cicco[2], Marco Mellia[3], and Dario Rossi[4]

[1] Télécom ParisTech, Paris, France
enrico.bocchi@telecom-paristech.fr
[2] Politecnico di Bari, Bari, Italy
luca.decicco@poliba.it
[3] Politecnico di Torino, Torino, Italy
marco.mellia@polito.it
[4] Ecole Nationale Supérieure des Télécommunications, Paris, France
dario.rossi@enst.fr

Abstract. This work focuses on the evaluation of Web quality of experience as perceived by actual users and in particular on the impact of HTTP/1 vs HTTP/2. We adopt an experimental methodology that uses real web pages served through a realistic testbed where we control network, protocol, and application configuration. Users are asked to browse such pages and provide their subjective feedback, which we leverage to obtain the Mean Opinion Score (MOS), while the testbed records objective metrics.

The collected dataset comprises over 4,000 grades that we explore to tackle the question whether HTTP/2 improves users experience, to what extent, and in which conditions. Findings show that users report marginal differences, with 22%, 52%, 26% of HTTP/2 MOS being better, identical, or worse than HTTP/1, respectively. Even in scenarios that favor HTTP/2, results are not as sharp as expected. This is in contrast with objective metrics, which instead record a positive impact with HTTP/2 usage. This shows the complexity of understanding the web experience and the need to involve actual users in the quality assessment process.

Keywords: Web · HTTP/2 · Page Load Time · MOS · User experience · QoE

1 Introduction

The Web keeps being at the center of our lives, thanks to a plethora of online services, from web searches to business applications, from personal communications to social networks and entertainment portals. HTTP is the de facto "thin waist" of the Internet [19], remaining almost unchanged from the original protocol defined at the end of the last century. Only recently a number of new protocols, namely HTTP/2 [3], SPDY [11] and QUIC [10], have been proposed and

© Springer International Publishing AG 2017
M.A. Kaafar et al. (Eds.): PAM 2017, LNCS 10176, pp. 47–59, 2017.
DOI: 10.1007/978-3-319-54328-4_4

are likely to change the Web status quo. Having reliable ways to compare performance benefits becomes crucial when massive deployments of new protocols take place. However, measuring Web users' Quality of Experience (WebQoE) is a challenging problem. Page complexity has grown to include hundreds of objects hosted on different servers, with browsers opening tens of connections to fetch them. While several studies pointed out the importance of latency [16,18] and its relationship with business value[1], it is less obvious how it impacts WebQoE.

Objective metrics have been defined and the Page Load Time (PLT) is the de-facto benchmark used for comparison [8,15,21–23], with the industry adopting it too (e.g., Alexa reports the quantiles of PLT). However, this family of metrics does not fully reflect users' quality of experience in the complex "waterfall" of network and browser events taking place during the page loading processes.

Subjective metrics, the Mean Opinion Score (MOS), allow one to measure the actual user's WebQoE, but it is extremely expensive to run MOS measurement campaigns. As such, approaches to estimate WebQoE have been proposed [6,9], but their relationship with actual users' experience is yet to be proved and their computational complexity makes them difficult to use in practice.

Recognizing intrinsic limits of objective metrics [5], we present the first study of MOS measurement of WebQoE: We engineer a methodology to collect volunteers' feedbacks in a controlled environment where users are asked to access actual pages while we control network, protocol, and application setup. In our effort towards a subjective, yet scientific, comparison of HTTP/1.1 (H1) and HTTP/2 (H2), we (i) collect a dataset of over 4,000 samples of subjective feedback augmented with objective metrics, and (ii) dig into the data to shed light on actual experience improvement when using H2 vs H1. Advantages appear to be less sharp than those shown by objective metrics: Users report no differences in over half of the cases, while H2 improves WebQoE in 22% of cases only.

2   Related Work

Since the original SPDY proposal [11], ended with the standardization in H2 [3], and the appearance of QUIC [10], researchers have been devoting increasing attention to the benchmarking and optimization of these protocols [4,7,8,15, 17,21–23]. In what follows, we contrast our investigation with related works considering experiment scale, testbed setup, set of pages, and collected metrics.

Experiments scale. In terms of experiments scale, works collecting objective metrics span from several thousands (active testbeds [7,8,17,21,22]) to several millions points (crawling [15] and server logs [23]). Conversely, studies employing actual user feedback (only [4] besides this paper) are inherently of smaller scale (i.e., tens of participants). Our work is based on the collection of actual user feedback from 147 participants, for a total of over 4,000 experiments.

Testbeds. Testbed setups are either based on proxies [7,8] or, as in this work, on locally controlled servers and networks [17,21,22]. Few works leverage actual

---

[1] http://www.fastcompany.com/1825005/how-one-second-could-cost-amazon-16-billion-sales.

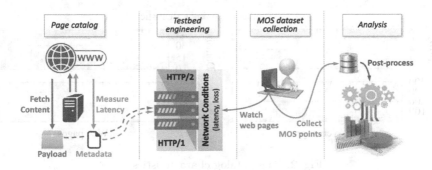

Fig. 1. Experimental workflow.

H2 servers in the Internet [15] or large corporate server logs [23]. Google Chrome is the most popular web browser followed by custom client implementations [21], or a mixture of clients [23]. As for network setup, both controlled [17,21,22] and uncontrolled [7,8,15] networks can be found, including 3G/4G access.

Page catalog. For what concerns pages used for testing, Alexa ranking is a popular source for the selection of websites. The number of sites ranges from 20 to 500, and page selection criterion (e.g., landing [7] vs non-landing [8]) differs. We use Alexa as well to drive our choice towards popular websites. As in [8], we select pages that are likely known by our users, i.e., pages popular in France. We consider pages optimized for desktop browsing and discard landing pages.

Measured metrics. Many works adopt the Page Load Time (PLT) as objective metric [7,8,15,21–23]. PLT limitations are well-known [6,9], yet only few works include more refined metrics to describe users' QoE, e.g., [5,17] consider the SpeedIndex [9]. MOS models for web traffic are dated back to 2002 and 2005 and therefore they should be re-assessed under recent architectures, technologies and designs. Involving end-users in subjective measurements is the best practice, with MOS being a simple and compact metric representative of their actual experience. MOS is the standard in audio and video quality comparison, but only recently it has been introduced for WebQoE assessment. To the best of our knowledge, only [4] presents a framework to collect volunteers' feedback on pre-recorded videos of web-browsing sessions: Side-to-side videos are shown, with the aim of identifying a winner. In contrast, we collect volunteers' feedback of actual browsing sessions, using the typical [1,5] MOS scale [13]. Both approaches have challenges: e.g., synchronization between videos, correlation between videos and actual browsing experience, ability to slow-down/pause video can affect results in [4]. Conversely, in our work the analysis is made complex by volunteers tendency to refraining from using the full scale of scores, as we shall see.

3 Methodology

As portrayed in Fig. 1, the methodology we employ to compare H1 and H2 consists of four phases: *1. Page catalog* (Sect. 3.1) – To build a realistic benchmark,

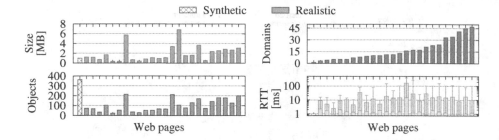

Fig. 2. Page catalog characteristics.

we fetch actual pages and characterize network paths towards servers. *2. Testbed engineering* (Sect. 3.2) – Pages and paths metadata are used to set up our testbed. Local servers host objects using multiple Apache instances while we control network (RTT, loss), protocol (H1/H2), and application (domain sharding) configuration. *3. MOS collection* (Sect. 3.3) – Volunteers browse pages served by our local infrastructure and provide a score in the range [1, 5]. At the same time, the testbed captures objective metrics. *4. Analysis* (Sects. 4–6) – At a later stage, we apply analytics to contrast H1 vs H2 performance.

3.1 Page Catalog

For collecting MOS grades, we aim at selecting pages users are familiar with. As our tests take place in Paris, we start from the top 100 in Alexa France ranking. We visit each page using Google Chrome and compile a list of URLs of objects being requested by the browser. We then mirror each object on a local server and measure the RTT towards each original domain using TCP-SYN packets.

We manually check each mirrored page from our local servers to both discard incomplete pages (e.g., object failing to download due to dynamic requests or cookies policies), landing pages [8] (e.g., Facebook login page), etc. We are left with 24 real pages covering a variety of categories, e.g., news, e-commerce, informative websites, leisure etc. At last, we add the toy page http://www.httpvshttps.com to the page catalog, for a total of 25 pages. For each considered page, Fig. 2 reports its size (top-left), the number of objects (bottom-left), the number of domains serving such objects (top-right), and the average per-domain RTT to contacted domains, with bars reporting the minimum and the maximum RTT (bottom-right). The figure shows that our catalog includes diverse scenarios, from pages hosted on few domains serving a handful of objects, to pages hosted on tens of domains and made of hundreds of objects.

3.2 Testbed Engineering

Server and network configuration. We design and setup a local testbed where we have full control on network conditions (RTT, loss), protocols (H1/H2), and content placement (domain sharding [12]). Our testbed is composed of six servers, each equipped with a quad-core processor, 4 GB of memory and two Gigabit network cards. Servers run Ubuntu 14.04 with Apache HTTP Server 2.4.18. Apache runs in its default configuration, with H2 and SSL modules enabled. Content is served using SSL by installing self-signed certificates.

We run multiple Apache instances configured to serve content through virtual hosts, which are both name-based and IP-based. We leverage name-based configuration to distinguish requests directed to different domains being hosted on the same machine, while the IP-based distinction is required to have domains mapped to specific network conditions. To control network conditions, we use Linux traffic control utility (tc) to enforce both network latency and packet loss. We next distribute content to each server, preserving the original placement of objects into domains, and map each domain to a static IP address using the 10.0.0.0/8 private range. Two separate virtual-hosts serve content using either H1 or H2 to avoid protocol switching or fall-backs on the client side. The choice of H1/H2 is performed by the client, which directs requests to the IP address of the server implementing the desired protocol.

Client instrumentation. We provide a preconfigured PC to each volunteer taking part in our campaign. Each PC runs Linux Mint 17.3 and is equipped with a set of scripts for experiment orchestration. In particular, such scripts (i) setup the local client to reflect the desired scenario, (ii) run Google Chrome to let the volunteer visit a page, (iii) collect the user's score and the objective measurement, and (iv) send the results to a central repository.

Each experiment requires several steps to complete. From the users' point of view, the experience starts with a GUI listing all the available websites of the page catalog. Volunteers (i) select a page from the list and (ii) observe it being loaded by Google Chrome. At the end, they (iii) input the MOS grade, and then (iv) watch again the same page, now served with the other protocol. At step (ii) the page is loaded using either H1 or H2 in a random fashion, then at step (iv) the complementary protocol is used. Therefore, users sequentially grade the same page under the same condition and for both protocols, although they are unaware about the protocol order.

From the implementation standpoint, once the volunteer has selected a page, the script (i) configures the system /etc/hosts file to direct browser requests to local servers instead of the public Internet.[2] Two hosts files are provided for each web page, one for H1 servers, the other for H2 servers. Next, the script (ii) starts Google Chrome in full screen mode, disabling the local cache and enabling the incognito mode. This ensures each page is loaded independently on previous tests and eventual cookies. We force Chrome to log network events, which we collect in the form of HTTP Archive (HAR) file for later stage analysis. Once the user has provided the (iii) MOS grade, (iv) all metadata for that experiment (i.e., HAR file, user's grade, and metadata with network configuration, etc.) are sent to a central repository.

---

[2] Due to the explicit binding between host names and IP addresses in hosts file, no DNS resolution takes place. This avoids potential bias due to resolution delay and DNS caching, enabling a fair comparison between H1 and H2 performance.

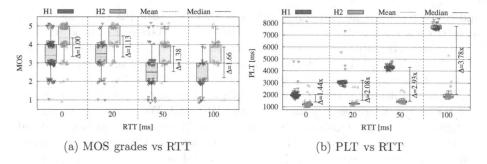

(a) MOS grades vs RTT   (b) PLT vs RTT

Fig. 3. MOS grades and PLT for homogeneous RTT in [0,100] ms. (Color figure online)

3.3 Scenarios and MOS Dataset Collection

We aim at collecting MOS grades in (i) realistic scenarios to provide answers of operational interest, but also in (ii) controlled scenarios that the scientific community has already targeted via objective metrics. Given the limited time available with volunteers, we focus our attention on the following scenarios.

- **Homogeneous network.** Objects are distributed on servers as originally observed. RTT and packet loss are artificially forced to be the same for all virtual servers. RTT can be chosen in $\{0, 20, 50, 100\}$ ms, and packet loss in $\{0, 1, 2\}\%$. Bandwidth is uncapped. These conditions are typically considered in literature.
- **Heterogeneous network.** As before, but latency reflects the original RTT measured during the collection process. No loss is introduced. Such configuration introduces realism into the dependency graph of objects download, which may not arise in case of homogeneous conditions.
- **Unsharded deployment.** All objects are hosted by a single server, on a single domain name and IP address. RTT to the server is forced in $\{0, 20, 50, 100\}$ ms. Bandwidth is uncapped, and no loss is introduced. Unsharded deployment is useful to contrast today's production scenarios (i.e., sharding over multiple domains) vs situations that are by now unrealistic (i.e., all content hosted on a single "unsharded" domain) where H2 benefits are expected to appear [12].

Volunteers are exposed to experiments by randomly choosing one scenario and by visiting the same page over H1 and H2 in unknown order. To avoid biased ratings, only the website name is disclosed to users. Experiments have been conducted in three sessions totaling to 147 volunteers who sampled a space of 25 pages with 32 different scenarios. We followed the best practices suggested by "The Menlo Report" [2], and in particular those for network measurements [1].

4   MOS on the Toy Page

We start the analysis of collected MOS grades focusing on the toy page https://www.httpvshttps.com, which contains a HTML document (18 kB) and 360

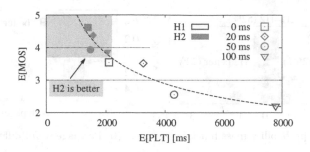

Fig. 4. Sub-linear dependency between PLT increase and MOS reduction.

identical non-cacheable images of 20×20 pixels (1.7 kB each), for a total of 630 kB. All the content is hosted on a single domain, mapped to a single IP address and served by a single server. This scenario is particularly adverse to H1 since the browser opens a large number of connections, each incurring in TCP and TLS handshake overhead and in TCP slow-start. In contrast, H2 takes full advantage of its capabilities by pipelining all requests over multiple streams encapsulated in a single TCP connection and by performing HPACK header compression. We expect H2 to reduce the PLT, ultimately providing a better WebQoE.

We use this toy page to validate the testbed and calibrate MOS grades. On the one hand, we aim at verifying whether expectations on H2 performance are satisfied. On the other hand, we aim at assessing the MOS gap between H2 and H1 by using this extreme scenario as a litmus paper [16,18,20]. We consider 4 different network setups, namely with RTT in $\{0, 20, 50, 100\}$ ms, collecting 487 MOS samples in total. Figure 3 shows MOS (left plot) and PLT (right plot) for H1 (red) and H2 (green). Each point corresponds to an experiment, adding jitter (to x-y axis for MOS and to x axis only for PLT) to enhance the representation.

Consider Fig. 3a first and notice that MOS consistently decreases with increasing RTT. This holds for H1 and H2, with H2 providing a better experience at both low and high latencies. Also, the difference (Δ) between the average of H1 and H2 MOS grades is always of at least 1 point, increasing along with RTT.

Consider now Fig. 3b, showing PLT. H1 is significantly more penalized than H2, with PLT peaking at 8 s for RTT = 100 ms, while H2 keeps PLT below 2 s in all scenarios. As expected, H2 outperforms H1 PLT, meeting the original design goal of "a 50% reduction in page load time" [11].

Next, we verify the existence of a sub-linear dependency of the subjective response to an objective impulse [20]. Here the impulse is the inflated RTT (translating into a longer PLT), while the response is the MOS degradation. Figure 4 reinterprets Fig. 3 as a scatter plot, where each point is the $(\mathbb{E}[PLT], \mathbb{E}[MOS])$ pair over all samples for a given RTT. The figure also reports the trend curve, clearly highlighting the expected sub-linear dependency.

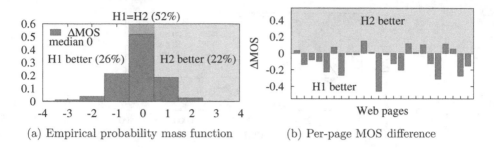

(a) Empirical probability mass function   (b) Per-page MOS difference

Fig. 5. H1 vs H2 MOS grades (ΔMOS) for all 4,000 tests in the dataset.

A final remark is that excellent MOS (i.e., 4 or higher) is bestow only to pages with a loading time lower than 1.25 s. This is in line with [14], which classifies pages as *reactive* if they render the above-the-fold content in less then 1 s.

5   MOS on Real Pages

We here focus on real pages to compare H1 and H2 from a subjective perspective. Our aim is to assess if and to what extent differences in user experience shown earlier still hold in real-life scenarios. To do so, we consider a set of pages served using multiple network and application configurations. On the one hand, we revisit known results from the unique user MOS perspective. On the other hand, we target the impact of less studied factors, such as implications of content sharding [12] over multiple domains and differences caused by homogeneous vs heterogeneous latency conditions towards servers.

5.1   Subjective MOS Differences

We start by assessing the per-user difference of H1 vs H2 MOS grades (ΔMOS) for each page in the catalog. Figure 5 shows ΔMOS = $MOS_{H2} - MOS_{H1}$ over all tests, detailing both the empirical probability mass function (Fig. 5a) and the per-page MOS difference (Fig. 5b). The figure is annotated with statistics (e.g., median) and visual references (e.g., light-gray area for H2 better than H1).

Some insightful observations can be drawn from the plot: The distribution is (i) monomodal with zero mean and median, (ii) bell shaped, but (iii) slightly skewed. In other words, (i) in 50% of cases, users equally score H2 and H1, (ii) cases where either H2 or H1 has higher score are roughly balanced, although (iii) there is a slight yet noticeable bias towards negative ΔMOS, where $MOS|_{H1}$ is higher than $MOS|_{H2}$. That is, contrary to the previous results, the difference between H2 and H1 is much more subtle and inconsistent.

This reinforces the need to perform experiments on real-world pages, as opposite to benchmark pages that inflate MOS differences. Results are only partially surprising. First, pages widely differ (see Fig. 2) and ΔMOS varies according to

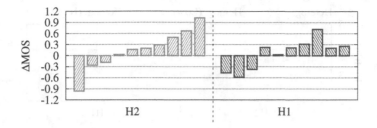

Fig. 6. ΔMOS for 10 pages where we contrast unsharded vs sharded versions.

the page being considered, as shown by Fig. 5b (the order of web pages is consistent with Fig. 2). Second, users have a different way to "value improvement", causing them to report the same score under both protocols, which contributes to ΔMOS = 0. Third, pages in our catalog are likely optimized for H1. Fourth, the H1 software has undergone decades of testing and optimization, while H2 is a relatively new protocol.

5.2   Impact of Page Sharding

We now consider sharding [12], i.e., distributing page content over multiple domains to exploit server parallelism. This practice helps in overcoming the limitation on the maximum number of connections a browser can establish towards the same domain. Given H2 benefits of using a single connection to a single domain [7,15,22], one would expect that unsharding helps in taking advantage of H2 pipelining features. In our evaluation, we consider 10 of the 25 pages of the catalog and modify them so to have all the content hosted on a single domain (i.e., unsharding the content). We then contrast MOS grades to assess the impact of (un)sharding for H2 and H1 independently.

Figure 6 shows the per-page difference between the average MOS for the unsharded and for the sharded content. In formulas, ΔMOS = E[MOS|$_{\text{unsharded}}$] − E[MOS|$_{\text{sharded}}$]. Pages are sorted increasingly according to ΔMOS for H2.

It is straightforward to notice that the impact of sharding is page-dependent: there are pages for which the user experience improves when they are served through the unsharded deployment (ΔMOS > 0), as well as pages suffering from usharding (ΔMOS < 0). 7 pages out of 10 show an improvement in MOS when unsharded, even though the difference in perceived quality greatly changes, from a minimum of 0.028 to a maximum of 1.020 ΔMOS points. H2 appears to benefit more of unsharding, but 3 pages gets a sensibly reduced MOS. H1 is less impacted, peaking at a difference of "only" 0.716 ΔMOS points.

5.3   Impact of Latency Diversity

Page latency is known to be impacted by client-server RTT. Here we investigate how much impact it has on MOS. We contrast scenarios with homogeneous

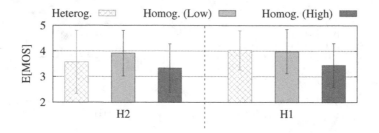

Fig. 7. $\mathbb{E}[MOS]$ for heterogeneous vs homogeneous RTT settings.

RTT (usually considered in literature [17,21]) against heterogeneous RTT to each domain. Clearly, homogeneous conditions are the ordinary solution in case of proxy-based proposals [7,8,22] and is typically justified in testbed studies with the assumption that sharding practice will ultimately be abandoned as countering H2 benefits. At the same time, sharding is by now a standard practice and page redesign would happen conditionally on unsharding benefits being proved and consistent. Total unsharding is unlikely as pages aggregate many contributions (e.g., twitter feeds, advertisement, etc.) coming from multiple content producers. As such, it is important to evaluate H2 performance also in controlled conditions that are as close as possible to the real ones.

For this experiment, we select a subset of 3 pages sampled by 95 users for a total of 362 experiments. Average MOS scores are reported in Fig. 7 for different RTT configurations and for H2 and H1 separately. It emerges that different RTT leads to opposite biases for H1 vs H2. For instance, in the case of H2, low-RTT homogeneous scenarios provide about 0.35 better MOS than heterogeneous RTT. When RTT is high (>50 ms), instead, MOS degrades loosing 0.58 points with respect to the low-RTT scenario. This happens in the case of H1 too, where high-RTT homogeneous scenarios lead to a loss of about 0.5 MOS points with respect to both heterogeneous and low-RTT homogeneous scenarios. Interestingly, H1 in heterogeneous RTT conditions performs much better than H2 in the same scenario. Similarly to [23], we noticed that macroscopic pages characteristics are not telling as for user MOS. The performance gap has its roots in page dependency graph [22], and homogeneous latencies may hide intricate interactions in such dependencies that arise only under heterogeneous conditions.

6   Objective Metrics on Real Pages

We finally study the H1 vs H2 difference using objective metrics (OBJ in short). As before, we quantify the difference in accessing the same page over the two protocols with $\Delta OBJ = OBJ_{H2} - OBJ_{H1}$, where OBJ is the Time to the First Byte (TTFB), the Document Object Model (DOM), or Page Load Time (PLT). We additionally consider the ObjectIndex, a replacement metric for the SpeedIndex [9] that has been shown to be strongly correlated with the latter [5].

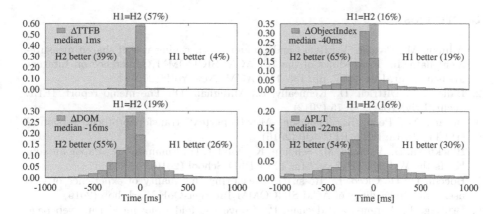

Fig. 8. Empirical probability mass function of ΔOBJ various objective metrics.

Figure 8 presents the results depicting the histogram of ΔOBJ using bins of 100 ms. The figure is annotated with statistics (notice that H2 better than H1 is represented by the negative semi-plane in this case). All OBJ exhibit an empirical probability mass function that is similar to that of the ΔMOS grades (i.e., roughly symmetric, peak close to zero, very low median). In addition, here ΔOBJ attributes a (slight) advantage to H2, unlike in the ΔMOS case.

Excluding the TTFB, which is known to be not the most appropriate metric for web pages performance assessment, H2 shows better results than H1 in at least 54% of tests. That is, H2 speeds up the page loading process and the time needed to load the DOM, but those improvements are not reflected in user experience that rates H1 and H2 with the same score in 55% of cases (see Fig. 5).

7   Conclusions

This paper presents the first study comparing the performance of H2 and H1 in terms of MOS. We contrast the two protocols using both subjective (i.e., a MOS corpus of over 4,000 points) and objective metrics using a dedicated testbed.

The emerging picture does not allow the election of a single winner. While H2 sensibly reduces the PLT on a toy page, ultimately improving the quality of experience, it is not as effective when serving real-world web pages. Objective metrics (e.g., DOM, PLT, etc.) show a performance improvement to the advantage of H2 in more than 50% of cases, but they fail to predict users' MOS that is reported to be higher in the case of H1.

This highlights the importance of users feedbacks and calls for future research on new models enhancing the correlation between MOS and QoE metrics.

Acknowledgments. This work has been carried out at LINCS (http://www.lincs. fr) and benefited from support of NewNet@Paris, Cisco's Chair "NETWORKS FOR THE FUTURE" at Telecom ParisTech (http://newnet.telecom-paristech.fr).

References

1. Allman, M., Paxson, V.: Issues and etiquette concerning use of shared measurement data. In: Proceedings of the 7th ACM SIGCOMM Conference on Internet Measurement, IMC 2007, pp. 135–140. ACM, New York (2007)
2. Bailey, M., Dittrich, D., Kenneally, E., Maughan, D.: The menlo report. IEEE Secur. Priv. **10**(2), 71–75 (2012)
3. Belshe, M., Peon, R., Thomson, M.: Hypertext transfer protocol version 2 (HTTP/2). In: IETF RFC7540 (2015)
4. Blackburn, B., Varvello, M., Schomp, K., Naylor, D., Finamore, A., Papagiannaki, K.: Is the Web HTTP/2 yet? In: TMA PhD School (2016)
5. Bocchi, E., De Cicco, L., Rossi, D.: Measuring the quality of experience of web users. In: Proceedings of ACM SIGCOMM Internet-QoE Workshop (2016)
6. Brutlag, J., Abrams, Z., Meenan, P.: Above the fold time: measuring web page performance visually. http://conferences.oreilly.com/velocity/velocity-mar2011/public/schedule/detail/18692. Accessed 15 Sept 2016
7. Butkiewicz, M., Wang, D., Wu, Z., Madhyastha, H.V., Sekar, V.: Klotski: reprioritizing web content to improve user experience on mobile devices. In: Proceedings of USENIX NSDI, pp. 439–453 (2015)
8. Erman, J., Gopalakrishnan, V., Jana, R., Ramakrishnan, K.K.: Towards a SPDY'Ier Mobile Web? In: Proceedings of ACM CoNEXT, pp. 303–314 (2013)
9. Google Inc. https://sites.google.com/a/webpagetest.org/docs/using-webpagetest/metrics/speed-index. Accessed 19 Sept 2016
10. Google Inc. QUIC. https://www.chromium.org/quic. Accessed 19 Sept 2016
11. Google Inc. SPDY. https://www.chromium.org/spdy/spdy-whitepaper. Accessed 19 Sept 2016
12. Grigorik, I.: HTTP/2 is here, let's optimize! http://bit.ly/http2-opt. Accessed 10 Oct 2016
13. International Telecommunication Union. Subjective testing methodology for web browsing. ITU-T Recommendation P.1501 (2014)
14. Irish, P.: Delivering the goods in under 1000 ms. http://bit.ly/1toUUA7 Accessed 10 Oct 2016
15. Varvello, M., Schomp, K., Naylor, D., Blackburn, J., Finamore, A., Papagiannaki, K.: Is the web HTTP/2 yet? In: Karagiannis, T., Dimitropoulos, X. (eds.) PAM 2016. LNCS, vol. 9631, pp. 218–232. Springer, Heidelberg (2016). doi:10.1007/978-3-319-30505-9_17
16. Miller, R.B.: Response time in man-computer conversational transactions. In: Proceedings of AFIPS Fall Joint Computer Conference, pp. 267–277 (1968)
17. Netravali, R., Sivaraman, A., Das, S., Goyal, A., Winstein, K., Mickens, J., Balakrishnan, H.: Mahimahi: accurate record-and-replay for HTTP. In: Proceedings of USENIX ATC, pp. 417–429 (2015)
18. Nielsen, J.: Response times: the 3 important limits.https://www.nngroup.com/articles/response-times-3-important-limits/ (1993). Accessed 19 Sept 2016
19. Popa, L., Ghodsi, A., Stoica, I.: HTTP as the narrow waist of the future internet. In: 9th ACM SIGCOMM Workshop on Hot Topics in Networks (2010)
20. Reichl, P., Egger, S., Schatz, R., D'Alconzo, A.: The logarithmic nature of QoE and the role of the Weber-Fechner law in QoE assessment. In: IEEE ICC (2010)
21. Wang, X.S., Balasubramanian, A., Krishnamurthy, A., Wetherall, D.: How speedy is SPDY? In: Proceedings of USENIX NSDI, pp. 387–399 (2014)

22. Wang, X.S., Krishnamurthy, A., Wetherall, D.: Speeding up web page loads with Shandian. In: Proceedings of USENIX NSDI, pp. 109–122 (2016)
23. Zarifis, K., Holland, M., Jain, M., Katz-Bassett, E., Govindan, R.: Modeling HTTP/2 speed from HTTP/1 traces. In: Karagiannis, T., Dimitropoulos, X. (eds.) PAM 2016. LNCS, vol. 9631, pp. 233–247. Springer, Heidelberg (2016). doi:10.1007/978-3-319-30505-9_18

Internet Scale User-Generated Live Video Streaming: The Twitch Case

Jie Deng$^{(\boxtimes)}$, Gareth Tyson, Felix Cuadrado, and Steve Uhlig

Queen Mary University of London, London, UK
{j.deng,gareth.tyson,felix.cuadrado,steve.uhlig}@qmul.ac.uk

Abstract. Twitch is a live video streaming platform used for broadcasting video gameplay, ranging from amateur players to eSports tournaments. This platform has gathered a substantial world wide community, reaching more than 1.7 million broadcasters and 100 million visitors every month. Twitch is fundamentally different from "static" content distribution platforms such as YouTube and Netflix, as streams are generated and consumed in real time. In this paper, we explore the Twitch infrastructure to understand how it manages live streaming delivery to an Internet-wide audience. We found Twitch manages a geo-distributed infrastructure, with presence in four continents. Our findings show that Twitch dynamically allocates servers to channels depending on their popularity. Additionally, we explore the redirection strategy of clients to servers depending on their region and the specific channel.

Keywords: Twitch.tv · Live video streaming · Video streaming infrastructure

1 Introduction

Online live streaming has long been a popular application. However, recently, there has been an interesting evolution, whereby everyday users provide streams of their own activities, *e.g.,* Facebook Live, Periscope [18], Meerkat. This is termed *user-generated live streaming*, and unlike other platforms (*e.g.,* YouTube [14,15] and Netflix [7,9]), often involves things like live social interaction. Thus, these platforms introduce two core innovations: (*i*) Any user can provide a personal live stream (potentially to millions of viewers); and (*ii*) This upload must occur in realtime due to live social interaction between consumers and producers. One of the most popular examples of this is *Twitch* [3,21]. This live broadcast platform is oriented towards video games, allowing users to broadcast their gameplay, as well as to watch large eSports tournaments with professional players. Though others have started similar services (*e.g.,* YouTube Gaming), they are yet to experience the demand of Twitch [17,18], which delivered 35 K streams to over 2 million concurrent users in real time during its peak [5].

The rapid expansion of user-generated live streaming platforms, like Twitch, comes with fundamental challenges for the management of infrastructure and

© Springer International Publishing AG 2017
M.A. Kaafar et al. (Eds.): PAM 2017, LNCS 10176, pp. 60–71, 2017.
DOI: 10.1007/978-3-319-54328-4_5

traffic delivery.[1] For example, in Twitch it is impossible to time-shift (cache) video content, and often uploaders are not geographically near or well connected to their subscribers. Further, live social interaction (*e.g.,* via web cams and chat feeds [16]) means that the *real-time* constraints are very strict. Thus, we argue that Twitch might offer some important insights into how such challenges can be overcome.

In this paper, we perform a large-scale measurement study of Twitch. Taking advantage of a global network of proxy servers, we map the infrastructure used by Twitch. We explore its content replication and server selection strategies, correlating them with both viewer and broadcaster location. Note that broadcaster selection is a unique aspect of personalised video streaming, as prior systems lack the concept of user-generated live broadcasters. In this paper, we analyse how Twitch has managed to scale-up to deal with its huge demand. In summary, we make the following contributions:

- We map the infrastructure and internetworking of Twitch. Unlike YouTube or Netflix which deploy thousands of caches in edge networks, Twitch serves millions of users directly from relatively few server locations in North America (NA), Europe (EU) and Asia (AS) (Sect. 3).
- Based on this, we expose how streams are hosted by Twitch at different locations (Sect. 4); we explore how Twitch scales-up depending on channel popularity, and how clients are redirected to Twitch servers.
- We evaluate the client redirection strategy (Sect. 5) on a global scale. We find multiple factors affecting the redirection policy, including channel popularity and the client network configuration (peering). Due to the lack of peering in Asia, 50% of the clients are exclusively served by NA servers.

2   Measurement Methodology

We begin by presenting our measurement methodology, which is driven by three goals. First, we wish to discover the location and number of servers in Twitch's infrastructure. Second, we want to know how Twitch allocates individual live streams onto these severs (note that this is a very different model to static video content, which is usually reactively cached wherever it is requested). Third, we want to understand how users are mapped to servers so that they can watch the stream they are interested in.

We built a Python crawler that allows us to automatically request video streams from Twitch channels. The responses to these requests allow us to inspect which server the client has been redirected to.[2] In order to comprehensively sample the infrastructure, and explore how different clients are redirected to Twitch servers, we ran this crawler in many geographic locations to achieve global coverage of Twitch's infrastructure. To achieve this, we utilised a global network of

---

[1] Note that Twitch is the fourth largest source of peak traffic in the US [4].
[2] We distinguish unique servers based on their IP address — we note that each IP address is also allocated a unique domain name.

open HTTP proxies[3] to launch the video requests from around the world. We validated that the client IP address exposed to the server is the proxy address, thus we can expect the Twitch server to redirect based on the proxy location. In total, we routed through 806 proxies, from 287 ASes located in 50 countries from Europe (154), Asia (372), Africa (24), Australia (4), North America (138) and South America (114). Though there are several limitations with using open proxies (e.g., unevenly distributed locations and no accurate feedback of the video streaming latency), we argue that the proxy platform provides sufficient information on Twitch infrastructure at scale.

We observed that Twitch frequently redirects a client to different servers when requesting the same channel multiple times, thus evidencing some mechanism of load balancing. For each channel we sent the request multiple times from each proxy in order to comprehensively sample the servers offered from that location. Each channel was requested a variable number of times (from 15 to 300) based on how many unique servers our queries discovered. We first ran the crawler for 5 months from December 2015 to April 2016. We continuously launched requests to all online channels listed from public Twitch API,[4] and collected over 700 K requests indicating the Twitch servers that clients in that region are redirected to.

Once we acquired the list of Twitch servers, we began to explore the strategy that maps streams onto servers. First, we requested all online channels via proxy servers in the countries in which Twitch servers are located; also each channel was requested multiple times to discover as many servers hosting the stream as possible. Second, we carried out the same experiment for around 30 selected popular channels every 5 min. This was done to observe how the most popular channels are managed over an extended period of time. A total of 1 m requests were collected from these two experiments.

Finally, to further understand Twitch's client redirection strategy on a global scale, we also requested all online channels through all proxies one-by-one. We then captured which server each proxy is redirected to. For each proxy, we requested the channels only once to emulate a typical client. This resulted in a further 1 m requests collected between April to June 2016.

3   Geographic Deployment of Twitch Infrastructure

We start the exploration of Twitch's infrastructure by describing the locations of its servers, as well as how they are connected to the Internet. Our logs show that all Twitch video streams are served from hls.ttvnw.net subdomains. Each domain consists of a server name with an airport code, hinting at a geographical location. For example, video11.fra01.hls.ttvnw.net is a server in Frankfurt (fra), Germany. We confirmed that there is a one-to-one mapping between each domain and an IP address by performing global DNS queries from locations around the world.

---

[3] These are servers that allow us to proxy web requests through them, thereby appearing as it our requests come from them: https://incloak.com/.

[4] https://github.com/justintv/Twitch-API.

In total, we discovered 876 servers distributed over 21 airport code subdomains from 12 countries.

It is unclear how accurate these location-embedded domains are and, therefore, we compare the airport codes against the locations returned by three IP geodatabases: ipinfo.io, DP-IP and Maxmind GeoLiteCity. Although the airport locations embedded within the domains are always in the same continent, we note that they are inconsistent with the locations returned from the databases. Instead, the geodatabases report that Twitch operates a centralised infrastructure. All servers were mapped to just 4 countries: Switzerland (Europe), Hong Kong (Asia), US (North America) and Sydney (Oceania). In total, our traces reveal 360 servers in the North America (NA), 257 servers in Europe (EU), 119 in Asia (AS) and 47 in Oceania (OC).

To explore the discrepancy between the databases and airport codes, we performed a TCP-based traceroute and ping campaign from 10 sites in East and West US, Europe, Asia Pacific and South America. From the traceroute path we see that servers sharing a prefix also pass through the same router when entering Twitch's AS, with only the last three hops differing. This, however, does not confirm physical locations. Hence, we also check the Round Trip Time (RTT) to each server using TCP ping. This shows a clear boundary between servers with different airport codes. Servers inside the same sub-domains tend to differ by under 5 ms; for servers on the same continent, the difference is within 50 ms; for servers on different continents, this increases beyond 100 ms. We found a minimal RTT of under 3 ms when accessing servers sharing the same country code. This suggests that the airport country codes are a good indicator of physical location. In other words, this highlights inaccuracy in the geolocation databases (this is perhaps reasonable, as geodatabases are well known to suffer limitations such as address registration [10]).

We gain additional confidence in our findings by checking the BGP routing tables.[5] Unlike other large content providers, we fail to find any third party hosting, as seen in other larger CDNs like Google [10] or Netflix. Instead, all servers are located within Twitch's own Autonomous System (AS46489). Importantly, we find the prefixes are only announced in their appropriate continents. For example, 185.42.204.0/22 is only announced in Europe and 45.113.128.0/22 is only announced in Asia. Thus, we are confident that the geolocations are at least accurate on a continent-level granularity

Finally, to dig deeper into the BGP interconnectivity of Twitch's AS, we utilise PeeringDB [2] to extract the locations of advertised public and private peering facilities used by the 153 Twitch peers listed in [1]. Figure 1 presents the number of *potential* peers that are collocated with Twitch in Internet Exchange Points (IXPs) and private peering facilities. Unsurprisingly, we find a tendency for more peering in countries where we also discover Twitch servers. For example, most of the *potential* peerings are located in IXPs in the Netherlands (AMS-IX), US (Equinix), UK (LONAP) and Germany (DE-CIX Frankfurt). Noteworthy is that the number of *potential* peerings in Asia is actually quite small, with the

---

[5] http://routeserver.org/.

bulk in America and Europe (we acknowledge this could be caused by inaccuracies in PeeringDB). We find from BGP route records[6] that the IP prefix for the Asia presence was first advertised in June 2015. This recency could explain the low number of peers. The same is for Oceania, which first was advertised in November 2015. The low number of peers could affect the performance in redirection, as we will illustrate later in Sect. 5.

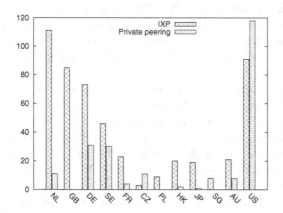

Fig. 1. Number of peers collocated with Twitch AS46489 at Internet Exchange Points and private peering facilities in each country (from PeeringDB). There is more peering in countries where Twitch servers are based.

The above results only allow us to definitively state that geolocations are accurate on a per-continent basis. Hence, for the rest of this paper, we focus our analysis on *continent-level* geolocation; where countries are mentioned, we use airport codes as the ground truth. Due to the low utilisation of Oceania servers, we will mainly focus on NA, EU and AS in the following sections.

4   Stream Hosting Strategy

The previous section has explored the location of Twitch's infrastructure. However, this says little about how it is used to serve its dynamic workload. Next, we look at how streams are allocated to Twitch's servers.

4.1   How Important Is Channel Popularity?

We first look at the number of servers a channel is hosted on, based on how many viewers it receives (*i.e.,* popularity). It might be expected that the number of servers hosting a channel scales linearly with the number of viewers. However, we find this is not the case for Twitch. Figure 2 presents the number of servers

---

[6] https://stat.ripe.net/.

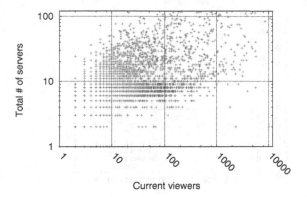

Fig. 2. Number of unique servers hosting each channel (found using requests from multiple vantage points all over the world) against number of current viewers. Channels with high view counts are replicated on a larger number of servers.

hosting a channel against the instant number of viewers per channel. Live viewer figures are acquired from the Twitch API. Although there is an upward trend, it is not that distinct (highest correlation is just 0.41). We also explored the total number of viewers (accumulated viewers over time), however the correlation with number of servers was not higher.

The low correlation suggests a more sophisticated methodology is used to manage the scaling — it is not solely based on the number of viewers. To understand this better, we take a temporal perspective to see how the number of servers utilised for a channel evolves over time. We manually selected 30 popular streamers from different countries and repeatedly requested their channels every 5 min from the proxies.

Figure 3 presents example results from a US streamer and a Chinese streamer. Both channels have an initial allocation of 3 servers when they start the streaming session. As more viewers join, the popularity is followed by an increase in the number of servers provisioned by Twitch. The figure also shows how drops in viewing figures are accompanied by a decrease in the number of servers. When looking at the number of servers per continent, it can be seen that the capacity is adjusted independently per region, with the Chinese streamer having only 3 instances in Europe and America. Again, this confirms that Twitch scales dynamically the number of servers allocated to a channel, depending on the view count. Moreover, it indicates that each region is scaled independently based on the number of viewers in that region.

4.2   Scaling of Servers Across Continents

The previous section shows that the number of servers hosting the channel is correlated with the number of viewers watching the channel per region. We next investigate how the scaling works across continents. Figure 4 presents the fraction of servers found in each continent for each channel (based on its number

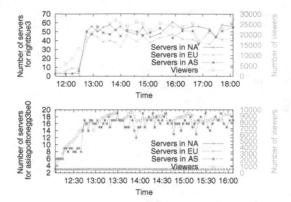

Fig. 3. (*a*) Number of servers found for channel nightblue3 (US streamer) as a time-series; (*b*) Number of servers found for channel asiagodtonegg3be0 (Asian streamer) as a timeseries. The number of servers are scaled independently in each region.

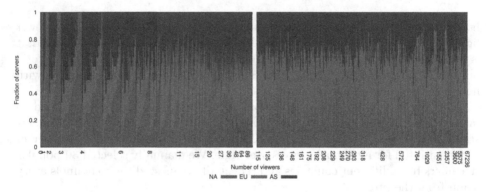

Fig. 4. Fraction of servers found from NA, EU and AS cluster for the bottom 70% (left) and top 10% channels (right). Only popular channels are replicated outside of NA (Color figure online)

of viewers). We present both the bottom 70% and top 10% of all channels during one snapshot.

We can see from Fig. 4 that channels with a small number of viewers tend to be predominantly served from NA only (red). 67% of channels with 0 viewers are exclusively hosted in the US; this drops to 63% for 1 viewer, 48% for 2 viewers, 40% for 4 viewers, and just 24% for 5 viewers. As the number of viewers increases, the fraction of US servers hosting the stream decreases (to be replaced by both EU and AS servers). Channels with over 50 viewers are nearly always served from all three continents. Figure 4 also shows the server distribution of the top 10% channels, with 21% of servers in NA, 53% in EU and 26% in AS overall.

Briefly, we also see distinct patterns within each continent. For example, in NA, channels are always first hosted in San Francisco (sfo) before being scaled out to other server locations in the region. The same occurs in EU and AS, with Amsterdam (ams) and Seoul (sel) usually hosting a stream before other continental locations.

5   Client Redirection and Traffic Localisation

The previous section has shown that Twitch tries to adapt to the global demand by progressively pushing streams to multiple servers on multiple continents. In this section, we explore the mapping of clients to these regions by utilising our full set of proxies. We perform a full channel crawl from each location, and see where the clients are redirected to (*cf.* Sect. 2). Table 1 provides a breakdown of the redirections between different continents. In the majority of cases, Twitch assigns a server from the nearest continent: 99.4% of the requests in North America and 96% of requests in South America are handled by servers in NA; 82% of the requests in Europe and 78.2% of the requests in Africa are served by EU servers.

Table 1. Traffic distribution of Twitch clusters globally.

Fraction (%)	NA cluster	EU cluster	AS cluster
North America	99.4	0.6	0
South America	96	4	0.01
Europe	17	82	1
Africa	21.8	78.2	0
Asia	34.4	20	45.6

Our results also contain some noticeable outliers. Asian servers handle only 45.6% of requests from Asian clients; more than one third of the requests are handled by NA servers. That said, the NA cluster also absorbs the vast majority of requests from other regions that are not resolved to their local servers, including AS and EU. In order to explore the reasons behind this apparent mismatch, we investigate for each proxy the fraction of redirections to its local (continental) servers when requesting the full list of channels. Figure 5 shows the empirical CDF of the fraction of local servers observed by each proxy. We separate the plots into each continent for comparison. A clear contrast can be seen among the three different regions: nearly 90% of the clients in North America are always served by NA servers; and almost 40% of the clients in Europe are always served by EU servers. However, for Asia, 50% of the clients are never served by the Asian servers, and only 10% are entirely served by Asian servers.

As previously noted, the number of servers that host a stream is closely related to the stream's popularity. Hence, we also inspect the relationship between channel popularity and the ability of clients to access streams from their local cluster. Figure 6 presents the fraction of requests that are redirected

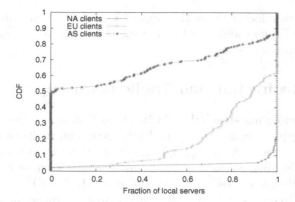

Fig. 5. Fraction of local servers observed for each proxy. Clients are grouped by continents for comparison. NA users are usually served locally, whereas most AS clients must contact servers outside of AS.

to a cluster on the same continent, plotted against the popularity of the channels. Again, it can be seen that European clients get far more local redirects, whilst Asian requests regularly leave the continent. This is consistent across all channel popularities, although in both cases, more popular channels receive a large number of local redirects.

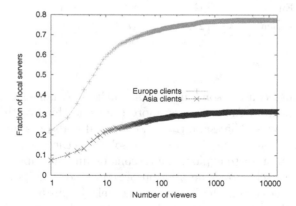

Fig. 6. The fraction of local servers used *vs.* the total number of viewer for a channel. More popular channels are more likely to be locally available on a continent.

An obvious question is why do the Asian clients suffer from such poorly localised redirects. Only 15% of our Asian clients exclusively utilise Asian servers; 50% are *never* redirected within Asia. To analyse why this might be the case, we revisit the peering policies of those particular networks. When inspecting the 15% of Asian clients that exclusively rely on Asian servers, we see that they all share the same private peering facilities with Twitch (based on PeeringDB). For example, AS36351, AS9381 and Twitch are all registered in Equinix, Hong Kong. In contrast, the remaining networks do not peer. Therefore, it is likely that Asia fails to localise its requests because of these poor existing peering arrangements (Sect. 3). Even if the servers in Asia are geographically nearby, their network distance might be higher. Similar scenarios can be found in previous work [13], highlighting that topology and peering is far more important than geographic distance.

6   Related Work

Live video streaming is challenging due to the size of video content and the time constraints involved. Various architectures have been developed to support these challenges. Peer-to-Peer (P2P) video streaming has emerged as one promising solution, leveraging the resources of end users. For example, LiveSky [23] and PPLive (CoolStreaming [22]) are two examples of deployed systems, relying on P2P assistance. Other approaches rely on cloud assistance; Chen *et al.* used Amazon Cloud, Microsoft Azure and Planetlab nodes to build an elastic system to support various loads in live video streaming [11].

To date, this is the first work revealing the content delivery infrastructure of Twitch; we believe this could be very influential when designing future Twitch-like systems. That said, there has been a wealth of work looking, more generally, at content delivery infrastructures in Video on Demand and live video streaming. For example, in [8], the authors use PlanetLab nodes to measure YouTube's infrastructure. They found that YouTube uses many different cache servers hosted inside edge networks. Torres *et al.* [19] captured traces from a campus network, showing that the server selected in the YouTube CDN is usually the closest one to the user. There has also been work looking at various other systems, *e.g.,* Netflix [7,9], YouPorn [20] and Hulu [6]. However, whereas previous work has focussed on platforms in which static (*i.e.,* non-live) content is being delivered, Twitch suffers from far greater constraints due to its live real time nature (making caching redundant). Critically, Twitch is the first major platform to employ *user generated* live video streaming. In our past work [12], we explored the nature of channel and game popularity to confirm the significant scale of Twitch (channel peaks exceeding 1.2 million viewers).

7   Conclusion

In this paper, we have studied Twitch as an example of modern user generated live streaming services. We have made a number of findings, which reveal how Twitch's infrastructure differs from traditional "static" streaming platforms like YouTube. Through empirical measurements, we have shown that Twitch operates a much more centralised infrastructure — in a single AS with POPs on four continents (compared to the thousands used by YouTube). This is likely because the benefits of using highly decentralised caches are less than for that of live streaming (as time-shifted caching cannot take place for live streams). These design choices naturally lead to a different scale-up strategy to that of content delivery networks like YouTube, which typically rely on reactive caching. Driven by the delay sensitivity of live streaming, Twitch progressively and proactively replicates streams across servers only after sufficient demand is observed. Critically, this occurs on a pre-region basis, dynamically replicating streams based on *local* demand. This more centralised approach places a much greater reliance on effective peering and interconnection strategies (as Twitch does not place caches inside other networks). We observed the challenges this brings in Asia, where clients were redirected to NA due to poor local interconnectivity with Twitch's AS.

Although Twitch is only one example of user generated live streaming, we believe its scale and success indicates that its architecture could be an effective design choice for other similar platforms. Hence, there are a number of future lines of work that can build on this study. We are interested in exploring a range of system improvements for Twitch-like platforms, including a more sophisticated control plane that redirects on several factors, expanding their multicast design, introducing peer-to-peer techniques, or addressing issues with peering. We would also like to expand our study by measuring realtime streaming performance and comparing with other platforms, such as YouTube's recent gaming service. Only through this will it be possible to evaluate the best architecture(s) for future user generated streaming platforms.

References

1. AS46489 Twitch.tv IPv4 Peers. http://bgp.he.net/AS46489#_peers
2. PeeringDB - AS46489 Twitch.tv. https://www.peeringdb.com/net/1956
3. Twitch. https://www.twitch.tv/
4. Twitch is 4th in Peak US Internet Traffic. https://blog.twitch.tv/
5. Twitch: The 2015 Retrospective. https://www.twitch.tv/year/2015
6. Adhikari, V.K., Guo, Y., Hao, F., Hilt, V., Zhang, Z.L.: A tale of three CDNs: an active measurement study of Hulu and its CDNs. In: 2012 IEEE Conference on Computer Communications Workshops (INFOCOM WKSHPS), pp. 7–12. IEEE (2012)
7. Adhikari, V.K., Guo, Y., Hao, F., Varvello, M., Hilt, V., Steiner, M., Zhang, Z.L.: Unreeling netflix: understanding and improving multi-CDN movie delivery. In: 2012 Proceedings of IEEE INFOCOM, pp. 1620–1628. IEEE (2012)
8. Adhikari, V.K., Jain, S., Chen, Y., Zhang, Z.L.: Vivisecting YouTube: an active measurement study. In: 2012 Proceedings of IEEE INFOCOM, pp. 2521–2525. IEEE (2012)
9. Böttger, T., Cuadrado, F., Tyson, G., Castro, I., Uhlig, S.: Open connect everywhere: a glimpse at the internet ecosystem through the lens of the netflix CDN (2016). arXiv:1606.05519
10. Calder, M., Fan, X., Hu, Z., Katz-Bassett, E., Heidemann, J., Govindan, R.: Mapping the expansion of Google's serving infrastructure. In: Proceedings of the 2013 ACM Conference on Internet Measurement (IMC 2013), pp. 313–326. ACM (2013)
11. Chen, F., Zhang, C., Wang, F., Liu, J., Wang, X., Liu, Y.: Cloud-assisted live streaming for crowdsourced multimedia content. IEEE Trans. Multimed. **17**(9), 1471–1483 (2015)

12. Deng, J., Cuadrado, F., Tyson, G., Uhlig, S.: Behind the game: exploring the Twitch streaming platform. In: 2015 14th Annual Workshop on Network and Systems Support for Games (NetGames). IEEE (2015)
13. Fanou, R., Tyson, G., Francois, P., Sathiaseelan, A., et al.: Pushing the frontier: exploring the African web ecosystem. In: Proceedings of the 25th International Conference on World Wide Web (WWW 2016). International World Wide Web Conferences Steering Committee (2016)
14. Finamore, A., Mellia, M., Munafò, M.M., Torres, R., Rao, S.G.: YouTube everywhere: impact of device and infrastructure synergies on user experience. In: Proceedings of the 2011 ACM Conference on Internet Measurement (IMC 2011), pp. 345–360. ACM (2011)
15. Gill, P., Arlitt, M., Li, Z., Mahanti, A.: YouTube traffic characterization: a view from the edge. In: Proceedings of the 2007 ACM Conference on Internet Measurement (IMC 2007), pp. 15–28. ACM (2007)
16. Hamilton, W.A., Garretson, O., Kerne, A.: Streaming on Twitch: fostering participatory communities of play within live mixed media. In: Proceedings of the 32nd Annual ACM Conference on Human Factors in Computing Systems, pp. 1315–1324. ACM (2014)
17. Pires, K., Simon, G.: YouTube live and Twitch: a tour of user-generated live streaming systems. In: Proceedings of the 6th ACM Multimedia Systems Conference, MMSys 2015, pp. 225–230. ACM, New York (2015)
18. Siekkinen, M., Masala, E., Kämäräinen, T.: A first look at quality of mobile live streaming experience: the case of periscope. In: Proceedings of the 2016 ACM on Internet Measurement Conference, pp. 477–483. ACM (2016)
19. Torres, R., Finamore, A., Kim, J.R., Mellia, M., Munafo, M.M., Rao, S.: Dissecting video server selection strategies in the YouTube CDN. In: 2011 31st International Conference on Distributed Computing Systems (ICDCS), pp. 248–257. IEEE (2011)
20. Tyson, G., El Khatib, Y., Sastry, N., Uhlig, S.: Measurements and analysis of a major porn 2.0 portal. In: ACM Transactions on Multimedia Computing, Communications, and Applications (ACM ToMM) (2016)
21. Wang, B., Zhang, X., Wang, G., Zheng, H., Zhao, B.Y.: Anatomy of a personalized livestreaming system. In: Proceedings of the 2016 ACM on Internet Measurement Conference, pp. 485–498. ACM (2016)
22. Xie, S., Li, B., Keung, G.Y., Zhang, X.: Coolstreaming: design, theory, and practice. IEEE Trans. Multimed. 9(8), 1661–1671 (2007)
23. Yin, H., Liu, X., Zhan, T., Sekar, V., Qiu, F., Lin, C., Zhang, H., Li, B.: Design and deployment of a hybrid CDN-P2P system for live video streaming: experiences with livesky. In: Proceedings of the 17th ACM International Conference on Multimedia, pp. 25–34. ACM (2009)

Internet Access for All: Assessing a Crowdsourced Web Proxy Service in a Community Network

Emmanouil Dimogerontakis[✉], Roc Meseguer, and Leandro Navarro

Universitat Politècnica de Catalunya, Barcelona, Spain
{edimoger,meseguer,leandro}@ac.upc.edu

Abstract. Global access to the Internet for all requires a dramatic reduction in Internet access costs particularly in developing areas. This access is often achieved through several proxy gateways shared across local or regional access networks. These proxies allow individuals or organisations to share the capacity of their Internet connection with other users. We present a measurement study of a crowdsourced Internet proxy service in the guifi.net community network that provides free Web access to a large community with many small proxy servers spread over the network. The dataset consists of Squid proxy logs for one month, combined with network topology and traffic data. Our study focuses on a representative subset of the whole network with about 900 nodes and roughly 470 users of the web proxy service. We analyse the service from three viewpoints: Web content traffic from users, performance of proxies and influence of the access network. We find clear daily patters of usage, excess capacity and little reuse of content which makes caching almost unnecessary. We also find variations and small inefficiencies in the distribution of traffic load across proxies and the access network, related to the locality and manual proxy choice. Finally, users experience an overall usable Internet access with good throughput for a free crowdsourced service.

Keywords: Community network · guifi.net · User experience · Proxy service

1 Introduction

The majority of the world's population does not have any or an adequate Internet access [12], implying that the Internet cannot provide service and reach everyone without discrimination. Global access to the Internet for all requires a dramatic reduction in Internet access costs especially in geographies and populations with low penetration [9]. Community Networks (WMNs) [17] allow local communities to build their own network infrastructures and provide affordable internetworking with the Internet including the deepest rural communities worldwide [15]. Internet companies have also tried to address the digital divide with

© Springer International Publishing AG 2017
M.A. Kaafar et al. (Eds.): PAM 2017, LNCS 10176, pp. 72–84, 2017.
DOI: 10.1007/978-3-319-54328-4_6

initiatives such as Facebook's FreeBasics [16] or the Google Global Cache. Sharing resources, such as local access infrastructure or global Internet transport, is encouraged at all levels [7,11] to lower the cost of network infrastructures and Internet services.

Among many other community networks, guifi.net exemplifies how regional communities can develop their own network infrastructures governed as a commons [2], using wired and wireless links to create a regional IP network, and sharing several Internet gateways among all their participants. These gateways are usually web proxies for Web access, the most popular traffic, but can accommodate other traffic through HTTP CONNECT, SOCKS or tunneling. Proxies, not exempt from the drawbacks of middleboxes, have also additional advantages: some content and DNS resolution can be shared in caches, and most important, proxies can protect the privacy of end users if they trust the proxy provider. Access to the Internet through Web proxy gateways relies on individuals or organisations sharing the full or spare capacity of its Internet connection with other guifi.net users. However, these crowdsourced gateway nodes have limited processing and Internet transfer capacity and might be overloaded by the demand.

In this paper we contribute an analysis of a large crowdsourced proxy service in a regional community network. A large population of C clients can browse the Web taking advantage of the aggregated capacity of a pool of P contributed web proxies, with $C > P$, spread over a regional network infrastructure, at a fraction of the cost of C Internet connections.

We first describe the guifi.net network, its proxy service and the collected datasets in Sect. 2. Then we analyse the service from three viewpoints: (1) service usage by end-users: patterns of usage and content in Sect. 3, (2) the proxy, Sect. 4, in terms of caching, users, performance and variability, and (3) the local network, Sect. 5, in terms of topology and usage. Our measurements describe the effectiveness of a simple setup of a regional network sharing a set of Web proxies in delivering free basic Web access to a large population.

2   The guifi.net Proxy Service

guifi.net is an open, free, and neutral network built by citizens and organisations pooling their resources to build and operate a local network infrastructure, governed as a common pool resource [2]. The network infrastructure is mostly wireless [17] with a fiber backbone. Participants can extend the network to reach new locations and use it to access intranet services like the web proxy service.

The most popular application in community networks is web access and guifi.net is no exception. Web proxy nodes connected both to guifi.net and an ISP act as free gateways to the Internet to the community network users. Proxies run on simple servers and take advantage of individuals or organisations (like libraries or municipalities) offering their Internet access to other guifi.net users. Using web proxies, public entities can provide free Internet access without infringing telecom market competence regulations. While some of the web proxies are kept as a private service, 356 out of the 477 registered web proxy servers in the network (May 2016) are shared with all the network registered participants (12,500). A registered member is allowed to use any proxy of their convenience, although recommended to use one nearby. Users can select or change its choice based on quality of experience. Therefore, while some proxies may become popular and highly used, others may remain underused.

Data collection: For our analysis we chose to study the Llucanes guifi.net zone, a region in the Osona county of Catalunya, Spain. As explained in [6], this zone is representative of other rural guifi.net networks. Furthermore, Llucanes is the only guifi.net zone with published anonymized logs for all (four) involved operational proxies. Even-day proxy log entries anonymise the client IP address and show information about the requested URLs, while odd-day proxy logs show the opposite. We assisted in the preparation and publication of these logs. The logs combined with other openly accessible information about network topology, network links and network traffic information, provide a consistent and complete view of this regional network.

3   Service Usage Viewpoint

The behavior of the users and the service can be described at macro-level as a set of time series concerning metrics that can be extracted from the monthly logs, namely bytes per request, number of requests and number of users.

The traffic time series for the aggregate set of proxies shows a daily repetitive pattern, but also strong aperiodic negative spikes, which were statistically verified as a dominant period of 1 day, and the second largest peak at 12 h.

Service usage: The majority of the traffic is due to a relatively small number of large requests (20% of the requests produce 97% of the traffic), while the rest of the requests present little variation in size. Additionally, as expected, the majority of the traffic (90%) is created by 15% of the users. However, in contrast to the distribution of request size, the distribution of traffic and number of requests per user varies exponentially across users. For the analysis of the service processing rate we calculated the **request processing throughput** as the bits per time elapsed for each request, depicted in Fig. 1, ranging from less than 10^7 for the worst 10% to at least 10^8 for more than 80% of the requests.

Content analysis: Using the even-day proxy logs we looked at the request types and target URL of the users' requests. The majority of the traffic, almost 50%, consists of HTTP CONNECT requests, which is the method to establish TCP tunnels over HTTP, mostly all HTTPS which is indisputably the main usage appearing in the logs. While for HTTP CONNECT we cannot know the corresponding content type, the most common type for the rest of the requests is the generic *application/** with 23%, followed by *video/** (19%) and *image/** (5.5%).

The traffic for all analysed proxies in Table 1, including HTTP CONNECT, shows that the top video portal traffic occupies 36% of the traffic, which is an impressive large amount. For completeness, we mention that this is not reflected

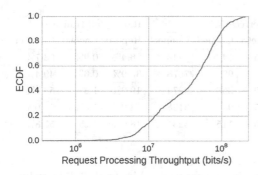

Fig. 1. Processing rate per request

Table 1. Top domains by traffic

Domain	Traffic fraction
googlevideo	27.85%
mega	16.73%
fbcdn	5.40%
rncdn3	2.80%
nflxvideo	2.70%
xvideos	2.60%
tv3	2.54%
level3	2.51%
google	1.96%
apple	1.78%

in the number of requests, therefore it is attributed on the size of the objects requested. Since video is by far the HTTP type with most traffic, it is not surprising to find that 4 out of 10 top domains are video portals. We also found that the distribution of web traffic per URL can roughly approximate a Zipf distribution, equivalent to results in [14] with domestic Internet connections.

4   The Proxy Viewpoint

In this section we investigate the capabilities and influence of the proxy servers involved. Our dataset concerns the only 4 proxies operating in the Llucanes zone. Table 2 shows the CPU and RAM characteristics of the proxy servers, as well as the nominal maximum throughput of the Internet connection they offer. They are very diverse, with great differences in Internet throughput (4–80 Mbps). We also observe that proxy 11252 has the slowest combined characteristics. Despite that these servers provide other services, e.g. SNMP, the interference caused by other services is expected to be negligible.

Table 2. Characteristics of the proxies

Id	CPU	RAM	Max throughput
3982	Intel amd64 2-core 2.6 GHz	2 GB	80 Mbps
10473	Intel x86 2-core 2.6 GHz	0.5 GB	6 Mbps
11252	AMD Athlon(tm) XP 1700+	0.5 GB	4 Mbps
18202	Intel amd64 2-core 2.7	2 GB	8 MBps

Table 3. Average volume of data in all proxies and ratios in a month of logs

Proxy	Different data (MB)			Data transferred (MB)				Ratio (/all transfrd)		
	All	Repetd	Cached	All	Repetd	Cached	Connect	Repetd	Cached	Connect
10473	606	37	9.2	1481	95	14.3	943	6.4%	0.9%	63.7%
11252	3572	1234	28	15352	5512	99	7578	35.9%	0.6%	49.4%
18202	6384	1498	151	15963	3039	253	9274	19.0%	1.6%	58.1%
3982	2542	435	55	6019	855	96	3128	14.2%	1.6%	52.0%
Avg	3276	801	61	9704	2376	115	5231	18.9%	1.2%	55.8%

The analysis of logs for the four proxies is summarized in Table 3. The values are averages for each proxy over a month of daily logs. The first group of columns (Different data) shows a data object storage perspective, with the amount of different data objects requested (disregarding the number of requests for each). The second group (Data transferred) shows a data transfer perspective, with the amount of traffic in each category. The third group shows data transfer ratios to the total transferred. We distinguish between "All" content, seen or transferred by the proxy, content requested repeatedly (same URL, cacheable or not), content served from the cache (checked or not against the server), and content that is invisible (Connect method, typically HTTPS, passed through blindly).

Cache effectiveness: As introduced before, the passed-through content (HTTPS) represents the majority of the proxy traffic (49.4–64%). Although URLs repeat significantly (6.4–36% of proxy traffic), the content successfully served from the cache (after validation or not) only represents a negligible amount (1–1.6%). Considering the number of requests instead of the amount of data, despite URLs repeat often (20–41%), the content does not seem cache friendly, as cache hits only represent a very small portion (3–10%). The analysis in number of requests compared to byte count indicates that cached content usually corresponds to small objects. Bad cache performance can be attributed to characteristics of the proxy service, such as small cache size, small number of concurrent users per proxy, or to increasingly non-cacheable served content. We next look at how these apply to our scenario, claiming that non-cacheable content is the main factor affecting cache performance.

Cache size: As far as the cache size, the default allocated cache size in guifi.net proxy settings is 10 GB of secondary storage, while in some proxies caching is not even enabled. However, we discovered that cached content that results in cache hits only accounts for a maximum of 151 MB (if all repeated URLs were cacheable) and an average of 61 MB (based on cache HITs) of data per day. In the extreme case where all content were cacheable and discounting the transparent CONNECT/HTTPS data, the amount of daily data seen (i.e. all content for all URL seen) accounts for a maximum of 1.5 GB or 801 MB on average, easily achievable with RAM-based caches.

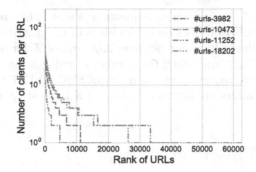

Fig. 2. Rank of URLs by number of clients requesting them per proxy

Sharing across clients: Proxies can provide the benefit of sharing network resources, reusing not only HTTP content, but also reusing DNS resolution data as client web browsers delegate, or even reusing (pooling) established TCP connections among different clients. Figure 2 shows the popularity of URLs across different clients in each proxy over a month, with top values between 60 to 212 different clients accessing each given URL. The number is related to the structure of the service, with many decentralized proxies with few users each and no inter-cache cooperation, which limits the potential of sharing cached content across more users.

Proxy selection: Users are instructed to check the public list of nearby proxies (in their network zone) in the public network management directory of the community network with shows a list of nearby proxies, including status and availability ratio, or follow the advice of trusted neighbors with previous usage experience. Therefore the choice is influenced by social factors and the reputation of each proxy, but in most cases the first choice is the nearest operational proxy with acceptable availability or reputation. Typically several nearby Web proxy services are configured in client Web browsers. As all federated proxies use the same authentication service, users are free to choose whatever proxy they prefer. The choice of proxy is rather fixed and prioritized, only switching to lower choice proxies when the first fails to reply.

Users and proxies: Figure 3 presents the distribution of the average number of users per hour. The different proxies show similar distributions, though we observe that proxy 10473 has a differentiated demand, with 40% of time without any user and a maximum of 10 users per hour. The rest of proxies, the majority of time (60%) have an almost linear distribution between 5 and 25 users, with near equally distributed values, and an average of around 17 users per hour for proxies 11252 and 18202, and an average of 12 users for proxy 3982. The different distributions among proxies is a result of preference for proximity and manual selection. To complete the picture, we found an average of 10 users in periods of 10 s, an average of 76 different users per proxy and day, and a maximum of 254 in a month. The user's distribution among proxies has a clear impact in the distribution of the number of requests in Fig. 4. The ordering of proxies according to the number of users remains visible in the distribution of requests. Also, there is near-linear behavior between 20% and 60% for all proxies except 10473. For proxies 11272 and 18202 the number of requests per hour is typically between 1 K and 10 K requests, with a mean of 8187 and 6716 respectively. In proxy 3982 typical values are between 500 and 1 K requests per hour.

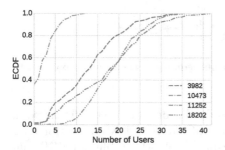

Fig. 3. Hourly average users per proxy

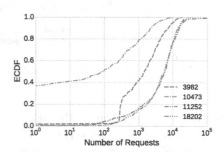

Fig. 4. Hourly average requests per proxy

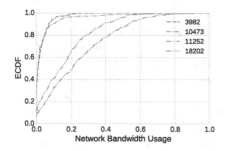

Fig. 5. Network usage per proxy

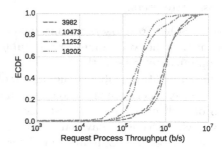

Fig. 6. Hourly average request processing throughput per proxy

Regarding the number of clients seen by a proxy every day, the values (min, average, max) range from the lowest in proxy 10473 (14, 20, 27) to the highest in proxy 3982 (59, 82, 101). These numbers reflect the spirit of a highly decentralized service with many small capacity local proxies.

Internet connection and processing performance: Figure 5 provides the distribution of the Internet connection usage per proxy, calculated as the approximate instant connection throughput of each proxy normalized by its maximum Internet throughput as provided in Table 2. All proxies show low utilization of their network resources, being approximately less than 0.3 (30%) for all the proxies for 80% of the time. Nevertheless, proxies 11252 and 18202 have significantly

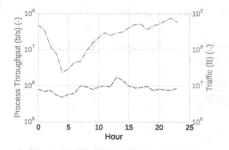
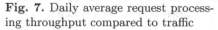
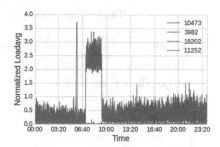

Fig. 7. Daily average request processing throughput compared to traffic

Fig. 8. Daily median loadavg per
proxy normalized by #CPUs

higher traffic. Moreover, Fig. 6 shows the distributions of the request processing
throughput. We observe that all proxies have almost identical distribution but
around different mean values, depending on the individual characteristics of the
proxy. Moreover, we can see that a significant percentage (>60%) of the time
proxies serve at a very narrow range of processing throughput, meaning they
can offer a stable service. Even in the worst cases, the service does not suffer
from extreme degradation, while remaining higher than 100 Kbps 80% of the
time. We also observe that for proxies 3982 and 11252, the processing throughput distribution resembles the number of requests distribution in Fig. 4 possibly
indicating, as before, that the proxies are not saturated.

To gain a more complete perspective we also studied the daily aggregates of
the traffic, users and requests clearly observing not only the expected human
daily pattern but also a clear effect of the different way each proxy receives and
serves request as a result of the users' manual proxy selection. Moreover, studying the mean daily patterns, we noticed that, as seen in Fig. 7, the processing
throughput presents very small variations implying a stable service behavior.
Furthermore, the traffic volume varies more than 1.5 orders of magnitude. The
fact that the processing throughput is not affected by the traffic size confirms our
observation that the servers are not saturated. Additionally, in order to verify
that the processing capabilities of proxies are not a bottleneck for the service,
we monitored the proxies' CPU using the *loadvg* Linux metric. The results, presenting a strong daily cyclic pattern, are summarized in Fig. 8 that shows the
daily median of the per-minute loadavg for each proxy normalized by the number of CPUs. Except from 3982, affected by other co-located network services,
the proxies are not overloaded. The brief daily peak in each proxy is due to the
daily restart of the proxy that includes a cache reindexing. Even at that small
scale, we observed the daily cycle of human activity with preference for evenings
and really reduced traffic during the first hours of the day. The pattern is visible
in all the described metrics in different degrees.

From all the above we can conclude that the proxies are able to offer a stable
service, with respect to the traffic load, allowing them to be used as an alternative
domestic Internet connection. Moreover, in our concrete scenario, the network

Table 4. Summary of Llucanes network graph

Graph	Nodes	Edges	Degree max/mean/min	Diameter
Base-graph	902	914	98/2.04/1	11
Proxy-clients-graph	463	472	60/2.04/1	10
Backbone-graph	47	56	10/2.38/1	9

capacity of the proxies is underutilized assuming that no other services co-located in the host of the proxy are heavily using the Internet network capacity.

5   The Local Network Viewpoint

The local network infrastructure has also an influence in the final user experience. For the analysis we used information extracted from odd day logs that provide these details while hiding URL destinations.

Network structure: We refer to the entire zone network as the *base graph*. Moreover, we refer as *proxy-clients graph* to the part of the Llucanes network including only the nodes (clients, routers, proxies) that participate in the proxy service. Similarly to many rural community network deployments, the network consists of a small set of interconnected routers, the *backbone graph*, where each router is connected with a large number of end nodes, mostly 802.11b wireless links [17]. Users access the entire guifi.net network from the end nodes. Some of the routers act also as hosts for various guifi.net services, including the proxy service. More information concerning the network structure, hardware characteristics, and protocols used in guifi.net is available in [17].

Table 4 describes the main characteristics of the aforementioned graphs. We notice that the mean degree of the base graph and of the proxy-clients graph is very low since the end-nodes dominate the distribution of degrees. The low mean degree value in the backbone graph is more interesting though, since it implies that the majority of the routers have only two neighbors. Figures 9 and 10 provide a view of the proxy-clients graph and the backbone graph. The colors of the participating nodes and routers indicate that they are using the proxy with the same color. Moreover, in Fig. 10 the darkness of the link color denotes the cost in latency for a byte to cross this link, therefore the darker the color the more expensive is the link to use.

Network usage: Due to the almost static (manual) proxy selection, the analysis of local network usage can show the effect of selection on local network usage and the perceived user experience. Towards that end, we first analyse metrics of distance between the users and the proxies. Figure 11 shows the distribution of the number of hops between users and their selected proxies. The distribution is almost uniform for 95% of the users with values from 1 to 6 hops. The remaining 5% is split between 7 and 8 hops. Nevertheless, we observe that manual choices result to a slight increase in number of hops, possibly introducing small

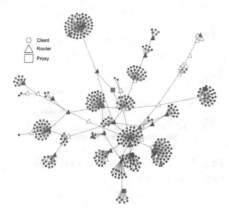

Fig. 9. Llucanes proxies and clients (Color figure online)

Fig. 10. Llucanes backbone (Color figure online)

unnecessary overheads. The latency involved, depicted in Fig. 12, shows a different behavior. Almost 80% of the users experience an average latency smaller than 15 ms to reach their proxy. The remaining 20% lies between 20 ms to 35 ms. Despite the almost uniform distribution of hops, latency values vary much less, implying that during normal network conditions, the distance between the users and proxies is not significantly deteriorating the user experience for web services.

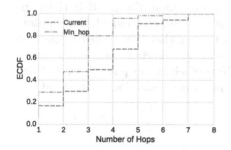

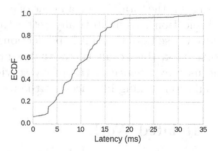

Fig. 11. Number of network hops between users and their selected proxies

Fig. 12. Average latency between users and their selected proxies

Download throughput: As described earlier, the request processing throughput is calculated using the request elapsed time, which includes the time the proxy requires until the last byte of the web object is sent to the client. Therefore, any significant local network deterioration affects the throughput behavior. Based on this observation we can utilize the request processing throughput metric for objects larger than 1 MB, in order to estimate significant degradation on the user experience. Including smaller objects would give unreliable throughput results due to the noticeable influence of network buffering in the proxy, DNS

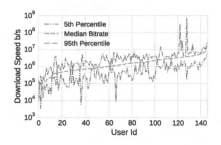
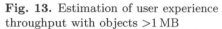
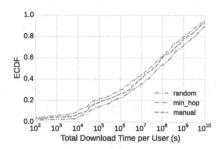

Fig. 13. Estimation of user experience throughput with objects >1 MB

Fig. 14. User cost as sum of download times (1 month)

caching and network latency variations for short connections. Figure 13 illustrates the individual user experience in throughput estimated for objects larger than 1 MB, under the simplifying assumption that users focus on few or a single large object at a time. If so, our measures could be taken as a lower bound for the experienced individual download throughput. Median values of download throughput appear quite stable with median values ranging from 0.1 Mbps to 10 Mbps for different users. A quite good result for the many users of a free crowdsourced service.

Furthermore, in order to show the margin for improvement in the user experience using other proxy selection strategies, we simulated the traffic of the users using a *min_hop* and a random strategy considering local link latencies. As seen in Fig. 14, the total download time of each user throughout the month in the manual selection is asymptotically better than the random selection while asymptotically worse than the min_hop selection. Considering that the proxies are not the bottleneck, this result shows that a proxy selection mechanism could improve the user experience of the proxy service. Nevertheless, we plan to extend our simulations taking into account the proxies processing and download speed.

6   Related Work

Most work on wireless networks focuses on usage traffic patterns, link level characteristics and topologies, but not user experience, e.g. MadMesh [4], Google WiFi [1] and Meraki [3] networks. In these studies, Internet access is direct instead of using proxies, and these wireless networks are homogeneous. Thus, measurement results cannot easily be compared with this. In the Google WiFi and MadMesh transfer rates are limited to 1 Mbps, but 80% getting less than 80 Kbps in Google WiFi. In MadMesh 80% get less than 1 Mbps with 85% of the clients connected within 3 hops to Internet, comparable with our results that achieve higher speed but more hops to a web proxy.

Facebook's Free Basics [16] shows comparable performance (80–600 Kbps for FB vs. 0.1–10 Mbps median speeds) better in our case, despite significant differences: in clients (mobile devices vs. any device), access network (cellular mobile carrier vs. wireless fixed community network), web proxies (centralized large servers vs. distributed small servers with network locality), and web service and content providers (redesigned and optimized vs. unmodified content).

The web proxy business has changed significantly over the years. The percentage of cacheable content has been decreasing, coupled with a dramatic increase of HTTPS traffic. The performance of web proxies is not only about high-level metrics such as hit rates. Low-level details such as HTTP cookies, aborted connections, and persistent connections between clients and proxies as well as between proxies and servers have a visible impact on performance, particularly in heterogeneous bandwidth environments [8]. In [5], authors analyse a mobile network topology with a two level cache hierarchy. Their claim that a caching system can be efficient when 5.1% of traffic is suitable for caching, shows that the lower rates of caching in our case may not be that beneficial.

Wireless network user experience has been characterized previously. The first [13] focuses on web traffic and the use of proxies to access Internet content in rural areas. Five years ago, using a single high latency and slower VSAT Internet connection (64–128 Kbps) obtained RTT values sometimes over 10 s, closer to a DTN case, and cache hit rates of 43%. There are also complementary lessons, about security or that content from CDN is usually not cacheable, but the scenarios are too different. The second study [10] looks at web traffic patterns and content caching. They mention the decreasing cache hit rates over previous studies, even lower in our study 5 years later with a dramatic increase of HTTPS traffic.

7   Summary of Lessons Learned

The analysis of the guifi.net proxy service describes a crowdsourced, social solidarity driven, free basic Internet service built from many small proxy servers spread across a regional community network, contributed by locals for locals. These proxies act as gateways to Web content and DNS, that can be cached and shared among clients or act as middleboxes for HTTPS transfers, the majority of traffic. Being in the middle can also help protect the privacy of clients.

The analysis confirms the trend to non-cacheable content, small cacheable objects, and therefore small object caches that can even fit in RAM. Each proxy has a small number of clients, ranging from 14 to 101 per day. Moreover, there is a good balance of traffic and number of clients per proxy despite the manual proxy selection, driven by locality (same zone), end-user choice and advice from people living nearby. The system is simple and resilient since each proxy is independent and clients just switch to their next choice in case of failure of their proxy.

The service has satisfactory performance (0.1–10 Mbps, good client-proxy latency), without perceived Internet, access network or service congestion, despite the typical daily usage patterns. That can be attributed to the structure of the service with many small servers across a regional access network, close to end-users with locality preference. Nevertheless, scaling or coordination between services between different zones is not trivial. Future work lies in exploring optimization by automating service selection with a global perspective, under diverse cost and performance metrics.

In summary, a crowdsourced service that fulfills the goal of an usable, satisfactory and inexpensive free basic alternative Internet access service for many.

Acknowledgments. This work was partially supported by the EU funded Erasmus Mundus Joint Doctorate in Distributed Computing (EMJD-DC) (FPA 2012-0030), the EU Horizon 2020 project netCommons (H2020-688768), the Spanish government (TIN2016-77836-C2-2-R), and the Generalitat de Catalunya (2014-SGR-881). Our thanks to Davide Vega, Roger Baig and several guifi.net members that have made this work possible.

References

1. Afanasyev, M., Chen, T., Voelker, G., Snoeren, A.: Usage patterns in an urban wifi network. IEEE/ACM Trans. Netw. **18**(5), 1359–1372 (2010)
2. Baig, R., Roca, R., Freitag, F., Navarro, L.: guifi.net, a crowdsourced network infrastructure held in common. Comput. Netw. **90**, 150–165 (2015)
3. Biswas, S., et al.: Large-scale measurements of wireless network behavior. ACM SIGCOMM Comput. Commun. Rev. **45**(4), 153–165 (2015)
4. Brik, V., et al.: A measurement study of a commercial-grade urban wifi mesh. In: Internet Measurement Conference (IMC), pp. 111–124 (2008)
5. Catrein, D., et al.: An analysis of web caching in current mobile broadband scenarios. In: New Technologies, Mobility and Security (NTMS), pp. 1–5 (2011)
6. Cerdà, L.: On the topology characterization of guifi.net. In: Wireless and Mobile Computing, Networking and Communications (WiMob), pp. 389–396 (2012)
7. European Parliament and Council: Directive 2014/61/EU on measures to reduce the cost of deploying high-speed electronic communications networks, May 2014
8. Feldmann, A., et al.: Performance of web proxy caching in heterogeneous bandwidth environments. In: INFOCOM, pp. 107–116 (1999)
9. Gaia, W.G.: Global access to the internet for all research group. https://irtf.org/gaia (2016). Accessed 14 Sept 2016
10. Ihm, S., Pai, V.S.: Towards understanding modern web traffic. In: Internet Measurement Conference (IMC), pp. 295–312 (2011)
11. International Telecommunication Union: Trends in telecommunication reform 2008: six degrees of sharing (d-pref-ttr.10), July 2009
12. Internet Society: Global internet report 2015, October 2015
13. Johnson, D.L., Pejovic, V., Belding, E.M., van Stam, G.: Traffic characterization and internet usage in rural Africa. In: World Wide Web, pp. 493–502 (2011)
14. Maier, G., et al.: On dominant characteristics of residential broadband internet traffic. In: Internet Measurement Conference (IMC), pp. 90–102 (2009)
15. Rey-Moreno, C., et al.: Experiences, challenges and lessons from rolling out a rural wifi mesh network. In: ACM Computing for Dev (ACM-DEV), p. 11 (2013)
16. Sen, R., et al.: on the free bridge across the digital divide: assessing the quality of Facebook's free basics service. In: Proceedings of the 2016 ACM on Internet Measurement Conference (IMC), pp. 127–133 (2016)
17. Vega, D., et al.: A technological overview of the guifi.net community network. Comput. Netw. **93**, 260–278 (2015)

Security

A First Look at the CT Landscape: Certificate Transparency Logs in Practice

Josef Gustafsson[1], Gustaf Overier[1], Martin Arlitt[2], and Niklas Carlsson[1(✉)]

[1] Linköping University, Linköping, Sweden
niklas.carlsson@liu.se
[2] University of Calgary, Calgary, Canada

Abstract. Many of today's web-based services rely heavily on secure end-to-end connections. The "trust" that these services require builds upon TLS/SSL. Unfortunately, TLS/SSL is highly vulnerable to compromised Certificate Authorities (CAs) and the certificates they generate. Certificate Transparency (CT) provides a way to monitor and audit certificates and certificate chains, to help improve the overall network security. Using an open standard, anybody can setup CT logs, monitors, and auditors. CT is already used by Google's Chrome browser for validation of Extended Validation (EV) certificates, Mozilla is drafting their own CT policies to be enforced, and public CT logs have proven valuable in identifying rogue certificates. In this paper we present the first large-scale characterization of the CT landscape. Our characterization uses both active and passive measurements and highlights similarities and differences in public CT logs, their usage, and the certificates they include. We also provide insights into how the certificates in these logs relate to the certificates and keys observed in regular web traffic.

1 Introduction

The internet today involves billions of devices and millions of services that require private or confidential communication. Unfortunately, it is unthinkable to trust that every entity on the internet is who they claim to be. Instead, protocols such as Transport Layer Security (TLS) and its predecessor Secure Sockets Layer (SSL) rely heavily on the trust in Certificate Authorities (CAs) [2].

With TLS/SSL, CAs are responsible for verifying the identity of entities and issuing electronic proof in the form of X.509 certificates. For example, in the case of HTTPS, a server or domain that wants to prove its identity typically pays a CA (or an organization that a CA has delegated trust to, using chained certificates) to create a signed certificate that connects its identity with a public key that others can use to securely communicate with the server/domain. If that CA's root certificate is available in the browser's root store, the browser can then use the root certificate to validate this certificate. Once validated, the browser trusts that the public key belongs to the claimed server/domain.

Conceptually, certificates enable a user to trust that a service provider they want to use is who they say they are. However, in practice, there are numerous

© Springer International Publishing AG 2017
M.A. Kaafar et al. (Eds.): PAM 2017, LNCS 10176, pp. 87–99, 2017.
DOI: 10.1007/978-3-319-54328-4_7

issues that can undermine that trust, including human error, intentional fraud, etc. [13]. Many of these issues stem from every CA having the power to issue certificates for any domain and that there are no mechanisms to inform the domain owners of issued certificates. This has resulted in many hard-to-detect incidents, including a recent incident where Symantec issued test certificates for 76 domains they did not own (including domains owned by Google) and another 2,458 unregistered domains [23].

To improve the situation, the use of Certificate Transparency (CT) [17] has been proposed and standardized through IETF. In fact, after the Symantec incident mentioned above, Google demanded that Symantec log all of their certificates in public CT logs. With CT, certificates should be published in public append-only logs, whose content is verified by monitors, and whose cryptographic integrity are verified by auditors. Any organization or individual can operate a monitor to verify these public records.

Google's Chrome browser was the first to enforce CT, with Chrome 41 and later requiring CT for Extended Validation (EV) certificates (issued after Jan. 1, 2015). Before displaying visual cues to the user that normally come with EV certificates, the certificate needs to be accompanied by Signed Certificate Timestamps (SCTs), where an SCT is a promise that the certificate is included in a public log. Chrome requires an EV certificate to be included in at least one Google operated log and one non-Google operated log [15]. The choice to start with EV certificates was motivated by the EV certificates themselves being intended to follow stricter issuing criteria than regular Domain Validated (DV) and Organization Validated (OV) certificates.[1] Mozilla is currently drafting their own CT policies (expected to require that certificates are present in logs operated by two organizations separate from the CA) and are on track to start enforcing CT for EV later 2017. Both Chrome and Mozilla are expected to enforce CT also for DV some time in the future.

Although CT is standardized [17] and used at large scale, it is not publically known how CT logs are used in practice. In this paper we present the first large-scale characterization of the CT landscape. First, we implemented a basic CT monitor [17] that actively monitors all public logs submitted to Chrome up to Dec. 2015 (3 Google operated and 7 CA operated) and one large log operated by NORDUnet.[2] Second, we characterize both differences in basic properties related to how different policies are implemented at the logs and properties related to the log content itself, including the certificates they include, their overlap in coverage, as well as temporal differences between the logs and their usage. Third, to glean some insight into how the certificates in these logs and their usage relate to that seen in regular web traffic, we also use the certificates observed across 232 million HTTPS sessions observed on a university network.

---

[1] EV certificates were themselves introduced to address waning user trust.

[2] Technically, Google is also a CA. At the time of the measurements, no other production logs were known - only logs for testing purposes - although more production logs have appeared since. https://www.certificate-transparency.org/known-logs.

Our results highlight differences and similarities between the different logs. In general, there are significant differences in the certificates included in Google operated logs (that relies heavily on web crawls to identify certificates) and smaller CA operated logs. The coverage of the logs is broad. For example, for almost all domains observed in the university traces, there is at least one log with a valid DV certificate (despite such logging being voluntary for all CAs except Symantec), and for EV certification there are only small differences between the certificates that are included in Google logs and in CA operated logs.

The remainder of the paper is organized as follows. We first give a brief overview of CT (Sect. 2) and describe our collection methodology (Sect. 3). Next, we characterize the logs from the perspective of their properties alone (Sect. 4) and then based on the HTTPS traffic observed on campus (Sect. 5). Finally, related work (Sect. 6) and conclusions (Sect. 7) are presented.

2   Certificate Transparency

Certificate Transparency attempts to address flaws in the TLS/SSL certificate system [17,18]. CT extends classic TLS/SSL operation with CT logs, auditors, monitors, as well as new communication interfaces between all these entities. With CT, each log maintains an append-only hash tree based on a binary Merkle Hash Tree [20] and newly issued certificates are appended to one or more CT log. The logs return a signed promise of inclusion, called an SCT, which is used by the TLS server to prove to clients that the certificate is logged.

Logs commit to publishing a Signed Tree Head (STH) within a fixed amount of time of issuing the SCT, called the Maximum Merge Delay (MMD). The STH can be used to prove both that a certain entry was included at a certain point in time and that the log maintains consistency over time (i.e., every new tree is a superset of every old tree). A log that cannot prove consistency between two STHs is likely to be distrusted immediately. In practice, the inclusion process can be broken into an update interval (UI) and the time to publish (TTP), where UI is the time between issuing an SCT and incorporating the corresponding entry into the STH and TTP is the time between signing and publishing STHs. In general, a CT log is itself considered compliant with regards to the MMD (offering an acceptably small attack window) if UI+TTP < MMD.

Once the STH is published, monitors will have access to the certificate chain to detect any irregularities. A log can prove that a certain certificate has been included using an inclusion proof [17]. Auditors and monitors cooperate to ensure that logs are behaving correctly and that the log content corresponds to what the domain owners intended. In contrast to CAs, the CT logs are publicly auditable and enable anyone to verify claims of correctness. Furthermore, anyone can operate logs, monitors and auditors, making it infeasible for an adversary to control all instances.

3   Methodology and Datasets

For our data collection we implemented a basic CT monitor [17] in Python, which monitors the public logs and various domains, but that does not try to determine the legitimacy of the certificates. For the purpose of our study, we collected all certificates that have been added to eleven CT logs: the ten public logs submitted to Chrome (3 operated by Google and 7 CA operated logs) at the time of our last measurement (Dec. 2015) and one (non-production) log operated by NORDUnet. We recorded all fields of the individual certificates and validated the certificates against the Mozilla root store, as observed on Dec. 1, 2015.

Furthermore, to understand how representative the observed certificates of the different logs are compared with what a typical internet user sees, we also use a one-week long complementary dataset collected by passively monitoring the internet traffic to/from the University of Calgary, Canada [22]. Using Bro, we log specific information about the non-encrypted part of the TLS/SSL handshake, including all digital certificates sent. This dataset was collected Oct. 11–17, 2015, and covers 232 million HTTPS sessions, 67,644 unique certificates, and 552 million certificate exchanges. For most of our analysis we focus on the CT logs, and use the university dataset as a reference point.

4   Analysis of Logs

4.1   Basic Log Properties and Operational Measures

Table 1 summarizes the basic properties of the eleven logs we used. The logs are ordered based on when they were submitted to Chrome (second column). All logs allow HTTPS to be used when accessing the logs. Furthermore, all logs except Venafi (who uses RSA with SHA-256) use ECDSA (over the NIST P-256 curve)

Table 1. Basic properties of the CT logs.

Log name	Operated by	Submitted	URL	Roots	MMD	UI	TTP
Pilot	Google	2013-03-25	ct.googleapis.com/pilot	474	24 h	1 h	22 min
Aviator	Google	2013-09-30	ct.googleapis.com/aviator	474	24 h	1 h	22 min
Rocketeer	Google	2014-09-01	ct.googleapis.com/rocketeer	474	24 h	30 min	34 min
Digicert	Digicert	2014-09-30	ct1.digicert-ct.com/log	57	24 h	1 h	12 h
Izenpe	Izenpe	2014-11-10	ct.izenpe.com	40	24 h	1 min	< 1 min
Certly	Certly	2014-12-14	log.certly.io	183	24 h	10 min	< 1 min
Symantec	Symantec	2015-05-01	ct.ws.symantec.com	19	24 h	6 h	< 1 min
Venafi	Venafi	2015-06-11	ctlog.api.venafi.com	357	24 h	2 h	3 min
WoSign	WoSign	2015-09-22	ct.wosign.com	12	24 h	1 min	< 1 min
Vega	Symantec	2015-11-13	vega.ws.symantec.com	19	24 h	6 h	< 1 min
Plausible	NORDUnet	Not Subm	plausible.ct.nordu.net	442	24 h*	12 min	2 min

*Plausible operates with an unofficial MMD of 24 h.

to sign data structures (STHs and SCTs). Both techniques are recommended in RFC6962 [17] and are expected to provide roughly the same security.

The last four columns indicate large differences in how the logs are implemented and maintained. The *roots* column shows the number of accepted certificate-chain roots for the logs. We used the APIs provided by the CT logs to download all roots accepted by each log. Out of the 503 unique roots we observed across all logs, the three Google logs included 474 in their root store. In contrast, the CA operated logs typically included much fewer roots. For example, the two Symantec logs (Symantec and Vega) and the WoSign log only allowed certificates signed by 19 and 12 of the roots, respectively. These observations point to differing usage patterns. Based on the Google CT policy, for example, CAs may be incentivized to log any certificates they issue themselves, but there is little incentive for them to log certificates issued by competitors. In contrast, browser vendors may prefer to log at least the certificates accepted by the browser.

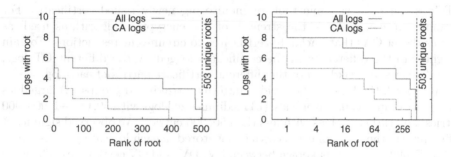

Fig. 1. Number of logs accepting each root for submitted entries.

With browsers increasingly requiring certificates to be found in multiple logs, many roots are starting to be included in several logs. Figure 1 shows the number of logs that include each root. In general, we have found that roughly 10% of the roots are included in six or more of the logs' root stores, and most of the roots are included in 3–5 of the root stores. Again, the three Google operated logs include the majority of the observed roots.

The last two columns provide insights into the time granularity at which the logs operate and how well the MMD is satisfied. First, referring to Sect. 2, remember that UI+TTP must be less than the MMD for the log to be considered compliant. In general, the (load dependent) UIs are substantially smaller than the 24-hour MMDs, suggesting that all logs typically require much less time to merge the certificate chain than the upper bound. However, the UIs differ substantially between logs. For example, the median UI observed in Table 1 varies from minute scale (e.g., Izenpe and WoSign) to hours (e.g., the Symantec and Google logs). In fact, on Oct. 16, 2016, the Aviator log (Google operated) overshot its MMD by 2.2 h. As a result, since Dec. 1, 2016, the log has been frozen and is no longer accepting new submissions.[3] This is a form of "soft untrusting"

---

[3] https://bugs.chromium.org/p/chromium/issues/detail?id=389514.

as old SCTs issued by Aviator are still honored. The incident has sparked a debate on if the policy needs to be updated. In general, a shorter interval can be convenient for both operators and clients, as it reduces the size of each merge and reduces the time until clients can request inclusion proofs.

The TTPs also differ substantially between logs. The notable outlier is Digicert with a 12-hour delay between signing and publishing STHs. When we asked, Digicert said that they sign STHs every hour, but use the extra delay for synchronizing between servers located in multiple datacenters. All other logs publish STHs within 1 h, although some have much shorter TTPs. While Table 1 reports median values, UIs and TTPs were relatively stable with small variations over the time we monitored the logs (up to Dec. 2015). The spike in UI that Aviator saw on Oct. 16, 2016, shows that there since have been larger variations.

4.2   Certificate Analysis

CT logs can be a valuable tool for monitoring newly issued certificates. For example, we can examine the strength of the encryption algorithms used, as well as detect CAs that backdate certificates to circumvent restrictions. To gain insight into the differences in the certificates logged by the different CT logs, Table 2 shows a breakdown of the different certificate entries of each log.

In general, the logs can be divided into three size-based groups: (i) large logs with more than $5,000,000$ entries, (ii) medium-sized logs with $50,000-1,000,000$ entries, and (iii) small logs with less than $50,000$ entries. We observed significant differences in the types of certificates being stored in each log category. Columns 2–4 in Table 2 show a breakdown between EV, DV, and OV certificates. The large difference in the ratio between DV and EV certificates observed for the four large logs (Pilot, Aviator, Rocketeerer, and Plausible; each with 5% EV certificates) and the top-four CA operated logs (Digicert, Izenpe, Certly, and Symantec; all in the 61–78% range) can be explained by the relative log sizes and differences in how the certificates are submitted. While the Google logs and Plausible have been populated by crawling the internet and submitting encountered certificates (capturing all types of certificates, including certificates of domains that may not themselves have chosen to participate in CT), it appears that Digicert, Izenpe, Certly, and Symantec primarily use the logs to store entries with the intent of using the SCTs in EV validation. The focus on EV certificates of both Digicert and Symantec is also visible in the university dataset, where these two CAs are responsible for 27.6% and 56.2% of the EV sessions (and a combined 37.9% of the unique EV certificates). However, in absolute numbers, the four large logs all include more EV certificates than the CA logs. We also note that the fraction of EV certificates observed in the three Google operated logs and Plausible are similar to the fractions observed in the wild. For example, in our university dataset EVs are observed in 4.9% of the observed leaf certificates and 6.3% of all sessions. The small logs (Venafi, WoSign, and Vega) are younger logs that at the time of the measurements still contained a large fraction of test entries, rather than entries intended for CT. These logs therefore have substantially different properties than the other categories.

Table 2. Distribution of certificate validation types and signature hashes.

Log name	Operated by	Entries	Validation			Encryption algorithm			
			DV	OV	EV	RSA (1024)	RSA (2048)	RSA (4096)	EC (256)
Pilot	Google	10,831,024	87%	8%	5%	2%	79%	3%	16%
Aviator	Google	10,069,865	87%	8%	5%	1%	78%	3%	17%
Rocketeer	Google	8,140,991	87%	8%	5%	1%	75%	4%	21%
Digicert	Digicert	229,858	18%	5%	78%	0%	96%	3%	0%
Izenpe	Izenpe	65,812	31%	1%	68%	0%	95%	5%	0%
Certly	Certly	161,740	36%	3%	61%	0%	94%	5%	0%
Symantec	Symantec	113,674	21%	5%	74%	0%	97%	2%	0%
Venafi	Venafi	4,626	85%	10%	5%	0%	93%	5%	1%
WoSign	WoSign	11,188	97%	1%	2%	0%	99%	1%	0%
Vega	Symantec	80	95%	0%	5%	0%	95%	0%	2%
Plausible	NORDUnet	5,893,906	88%	7%	5%	3%	90%	3%	4%

In general, the logging of other certificates than EV certificates can be used for testing and to preserve public records of certificates. The use of public logs provides the true owners of domains (or monitors) a much easier means to identify rogue certificates than having to search the web, especially since many rogue certificates may not be reachable from the internet. This has proven valuable in identifying certificates violating regulations, including improper certificates from both Comodo[4] and Symantec[5]. Finally, we note that the certificate ratios of the CA operated logs are expected to change as browsers start to require logging of DV and OV certificates too.

In general, most logged certificates we observed use strong algorithms, with the majority of certificates in all logs using RSA with 2048 bit keys ($\geq$75%). Columns 5–8 in Table 2 break down the distribution of algorithms used for the certificates in each log. In addition to RSA keys (of different lengths), we note that the three Google logs include a significant number (16–21%) of certificates using Elliptic Curve (EC) signatures.

However, the logs also capture many certificates with weak keys or signatures. First, despite that NIST recommended to stop using 1024-bit RSA keys in 2013 [4], before the first entries of any of the CT log, we observed a non-negligible use of such short keys in the logs that use crawling of the web to fill their records. All these four logs include 1–3% such entries. This is consistent with the 1.3% authority and 5.6% leaf certificates we observed on campus [22].

---

[4] https://cabforum.org/pipermail/public/2015-November/006226.html.
[5] https://security.googleblog.com/2015/10/sustaining-digital-certificate-security.html.

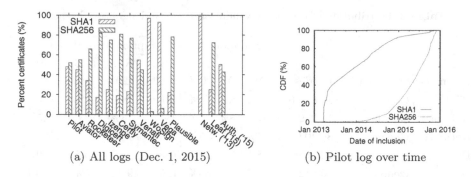

(a) All logs (Dec. 1, 2015)   (b) Pilot log over time

Fig. 2. Signatures used for certificates.

Second, despite that the SHA1 hash algorithm is susceptible to known attacks and CAs no longer sign new certificates with SHA1, SHA1 is observed in $17-97\%$ of signatures across the logs. Figure 2(a) breaks down the use of SHA1 and SHA256 across the logs. As reference points we also include values by Durumeric et al. [9] (Aug. 2013) and the university dataset (Oct. 2015) [22]. We note that most of the logs have numbers in-between those observed in the wild in 2013 and 2015, and that Plausible has a smaller fraction SHA1 usage than the three older Google logs. Given the append-only properties of these logs, this is to-be expected and supports observations that there is a reduction of SHA1 usage for new certificates. To understand the shift, Fig. 2(b) shows the cumulative distribution function (CDF) of all SHA1 and SHA256 certificates inserted as a function of time for the oldest and largest log (Pilot). As expected, the SHA1 inclusion rate is steadily decreasing, while the SHA256 rate is steadily increasing. Again, the newer logs (with fewer entries) stick out with a large fraction SHA1 certificates. These certificates have been added relatively recently and include a large fraction weaker self-signed SHA1 test certificates from Google CT.

One explanation that the outphasing of SHA1 is taking a long time is that many service providers, including Facebook and Twitter, are concerned that millions of users with older devices would lose access to their services and therefore want to delay the outphasing of SHA1[6]. With Facebook and Twitter only being responsible for 287 and 9 of the 250,000 most recently logged SHA1 certificates in the Pilot log, many other service providers also appear to be stalling.

As mentioned, the small logs (Venafi, WoSign, and Vega) have quite different key strength properties than the other logs. These logs stick out even more when looking at the validity of the certificates in the logs. Figure 3 shows the percent of the certificates in each log that validate using the Mozilla root store. The large fraction of invalid certificates is again explained by a relatively large fraction of test certificates. For these logs almost none of the invalid certificates are due to expired roots. In contrast, for the other logs about half of the invalid certificates are due to expired roots. However, despite all logs being append-only

---

[6] https://blog.cloudflare.com/sha-1-deprecation-no-browser-left-behind/.

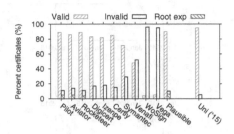

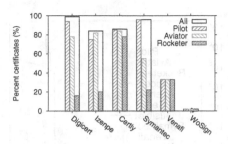

Fig. 3. Validation tests using the Mozilla root store.

Fig. 4. Percent of entries in CA operated logs seen in at least one Google log.

and certificates eventually expiring, most of the observed certificates for the other logs are still valid. Furthermore, we again observe similar characteristics for the large crawled logs (86–90% still valid certificates) and campus (94.8% as measured by the fraction of HTTPS sessions that had a valid certificate).

4.3 Cross-Log Publication

To improve security and increase assurance, several SCTs can be used when validating certificates. For example, to pass Chrome's CT checks, an EV certificate must be accompanied by multiple valid SCTs: one operated by Google, one by another operator, and in some cases (depending on the validity period of the certificate) additional SCTs [15]. While Mozilla currently is drafting their own CT policies, it appears that their requirement of at least two independent logs will be similar in flavor to the policy applied by Chrome.

Motivated by Chrome's policy, we considered what fraction of the certificates in the six CA operated logs with at least 10,000 entries was included in at least one Google operated log. Figure 4 shows that at least 80% of the entries in each of the four large CA logs (Digicert, Izenpe, Certly, and Symantec) also are included in at least one of the three Google operated logs. Again, it appears that the remaining two smaller logs (Venafi and WoSign) contain a larger fraction of test certificates. This is expected to change when they become more mature.

The use of the Google logs also varies among the certificates in the top-four CA logs. For example, Certly certificates appear to be submitted to all three logs, whereas the certificates of the other three (Digizert, Izenpe, and Symantec) primarily are submitted to Pilot and Aviator. Part of the bias towards Pilot may be due to it being the first public log and rich-get-richer effects.

4.4 Temporal Analysis

All CT logs are strictly append-only. Figure 5 shows the number of certificate entries (logarithmic scale) as a function of time for the different logs. To tie with the above discussion, we order the logs based on their start dates. While the

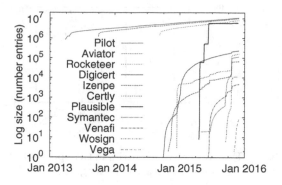
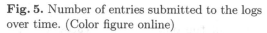
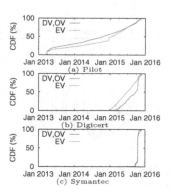

Fig. 5. Number of entries submitted to the logs over time. (Color figure online)

Fig. 6. Submissions of certificates for three example logs.

Google logs (red curves) have a strict size ordering, the size-order changes over time among the CA operated logs (blue). The generally increasing growth rates can be explained by increasing use of short-lived certificates and general use of HTTPS. Some of the spikes can be explained by bulk registrations of certificates and the advent of enforcing CT for DV certificates.

Among the crawl-based logs we have observed steady inclusion rates of DV and OV certificates (e.g., Fig. 6(a)), whereas the inclusion rates of EV certificates have been increasing. This suggests a relative increase in the use of EV certificates in the wild, but may also be affected by how Google extracts certificates. We also observe a significant peak in additions around Jan. 1, 2015, when Chrome's EV policy took effect. This is also around the time that Digicert (Fig. 6(b)) started its log. Since then, Digicert have added EV certificates at a fairly steady rate. We also include results for Symantec (Fig. 6(c)) as an example where the insertion rates of EV and DV certificates goes hand-in-hand. Again, Google requires Symantec to log all their certificates; not only EVs.

5   Popularity-Based Analysis

We next look at the certificates of the domains associated with the HTTPS sessions on campus. For this analysis we extract the domain name associated with each HTTPS session and map them to the certificates observed in the public logs (excluding Plausible). Furthermore, we rank each domain from most popular to least popular and report statistics for domains of different popularity.

Figure 7(a) shows the average number of logs (broken down into Google and non-Google logs) that domains in each popularity category observed (each category given a logarithmic-sized bucket of popularity ranks). The top-10 domains (google.com, apple.com, facebook.com, icloud.com, live.com, fbcdn.net, akamaihd.net, gstatic.com, microsoft.com, doubleclick.net) are observed in more logs than the less popular domains. The difference is largest for the EV certificates, although we see a decrease also for the other types. On average the EV

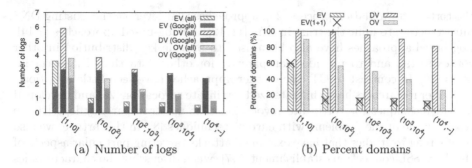

(a) Number of logs   (b) Percent domains

Fig. 7. Average number of public logs that domains with different popularity occur in.

certificates of this top category are observed in 3.5 logs, while DV and OV certificates are seen in 6 and 4 logs, respectively. In general, however, the CA logs have much worse coverage of the less popular domains. Perhaps more encouraging is that the Google logs include DV certificates for almost all domains (regardless of popularity). The total coverage is shown in Fig. 7(b). The fraction of domains that have valid EV (or OV) certificates inserted in at least one log is smaller, and sharply decreasing with the domains popularity. We also note that the fraction of domains that satisfies Chrome's 1+1 requirement is even less. This is indicated by the × markers.

When interpreting the above results, note that the top-10 are responsible for 39% of the sessions and the top-100 for 75% (36% if not including the top-10). This shows that the average session is more likely to be to a domain included in at least one log than if considering a random domain from across all popularities) and that the more popular domains may be more willing to pay the extra cost of EV certificates. It will be interesting to see how websites will adopt if and when browsers start applying stricter CT policies also for non-EV certificates.

6   Related Work

Certificate Transparency (CT) is a fairly new topic. Measurement-based research has instead often focused on the TLS/SSL landscape with CT excluded and only commented that it may significantly change the landscape. Related studies include works that have analyzed the trust graphs in the HTTPS ecosystem [2], identified occurrences of man-in-the-middle attacks on Facebook [13], considered the trustworthiness of CAs and the countries they represent [10], and identified SSL error codes and their reasons [1].

CT is not the only attempt to reinforce the CA-based authentication system of TLS/SSL. Most approaches try to reduce the reliance on the trust of the CAs. This includes client-centric approaches that try to bypass the CAs during the certificate validation process [24], approaches that leverage the existing DNS infrastructure to limit the trust in CAs [11,12], and log-based approaches [5,14]. Log-based approaches have also been used to provide key distribution in other contexts [19], and to provide transparency for other data than X.509 certificates [26]. In contrast to CT, these other approaches have seen little adoption.

Other researchers have characterized certificate revocation [25] and developed hybrid techniques for certificate revocation that use transparency logs [16] to resolve some of the problems with current techniques [8]. In this article, we also briefly refer to studies that have examined attacks targeting particular aspects of the TLS/SSL connection establishment [3,7], when discussing the characteristics of the certificates themselves and the included public keys.

7   Conclusions

This paper presents the first large-scale characterization of the CT landscape. Using both active measurements obtained with a basic CT monitor and passively collected measurements in a university network, we characterize eleven CT logs and highlight similarities and differences across multiple dimensions. We find significant differences in the selection of root stores and how new certificates are added. For example, Google operated logs use large root stores and add certificates primarily through crawling, resulting in these logs including broad categories of certificates. The certificates in these crawl-based logs are more representative of the web traffic that browsers may see (e.g., on campus) than the certificates in the CA operated logs are. In general, the crawl-based logs have greater diversity in the types of certificates observed, are much larger, and include many certificates with weak keys or hashes. Analysis of the large CA operated logs and cross-log submissions suggest that CAs try to comply to Chrome's EV certificate policy, but that the submission rates of DV certificates have differed over time between CAs. In addition, by comparing with the certificates, keys, and domains observed in 232 million HTTPS sessions on a university network, we demonstrate how the coverage of the crawled logs captures the certificates observed during typical internet usage and that popular domains appear to be more willing to pay the extra cost of EV certificates. Future work could try to intercept the exchange of SCTs, so to also capture the potential validation that clients could do directly with the CT logs or the additional protection against partitioning that gossiping [6,21] and client-to-client communication may offer.

Acknowledgements. The authors are thankful to our shepherd Ralph Holz and the anonymous reviewers for their feedback. This work was funded in part by the Swedish Research Council (VR) and the Natural Sciences and Engineering Research Council (NSERC) of Canada.

References

1. Akhawe, D., Amann, B., Vallentin, M., Sommer, R.: Here's my cert, so trust me, maybe?: understanding TLS errors on the web. In: Proceeding of WWW (2013)
2. Amann, B., Sommer, R., Vallentin, M., Hall, S.: No attack necessary: the surprising dynamics of SSL trust relationships. In: Proceeding of ACSAC (2013)
3. Beurdouche, B., et al.: A messy state of the union: Taming the composite state machines of TLS. In: Proceeding of IEEE S&P (2015)
4. Barker, E., Barker, W., Burr, W.P.W., Smid, M.: Recommendation for key management, part 1: General (rev. 3). NIST Special. Publication 800–57 (2012)
5. Basin, D., Cremers, C., Kim, T.H.-J., Perrig, A., Sasse, R., Szalachowski, P.: Arpki: Attack resilient public-key infrastructure. In: Proceeding of ACM CCS (2014)
6. Chuat, L., Szalachowski, P., Perrig, A., Laurie, B., Messeri, E.: Efficient gossip protocols for verifying the consistency of certificate logs. In: Proceeding of IEEE CNS (2015)
7. Adrian, D., et al.: Imperfect forward secrecy: how Diffie-Hellman fails in practice. In: Proceeding of ACM CCS (2015)
8. Duncan, R.: How certificate revocation (doesn't) work in practice (2013)
9. Durumeric, Z., Kasten, J., Bailey, M., Halderman, J.A.: Analysis of the HTTPS certificate ecosystem. In: Proceeding of IMC (2013)
10. Fadai, T., Schrittwieser, S., Kieseberg, P., Mulazzani, M.: Trust me, I'm a root CA! Analyzing SSL root CAs in modern browsers and operating systems. In: Proceeding of ARES (2015)
11. Hallam-Baker, P., Stradling, R.: RFC6844: DNS Certification Authority Authorization (CAA) Resource Record. IETF (2013)
12. Hoffman, P., Schlyter, J.: RFC6698: The DNS-Based Authentication of Named Entities (DANE) Transport Layer Security (TLS) Protocol: TLSA. IETF (2012)
13. Huang, L., Rice, A., Ellingsen, E., Jackson, C.: Analyzing forged SSL certificates in the wild. In: Proceeding of IEEE S&P (2014)
14. Kim, T.H.-J., Huang, L.-S., Perrig, A., Jackson, C., Gligor, V.: Accountable key infrastructure (AKI): A proposal for a public-key validation infrastructure. In: Proceeding of WWW (2013)
15. Laurie, B.: Improving the security of EV certificates (2015)
16. Laurie, B., Käsper, E.: Revocation transparency. Google Research, September 2012
17. Laurie, B., Langley, A., Käsper, E.: RFC6962: Certificate Transparency. IETF (2013)
18. Laurie, B., Langley, A., Käsper, E., Messeri, E., Stradling, R.: RFC6962-bis: Certificate Transparency draft-ietf-trans-rfc6962-bis-10. IETF (2015)
19. Melara, M., Blankstein, A., Bonneau, J., Felten, E., Freedman, M.: Coniks: Bringing key transparency to end users. In: Proceeding of USENIX Security (2015)
20. Merkle, R.: Merkle Tree Patent, US4309569A (1979)
21. Nordberg, L., Gillmor, D.K., Ritter, T.: Gossiping in CT. IETF (2015)
22. Ouvrier, G., Laterman, M., Arlitt, M., Carlsson, N.: Characterizing the HTTPS trust landscape: a passive view from the edge. Technical report (2016)
23. Sleevi, R.: Sustaining digital certificate security, Google Security Blog, 28 October 2015. https://security.googleblog.com/2015/10/sustaining-digital-certificate-security.html
24. Wendlandt, D., Andersen, D.G., Perrig, A.: Perspectives: improving SSH-style host authentication with multi-path probing. In: Proceeding of USENIX ATC (2008)
25. Liu, Y., et al.: An end-to-end measurement of certificate revocation in the web's PKI. In: Proceeding of IMC (2015)
26. Zhang, D., Gillmor, D.K., He, D., Sarikaya, B.: CT for Binary Codes. IETF (2015)

Where Is the Weakest Link? A Study on Security Discrepancies Between Android Apps and Their Website Counterparts

Arash Alavi[1]([✉]), Alan Quach[1], Hang Zhang[1], Bryan Marsh[1], Farhan Ul Haq[2], Zhiyun Qian[1], Long Lu[2], and Rajiv Gupta[1]

[1] University of California, Riverside, Riverside, USA
{aalav003,quacha,hzhan033,marshb,zhiyunq,gupta}@cs.ucr.edu
[2] Stony Brook University, Stony Brook, USA
{fulhaq,long}@cs.stonybrook.edu

Abstract. As we move into the mobile era, many functionalities in standard web services are being re-implemented in mobile apps and services, including many security-related functionalities. However, it has been observed that security features that are standardized in the PC and web space are often not implemented correctly by app developers resulting in serious security vulnerabilities. For instance, prior work has shown that the standard SSL/TLS certificate validation logic in browsers is not implemented securely in mobile apps. In this paper, we study a related question: given that many web services are offered both via browsers/webpages and mobile apps, are there any discrepancies between the security policies of the two?

To answer the above question, we perform a comprehensive study on 100 popular app-web pairs. Surprisingly, we find many discrepancies – we observe that often the app security policies are much weaker than their website counterparts. We find that one can perform unlimited number of login attempts at a high rate (*e.g.*, 600 requests per second) from a single IP address by following the app protocol whereas the website counterpart typically blocks such attempts. We also find that the cookies used in mobile apps are generally more valuable as they do not expire as quickly as the ones used for websites and they are often stored in plaintext on mobile devices. In addition, we find that apps often do not update the libraries they use and hence vulnerabilities are often left unpatched. Through a study of 6400 popular apps, we identify 31 apps that use one or more vulnerable (unpatched) libraries. We responsibly disclosed all of our findings to the corresponding vendors and have received positive acknowledgements from them. This result is a vivid demonstration of "security is only as good as its weakest link".

1 Introduction

Many web services are now delivered via mobile apps. Given that a large number of services already exist and are offered as traditional websites, it is expected that many apps are basically remakes or enhanced versions of their website

© Springer International Publishing AG 2017
M.A. Kaafar et al. (Eds.): PAM 2017, LNCS 10176, pp. 100–112, 2017.
DOI: 10.1007/978-3-319-54328-4_8

counterparts. Examples of these include mobile financial applications for major banking corporations like Chase and Wells Fargo or shopping applications like Amazon and Target. The software stack for the traditional web services has been well developed and tested, including for both browsers and web servers. The security features are also standardized (*e.g.,* cookie management and SSL/TLS certificate validation). However, as the web services are re-implemented as mobile apps, many of the security features need to be re-implemented as well. This can often lead to discrepancies between security policies of the websites and mobile apps. As demonstrated in a recent study [9], when the standard feature of SSL/TLS certificate validation logic in browsers is re-implemented on mobile apps, serious flaws are present that can be exploited to launch MITM attacks. Such an alarming phenomenon calls for a more comprehensive analysis of aspects beyond the previous point studies.

In this paper, we examine a number of critical website security policies that need to be re-implemented in mobile apps. We hypothesize that such security policies in mobile apps are significantly weaker than those in traditional website environment, due to the following observations: (1) mobile devices are much more limited in terms of power and screen size; thus, many of the stringent security features such as CAPTCHAs are likely to be relaxed; (2) many mobile apps are newly developed and may naturally lack the maturity of web services that are developed and tested for a much longer period of time.

To verify our hypothesis, we study the top 100 popular Android apps (each of which has more than 5,000,000 installs) from various categories in Google play, as well as their website counterparts, to perform a comprehensive study about their security discrepancies. The contributions of the paper can be summarized as follows:

- We identify a set of critical security policies that are commonly employed by (app, web service) pairs. Since such pairs represent essentially the same services, the discrepancy in security policies effectively lowers the security of the overall service.
- For the authentication related security policies, we find significant differences in the way their backend services handle login attempts (even when they are essentially the same company, *e.g.,* Expedia app vs. Expedia website). We report 14 high-profile apps without any obvious security layer against failed login attempts while their website counterparts do have security protections. Thus these apps allow unlimited number of login attempts at a high rate that can be used for dictionary attacks. We also find that in 8 apps, the discrepancy allows one to perform an unlimited number of requests and learn whether a user ID has been registered with the service.
- For the cookie management related security policies, we find that cookies managed by mobile apps are generally (1) easier to steal as they are often stored in plaintext and accessible in a number of ways; (2) more valuable to steal as many of them do not expire any time soon; and (3) more usable by an attacker as they can be used from almost any IP address in the world.

- For the use of libraries, we find 2 of the above 100 apps use vulnerable versions of libraries. By extending our study to 6400 apps, we find 31 potential vulnerable apps due to their use of vulnerable libraries.

The rest of this paper is organized as follows. We first introduce the necessary background information for the rest of the paper in Sect. 2. Then we discuss the methodology and implementation details in Sect. 3. We describe our observations for different tests that we have performed in Sect. 4. Section 5 lists the related works and Sect. 6 concludes the paper.

2   Background

In this section, we begin with the introduction to different authentication security policies, and then we discuss the storage encryption methods that are used by different browsers and in mobile apps. Finally, we give a brief overview of library use in Android apps and how it differs from the browser scene.

Authentication Security Policies. We anticipate to see many different forms of authentication security policies in place for both apps and websites. One of the most common forms of authentication policies that can be seen are CAPTCHAs. Others include a mandatory wait period or denial of access either to an account or service. All three of these have potential to be IP/machine-based or global.

*C*APTCHA. Though CAPTCHAs are designed with the purpose of defeating machines, prior research has shown that they can be defeated by machines algorithmically [14] or via speech classification [18]. Due to the possibility of CAPTCHA replay attacks, Open Web Application Security Project (OWASP) recommends that CAPTCHA be only used in "rate limiting" applications due to text-based CAPTCHAs being crackable within 1–15 s [16].

*W*aiting Time. A less common method of authentication policy is the usage of waiting periods to limit the number of logins that can be attempted. The response is in the form of an explicit message or disguised through a generic "Error" message. Waiting periods, either for a single IP or for the user account is a very effective method to slow down and mitigate aggressive online credential guessing attacks. Depending on the implementation, it may operate on a group of IPs (*e.g.,* belonging to the same domain).

*D*enial of Access. An extreme policy is the denial of access, where an account is essentially "locked" and additional steps are necessary to regain access (*e.g.,* making a phone call) [19]. If an attacker knows the login ID of an account, then he can lock the account by repeatedly failing the authentication. Though very secure against online password guessing attacks, OWASP recommends that such methods be used in high-profile applications where denial of access is preferable to account compromises [15].

Storage Encryption Methods. Browsers on PCs by default encrypt critical data for long term storage. In the case of Chrome on Windows, after a successful login into a website, by clicking "Save Password", the browser stores the password in encrypted form using the Windows login credential as the key. It is not the same for mobile apps. For instance, the APIs for managing cookies do not require the cookies to be encrypted.

Libraries. Mobile apps use libraries for different functionalities such as advertisements, audio and video streaming, or social media. Previous studies [1, 7, 11] have shown security and privacy issues that arise by use of some libraries which can lead to leakage of sensitive user information, denial-of-service, or even arbitrary code execution. For services delivered through websites on the other hand, no website-specific native libraries are loaded. Unlike libraries embedded in apps that may be out-of-date and vulnerable, libraries used in browsers (*e.g.,* flash) are always kept up-to-date and free of known vulnerabilities.

3 Methodology and Implementation

In this section we describe our methodology and implementation details of our approach to analyze app-web pairs. We selected the top 100 popular Android apps (each of which has more than 5,000,000 installs) from popular categories such as shopping, social, news, travel & local, etc. in Google play. All apps have a corresponding website interface that offers a similar functionality. For each app-web pair, we created legitimate accounts using default settings. This was done to mimic the processes of an actual user interacting with an app or website.

Login Automation Analysis. We automate logins and logging for apps and websites for the purposes of this study. For each app-web pair, we perform 101 login attempts automatically using randomly generated alphanumeric passwords for the first 100 attempts followed by an attempt with the correct password. 100 attempts was chosen as this was an order of magnitude larger than what an average user would perform within a span of 24 h [6]. Allowing unlimited number of login attempts is a security vulnerability because it allows an attacker to perform brute force or dictionary attacks. Another security aspect of login attempts is that if the system leaks the user ID (*e.g.,* email) during the login authentication checking, by returning error messages such as "wrong password" either in the UI or in the response message, then an attacker can send a login request and learn whether a user ID has been registered with the service. Therefore, we also compare the servers' responses to login requests, either shown in the UI or found in the response packet, for both apps and websites.

Sign Up Automation Analysis. Besides login tests, we perform the sign up tests that can also potentially leak if the username has been registered with the service. Again, we simply need to compare the servers' responses to sign up requests for apps and websites. For both login and sign up security policies, if a service where the website allows for only a limited number of logins/sign-ups before a CAPTCHA is shown whereas the mobile app never prompts with a CAPTCHA, an attacker would be inclined to launch an attack following the mobile app's protocol rather than the website's. Test suites for the purposes of testing mobile apps and websites were created using *monkeyrunner* and *Selenium Webdriver*, respectively.

Authentication Throughput Analysis. From the login automation analysis, we collect the set of app-web pairs where we find different behaviors between the app and the website counterpart, we call this set "discrepancy list". Using the network traffic monitoring tools *Fiddler* and *mitmproxy*, we log network traffic traces for all app-web pairs in the discrepancy list. Using the information in the network traffic traces, we analyze how authentication packets are structured for each client as well as finding what sort of information is being shared between a client and server. This enables us to determine whether the app-web pair has the same authentication protocol and share the same set of backend authentication servers. In addition, this allows us to construct tools capable of sending login request packets without actually running the mobile app, pushing for higher throughput of authentication attempts. The tool also logs all responses received from a server. To push the throughput even further, we can optionally parallelize the login requests (from the same client) by targeting additional backend authentication server IPs simultaneously. Our hypothesis is that the throughput can be potentially multiplied if we target multiple servers simultaneously.

IP-Changing Clients Analysis. Using *VPN Gate* and a sequence of 12 IP addresses from different geographical locations, including 3 from North America and 9 from other countries, we test the apps and websites regarding their response to accounts being logged in from multiple locations separated by hundreds of miles in a short span of time. The motivation of this analysis was to determine whether app/website has a security policy against IP changes can indicate session hijacks [8]. If not, then an attacker can use the hijacked cookies anywhere without being recognized by the web service. For example an attacker can use a stolen cookie from an app with any IP address to obtain personal and/or financial information pertaining to the user account.

Cookie Analysis. For each app-web pair, we analyze the cookies that are saved on the phone/PC. We collect all the cookies and analyze cookie storage security policies to find whether they are stored in plaintext and more easily accessible. We also perform expiration date comparison testing on 18 shopping app-web pairs from our list of app-web pairs. The hypothesis is that mobile apps run on small screens and it is troublesome to repeatedly login through the small software keyboard; therefore the corresponding app's servers will likely have a more lenient policy allowing the cookies to stay functional for longer time periods.

Vulnerable Library Analysis. While both apps and websites execute client-side code, app code has access to many more resources and sensitive functionalities compared to their website counterpart, *e.g.,* apps can read SMS on the device while javascript code executed through the browser cannot. Therefore, we consider the app code more dangerous. Specifically, vulnerable app libraries running on the client-side can cause serious attacks ranging from denial of service (app crash) to arbitrary code execution. Because of this, for each app, we identify if it uses any vulnerable libraries. We conduct the analysis beyond the original 100 apps to 6400 apps in popular categories. Ideally the libraries should be tagged with versions; unfortunately, we discover that most libraries embedded in Android apps do not contain the version information as part of their metadata. Therefore, in the absence of direct version information, we perform the following steps instead. First, we search the extracted libraries through the CVE database. If there is any library that is reported to have vulnerabilities, we perform two tests to conservatively flag them as vulnerable. First is a simple time test: we check if the last update time of the app is before the release time of patched library. Obviously, if the app is not updated after the patched library is released, then the app must contain a vulnerable library. If the time test cannot assert that the library is vulnerable, we perform an additional test on the symbols declared in the library files. Specifically, if there is a change (either adding or removing a function) in the patched library, and the change is lacking in the library file in question, then we consider it vulnerable. Otherwise, to be conservative, we do not consider the library as vulnerable.

4 Observations

We present our results obtained from following the methodology outlined earlier.

Security Policies Against Failed Login and Sign up Attempts. By performing login attempts automatically for each pair of app and website, many interesting discrepancies in security policies have been found. Figure 1 summarizes the main results for all 100 pairs, considering their latest versions at the time of experiment. In general, we see that the security policy is weaker on the app side. There are more apps without security policies than websites. We also see that there are significantly fewer apps asking for CAPTCHA, presumably due to the concern about usability of the small keyboards that users have to interact with. Interestingly, in the case when CAPTCHAs are used both by app and website, the CAPTCHA shown to app users is usually simpler in terms of the number of characters and symbols. For instance, LinkedIn website asks the user to enter a CAPTCHA with 2 words while its app CAPTCHA only has 3 characters. Unfortunately, an attacker knowing the difference can always impersonate the mobile client and attack the weaker security policy. We also observe

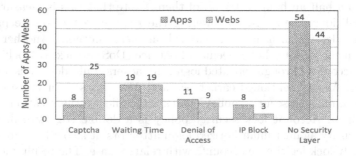

Fig. 1. Security policies against failed login attempts in apps vs. websites

that more apps employ IP block policies for a short period of time. This is effective against naive online credential guessing attacks that are not operated by real players in the underground market. In reality, attackers are likely operating on a large botnet attempting to perform such attacks, rendering the defense much less effective than it seems. In fact, if the attackers are aware of the discrepancy, they could very well be impersonating the mobile client to bypass stronger protections such as CAPTCHA (which sometimes requires humans to solve and is considered additional cost to operate cyber crime).

Table 1 lists app-web pairs in detail where apps operate without any security protections whatsoever, at least for the version when we began our study but their websites have some security policies. In total, we find 14 such app-web pairs; 8 apps have subsequently strengthened the policy after we notified them. There are however still 6 that are vulnerable to date. We also provide a detailed list of all 100 app-web pairs on our project website [2]. To ensure that there is indeed no security protection for these apps, we perform some follow-up tests against the 14 applications and confirm that we could indeed reach up to thousands of attempts (without hitting any limit). Note that our approach ensures that no hidden security policy goes unnoticed (such as the account being silently blocked), as our test always concludes with a successful login attempt using the correct password, indicating that it has not been blocked due to the failed attempts earlier. In the table, we also list the URLs that correspond to the login requests. Since both the domain names and resolved IP addresses (which we did not list) are different, it is a good indication that apps and websites go through different backend services to perform authentications, and hence there are different security policies.

Impact of Online Credential Guessing Attacks. To perform online password guessing attacks, one can either perform a brute force or dictionary attack against those possibilities that are deemed most likely to succeed. As an example, the recent leakage of passwords from Yahoo [4] consisting of 200 million entries (without removing duplicates). According to our throughput result, at 600 login attempts per second (which we were able to achieve against some services), one can try every password in less than 4 days against a targeted account (if we eliminate duplicate passwords the number will be much smaller). Let us consider an attacker who chooses the most popular and unique 1 million passwords; it will take less than half an hour to try all of them. Note that this is measured from a single malicious client, greatly lowering the requirement of online password guessing attacks, which usually are carried out using botnets. Another type of attack which can be launched is Denial of Service (DoS) attack. By locking large amount of accounts through repeated logins, attackers could deny a user's access to a service. As we mentioned earlier, we find more apps than websites which have the account lock security policy against the failed authentication (11 apps vs. 9 websites). Account lock security policy is a double edge sword: while it provides security against unauthorized login attempts, it also allows an attacker to maliciously lock legitimate accounts with relative ease. The result shows that this kind of attack can be more easily launched on the app side. We verify this

Table 1. Discrepancy of authentication policies among app-web pairs. In all cases, the apps have no security policy while their website counterparts do have security policies. This allows attackers to follow the app protocol and gain unlimited number of continuous login attempts (confirmed with 1000+ trials). A subset of them (8) have subsequently patched the security flaw after our notifications.

App-web	App security layer (app version)	Website security layer	App host	Website host
Babbel	None (5.4.072011) Account lock (5.6.060612)	Account lock	www.babbel.com/api2/login	accounts.babbel.com/en/ accounts/sign_in
Ebay	None (3.0.0.19) IP block (5.3.0.11)	Captcha	mobiuas.ebay.com/servicesmobile/ v1/UserAuthenticationService	signin.ebay.com/ws/ eBayISAPI.dll
Expedia	None (5.0.2)	Captcha	www.expedia.com/api/user/signin	www.expedia.com/user/login
Hotels.com	None (12.1.1.1) IP block (20.1.1.2)	Captcha	ssl.hotels.com/device/signin.html	ssl.hotels.com/profile/ signin.html
LivingSocial	None (3.0.2) IP block (4.4.2)	Wait time	accounts.livingsocial.com/v1/ oauth/authenticate	accounts.livingsocial.com/ accounts/authenticate
OverDrive	None (3.5.6)	Captcha	overdrive.com/account/sign-in	www.overdrive.com/account/sign-in
Plex	None (4.6.3.383) IP block (4.31.2.310)	IP block	plex.tv/users/sign_in.xml	plex.tv/users/sign_in
Quizlet	None (2.3.3)	Wait time	api.quizlet.com/3.0/directlogin	quizlet.com/login
Skype	None (7.16.0.507)	Wait time & Captcha	uic.login.skype.com/login/ skypetoken	login.skype.com/login
SoundCloud	None (15.0.15) IP block (2016.08.31-release)	Captcha	api.soundcloud.com/oauth2/token	sign-in.soundcloud.com/sign-in/password
TripAdvisor	None (11.4) IP block (17.2.2)	Captcha	api.tripadvisor.com/api/ internal/1.5/auth/login	www.tripadvisor.com/ Registration
Twitch	None (4.3.2) Captcha (4.11.1)	Captcha	api.twitch.tv/kraken/oauth2/login	passport.twitch.tv/authorize
We Heart It	None (6.0.0)	Captcha	api.weheartit.com/oauth/token	weheartit.com/login/ authenticate
Zappos	None (5.1.2)	Captcha	api.zappos.com/oauth/access_token	secure-www.zappos.com/ authenticate

claim against our own account and confirm that we are unable to login with the correct password even if the login is done from a different IP address.

To perform online account-ID/username guessing attacks, we report the result of the sign up (registration) security policy testing, which aligns with the login results. We find 5 app-web pairs — 8tracks, Lovoo, Newegg, Overdrive, Stumble-Upon — where the app has no security protection against flooded sign up requests while the website has some security protection such as CAPTCHA. We also find that 14 websites leak the user email address during the authentication checking by returning error messages such as "wrong password". In contrast, 17 apps leak such information. The three apps with weaker security policies are AMC Theaters, Babbel, and We Heart It. The discrepancy allows one to learn whether a user ID (e.g., email) has been registered with the service by performing unlimited registration requests. Combined with the password guessing, an attacker can then also attempt to test a large number of username and password combinations.

Throughput Measurement. In throughput testing, we tested authentications-per-second (ApS) that are possible from a single desktop computer. Table 2 shows the throughput results for login testing. An interesting case was Expedia, which allowed ~150 ApS when communicating with a single server IP and upwards of ~600 ApS when using multiple server IPs during testing. The existence of multiple server IPs, either directly from the backend servers or CDN, played a role in the amplification of an attack. It is interesting to note that in the case of Expedia, different CDN IPs do not in fact allow amplification attacks. We hypothesize that it is due to the fact that these CDNs still need to access the same set of backend servers which are the real bottleneck. To identify backend server IPs, we perform a step we call "domain name scanning" and successfully locate a non-CDN IP for "ftp.expedia.com". From this IP, we further scan the subnet and find 19 other IPs capable of performing authentication. By talking to these IPs directly, we are able to improve the throughput from 150 to 600.

Finally, we also obtain throughput results for 4 of the applications in sign up testing and their average throughput is around 90 to 240 ApS.

Client IP Changing. During IP address testing, we find that 11 app-web pairs have client IP changing detection and associated security policy on the server side. The remaining 89 app-web pairs have no visible security policy. Among them there are 8 app-web pairs for which both the app and the website have the same behavior against IP changing. For the remaining 3 pairs, — Target, Twitch, Steam — the app and website have different behaviors where the website returns an access denied error for some IP address changes (in the case of Target and Twitch) or forces a logout for any change of the IP address (in the case of Steam) but the app allows changing client IP address frequently.

One main consequence is that when an app/website has no security policy against IP changing, an attacker can perform HTTP session hijacking with stolen cookies more easily without worrying about what hosts and IP addresses to use in hijacking. For instance, Steam is a gaming client; it does have security protection in its websites. When a cookie is sent from a different IP, the website immediately invalidates the cookie and forces a logout. However, using the Steam app and the associated server interface, if the attacker can steal the cookie, he can impersonate the user from anywhere (i.e., any IP address).

Table 2. Throughput results for login testing.

App	ApS (Single-server-IP)	ApS (Multi-server-IP)	# of IPs found	CDN/Host
Ebay	~77	~100	2	Ebay
Expedia	~150	~600	20	Akamai/Expedia
SoundCloud	~77	~178	2	EdgeCast
We Heart It	~83	~215	5	SoftLayer/ThePlanet.com
Zappos	~84	~188	20	Akamai

Cookies. Cookies are commonly used for web services as well as mobile apps. In browsers, cookie management has evolved over the past few decades and gradually become more standardized and secure. However, on the mobile platform every app has the flexibility to choose or implement its own cookie management, i.e. cookie management is still far from being standardized.

We observe that many apps store their cookies unencrypted (47 apps among all 100 apps). An attacker can access the cookie more easily as compared to browsers on PCs. First, smartphones are smaller and more likely to be lost or stolen. Therefore, a simple dump of the storage can reveal the cookies (assuming no full-disk encryption). In contrast, in the case of browsers on PCs, cookies are often encrypted with secrets unknown to the attacker even if the attacker can gain physical access to the device. For instance, Windows password (used in Chrome) and master password (used in Firefox) are used to encrypt the cookies [20]. Second, if the device is connected to an infected PC (with adb shell enabled), any unprivileged malware on PC may be able to pull data from the phone. For instance, if the app is debuggable then with the help of *run-as* command, one can access the app data such as cookies. Even if the app is not debuggable, the app data can still be pulled from the device into a file with .ab(android backup) format [12].

We also report another type of important discrepancy — cookie expiration time. Here we focus on 18 shopping app-web pairs (a subset from the list of 100 pairs). We observe that app cookies remain valid for much longer time than web cookies. The cookie expiration time in all 18 shopping websites is around 3 h on average, whereas it is several months in their app counterparts. The result is shown in Table 3. We find that 6 apps have cookie expiration time set to at least 1 month while their websites allow only minutes before the cookies expire. An attacker can easily use a stolen cookie for these apps and perform unwanted behavior such as making purchases as the cookie is not expired. For instance, based on our personal experience, Amazon app appears to use cookies that never expire to give the best possible user experience. We confirmed that a user can make purchases after 1 year since the initial login in.

Vulnerable Libraries. During vulnerable library testing, we find two apps (Vine and Victoria's Secret) use unpatched and vulnerable libraries from FFmpeg [3]

Table 3. Cookies expiration time.

App-web	App cookies expiration time	Website cookies expiration time
AliExpress	Several months	60 min
Amazon	Several months	14 min
Best Buy	Several months	10 min
Kohl's	Several months	20 min
Newegg	Several months	60 min
Walmart	Several months	30 min

Table 4. Vulnerable libraries used by apps.

Library	Vulnerabilities	# of apps	Example vulnerable apps (version) (# of installs)
libzip	DoS or possibly execute arbitrary code via a ZIP archive	13	com.djinnworks.StickmanBasketball (1.6) (over 10,000,000) com.djinnworks.RopeFly.lite(3.4) (over 10,000,000)
FFmpeg[a]	DoS or possibly have unspecified other impact	9	co.vine.android (5.14.0) (over 50,000,000) com.victoriassecret.vsaa (2.5.2) (over 1,000,000)
libxml2	DoS via a crafted XML document	8	com.avidionmedia.iGunHD (5.22) (over 10,000,000) com.pazugames.girlshairsalon (2.0) (over 1,000,000)
	Obtain sensitive information	5	com.pazugames.girlshairsalon (2.0) (over 1,000,000) com.flexymind.pclicker (1.0.5) (over 100,000) com.pazugames.cakeshopnew (1.0) (over 100,000)
	DoS or obtain sensitive information via crafted XML data	5	
	DoS via crafted XML data	5	
libcurl	Authenticate as other users via a request	1	sv.com.tigo.tigosports (6.0123) (over 10,000)

[a]FFmpeg includes 7 libraries: libavutil, libavcodec, libavformat, libavdevice, libavfilter, libswscale, and libswresample.

framework, which motivates us to look at a larger sample of 6,400 top free apps in different categories. Table 4 summarizes our observation for vulnerable libraries with the number of apps using them. For example, an attacker can cause a DoS (crash the application) or possibly execute arbitrary code by supplying a crafted ZIP archive to an application using a vulnerable version of libzip library [5]. As we discussed before, javascript vulnerabilities are unlikely to cause damage to the device compared to app libraries, especially given the recent defences implemented on WebView [10].

5   Related Work

As far we know, there are no in depth studies that explicitly analyze the similarities and differences between mobile applications and their website counterparts in terms of security. Fahl et al. [9] understood the potential security threats posed by benign Android apps that use the SSL/TLS protocols to protect data they transmit. Leung et al. [13] recently studied 50 popular apps manually to compare the Personally Identifiable Information (PII) exposed by mobile apps and mobile web browsers. They conclude that apps tend to leak more PII (but not always) compared to their website counterparts, as apps can request access to more types of PII stored on the device. This is a demonstration of the discrepancy of privacy policies between apps and websites. In contrast, our work focuses on the discrepancy of security (not so much privacy) policies between apps and websites. Zuo et al. [21] automatically forged cryptographically consistent messages from the client side to test whether the server side of an app lacks sufficient security layers. They applied their techniques to test the server side implementation of 76 popular mobile apps with 20 login attempts each and conclude that many of them are vulnerable to password brute-forcing attacks, leaked password probing attacks, and Facebook access token hijacking attacks. Sivakorn et al. [17] recently conducted an in-depth study on the privacy threats that users face when attackers have hijacked a user's HTTP cookie. They evaluated the extent of cookie hijacking for browser security mechanisms, extensions, mobile apps, and search bars. They observed that both Android and iOS platforms have official apps that use unencrypted connections. For example, they find that 3 out of 4 iOS Yahoo apps leak users' cookies.

6   Conclusion

In this paper, we identify serious security related discrepancies between android apps and their corresponding website counterparts. We responsibly disclosed all of our findings to the corresponding companies including Expedia who acknowledged and subsequently fixed the problem. The lesson learnt is that, for the same web service (*e.g.*, Expedia), even though their websites are generally built with good security measures, the mobile app counterparts often have weaker or non-existent security measures. As a result, the security of the overall service is only as good as the weakest link — more often than not, the mobile apps.

Acknowledgments. We would like to thank our shepherd Kanchana Thilakarathna for his feedback in revising the paper. This work is supported by NSF grant CNS-1617424 to UC Riverside.

References

1. The Hacker News. Warning: 18,000 android apps contains code that spy on your text messages. http://thehackernews.com/2015/10/android-apps-steal-sms.html. Accessed 10 Nov 2016
2. Authentication Policy Table. http://www.cs.ucr.edu/~aalav003/authtable.html. Accessed 10 Nov 2016
3. FFmpeg. https://ffmpeg.org/. Accessed 10 Nov 2016

4. Hacker Selling 200 Million Yahoo Accounts On Dark Web. http://thehackernews. com/2016/08/hack-yahoo-account.html. Accessed 10 Nov 2016
5. Red Hat Bugzilla Bug 1204676. https://bugzilla.redhat.com/show_bug.cgi?id= CVE-2015-2331. Accessed 10 Nov 2016
6. Amber. Some Best Practices for Web App Authentication. http://codingkilledthe cat.wordpress.com/2012/09/04/some-best-practices-for-web-app-authentication/. Accessed 10 Nov 2016
7. Book, T., Pridgen, A., Wallach, D.S.: Longitudinal analysis of android ad library permissions. CoRR, abs/1303.0857 (2013)
8. De Ryck, P., Desmet, L., Piessens, F., Joosen, W.: Secsess: keeping your session tucked away in your browser. In: Proceedings of the 30th Annual ACM Symposium on Applied Computing (SAC 2015) (2015)
9. Fahl, S., Harbach, M., Muders, T., Baumgärtner, L., Freisleben, B., Smith, M.: Why eve and mallory love android: an analysis of android SSL (in)security. In: ACM CCS (2012)
10. Georgiev, M., Jana, S., Shmatikov, V.: Breaking and fixing origin-based access control in hybrid web/mobile application frameworks. In: 2014 Network and Distributed System Security (NDSS 2014), San Diego, February 2014
11. Grace, M.C., Zhou, W., Jiang, X., Sadeghi, A.-R.: Unsafe exposure analysis of mobile in-app. advertisements. In: WiSeC (2012)
12. Hwang, S., Lee, S., Kim, Y., Ryu, S.: Bittersweet ADB: attacks and defenses. In: Proceedings of the 10th ACM Symposium on Information, Computer and Communications Security, ASIA (CCS 2015) (2015)
13. Leung, C., Ren, J., Choffnes, D., Wilson, C.: Should you use the app for that?: Comparing the privacy implications of app- and web-based online services. In: Proceedings of the 2016 ACM on Internet Measurement Conference (IMC 2016), New York, NY, USA, pp. 365–372. ACM (2016)
14. Mori, G., Malik, J.: Recognizing objects in adversarial clutter: breaking a visual captcha. In: Proceedings of the 2003 IEEE Computer Society Conference on Computer Vision and Pattern Recognition (2003)
15. OWASP. Blocking Brute Force Attacks. http://www.owasp.org/index.php/ Blocking_Brute_Force_Attacks. Accessed 10 Nov 2016
16. OWASP. Testing for Captcha (OWASP-AT-012). http://www.owasp.org/index. php/Testing_for_Captcha_(OWASP-AT-012). Accessed 10 Nov 2016
17. Sivakorn, S., Polakis, I., Keromyti, A.D.: The cracked cookie jar: http cookie hijacking and the exposure of private information. In: Proceedings of the 2016 IEEE Symposium on Security and Privacy. IEEE (2016)
18. Tam, J., Simsa, J., Hyde, S., Ahn, L.V.: Breaking audio captchas. In: Koller, D., Schuurmans, D., Bengio, Y., Bottou, L., (eds.) Advances in Neural Information Processing Systems, vol. 21, pp. 1625–1632 (2008)
19. Wolverton, T.: Hackers find new way to milk eBay users. In: Proceedings of the 1998 Network and Distributed System Security Symposium (2002)
20. Wright, J.: How Browsers Store Your Passwords (and Why You Shouldn't Let Them). http://raidersec.blogspot.com/2013/06/how-browsers-store-your-passwords-and.html/. Accessed 10 Nov 2016
21. Zuo, C., Wang, W., Wang, R., Lin, Z.: Automatic forgery of cryptographically consistent messages to identify security vulnerabilities in mobile services. In: NDSS (2016)

Patch Me If You Can: A Study on the Effects of Individual User Behavior on the End-Host Vulnerability State

Armin Sarabi[1]([✉]), Ziyun Zhu[2], Chaowei Xiao[1], Mingyan Liu[1], and Tudor Dumitraş[2]

[1] University of Michigan, Ann Arbor, USA
{arsarabi,xiaocw,mingyan}@umich.edu
[2] University of Maryland, College Park, USA
{zhuziyun,tdumitra}@umiacs.umd.edu

Abstract. In this paper we study the implications of end-user behavior in applying software updates and patches on information-security vulnerabilities. To this end we tap into a large data set of measurements conducted on more than 400,000 Windows machines over four client-side applications, and separate out the impact of user and vendor behavior on the vulnerability states of hosts. Our modeling of users and the empirical evaluation of this model over vulnerability states of hosts reveal a peculiar relationship between vendors and end-users: the users' promptness in applying software patches, and vendors' policies in facilitating the installation of updates, while both contributing to the hosts' security posture, are overshadowed by other characteristics such as the frequency of vulnerability disclosures and the vendors' swiftness in deploying patches.

1 Introduction

Software vulnerabilities represent a valuable resource for attackers. Exploits for these vulnerabilities can allow miscreants to control the vulnerable hosts remotely. Unpatched vulnerabilities also present a threat for enterprises, as an outward facing machine with an exploitable vulnerability can provide unauthorized access to the company's internal network [26]. Moreover, the emergence of exploit kits [14], makes it easy for attackers to compromise hosts in an automated fashion. To counter these threats, software vendors create and disseminate patches that users then install to remove vulnerabilities on their machines. Vendors have also increased the automation of their software updating mechanisms [9,13] in an attempt to accelerate the patching process to sidestep possible tardiness on the part of the end users.

It follows that the vulnerability state of any given end-host at any given time, reflected in the number of *known but unpatched vulnerabilities*, and *unpatched vulnerabilities with known exploits*, is the result of a combination of factors, including (1) the user's updating behavior, (2) the software products' patch release timeliness with respect to the disclosure of vulnerabilities,

© Springer International Publishing AG 2017
M.A. Kaafar et al. (Eds.): PAM 2017, LNCS 10176, pp. 113–125, 2017.
DOI: 10.1007/978-3-319-54328-4_9

Table 1. Summary of findings. $+/-$ indicate positive and negative impacts.

	Findings	Implications
+	The user behavior can be summarized using single parameter distributions	Users' willingness to patch does not seem to depend on the type of improvements in new releases
+	The geometric distribution provides a good fit, even for products with silent updates	This simple model significantly simplifies the analysis of the relationship between user behavior and the vulnerability state of their machines
+	Silent updates lead to shorter windows of vulnerability for end-hosts (as expected)	The product vendors can improve the vulnerability state by adopting a silent updating mechanism
−	Even with silent updates, the majority of hosts have long windows of vulnerability	The large number of security flaws in client-side applications limits the benefits of silent updates
−	Many hosts have long windows of susceptibility to known exploits	Exploit kits present a direct threat to these hosts

(3) the update mechanisms employed to deploy patches on hosts, and (4) the frequency at which vulnerabilities are disclosed and exploits are developed. While the latter three elements have been extensively studied in the literature—see e.g., [2–5,7,8,18,20,22,25] on vulnerability disclosure and patch releases, [11,17,21,23,30] on patch deployment, and [4,6,14,24] on exploits—relatively less is known about the impact of individual user behavior. Prior work in this area has introduced several hypotheses on why users might delay patching vulnerabilities [15,16,29], and aggregated patching measurements for individual vulnerabilities over the general population and over selected groups of users [17].

In this paper, we present a broad field study of individual user behavior, including more than 400,000 users over a period of 3 years (01/2010 to 12/2012), and their updating activities concerning 1,822 vulnerabilities across 4 software products. The updating automation for these applications ranges from prompting users to install patched versions to silent updates, which require minimal user interaction. Our goal is to understand (1) how users behave on an individual level, and (2) how different updating behaviors relate to the vulnerability state of their machines, and how this relationship differs across products.

To achieve the above goal, we employ a combination of empirical analysis and mathematical modeling. In summary, our main contributions are as follows. We propose methods for quantifying the user updating behavior from field measurements of patch deployment. Furthermore, we conduct a systematic study of vulnerability patching, from the perspective of individual users (rather than individual vulnerabilities), and quantify the corresponding vulnerability state of the users' machines. Finally, building on insights from our measurements, we create and evaluate a parameterized model for individual patching behavior, and discuss its implications for end-host security. Table 1 summarizes our findings.

2   Data Sets and Their Processing

We utilize a corpus of patch-deployment measurements collected by Nappa et al., on user hosts that include average users, as well as professionals, software developers, and security analysts, and mostly consist of Windows XP/Vista/7 machines[17]. These measurements were conducted by observing the installation of subsequent versions of different applications, and are derived from the WINE data set [10]. The set of security flaws affecting each version are extracted from NVD [19], using the CVE-ID of the vulnerability, resulting in 1,822 vulnerabilities. We analyze users' patching behavior over 4 products: Google Chrome, Mozilla Firefox, Mozilla Thunderbird, and Adobe Flash Player, and only include hosts that have recorded more than 10 events for at least one application. This results in a data set consisting of 11,017,973 events over 426,031 unique hosts, 99.3% of which are between 01/2010 and 12/2012.

Although an open vulnerability indicates that the application could be exploited, few vulnerabilities are actually exploited in the wild. We collect exploit data from (1) public descriptions of Symantec's anti-virus signatures [28] and (2) metadata about exploit kits from Contagiodump [12]. Combining both sources of exploit information results in exploit release dates for 21 CVEs. The median time between vulnerability disclosure and an exploit kit targeting it is 17 days.

For Firefox, Flash Player, and Thunderbird, we manually scrape release history logs, either provided on the vendor's website, or collected by a third party, to find out when each version is released to the public. We have collected the results along with the source for each entry in a single document [27].

2.1   Curated Data

Host state. Each update event corresponds to a *(machine ID, product, version, timestamp)* tuple, indicating the installation of a software on the host. However, the WINE database provides no information on when the product has been removed, or if the user has installed multiple product lines in parallel (e.g. Firefox 3.6, and 4.0). We utilize the following heuristic to update the state of a machine after each event. Assume that an event at time t signals the installation of version v belonging to product line ℓ, and we have detected the presence of versions $S_{t-} = \{(\ell_1, v_1), \ldots, (\ell_n, v_n)\}$ on the machine prior to the event. For each ℓ_i in S_{t-}, if there are no observations for the same line within 6 months of the current event, we remove the (ℓ_i, v_i) pair from S_{t-}. We then add the (ℓ, v) pair, or update the corresponding pair in S_{t-} if the same product line is already installed on the host, to obtain the state S_t after the event. We then take the union of vulnerabilities that affect each version in S_t from NVD, as the set of vulnerabilities present on the host. The subset of vulnerabilities that have already been disclosed, or exploited, represent the machine's security posture.

Version release date. For Firefox, Flash Player, and Thunderbird, we can obtain the official release dates for each version by scraping version release notes from the vendor, or release histories collected by a third party. For Chrome, we tap into the patch measurement data to estimate release dates for each version. In previous work, Nappa et al. [17] identify the release date automatically, by selecting the first date when the version appears in WINE. However, we found that this approach can be unreliable in some cases. The binary that corresponds to a new version might appear in the wild half a year before it is made available on the release channel. We observe that on a release date there is usually a high volume of patching events. We thus first rank the dates by the count of patching events, and then identify the patch release date as the earliest day among the 10 dates with top ranks. We compared the results from this method with the release dates for Firefox and we found that they match for all the versions.

Purpose of updates. To determine if users are influenced by the purpose of the updates, we identify four types of software releases: introducing new features I_{feats}, fixing bugs I_{bugs}, patching security vulnerabilities I_{vulns}, or introducing a new product line I_{majVer}. Using these four categories, we manually label the versions for Firefox and Flash Player. Since the release notes are not available for every build and they switched to silent updates on 2012-08-28 and 2012-03-28, respectively, the number of versions we labeled is 30 and 39, respectively.

User updates. To study the frequency of irregular user behavior, we first obtain the number of events that result in the presence of more than one product line on a host. For Chrome, Flash Player, Firefox, and Thunderbird, 0.9%, 4.9%, 1.2% and 0.3% of events lead to the installation of more than one product line. For Flash Player, we further analyze the number of vulnerabilities associated with each product line. On average, in the presence of multiple product lines, 79.5% of vulnerabilities come from the lowest product version installed on the machine. Therefore, we take the lowest application version on the machine as its current state, and only consider a new event as a version upgrade if it updates the lowest installed version. Note that for evaluating whether a machine is prone to a known vulnerability, we will still use the complete set of installed versions.

Finally, for each state transition that updates the lowest installed version, we need to extract the user's delay in applying the update. We first take the timestamps for the current and previous events (denoted by T_u^k and T_u^{k-1}), and extract the first time an update was released for the previously installed version (denoted by T_r). The user's delay is then $S_u^k := T_u^k - \max(T_u^{k-1}, T_r)$. This means that we measure the users' delay from the day an update is available for the installed version, or the product installation date, whichever comes last; the latter takes effect when the user installs an outdated version. Note that successive versions do not necessarily follow a chronological order, as multiple product lines are often developed in parallel. For each release, we take the next version in the same line to be the update for that release. For end-of-life releases, we pick the first version in the subsequent line as the next logical update.

Figure 1a depicts a sample scenario for 4 successive releases of Firefox, released at times $t = 0, 35, 50, 75$ ($t = 0$ corresponds to "2012-09-11"). Firefox

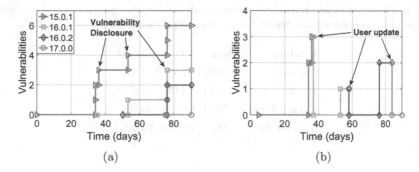

Fig. 1. The number of vulnerabilities in successive Firefox versions (left) and following a user's update events (right). Each color represents a single version. (Color figure online)

v15.0.1 is prone to 6 vulnerabilities, all of which are undisclosed at the time of release. However, these vulnerabilities are made public at times $t = 34, 36, 53, 76$, and patched in subsequent versions. Figure 1b illustrates a sample user in our data set who installs these versions at $t = 5, 37, 58, 84$, respectively. Note that with each update, the user inherits the set of vulnerabilities in the new release. An update is made available for the first version at time $t = 35$, and the user initiates a software update at time $T_u^1 = 37$, therefore the user's delay for the first update event is $S_u^1 = 2\ days$. Similarly, $S_u^2 = 8\ days$, and $S_u^3 = 9\ days$.

3   Analysis of User Behavior and Its Security Implications

3.1   Modeling a User's Patching Delay

We assume that the user's update delays are drawn from a probability distribution specific to the $(user, product)$ pair. In previous work, the survival function for number of hosts without a security patch has been modeled as an exponential decay process [21,23]. We note that a geometric distribution for a user's delay in applying a software update leads to the same model for the survival function. We independently test this assumption by performing a chi-squared goodness-of-fit test between each sequence and a geometric distribution whose parameter is calculated using a maximum likelihood estimate. The output of the test is a p-value: small p-values reject the null hypothesis "The samples are drawn from a geometric distribution". Table 2 summarizes our results, for each product we have included the number of users tested, and the percentage with p-values higher than significance levels of 5% and 1%. For the test, we ignore users with fewer than 20 update events. Our results show that for the majority of users the geometric distribution is a good fit.

The above results suggest that the users' response to new product releases are fairly "simple-minded", in the sense that they can be well-modeled using a one-parameter distribution. In what follows, we examine the relationship between

Table 2. Chi-squared test results over user update delays. We cannot reject the hypothesis that these sequences are drawn from a geometric distribution.

Product	Users	>0.05	>0.01
Chrome	167592	87.8%	97.6%
Firefox	21174	74.6%	93.0%
Flash Player	7722	98.2%	99.9%
Thunderbird	1857	86.5%	97.5%

patch delays and vulnerability states. Note that due to this single-parameter characterization, the average patching delay is sufficient for summarizing user behavior, and we shall only rely on sorting users by this measure.

3.2 Vulnerability State

We take the fraction of time that a host remains susceptible to at least one known vulnerability as an indicator of its security posture or *vulnerability state*. Figures 2a, c, and e display scatter plots of this measure for Chrome, Firefox, and Flash Player, respectively. For each figure we have randomly selected 5000 users, where each point represents one user. A point's x and y coordinates correspond to the average patch delay of that host, and its measured vulnerability state. The histogram at the bottom of each plot shows the distribution of users with respect to their average patch time; generated for users with an observation interval of at least one year, resulting in 140,588 sample points for Chrome, 64,016 for Firefox, and 55,042 for Flash Player. Note that the majority of hosts are observed for intervals smaller than 3 years, and we have omitted hosts with less than 10 update events (see Sect. 2). Therefore, our study does not capture users with average patch delays greater than roughly 100 days; longer observation windows are required to accurately assess the behavior of such users.

Vulnerability state as a function of average patch delay. We further group users with similar behavior by sorting them according to their estimated patch delay, and create bins consisting of 500 users. We calculate the median vulnerability duration, and the first and third quartiles in each bin; the results are illustrated in Figs. 2b, d, and f. We observe that a user with equal delays in each product experiences similar vulnerability duration. At 20 days, the user will remain vulnerable for 60% of the time, at 40 days this increases to 80%.

Across the three products, Chrome users clearly are more likely to have a lower patch delay (as shown in the histograms), likely the effect of silent updates, whereas Flash users are the most tardy. However, given the same average delay, the amount of vulnerabilities a user faces is very consistent across all products.

Outliers. In Fig. 2c we see high variability in vulnerability durations for users with similar patch times. Upon further inspection, we discovered two vulnerabilities for Firefox, CVE-2010-0654 and CVE-2010-1585, that were published on

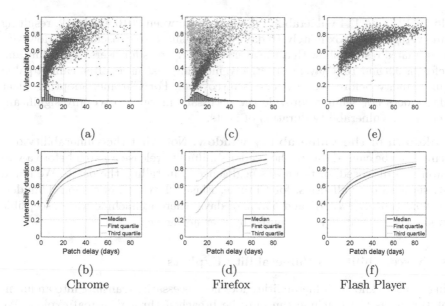

(a)   (c)   (e)

(b)   (d)   (f)

Chrome   Firefox   Flash Player

Fig. 2. Scatter plots of normalized vulnerability duration vs. average user delay in days (top), and the mean, and first and third quartiles for different user types (bottom). Each point in the scatter plots corresponds to a single user. In c the yellow/red dots are users active in 2010/only active starting 2011. (Color figure online)

"2010-02-18" and "2010-04-28", but first patched on "2010-07-20" and "2011-03-01", respectively. As a result, users that have been observed during 2010, have remained vulnerable for most of that year, regardless of their behavior. In Fig. 2c, we have used a lighter color to display hosts that have been observed at any time during 2010. The rest of the hosts (those that have opted in after 2010), exhibit similar variability to Chrome and Flash Player users.

Comparison across products. We further calculated the average vulnerability duration, over all users of each application. Note that these values are affected by the following properties of each product: (i) the distribution of different user types (the histograms in Fig. 2), and (ii) the expected vulnerability duration for each user type (Figs. 2b, d, and f). For Chrome, Firefox, Flash Player, and Thunderbird, the average host was susceptible to at least one vulnerability for 53.5%, 59.9%, 68.7%, and 55.7% of days. It follows that the improvement provided by different updating mechanisms in these applications is marginal.

A host's vulnerability state is influenced by two conditions. First, for a single vulnerability, the patch should be applied before the vulnerability is publicly disclosed. Nevertheless, even if the user misses the disclosure date, the damage can be minimized by prompt patching. However, when taking into account successive vulnerabilities, if the user does not apply the patch before the next vulnerability is disclosed, the clock is reset, and now they will have to apply a new patch to secure their machine. Quantitatively, for Chrome and Firefox, our data set includes 124, and 114 vulnerability disclosures between 2010 and 2012, resulting in an average of approximately 10 days between successive disclosures. However, our estimated results show that the average patch times for users of Chrome and Firefox, is 9.9 and 15.6 days, respectively, meaning that users often cannot patch a vulnerability before the next one is discovered. For Chrome, adopting silent updates does not seem to provide the necessary margin to see any significant effect on the vulnerability duration of hosts.

Breakdown of the vulnerability window. Note that the vulnerability of a machine can be caused due to the vendor's failure to release a patch before a vulnerability is disclosed, or the user's negligence in installing the patch. We found that, summed over all users, for Chrome, Flash Player, Firefox, and Thunderbird, 59.3%, 61.6%, 47.9% and 55.7% of days where a machine was susceptible to a known vulnerability was caused by user negligence.

3.3 Susceptibility to Vulnerability Exploits

Being prone to known vulnerabilities does not necessarily translate into an imminent threat, as the machine can only be breached through a real exploit. We perform a similar study on the percentage of days that a host remains susceptible to an exploitable vulnerability. Figures 3a and b display the scatter plot and vulnerability trends for 15 exploits of Flash Player. We did not have a sufficient amount of exploits for Chrome and Firefox, we were only able to find one known exploit for Chrome, and 2 for Firefox. Comparing these plots to 2a–f, we observe the same correlation between average patch times and vulnerability states. However, for similar patching delays, we generally see lower risk for known exploits. This is due to the small number of exploited vulnerabilities for Flash. Nevertheless, we observe that many hosts are susceptible to exploits more than 50% of the time, highlighting the threat exploit kits present to end-hosts.

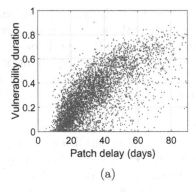

(a)

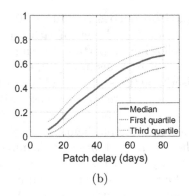

(b)

Fig. 3. Scatter plot (left) and mean, and first and third quartiles (right) for exploited vulnerabilities of Flash Player.

3.4 Factors that Impact User Behavior

Version-specific factors. Suppose we take an interval of size $2T$ and look at the total number of updating events that occur within the first and second half of the interval, across all users and for a specific subset of releases of a given product, and denote these by N_1 and N_2, respectively. We can then define a population-wide *willingness to update* as $W = 1 - (N_2/N_1)^{1/T}$. When looking at a period immediately following a release, if more users consider a new patch important and apply the patch promptly, then W tends to be high. Conversely, if more users hesitate to install the new patch, then more patching events occur at the second half of observation period resulting in a lower W.

For Firefox and Flash Player, we extract four features I_{vulns}, I_{bugs}, I_{feats}, and I_{majVer}, as described in Sect. 2. For each feature, we split the versions into two groups: those that have the feature and those that do not, and measure W within each group. We then conduct a statistical hypothesis test to determine if the updates from one group are deployed faster than the ones from the other group. Specifically, we perform a T-test between two groups with the null hypothesis "There is no difference in the mean of W". Low p-values from the T-test indicate that the factor affects the user's behavior. Here, we choose the significance level $\alpha = 0.05$. As we perform multiple hypothesis tests on the same data set, increasing the likelihood that we will find a significant result by pure chance, we apply the Bonferroni correction [1], by dividing α by the number of hypotheses tested. The adjusted α is 0.0125. The results are shown in Table 3. I_{majVer} for Firefox is the only factor with p-value below 0.05. However, this is not statistically significant after applying Bonferroni correction. This indicates that changes in versions have no statistically significant effect on user behavior.

Note that our results do not necessarily reflect users' indifference to these categorizations. In a recent user study [15], 80% of users state that update categories can influence their decision on applying a software update, and two-thirds react positively to a prototype that tags each update with one of five categories. Our results indicate that for the examined products, this information may not be readily available (we had to manually tag the release notes ourselves), which in turn causes users to behave independently of the update's intent.

Different countries and patch delivery. Table 4 shows the average time to patch for the top 10 countries with the largest numbers of users. Note that Chrome uses silent updates, and therefore has the lowest patch times. Firefox and Thunderbird versions prior to 15.0, and 16.0 (released 2012-08-28, and 2012-10-09, respectively) download updates in the background and prompt users for installation. Flash Player versions prior to 11.2 (released 2012-03-28) prompt users to download and install updates, and consequently exhibit the longest patch times. All three products switch to silent updates after the indicated dates; however these changes do not apply to the majority of our samples. For all four products, patching behavior is remarkably consistent, suggesting that cultural differences among these countries do not play a significant role in user behavior.

Table 4. Average patch times by country.

Country	Chrome	Firefox	Flash	Thunderbird
All	9.9	15.6	29.7	15.2
AU	10.6	16.3	30.1	15.1
CA	10.4	15.6	30.7	14.6
DE	10.9	15.3	24.9	14.7
FR	10.4	16.2	28.8	14.4
IT	8.8	15.9	26.1	13.5
JP	13.0	14.2	26.6	16.3
NL	10.4	15.2	28.5	14.7
PL	8.2	13.8	26.9	14.2
UK	9.2	15.7	28.3	13.9
US	10.5	15.5	32.1	15.4

Table 3. p-values from T-test on version-specific factors.

Application	I_{vulns}	I_{bugs}	I_{feats}	I_{majVer}
Flash Player	0.860	0.416	0.736	0.419
Firefox	0.109	0.226	0.126	0.027

4 Related Work

Rescorla [23] studied a 2002 OpenSSL vulnerability and observed two waves of patching: one in response to the vulnerability disclosure and one after the release of the Slapper worm exploit. Ramos [21] analyzed several remotely-exploitable vulnerabilities and reported a slow decay rate in some cases and some vulnerabilities that did not decay at all. Yilek et al. [30] scanned OpenSSL servers affected by a 2008 key generation vulnerability in Debian Linux and found a high patch rate in the first 30 days, followed by patching waves for the next six months. Durumeric et al. [11] showed that more than 50% of servers affected by the recent Heartbleed vulnerability in OpenSSL remained vulnerable after three months. Zhang et al. [31] showed that, even after patching OpenSSL, most websites remained vulnerable because they had not revoked certificates that may have been compromised owing to Heartbleed. The rate of updating is considerably higher for systems that employ automated updates [9,13]. Gkantsidis et al. [13] concluded that 80% of Windows Update users receive patches within 24 h after their release. Dübendorfer et al. [9] suggested that Google Chrome's silent update mechanism is able to update 97% of active browser instances within 21 days. Nappa et al. [17], measured vulnerability decay in 10 client-side applications and identified security threats presented by multiple installations of the same program and by shared libraries distributed with several applications. Alhazmi and Malaiya [2] examined five different vulnerability discovery models, fitting the models using data from three operating systems.

On factors that may affect vulnerability patching and user behavior, Schneider and Schneider [16] proposed several hypotheses, including an under-appreciation of risks and a fear of destabilizing other software. Vaniea et al. [29] suggested that negative experiences with past updates affect the users' willingness to deploy patches. Mathur et al. [15] study 30 users' updating practices, and design and evaluate a prototype updating interface based on their feedback.

5   Conclusions

In this paper we have conducted an in-depth analysis of the dynamics between vendors and consumers when it comes to software security. To the best of our knowledge, this is the first study on how individual behavior can influence the security state of a user's machine over long periods, where the continuous discovery of vulnerabilities, patch deployment by vendors, and the installation of patches create windows of opportunities for malicious entities to exploit open vulnerabilities on the machine. We have shown that frequent updating, and steps taken by vendors to speed up the installation of patches, provide marginal benefits when the rate at which new vulnerabilities are introduced into the product's code is high. Consequently, developers' should exercise due diligence when shipping new products to end-users, as the detrimental effects of releasing vulnerable applications to the public often cannot be eliminated by prompt patch deployment.

Our results also represent a first step toward understanding the *deployment-specific barriers* for updating software. We observe that user behavior can be modeled well using a simple and elegant mathematical model. We do not observe clusters of users with respect to the patching delay or the vulnerability state. Moreover, users do not make patching decisions depending on the type of improvements introduced with each new release (possibly due to how this information is presented), and the willingness to patch does not vary significantly across different countries. However, users seem to exhibit different behavior for different products, suggesting that vendors may be able to influence the users' patching delays. For example, Fig. 2 suggests that the vulnerability duration for Flash Player exhibits a lower variability than for Chrome and Firefox, despite the lack of a silent updating mechanism. This consistency may result from the fact that users are compelled to upgrade when sites remove backward compatibility for older Flash versions. A deeper understanding of these barriers could enable improvements in the software updating process.

Although we have shown that users' behavior can effectively be explained using a simple model, we are not able to build similar profiles for vendors. This is partly due to lack of a large data set on software vulnerability cycles. The set of unique vulnerability disclosures and patch deployments concerning the products under examination was too small to carry out a comprehensive study on product behavior. Such an analysis could close the loop when assessing the security posture of an end-user, by predicting the host's vulnerability state across different products, or for new products entering the market. Finally, leveraging additional data sources that can reveal the whole extent of user behavior, such as extending the study to other operating systems, and measuring periods of time where the system or a specific application are not used (this would lead to an overestimation of the vulnerability window in our current analysis) are other possible directions for future work.

References

1. Abdi, H.: Bonferroni and Šidák corrections for multiple comparisons. Sage (2007)
2. Alhazmi, O., Malaiya, Y.: Modeling the vulnerability discovery process. In: International Symposium on Software Reliability Engineering (2005)
3. Alhazmi, O., Malaiya, Y., Ray, I.: Measuring, analyzing and predicting security vulnerabilities in software systems. Comput. Secur. **26**(3), 219–228 (2007)
4. Arbaugh, W., Fithen, W., McHugh, J.: Windows of vulnerability: a case study analysis. IEEE Comput. **33**(12), 52–59 (2000)
5. Arora, A., Krishnan, R., Nandkumar, A., Telang, R., Yang, Y.: Impact of vulnerability disclosure and patch availability - an empirical analysis. In: Workshop on the Economics of Information Security (2004)
6. Bilge, L., Dumitraş, T.: Before we knew it: an empirical study of zero-day attacks in the real world. In: ACM Conference on Computer and Communications Security (2012)
7. Cavusoglu, H., Cavusoglu, H., Raghunathan, S.: Emerging issues in responsible vulnerability disclosure. In: Workshop on Information Technology and Systems (2004)
8. Clark, S., Collis, M., Blaze, M., Smith, J.: Moving targets: security and rapid-release in Firefox. In: ACM SIGSAC Conference on Computer and Communications Security (2014)
9. Duebendorfer, T., Frei, S.: Web browser security update effectiveness. In: Rome, E., Bloomfield, R. (eds.) CRITIS 2009. LNCS, vol. 6027, pp. 124–137. Springer, Heidelberg (2010). doi:10.1007/978-3-642-14379-3_11
10. Dumitraş, T., Shou, D.: Toward a standard benchmark for computer security research: the worldwide intelligence network environment (WINE). In: Workshop on Building Analysis Datasets and Gathering Experience Returns for Security (2011)
11. Durumeric, Z., Kasten, J., Adrian, D., Halderman, J.A., Bailey, M., et al.: The matter of heartbleed. In: Internet Measurement Conference (2014)
12. Exploit kits. http://contagiodump.blogspot.com
13. Gkantsidis, C., Karagiannis, T., Rodriguez, P., Vojnovic, M.: Planet scale software updates. In: ACM SIGCOMM Computer Communication Review (2006)
14. Grier, C., Ballard, L., Caballero, J., Chachra, N., Dietrich, C., et al.: Manufacturing compromise: the emergence of exploit-as-a-service. In: ACM Conference on Computer and Communications Security (2012)
15. Mathur, A., Engel, J., Sobti, S., Chang, V., Chetty, M.: "They keep coming back like zombies": improving software updating interfaces. In: Symposium on Usable Privacy and Security (2016)
16. Mulligan, D., Schneider, F.: Doctrine for cybersecurity. Daedalus, J. Am. Acad. Arts Sci. **140**(4), 70–92 (2011)
17. Nappa, A., Johnson, R., Bilge, L., Caballero, J., Dumitraş, T.: The attack of the clones: a study of the impact of shared code on vulnerability patching. In: IEEE Symposium on Security and Privacy (2015)
18. Neuhaus, S., Zimmermann, T., Holler, C., Zeller, A.: Predicting vulnerable software components. In: ACM Conference on Computer and Communications Security (2007)
19. NIST: National Vulnerability Database. https://nvd.nist.gov
20. Ozment, A., Schechter, S.: Milk or wine: does software security improve with age? In: USENIX Security Symposium (2006)

21. Ramos, T.: The laws of vulnerabilities. In: RSA Conference (2006)
22. Rescorla, E.: Is finding security holes a good idea? In: IEEE Security and Privacy (2005)
23. Rescorla, E.: Security holes... who cares. In: USENIX Security Symposium (2003)
24. Sabottke, C., Suciu, O., Dumitraş, T.: Vulnerability disclosure in the age of social media: exploiting Twitter for predicting real-world exploits. In: USENIX Security Symposium (2015)
25. Shahzad, M., Shafiq, M., Liu, A.: A large scale exploratory analysis of software vulnerability life cycles. In: International Conference on Software Engineering (2012)
26. Shankland, S.: Heartbleed bug undoes web encryption, reveals Yahoo passwords (2014). http://www.cnet.com/news/heartbleed-bug-undoes-web-encryption-reveals-user-passwords
27. Software release dates. http://bit.ly/2jKrMPj
28. Symantec Corporation: Symantec threat explorer (2012). http://www.symantec.com/security_response/threatexplorer/azlisting.jsp
29. Vaniea, K., Rader, E., Wash, R.: Betrayed by updates: how negative experiences affect future security. In: ACM Conference on Human Factors in Computing (2014)
30. Yilek, S., Rescorla, E., Shacham, H., Enright, B., Savage, S.: When private keys are public: results from the 2008 Debian OpenSSL vulnerability. In: Internet Measurement Conference (2009)
31. Zhang, L., Choffnes, D., Dumitraş, T., Levin, D., Mislove, A., et al.: Analysis of SSL certificate reissues and revocations in the wake of Heartbleed. In: Internet Measurement Conference (2014)

Performance

Application Bandwidth and Flow Rates from 3 Trillion Flows Across 45 Carrier Networks

David Pariag[1] and Tim Brecht[2](✉)

[1] Sandvine Incorporated, Waterloo, Canada
[2] Cheriton School of Computer Science, University of Waterloo, Waterloo, Canada
brecht@cs.uwaterloo.ca

Abstract. Geographically broad, application-aware studies of large subscriber networks are rarely undertaken because of the challenges of accessing secured network premises, protecting subscriber privacy, and deploying scalable measurement devices. We present a study examining bandwidth consumption and the rate at which new flows are created in 45 cable, DSL, cellular and WiFi subscriber networks across 26 countries on six continents. Using deep packet inspection, we find that one or two applications can strongly influence the magnitude and duration of daily bandwidth peaks. We analyze bandwidth over 7 days to better understand the potential for network optimization using virtual network functions. We find that on average cellular and non-cellular networks operate at 61% and 57% of peak bandwidth respectively. Since most networks are over provisioned, there is considerable room for optimization.

Our study of flow creation reveals that DNS is the top producer of new flows in 22 of the 45 networks (accounting for 20–61% of new flows in those networks). We find that peak flow rates (measured in thousands of flows per Gigabit) can vary by several orders of magnitude across applications. Networks whose application mix includes large proportions of DNS, PeerToPeer, and social networking traffic can expect to experience higher overall peak flow rates. Conversely, networks which are dominated by video can expect lower peak flow rates. We believe that these findings will prove valuable in understanding how traffic characteristics can impact the design, evaluation, and deployment of modern networking devices, including virtual network functions.

1 Introduction

The Internet continues to grow in geographic reach and data volume. This growth is facilitated by considerable investment from fixed and cellular service providers into network infrastructure. This infrastructure includes numerous devices such as switches, routers, caches, middle boxes and other devices to supply provider branded services (e.g., streaming video). Traffic incurs higher cost and increased latency as it moves from the network's edge towards its core. This offers a natural incentive for providers to invest in infrastructure that reduces traffic to Internet Exchange Points (IXPs) and backbone networks by placing devices closer to subscribers. However, there are relatively few studies which provide an *application-aware* view of broad scale traffic across multiple ISP networks. This is primarily

© Springer International Publishing AG 2017
M.A. Kaafar et al. (Eds.): PAM 2017, LNCS 10176, pp. 129–141, 2017.
DOI: 10.1007/978-3-319-54328-4_10

due to the difficulty of building and deploying scalable measurement devices in independent, geographically distributed networks. We believe that a large scale, application-aware study of Internet traffic can provide valuable insights into how application protocols drive consumption of bytes and flows in network devices.

In this paper, we conduct a detailed analysis of data that has been gathered as part of Sandvine's series of Internet Phenomena reports [27]. The collection of this data is facilitated by an ongoing partnership between Sandvine and participating ISPs. Our key contributions in this paper are:

- We find that there is a wide variety in the bandwidth consumed and rate at which new flows are created by the same application or service across networks. This makes it very difficult to describe a "typical network".
- We analyze bandwidth over time with respect to peak bandwidth and show that, on average, non-cellular and cellular networks operate at 57% and 61% of peak bandwidth, respectively. Since most networks are over provisioned, this suggests that the use of virtual network functions to offer elastic bandwidth may offer significant reductions in operating costs.
- We find that DNS is the top producer of flows in 22 of 45 networks, accounting for 20% to 61% of flows in those networks. We believe this places a significant load on flow-aware network devices including SDN routers, security middle boxes, and subscriber billing systems.

2   Methodology

Table 1 details the size and scope of the data used in our study. The dataset covers 22 3G and 4G subscriber networks (which we refer to as either cellular or mobile) and 23 cable, DSL and WiFi (fixed or non-cellular) subscriber networks across 26 countries on six continents. These networks range from a cellular network with peak bandwidth of 240 Mbps to a fixed network with peak bandwidth of nearly 600 Gbps. In total, our dataset covers 7 days in each network for a total of 62.8 PB and over 3 trillion flows of anonymized traffic.

This data was obtained from networks which have deployed Sandvine's Policy Traffic Switch (PTS). The PTS is a family of programmable network appliances which can be configured for applications including traffic inspection, subscriber billing, and network attack mitigation. It is a high performance device, capable of inspecting traffic in real time at network line rates. As such, our methodology does not rely on flow or packet sampling. We are able to inspect every packet of every flow. The PTS is usually deployed at the *edge* of the network, typically connected to termination points for cable and/or digital subscriber lines. The PTS is often used for subscriber billing purposes, which guarantees visibility of all subscriber traffic. Other deployments are possible, but we believe them to be uncommon in our dataset.

The PTS software stack examines packet headers at Ethernet, IP, and TCP/UDP layers as well as packet payloads at higher network layers. In concert with information gathered from lower layers, packet payloads are matched against an extensive collection of known signatures. Strong signatures can identify an application after a single packet. Other signatures may require multiple consecutive packets before a match is returned. Categorization of encrypted traffic relies on heuristic methods instead of payload inspection. For example, encrypted HTTPS traffic is usually immediately preceded by a DNS request from the client endpoint. The IP address in the DNS response primes the PTS to *expect* a new flow from the client to the resolved hostname in the near future. Similarly, SSL handshakes are sent as clear text and include information that identifies the server endpoint. These methods allow the PTS to identify services being delivered over HTTPS with a high degree of confidence. The accuracy of the Sandvine recognition engine is verified using a regression suite consisting of several thousand flows generated from live application testing (i.e., ground truth data). The recognition engine is updated on a monthly basis to account for new or changed application signatures.

Table 1. Scope of data collected

Region	Abbrev.	Countries	Sites	Traffic (PB)	New flows (billions)
Asia Pacific	APAC	3	3	1.0	152.9
Caribbean and Central America	CCA	5	7	1.7	162.1
Europe	ERP	8	13	22.7	949.1
Middle East and Africa	MEA	5	5	25.3	1,276.5
North America	NA	1	11	11.3	327.6
South America	SA	4	6	0.8	152.9
Total		26	45	62.8	3,021.0

The aforementioned recognition engine is run against every new flow in the network. A new flow is one whose 5-tuple (source IP, source port, destination IP, destination port, transport protocol) has no entry in the device flow table. Each new 5-tuple adds an entry to this flow table. For UDP flows, the flow entry is expired after 10 s without a packet transmission. Any subsequent packets transmitted with that 5-tuple are treated as a new flow. The 10 second UDP flow timeout is a default PTS configuration which conserves flow-related memory while accurately representing flow lifetimes. As a result, all UDP flows in our data are defined by this flow timeout. For TCP connections, the flow entry is terminated after a proper connection termination (i.e., after a TCP four-way handshake) or after the TCP TIME-WAIT timeout has expired without a packet transmission (i.e., at least 2 Maximum Segment Lifetimes, which is 240 s). The PTS classifies each new flow into one of nearly 2,000 application protocols. Once a flow is categorized, the PTS attributes all bytes and packets of that flow towards the identified application protocol. These application protocols include well-specified protocols such as DNS, FTP, SIP and MGCP. However, they also include traffic generated by well-known applications or services such as Skype, Windows Update, and WhatsApp. The popularity of HTTP as a transport protocol has led to several *refinements* of HTTP being classified as separate applications. For example, YouTube, Facebook, and Hulu are recognized as separate application protocols even though each is delivered over HTTP. In the interest of succinct analysis, we have created 21 application categories. Most categories are self-explanatory; those that require explanation are discussed when they are introduced. However, it is worth mentioning that the Misc category includes traffic that does not fit in any of the other 21 categories, as well as traffic that the PTS could not recognize.

Each PTS logs time-series data including byte, packet, and flow counts per application protocol to a centralized data store every 15 min. For the purposes of our study, we have retrieved the aforementioned time-series data from each network site for 7-day periods from June 2014 to September 2015. Note that packet payloads are not captured, only metadata gathered from payload inspection. Data collection and retention policies vary across operators, and as a result the 7-day periods vary across networks. Ownership of the data remains with the network operator and access to the data must be granted by each operator. Our analysis is based on post-processing data extracted from data stores.

3   Understanding Bandwidth Consumption

This section seeks to identify the applications which drive byte consumption and peak bandwidth in the networks under study. Figure 1 plots byte consumption by application category for all 45 networks. The x-axis lists each of the 21 application categories, and the y-axis shows the percentage of bytes consumed by each category. Fixed (non-cellular) networks are plotted to the left of the grid line using a green square, while mobile (cellular) networks are plotted to the right of the grid line using a red circle. Recall that the 7 day periods may differ across networks.

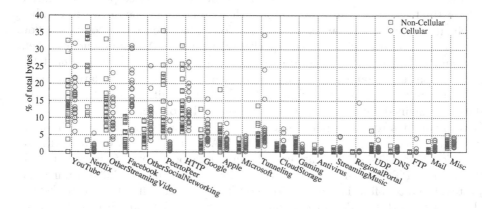

Fig. 1. Percentage of bytes by application (Color figure online)

As might be expected, video traffic (YouTube, Netflix and OtherStreamingVideo) is a significant consumer of bytes on many networks. The byte consumption ranges for YouTube are similarly large on both fixed and mobile networks, while Netflix consumption is noticeably lighter on mobile networks. Facebook byte consumption on many mobile networks is higher than seen on fixed networks. However, the most striking feature of Fig. 1 is that most application categories exhibit a large spread in byte consumption across many networks. For example, PeerToPeer traffic ranges from 0.35% of bytes in a Central American mobile network, to 35.49% of bytes in an Asian fixed network. Netflix, YouTube, Facebook, and other traffic categories exhibit similarly large spreads in either fixed or mobile networks. Figure 1 shows that there is wide diversity in the popularity of different application categories in different networks. We have examined traffic by region, and except for noting that several non-cellular North American networks are dominated by Netflix traffic, we find few similarities across different networks, even within the same region.

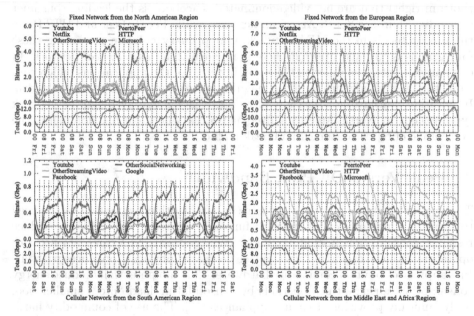

Fig. 2. Bandwidth in fixed North American (top-left), fixed European (top-right), mobile South American (bottom-left) and mobile African (bottom-right) networks

Figure 2 presents 7-day bandwidth versus time plots for four different networks. Data points are plotted every 15 min, with each point representing the average bandwidth over the previous 15 min. Each graph consists of two panels, with the top panel showing bandwidth for individual applications which consume more than 10% of bandwidth at any point during the week. The bottom panel plots total bandwidth for *all* applications over the week.

The top two graphs in Fig. 2 show video-dominated networks in North America (top-left) and Europe (top-right). The North American network is dominated by Netflix video. During peak bandwidth (which occurs at approximately 8 pm local time), Netflix consumes 40% of network bandwidth. Interestingly, the bandwidth plot also shows a local maxima just before noon on weekdays. As the bottom panel shows, the shape of the total bandwidth curve is shaped by Netflix usage patterns. More importantly, we have observed a similar degree of influence in nine other fixed North American networks where Netflix dominates bandwidth. The European network (top-right) is also video-dominated, with Netflix, YouTube and a regional provider (labelled OtherStreamingVideo, and intentionally anonymized) each consuming more than 10% of bandwidth. However, it is the regional service that exerts the greatest influence on peak bandwidth. Bandwidth for the regional service peaks between 8 pm and midnight on weekdays, and causes sharp but fairly short-lived peaks in total bandwidth.

The two lower graphs of Fig. 2 show a South American mobile network (bottom-left), and a network from the Middle East and Africa (MEA) region (bottom-right) that are not video-dominated. Facebook is the leading consumer of bandwidth in the South American network, while PeerToPeer and HTTP are the top protocols in the MEA network. Our primary point in presenting these four graphs is to illustrate that there is no such thing as a *typical* network. In our dataset, networks differ significantly in terms of the applications which consume the most bandwidth, and the magnitude and duration of peak bandwidth. In addition, we have not seen any clear patterns emerge by region or network type, except in North American fixed networks where Netflix dominates the percentage of bytes consumed and peak traffic.

4   Peak Versus Off Peak Bandwidth

This section examines how daily patterns in bandwidth consumption can be used to identify opportunities for network function virtualization (NFV) to reduce resource consumption (including energy conservation). NFV presents network operators with the opportunity to replace dedicated physical appliances with virtual appliances built on commodity hardware. This can potentially reduce energy consumption during off peak periods by consolidating load onto a smaller pool of dynamically provisioned virtual appliances [17]. The use of commodity hardware permits operators to take advantage of the power management technology leveraged in data centers [10,24,26]. The combination of Software Defined Networking (SDN) and NFV allows network operators to establish tradeoffs between power consumption and network performance [6], ultimately leading to significantly more efficient network infrastructures [5]. For example, Bolla et al. [4] have examined the traffic profiles of a Greek research network and a Telecom Italia subscriber network, and they argue that energy-efficient techniques may offer energy savings in excess of 60%.

Intuitively, networks with low night time troughs and sharp peaks offer greater opportunity for energy savings than networks with higher troughs and

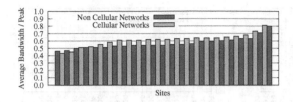

Fig. 3. Average bandwidth to peak ratio

Table 2. Reduction bounds

r	Cellular	Fixed
0	0.39	0.43
1	1.39	1.43
2	2.39	2.43
3	3.39	3.43

broad daytime plateaus. Figure 3 shows the average bandwidth consumed relative to the peak over the 7-day period for each network. This chart shows that the average bandwidth consumed relative to the peak is slightly higher for cellular than non-cellular networks. This is because many non-cellular networks tend to have sharper, more short-lived daily peaks than cellular networks.

At first glance, the potential for savings may not seem very large. For example, for the two networks with the highest bandwidth to peak ratios (0.80 and 0.81), the potential for reduction would seem to be no more than 20%. However, most networks are provisioned with capacity that exceeds the 7-day observed peak. If we denote peak bandwidth by p, capacity by c, and define r as the ratio of network capacity to the observed peak (i.e., $r = \frac{c}{p}$), then for networks which can dynamically adjust resources to meet demand, a bound on the possible bandwidth reduction is: $r + (1-$ average to peak bandwidth ratio).

Across the networks studied on average these reduction bounds are: $r + (1 - 0.61) = r + 0.39$ for cellular networks and $r + (1 - 0.57) = r + 0.43$ for non-cellular networks. Table 2 shows these reduction bounds for some values of r. If as one study has suggested, $r = 2$ [4], and more in some instances, then on average these networks provide significant opportunities for resource reductions by adjusting resources to efficiently meet demand.

5   Peak Flow Rates

Networking devices often store per-flow state in memory, and perform a flow lookup to associate each packet with a new or existing flow. Flow state is useful for detecting network threats [3, 21, 23] such as address scans, port scans, and reflector attacks. In addition, per-flow state is required for usage-based subscriber billing, which is required by many network operators.

In flow aware devices, which may include intrusion detections systems, carrier grade NATs, and some load balancers, the incoming packet rate determines the flow lookup rate, and the new flow rate determines the flow table *insertion rate*. The arrival of a new flow often triggers additional processing. For example, in an OpenFlow router, a new data flow may trigger a request to a controller node in order to complete the routing decision [12]. Similarly, the recognition engine of the Sandvine PTS executes on every new flow arrival. The new flow rate is thus an important determinant of performance for flow-aware systems as high new flow rates can lead to high processor load [13], and even flow exhaustion.

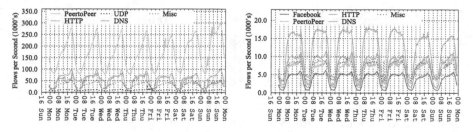

Fig. 4. New flow rates of fixed access (left) and mobile (right) European networks

In this section we study the applications that drive the creation of new flows. Figure 4 plots new flow rates over 7 days for fixed and mobile networks located in the same European country. As before, only applications which contribute more than 10% of total flows are plotted. In the fixed network (left graph), PeerToPeer applications are the chief creators of new flows, with peak new flow rates over 250,000 new flows/sec. At their peak, PeerToPeer flows constitute nearly 45% of all new flows. In the mobile network (right graph), it is DNS that drives flow creation with daily peak flow rates between 16,000 and 18,000 new flows/second. We offer these networks as examples of a broader trend: DNS and PeerToPeer applications account for the majority of new flows across all networks. DNS accounts for the highest percentage of new flows in 22 of 45 networks and more than 50% of all new flows in 3 networks. PeerToPeer flows account for the largest percentage of new flows in 22 of the remaining 23 networks, and comprise more than 50% of new flows in 8 networks. Interestingly, while PeerToPeer protocols dominate new flows in many fixed networks, they also account for the largest percentage of flows in several cellular networks.

The proportion of PeerToPeer flows is not unexpected because (1) The Bit-Torrent protocol is often served over uTP, which is a transport protocol layered on top of UDP [1]. (2) Some P2P implementations will actively change source and destination ports in an attempt to evade detection. (3) Peers send control messages (e.g., keep-alives) to each connected peer every two minutes. Many of these will count as new flows if the same 5-tuple is not reused within 10 s. The proportion of DNS flows captured by our data may be initially surprising. Early studies (circa 1997) [28] report that DNS constitutes less than 18% of flows. More recent work [8] tracks the incidence of DNS flows in a longitudinal dataset, and reports 22.55% to 54.87% of flows being DNS. However, we have identified several factors which help to explain the large proportion of DNS flows in many networks. First, many application protocols utilize DNS. If the name being resolved is not found in the local host's cache, this will result in DNS request(s). Second, DNS is commonly served over UDP, which is not connection oriented, causing each transaction to generate a separate sequence of datagrams. Operating system implementations now randomize the source port used in successive DNS requests [9,18] resulting in new 5-tuples (and thus flows) being generated. Third, popular web browsers such as Chrome, Firefox, and Internet

Explorer implement *DNS prefetching* in which the browser speculatively resolves hostnames for embedded page objects [19]. Modern web pages contain a median of 40 embedded objects, with 25% to 55% of pages requiring contact with *at least* 10 servers [7]. Lastly, many DNS responses use very short TTL values to better support load balancing and fault tolerance across multiple servers. As a result, even hostnames that are frequently referenced may require repeated DNS resolution.

5.1 Peak Flow Rates by Application

Intuitively, one would expect streaming video services and bulk download protocols like FTP to transfer a large number of bytes over a small number of flows. At the other extreme, one would expect DNS to transfer relatively little data over each flow. However, the *flow profile* of other applications (e.g., Facebook) is more difficult to intuit.

Figure 5 plots bandwidth normalized peak flow rates by application for all 45 networks. We calculate these rates by first identifying the 15 min window with the maximum flow rate (Flows/sec). This flow rate is broken down by application, and then normalized with respect to the bit rate (Gbps) over the 15 min window. This results in a ratio with units of Flows/Gbit. We only include data points if either the number of flows or bytes accounts for more than 0.5% of the application's flow or byte count, respectively. We normalize by bandwidth to compare networks of different sizes.

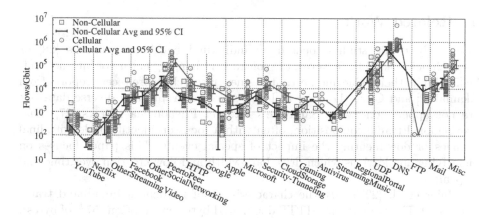

Fig. 5. Peak flow rates by application (log scale) (Color figure online)

In Fig. 5 the units on the y-axis are plotted using a log scale. Fixed networks are plotted to the left of the grid lines using a green square. Mobile networks are plotted in red and are offset to the right. Two trend lines are included to show the mean peak flow rates for each application along with 95% confidence intervals (CIs). Note that the CIs shown for Antivirus, RegionalPortal and FTP should be ignored because there were insufficient data points to compute CIs.

Figure 5 provides a number of key insights. First, we see that an individual application's peak new flow rates can vary by one or two orders of magnitude across different networks (e.g., YouTube ranges from 119 Flows/Gbit in one North American network to 2,347 Flows/Gbit in a MEA network). However, the variation across applications can be even larger, as can be seen by comparing the flow rates for Netflix and DNS in Fig. 5. Lastly, for several application groups the cellular networks have significantly higher peak new flow rates.

As expected, video services are at the low end of the spectrum with YouTube, Netflix and OtherStreamingVideo averaging, 352, 49, and 326 Flows/Gbit in fixed networks, respectively. At the other extreme, DNS averages 549,651 new flows per gigabit (and 936,399 in cellular networks). In fixed networks, application groups like Facebook, OtherSocialNetworking, PeerToPeer, and HTTP average 3,679, 4,484, 22,531, and 4,593 Flows/Gbit peak, respectively.

Networks whose application mix includes large proportions of DNS, Peer-ToPeer, social networking, and other flow-intensive applications can expect to experience higher overall peak flow rates. Conversely, networks which are dominated by video can expect lower peak flow rates. The overall peak flow rate can impact processing load for flow aware devices including OpenFlow routers, security devices, and billing systems. The large range of flow rates observed across different networks poses challenges when building and deploying cost-effective devices. We believe our data will be useful in the design, sizing, and testing of future devices.

6   Related Work

Very early traffic studies focused on individual backbone networks [28] or research networks [14]. However, the constantly changing nature of Internet traffic [20] limits their value and necessitates new research. More recent reports from Akamai [2] and Cisco [11] have included more geographically diverse data but are not application-aware. Sandvine's Internet Phenomena reports [27]) analyze regional traffic composition, often with a focus on identifying longitudinal changes or documenting the impact of special events. This paper focuses on identifying applications which drive bandwidth and flow creation over time and at peak.

Maier et al. [22] study the characteristics of residential broadband traffic circa 2009. They report that HTTP dominated byte consumption (57% of bytes), and that peer to peer traffic may not be as high (14% of bytes) as previously reported [15]. This study [22] covers a single digital subscriber line (DSL) network, and their application analysis is based on two 24 hour packet captures and fourteen 90 min captures. While their analysis of HTTP traffic reports HTTP content types, they do not differentiate *services* delivered over HTTP (e.g., Facebook).

Labovitz et al. [20] examine the evolution of inter-domain traffic from 2007 to 2009. They use deep packet inspection (DPI) to categorize traffic on five subscriber networks. They note the rise of legacy video protocols (e.g., RTSP), and the decline of peer to peer traffic over the study period. However, they do not separate video delivered over HTTP from other Web traffic. As a result, they attribute less than 3% of traffic to video.

Richter et al. [25] conduct an application-aware study of Internet traffic at one European IXP. Their methodology relies on random packet sampling (which may miss packets containing rich identifying information), and their application recognition examines just 74 bytes of TCP payload. They report that 57% of traffic is HTTP and 10% is HTTPS but offer no insight into the services that are delivered using those protocols.

As more services are delivered over HTTP, it is increasingly important to differentiate these services. As noted above, several earlier papers [16, 20, 22, 25] have broadly classified 20% to 58% of bytes as HTTP, Web, or browsing. Our methodology can inspect entire packet payloads, and reliably identify HTTP-based services as well as proprietary protocols (e.g., Skype). This is important because, as we have demonstrated, peak utilization can vary by service and understanding such patterns can enable more efficient network management. Additionally, our data set is taken from the *network's edge* and spans 45 provider networks across 26 countries. As a result, we measure traffic that may not be routed to IXPs (e.g., PeerToPeer and content that is cached near the edge). Both IXP and edge perspectives are valuable, but we believe that edge measurements provide an important view that is under-represented in the literature.

7   Conclusions

This paper presents an application and service aware analysis of bytes and flows from 7 days of Internet traffic from 22 cellular and 23 non-cellular networks across 26 countries to better understand how application traffic patterns impact network resource consumption. The analysis covers 62.8 PB *of payload data* and over 3 trillion flows, which makes it one of the largest such studies that we are aware of. We find that flow rates and bandwidth patterns are highly localized, with little similarity among networks or network types. In our analysis, we have not found factors which define a *typical* network.

We demonstrate that one or two applications can drive peak bandwidth and influence the shape of a network's bandwidth curve. This is important because the width and height of peak bandwidth and the depth of nightly troughs defines a *peak reduction bound* that can guide the deployment of NFV and SDN solutions which aim to reduce equipment and energy costs. We find that DNS traffic accounts for 25% of the three trillion flows examined and more than 50% of flows in several networks. We believe this is due to the large number of links embedded in modern web pages, aggressive DNS pre-fetching implemented in modern browsers, and short time-to-live settings for many DNS responses.

Acknowledgments. Tim Brecht's work was partially supported by a Natural Sciences and Engineering Research Council of Canada Discovery Grant. Thanks to Dan Deeth, Ian Wormsbecker, and Sau Cheng Lim at Sandvine for their assistance in gathering data, understanding network deployments, and for feedback on several drafts of this paper. We also thank Bernard Wong and S. Keshav from the University of Waterloo for their comments on an earlier version of this paper.

References

1. http://www.bittorrent.org/beps/bep_0029.html
2. Akamai Technologies Inc., Akamai's State of the Internet, vol. 7, no. 4, Q4 (2014)
3. Barford, P., Kline, J., Plonka, D., Ron, A.: A signal analysis of network traffic anomalies. In: 2nd ACM SIGCOMM Workshop on Internet Measurement (2002)
4. Bolla, R., Bruschi, R., Carrega, A., Davoli, F., Suino, D., Vassilakis, C., Zafeiropoulos, A.: Cutting the energy bills of internet service providers and telecoms through power management: an impact analysis. Comput. Netw. **56**(10), 2320–2342 (2012)
5. Bolla, R., Bruschi, R., Lombardo, C., Mangialardi, S.: Dropv2: energy efficiency through network function virtualization. IEEE Netw. **28**(2), 26–32 (2014)
6. Bolla, R., Bruschi, R., Lombardo, C., Suino, D.: Evaluating the energy-awareness of future Internet devices. In: IEEE Conference on High Performance Switching and Routing, July 2011
7. Butkiewicz, M., Madhyastha, H.V., Sekar, V.: Understanding website complexity: measurements, metrics, and implications. In: ACM IMC (2011)
8. Carela-Español, V., Barlet-Ros, P., Bifet, A., Fukuda, K.: A streaming flow-based technique for traffic classification applied to 12 + 1 years of Internet traffic. Telecommun. Syst. **63**(2), 191–204 (2016)
9. Castro, S., Zhang, M., John, W., Wessels, D., Claffy, K.: Understanding and preparing for DNS evolution. In: Ricciato, F., Mellia, M., Biersack, E. (eds.) TMA 2010. LNCS, vol. 6003, pp. 1–16. Springer, Heidelberg (2010). doi:10.1007/978-3-642-12365-8_1
10. Christensen, K., Reviriego, P., Nordman, B., Bennett, M., Mostowfi, M., Maestro, J.A.: IEEE 802.3 az: the road to energy efficient ethernet. IEEE Commun. Mag. **48**(11), 50–56 (2010)
11. Cisco Systems Inc. The Zettabyte Era: Trends and Analysis, May 2015
12. Curtis, A.R., Mogul, J.C., Tourrilhes, J., Yalagandula, P., Sharma, P., Banerjee, S.: Devoflow: scaling flow management for high-performance networks. In: ACM SIGCOMM (2011)
13. Estan, C., Keys, K., Moore, D., Varghese, G.: Building a better NetFlow. In: ACM SIGCOMM (2004)
14. Fomenkov, M., Keys, K., Moore, D., Claffy, K.: Longitudinal study of internet traffic in 1998–2003. In: Winter International Symposium on Information and Communication Technologies (2004)
15. Fraleigh, C., Moon, S., Lyles, B., Cotton, C., Khan, M., Moll, D., Rockell, R., Seely, T., Diot, C.: Packet-level traffic measurements from the sprint IP backbone. IEEE Netw. Mag. **17**(6), 6–16 (2003)
16. Fukuda, K., Asai, H., Nagami, K.: Tracking the evolution and diversity in network usage of smartphones. In: ACM IMC (2015)
17. Han, B., Gopalakrishnan, V., Ji, L., Lee, S.: Network function virtualization: challenges and opportunities for innovations. IEEE Commun. Mag. **53**(2), 90–97 (2015)

18. Kaminsky, D.: Black ops 2008: It's the end of the cache as we know it (2008). http://www.slideshare.net/dakami/dmk-bo2-k8
19. Krishnan, S., Monrose, F.: DNS prefetching and its privacy implications: when good things go bad. In: USENIX Conference on Large-scale Exploits and Emergent Threats (2010)
20. Labovitz, C., Iekel-Johnson, S., McPherson, D., Oberheide, J., Jahanian, F.: Internet inter-domain traffic. In: ACM SIGCOMM (2010)
21. Mai, J., Chuah, C.-N., Sridharan, A., Ye, T., Zang, H.: Is sampled data sufficient for anomaly detection? In: ACM IMC (2006)
22. Maier, G., Feldmann, A., Paxson, V., Allman, M.: On dominant characteristics of residential broadband internet traffic. In: ACM IMC (2009)
23. Moore, D., Shannon, C., Brown, D.J., Voelker, G.M., Savage, S.: Inferring internet denial-of-service activity. ACM Trans. Comput. Syst. **24**(2), 115–139 (2006)
24. Nedevschi, S., Popa, L., Iannaccone, G., Ratnasamy, S., Wetherall, D.: Reducing network energy consumption via sleeping and rate-adaptation. In: NSDI (2008)
25. Richter, P., Chatzis, N., Smaragdakis, G., Feldmann, A., Willinger, W.: Distilling the internet's application mix from packet-sampled traffic. In: Mirkovic, J., Liu, Y. (eds.) PAM 2015. LNCS, vol. 8995, pp. 179–192. Springer, Cham (2015). doi:10.1007/978-3-319-15509-8_14
26. Rotem, E., Naveh, A., Ananthakrishnan, A., Rajwan, D., Weissmann, E.: Power-management architecture of the Intel microarchitecture code-named Sandy Bridge. IEEE Micro **2**(2), 20–27 (2012)
27. Sandvine Inc., Global Internet Phenomena, December 2015. https://www.sandvine.com/trends/global-internet-phenomena/
28. Thompson, K., Miller, G., Wilder, R.: Wide-area Internet traffic patterns and characteristics. IEEE Netw. **11**(6), 10–23 (1997)

Measuring What is Not Ours:
A Tale of 3rd Party Performance

Utkarsh Goel[1]([⊠]), Moritz Steiner[2], Mike P. Wittie[1], Martin Flack[2],
and Stephen Ludin[2]

[1] Montana State University, Bozeman, USA
{utkarsh.goel,mwittie}@cs.montana.edu
[2] Akamai Technologies, Inc., San Francisco, USA
{moritz,mflack,sludin}@akamai.com

Abstract. Content Providers make use of, so called *3rd Party (3P)* services, to attract large user bases to their websites, track user activities and interests, or to serve advertisements. In this paper, we perform an extensive investigation on how much such *3Ps* impact the Web performance in mobile and wired last-mile networks. We develop a new Web performance metric, the 3rd `Party Trailing Ratio`, to represent the fraction of the critical path of the webpage load process that comprises of only *3P* downloads. Our results show that *3Ps* inflate the webpage load time (PLT) by as much as 50% in the extreme case. Using URL rewriting to redirect the downloads of *3P* assets on *1st Party* infrastructure, we demonstrate speedups in PLTs by as much as 25%.

1 Introduction

Content Providers (CPs) such as Facebook, Google, and others seek to attract large number of users to their websites and to generate high revenue. As a result, CPs strive to develop attractive and interactive websites that keep their users engaged. JavaScript libraries from online social networks, advertisements, and user tracking beacons allow CPs to personalize webpages based on end-users' interests, while various CSS frameworks make websites aesthetically pleasing [8, 10]. Further, webpage analytic APIs and performance monitoring tools allow CPs to monitor the user-perceived performance of their websites [9]. However, as CPs continue to evolve their websites with increasing number of features, the webpage load time (PLT) starts to increase – resulting in poor user experience [6,13].

To speed up the delivery of static Web content to end-users, CPs make contracts with Content Delivery Networks (CDNs), such as Akamai. CDN servers are distributed deep inside many last mile wired and mobile ISPs worldwide and thus provide low-latency paths to end-users [23,25]. Additionally, CDNs are motivated to adopt new and upcoming faster Internet technologies, such as HTTP/2 and IPv6 to achieve even faster content delivery for their CP customers [16,19,22]. Although CDNs are effective in reducing download times of Web objects they serve, as CPs continue to enhance their websites by embedding

© Springer International Publishing AG 2017
M.A. Kaafar et al. (Eds.): PAM 2017, LNCS 10176, pp. 142–155, 2017.
DOI: 10.1007/978-3-319-54328-4_11

external resources that the surrogate CDN does not serve, it becomes challenging for the CDN to speed up components of webpages beyond its control [15,17]. More generally, the usage of external resources have increased in last few years and have thus imposed a much harder challenge on CDNs to improve PLTs.

The performance of such *external* resources have been a great area of interest in the Web performance community. Previous attempts to classify *external* resources as *3rd Party* (*3P*) involves comparing object hostnames to the hostname of the base page URL. However, such techniques often lead to inaccurate classification. For example, while the two hostnames www.qq.com and btrace.qq.com appear to be from the same party, objects from www.qq.com are served from a surrogate CDN infrastructure, whereas objects from btrace.qq.com are served from an origin infrastructure. To bring clarity to classification of *3P* assets, we refer the server infrastructure that serves the base page HTML as the *1st Party* (*1P*) provider, such as a CDN provider acting as surrogate infrastructure for its CP customers. Additionally, we refer as to *3P* as any asset embedded in the webpage that is not served by the same infrastructure as the base page HTML. The downloads of such assets cannot be optimized by *1P* provider.

Current *3P* performance analysis techniques only investigate the overall load time of *3P* assets [6,11], however, such techniques fail to investigate the existence of *3P* assets on webpage critical path [27]. Moreover, previous work measures *3P* performance by comparing PLTs for a webpage with and without *3P* resources [3]. However, we show in Fig. 1 that such techniques may not result in accurate comparison of PLTs, as removing a *3P* resource may also remove other resources that are dependent on the removed resource. For example, while 50% of the *3P* resources initiate download of at least one other resource on the webpage, many *3P* resources initiate downloads of upto 10 other resources.

We argue that the key to minimize *3P* impact on PLT is to first understand which specific *3P* assets lie on webpages' critical path. In this paper, we extend our previous work of evaluating the impact of *3Ps* on PLT over mobile networks [21]. Specifically, we investigate *3P* impact on PLT over wired and well-provisioned datacenter networks and suggest a potential solution to mitigate their impact through experimental evaluation. Specifically, we make the following four contributions in this paper:

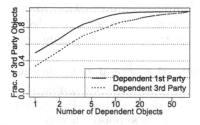

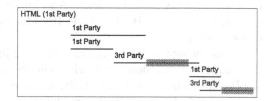

Fig. 1. Dependency on *3P* assets.

Fig. 2. A waterfall diagram with one *3P* and two *1P* objects.

Analysis of webpage structure: We make extensive use of the open-source data available at the HTTP Archive [2] to expose the characteristics of *3P* assets embedded into the top 16,000 Alexa webpages [7], currently served by four major CDN providers. Specifically, for *3P* assets in each webpage in our dataset, we calculate the number of unique domain names resolved, HTTP requests sent, total bytes, and total uncompressed bytes downloaded, among many other characteristics.

Extensive Measurement: To measure the impact of *3P* downloads on Web performance, we devise a new Web performance metric, 3^{rd}Party Trailing Ratio (3PTR), that represents the PLT fraction of the download time of *3P* assets on webpage critical path. As shown in Fig. 2, the 3PTR is the PLT fraction that is accounted for by the sum of the download times of *3P* objects whose download times do not overlap with any *1P* object, as highlighted by the shaded areas. To calculate 3PTR from HTTP Archive (HAR) files, we encourage readers to experiment with http:// nl.cs.montana.edu/tptr.

Next, using cellular and wired clients of Gomez Mobile and Gomez Last-Mile testbeds [4], we run several active experiments for three months in 2016 to calculate 3PTR for hundreds of webpages and identify which *3P* resources impact PLTs. We also use measurement data from HTTP Archive to calculate 3PTR for the top 16,000 Alexa webpages loaded from a well-provisioned datacenter network [2].

Problems Discovered and Solutions: In our analysis of *3P* performance, we discover two major problems. *First*, we identify that for many webpages, *3P* assets that lie on the webpage critical path contribute up to 50% of the total PLT. To the best of our knowledge, there is currently no known best-practice as to how *1Ps* could optimize *3P* downloads to mitigate their impact on the PLT.

Solution: We investigate how *1P* providers could safely redirect *3P* downloads onto their infrastructures for faster delivery of *3P* assets. Based on our measurements, we demonstrate that rewriting *3P* URLs in a way that enables *1P* servers to deliver *3P* assets improves PLTs by up to 25%. The faster PLTs are achieved as rewritten URLs eliminate DNS lookups to *3P* hostnames, the clients download *3P* assets from *1Ps* using an existing TCP connection to the *1P* server, and that the *1P* (surrogate CDN) servers are likely closer to clients than the *3P* servers. Additionally, *1P* servers could compress any uncompressed *3P* assets before transferring them to clients. And finally, *1Ps* could use new content delivery protocols, such as HTTP/2 and IPv6 for even faster delivery that many *3Ps* do not employ.

Second, using the HTTP Archive data we identify that several *3P* vendors do not compress Web objects even when clients indicate support for compression in HTTP request headers. Incidentally, we identify that some *1P* providers deliver uncompressed objects as well, even when clients indicate support for compression. Our investigation suggests that this behavior is due to misconfigured HTTP response headers on *1P* servers.

Solution: We made recommendations to several *1P* providers, providing them with a list of URLs to configure compression for the objects that they currently serve uncompressed.

2   Data Collection

We use the open-sourced HTTP Archive dataset, an initiative by Google, Mozilla, and other industry leaders, to analyze structures of different websites [2]. The HTTP Archive data is collected using the WebPageTest framework, where webpages are loaded over virtual machines inside a datacenter [14]. The page loads are then translated into a format similar to HTTP Archive format (HAR) containing the timing data and as well as the HTTP request and response headers for each object embedded in the webpage under test.

For our analysis, we extract only the HTTP request and response headers pertaining to the top 16,000 Alexa webpages. In particular, for each requested object we extract HTTP headers indicating the response size, `Cache-Control`, associated hostname, and whether the response was compressed when the client indicates support for compression in the HTTP request headers. Since many *3P* assets load after the `onLoad event` triggered by the Web browser and since we only focus on understanding how much *3P* downloads impact the PLT, we consider the measurement data for objects loaded only until the `onLoad event`.[1]

Next, for each hostname we perform a `dig` operation to check whether the hostname resolves to a canonical name (CNAME) associated with any of the four CDN providers we use in this study. If a hostname for an object does not resolve to a CNAME associated to the *1P* serving the base page HTML, we consider that object as a *3P* asset, with respect to that *1P*. Additionally, if the hostname does not resolve to any CNAME, we consider that hostname as *3P* for all four *1P* CDN providers. While many *1P* providers use anycast addressing for their CDN servers, the four CDN providers we use in this study perform DNS-based addressing and resolve hostnames to CNAMEs associated to them.

Finally, for each webpage, we calculate the total number of domain names resolved and HTTP requests sent for objects that we label as *3P*. We also calculate the total number of bytes, total number of uncompressed bytes, and total number of cacheable bytes delivered by various *3P* vendors by parsing the `Content-Encoding` and `Cache-Control` headers in the HTTP response, respectively. Our total dataset consists of structures for 16,000 webpages requesting a total of 1.6 M objects, out of which about 525 K (32%) objects belong to different *3P* providers.

To collect measurement data pertaining to *3P* impact on PLT, we conduct several active experiments using the Gomez Mobile testbed to load 60 mobile-specific webpages served by the production servers of a major CDN provider [1,4]. We also conduct active experiments using Gomez Wired Last-Mile testbed to load a set of 376 webpages designed for larger screens from

---

[1] We refer to the time Web browsers take to trigger the `onLoad event` as the webpage load time (PLT) [5].

the same CDN. The selected webpages are limited to a few hundred because of the operational costs related to running Gomez experiments and that the chosen webpages are among the most popular sites served by the CDN. Next, we configure both Gomez mobile and wired clients to load each website 400 times and record the browser exposed Navigation and Resource Timing data after each page load [5,12]. The Navigation and Resource Timing data we obtain from Gomez consists of timestamps when the page starts to load, timestamps when each object starts and finishes loading (including the time to perform DNS lookup, TCP handshake time, SSL handshake time, time to receive the first bit, and the object download time), and the timestamp when the *onLoad event* is triggered by the Web browser. Our configured Gomez clients also record the hostnames associated with each requested object, which we use to identify whether the object downloaded is a *3P* asset or a *1P* asset, similarly to how we identify this information using the HTTP Archive data. In addition to using Gomez clients, we use measurement data from the HTTP Archive to extract Resource Timing data pertaining to each object downloaded for the top 16000 Alexa webpages. Such a comprehensive measurement allows us to understand the impact of *3P* assets on PLTs when loaded under different network conditions, such as cellular, wired, and well-provisioned datacenter networks.

3   Exposing Characteristics of *3P* Assets

Using the HTTP Archive data, in Fig. 3 we show the distribution of the number of unique domain names resolved and total number of HTTP requests sent by clients to download *3P* assets for different webpages. In general, we observe that 50% of the webpages resolve atleast 10 unique *3P* domain names and issue a total of about 50 HTTP requests to different *3P* vendors. For mobile clients, where radio latency and the latency to cellular DNS servers is a few hundred milliseconds, resolving multiple *3P* domain names introduces significant latency to the overall PLT [22,23,26]. Further, such a large number of DNS lookups could result in many round trips to establish several new TCP connections to distant

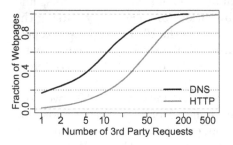

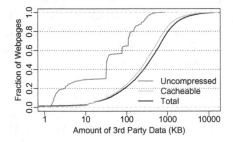

Fig. 3. Distribution of the number of DNS lookup and HTTP requests made to download *3P* assets.

Fig. 4. Distribution of total, uncompressed, and cacheable bytes downloaded from *3P* vendors.

3P servers – introducing additional delay to the object load times, especially during the TCP slow start phase of each connection.

Next, in Fig. 4, we show the distribution of the total amount of data downloaded from *3P* servers, and as well as the total number of uncompressed bytes transferred by *3P* servers, when clients indicate support for compression in the HTTP request headers. 50% of the webpages download atleast 400 KB data from different *3P* providers, out of which at least 40 KB of data is transferred uncompressed, and almost all of the data transferred by *3P* servers is cacheable by clients or any intermediate Web proxy. The opportunity to cache *3P* data allows *1Ps* to compress and serve requests from their infrastructures.

4   Third Party Trailing Ratio

3P assets embedded on a webpage require multiple DNS lookups and download of hundreds of kilobytes of data, however, *3P* assets that do not lie on the webpage critical path do not impact the PLT. Therefore, we investigate the time spent by *3P* downloads on the critical paths of webpages. For the purposes of this investigation, we devise a new Web performance metric, **3rd Party Trailing Ratio (3PTR)**, that represents the fraction of PLT that is spent only by *3P* downloads and during which no *1P* asset is downloading in parallel, as denoted by the two shaded areas in Fig. 2.

To calculate **3PTR**, we employ a two step process as follows: First, using start and end timestamps of all object downloads, we calculate all non-overlapping time intervals of *1P* and *3P* downloads independently [20]. Second, using the above time intervals, for each *3P* interval we identify whether there is any time duration that does not overlap with any *1P* interval. The sum of all such *3P* time intervals results in the *3P* delay. Finally, the percentage of PLT that belongs to *3P* delay is referred to **3PTR**.

In Fig. 5, we show the **3PTR** distributions for 60 webpages served by a major CDN provider, where we load each webpage 400 times from Gomez Mobile clients connected to cellular networks. For figure clarity, we sort pages along the x-axis based on the median **3PTR** value. In general, we observe that *3P* downloads do not impact PLT for about half of the webpages in our dataset. With these webpages, when *3P* assets are being downloaded, one or more longer *1P* assets are also being

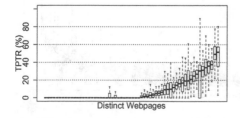 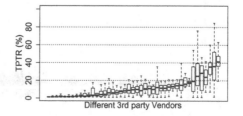

Fig. 5. 3PTR distributions for webpages served to Gomez Mobile.

Fig. 6.   3PTR   distributions   of   *3P* providers served to Gomez Mobile.

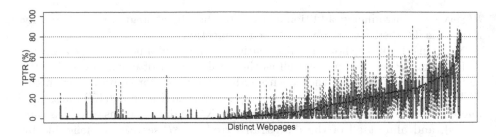

Fig. 7. 3PTR distributions for different webpages served to wired clients.

downloaded in parallel. Therefore, for these webpages, the *3P* downloads do not lie on the critical path. However, for other webpages, *3P* downloads contribute to up to 50% of the total PLT, in the median case. For these webpages, when *3P* assets are downloaded, none of the *1P* assets are being downloaded. Therefore, for these webpages, *3P* downloads lie on the webpage critical path and thus introduce additional latency to the overall PLT. Note that the variation in 3PTR in Fig. 5 arises from the variation in the network conditions, or server processing time. Specifically, as the load time of a *3P* asset changes, the 3PTR changes as well.

In Fig. 6, we separate 3PTR based on *3P* providers. Specifically, for each *3P* provider on the critical path, we show a boxplot distribution of the 3PTR contributed by that *3P* provider. From the figure we observe that while some *3P* providers impact PLT of some pages by as low as 5%, other *3Ps* contribute up to 40% of PLT for some webpages. Therefore, to speedup websites it is first important to understand which *3P* provider impacts PLT and then mitigate its impact.

We observe similar impact of *3P* on PLT when loading a different set of 376 webpages using Gomez Wired Last-Mile clients. In Fig. 7, we show that the median 3PTR is zero for about 40% of the webpages. For the rest 60% of the webpages, *3Ps* contribute as much as 50% of the PLT in the median case. As observed earlier, the variation in 3PTR comes from the variation in load times of

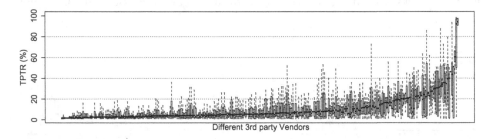

Fig. 8. 3PTR distributions for various *3P* providers for pages served to Gomez Wired Last-Mile clients.

3P assets. Additionally and similarly to Fig. 6, in Fig. 8 we observe that some *3Ps* impact PLTs of some webpages as low as 1%, while other *3Ps* impact PLT as much as 50%.

Finally, using the measurement data from HTTP Archive, in Fig. 9 we show the 3PTR distribution for the top 16,000 Alexa webpages. For example, we see that for about 50% of the webpages served by CDNs A, B, and C, *3Ps* contribute at least 20% of the total PLT, even when webpages are loaded from a cloud datacenter network. For webpages served by CDN D we see that about 65% of the webpages have zero 3PTR, because many webpages served by CDN D are for its own products that do not contain any *3P* assets.

5   Selecting Third Party Objects for Optimization

Based on our analysis of *3P* impact on PLT in different types of networks, we argue for *1Ps* (such as a CDN provider) to rewrite critical *3P* URLs and redirect requests onto their infrastructures to reduce 3PTR. Specifically, rewriting critical *3P* URLs eliminates DNS lookup time for multiple *3P* hostnames, as a rewritten URL can point to the hostname of the basepage that the browser has resolved already. Additionally, URL rewriting allows clients to connect to already warmed-up TCP connections to much closer *1P* servers and download *3P* content while eliminating TCP slow start and time to setup new TCP connections to distant *3P* servers.

Next, when the request to download a *3P* resource arrives at the *1P* server, the *1P* delivers the requested content in one of the following two ways: (1) either from the server's cache; or (2) by retrieving the requested resource from the *3P* server over a proactively established TCP connection. For example, while the first request for a *3P* resource is fetched from *3P* servers, subsequent requests for the same resource are served from *1P* cache. While it is possible that many clients request a specific resource URL, the response for which needs to be personalized according to the user profile, the *1Ps* will need to always fetch the resource from the original *3P* server. For such resources, the client requests contain a cookie in the HTTP headers that enables *3P* servers to customize responses accordingly.

Rewriting *3P* URLs for resources that require a *3P* cookie in the request, or in the response, introduces challenges for *1Ps* to reliably perform URL rewriting. Specifically, many *3P* providers process cookies to perform visitor counts for each resource, track user activities, generate responses based on user's recent activities, among others. Therefore, when *1Ps* proxy *3P* traffic on their infrastructure, requests may appear to originate from a smaller pool of *1P* server IP addresses – negatively impacting the visitor count and user tracking services for *3P* providers. Although, *1Ps* could add an x-Forwarded-For header in the forwarded HTTP requests, *3P* servers will need to process this header to accurately track users. Finally, if many *3P* requests containing user cookies originate from a unreasonably small pool of *1P* IP addresses, *3P* servers may interpret these requests as a part of a Denial-of-Service (DOS) attack.

In Fig. 10, we show the number of *3P* objects that require cookies in requests and/or responses for the top 16,000 Alexa webpages. From the figure we observe

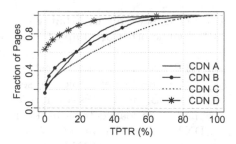

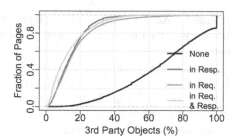

Fig. 9. 3PTR distribution for webpages served by four CDN providers.

Fig. 10. Distributions of cookie-based requests and responses.

that for about 50% of the total websites, at least 70% of the *3P* objects do not require cookies in requests and responses. Therefore, it is promising for *1P* providers to speed up webpages by rewriting URLs for those critical *3P* resources that do not require cookies neither in HTTP requests, nor in HTTP responses. We argue that for each webpage that a *1P* provider serves, the provider could proactively download *3P* resources to identify those that do not contain any cookies and thereafter apply URL rewriting to redirect requests for only those *3P* resources to its own infrastructure before sending the basepage HTML to the client.

6   Third Party Content Acceleration via URL Rewriting

We clone several webpages on a major CDN provider's infrastructure, where each webpage has two versions: (1) where *3P* resources are downloaded from *3P* servers, and (2) where URLs of *3P* resources are rewritten to download from *1P* servers. In Figs. 11, 12, 13, 14, 15 and 16, we show distributions of 200 PLTs for different webpages loaded under different mobile and wired network conditions. Note that the y-axis in these figures is on a log scale. To measure PLTs under different mobile network conditions, we utilize our previous work on simulating cellular networks [24]. For simulating wired network conditions, we only control end-to-end (E2E) latency between clients and servers, as in our observations packet loss on wired networks is minimal and bandwidth is not the limiting factor.

In Figs. 11 and 12, we select a webpage with 3PTR of about 49% and compare its PLTs in various mobile and wired network conditions respectively. Our results show that rewriting *3P* URLs for webpages with such high 3PTR values result in significantly lower PLTs compared to original page. For example, under *Fair* mobile conditions, the median PLT and the 3PTR is reduced by 28% by rewriting URLs of *3P* assets on the webpage critical path. Additionally, in a last-mile wired network with E2E latency of 20 ms (typical latency between clients and CDN providers), we observe that the median PLT and the 3PTR with rewritten *3P* URLs is 24% lower than original webpages.

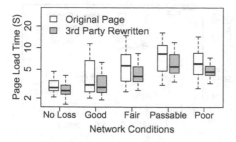

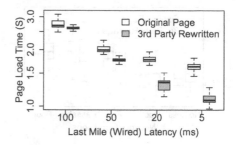

Fig. 11. PLTs in cellular conditions for a page with TPTR of 49%.

Fig. 12. PLTs in wired conditions for a page with TPTR of 49%.

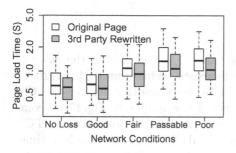

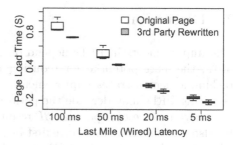

Fig. 13. PLTs in cellular conditions for a page with TPTR of 25%.

Fig. 14. PLTs in wired conditions for a page with TPTR of 25%.

Similarly, when comparing PLTs for webpages with 3PTR of 25% and 5% in Figs. 13, 14 and Figs. 15, 16 respectively, we observe reduced PLTs by rewriting *3P* URLs. However, for these webpages the improvements are less pronounced than we observe in Figs. 11 and 12, as the 3PTR for these webpages is less. For example in Figs. 13 and 14, the median PLTs and 3PTR of a webpage with rewritten *3P* URLs under *Fair* mobile conditions and 20 ms E2E wired latency are 15% and 10% lower than original webpage, respectively. Similarly, in Figs. 15 and 16, the median PLTs and the 3PTR under same conditions are 3% and 2.2% lower than for the original webpage.

Note: For CP customers that desire to enable *3P* content acceleration for their webpages, rewriting of all *3P* objects served over HTTPS should be performed only when the CDN provider makes legal agreements with individual *3P* providers to terminate HTTPS connections to their servers and cache the requested content. Additionally, URL rewriting does not introduce any operational complexity to CPs. As CDN providers fetch HTML from their CP customers, CDNs could parse the HTML and apply URL rewriting to *3P* objects that lie on the critical path. Further, as CDNs cache *3P* objects, these objects can be refreshed similarly to how CDNs refresh objects from their CP customers.

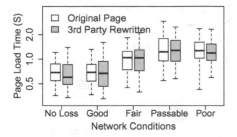
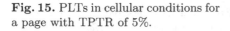

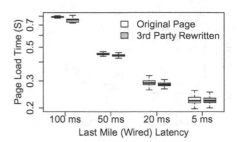

Fig. 15. PLTs in cellular conditions for a page with TPTR of 5%.

Fig. 16. PLTs in wired conditions for a page with TPTR of 5%.

7   Discussion

The improvements in PLTs depend on the value of **3PTR** – higher the value of **3PTR**, the more potential for reducing PLTs exists. While our URL rewriting technique demonstrates improvements in PLTs, we argue that for certain *3Ps*, rewriting URLs may degrade the performance. For example, in Fig. 17 we compare performance of a popular *3P* resource in terms of DNS lookup time, TCP handshake time, time to receive first bit, download time, and the total load time, when loaded from a major CDN provider network and *3P* servers respectively. We observe that DNS lookup time for the *3P* resource is significantly lower than the DNS lookup time for the *1P* CDN provider, likely because the *1P* domain name created for this experiment is not very popular and therefore is not cached by the local DNS resolver. The TCP handshake, first bit, and download time are similar when downloading the same object from *3P* or *1P* servers. As such, the total load time is governed by the DNS lookup time.

Similarly, in Fig. 18, we show the same performance metrics for a different *3P* resource. We observe that while DNS lookup time is still higher for a *1P* hostname, the TCP handshake, first bit times are significantly lower when downloading the resource from a *1P* server, which translates to a lower total load time with rewritten URLs. Therefore, we argue that careful performance analysis should be performed for each critical *3P* resource before transmitting

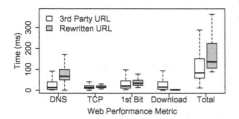
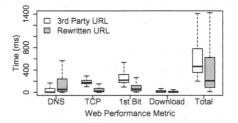

Fig. 17. Comparing performance metrics of a *3P* objects.

Fig. 18. Comparing performance metrics of another *3P* objects.

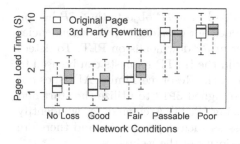 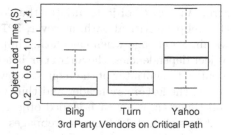

Fig. 19. PLTs distributions when rewriting URLs for an **h2** page.

Fig. 20. Distributions showing the variation in *3P* load times.

HTML with rewritten URLs to clients. For example, if DNS lookup time impacts the overall load time of the object, either the *3P* resource need not be rewritten, or the rewritten URL should use a hostname that client should have already resolved, or configure clients to coalesce TCP connections to multiple *3P* hostnames. In fact, a recent Internet draft by Microsoft and Mozilla details how to present additional certificates during an existing connection and serve content for the domains referenced in the additional certificates [18].

Next, in Fig. 19 we show the impact of URL rewriting when the base page is served over HTTP/2 (**h2**). This webpage uses many *3P* hostnames for which the client establishes several TCP connections. When rewriting such a webpage we rewrite all critical *3P* URLs to send requests to the basepage hostname – reducing the total number of connections from several dozen to just one **h2** connection. For such webpages, single TCP connection degrades PLTs as loss interpreted by TCP due to variable radio latency in cellular networks degrades HTTP/2 performance [24]. When measuring PLTs for the same page over **h2** in wired networks, we observe that without packet loss, **h2** offers faster PLTs. Therefore, we argue that for content delivery optimized for mobile networks, it is important to consider impact on PLT of the number of TCP connections that remain after rewriting URLs.

Finally, for another webpage with over 40 different *3P* hostnames and **3PTR** of about 30%, we identify that the performance variation from a few *3P* resources (for which we could not perform URL rewriting as they contain cookies) negate the benefits of URL rewriting for other *3P* resources. As shown in Fig. 20, the three *3P* resources downloaded from Bing, Turn, and Yahoo servers vary by over 1 second. For example, a resource loaded from Yahoo servers takes anywhere from 300 ms to 1.5 s. Therefore, we argue that for webpages that embed cookie-based *3P* objects with high performance variation may not assist the URL rewriting technique to improve PLTs.

Limitation: The one (minor) limitation of **3PTR** is that for some webpages, **3PTR** may give a lower bound on the impact of *3P* downloads on PLT. For example, when a *3P* object initiates the download of a *1P* object and the *3P* downloads in parallel with some other *1P* object, the TPTR is calculated as zero. As the *3P* object initiates the download of a *1P* object, that *3P* lies on the webpage critical path, however, 3PTR does not consider object dependencies within a webpage when calculating impact of *3P* downloads on PLT. To detect object dependencies, the `Referrer` header in the HTTP requests can be used to identify the initiator of the request. However, the Resource Timing API does not record the `Referrer` header and thus we designed 3PTR to utilize the start and end timestamps for each loaded object. Using HTTP Archive data, we identify that less than 2–10% of the webpages possess such dependencies and therefore 3PTR calculates accurate *3P* impact for majority of the webpages.

8   Conclusions

Our large scale investigation on 3rd *Party* performance reveals that *3Ps* can impact the overall webpage load time by up to 50%. Through extensive experimentation, we demonstrate that redirecting *3P* traffic to *1P* infrastructure improves webpage load times. We, therefore, make recommendations to *1P* providers to investigate the existence of *3P* resources the critical path of webpages and utilize URL rewriting to improve Web performance for end-users. In the future, we plan to perform even larger scale measurements on production Web traffic.

Acknowledgments. We thank Ilya Grigorik, Shantharaju Jayanna, Wontaek Na, and Kanika Shah for their help. We also thank National Science Foundation for supporting this work via grants CNS-1555591 and CNS-1527097.

References

1. Gomez Last-Mile Testbed, November 2009. https://goo.gl/BtwSWY
2. HTTP Archive: Interesting stats (2010). http://httparchive.org/
3. Performance of 3rd Party Content, February 2010. http://stevesouders.com/p3pc/
4. Gomez (Dynatrace Synthetic Monitoring), July 2015. https://goo.gl/4JTjJy
5. Navigation Timing, August 2015. http://w3c.github.io/navigation-timing/
6. The Truth Behind the Effect of Third Party Tags on Web Performance, December 2015. https://goo.gl/24f09c
7. Alexa Top Sites, July 2016. http://www.alexa.com/topsites
8. Facebook for Developers, June 2016. https://developers.facebook.com/
9. Google Analytics Solutions, June 2016. https://analytics.googleblog.com/
10. Google Fonts, June 2016. https://fonts.google.com/
11. Performance Measurement for the Real World, August 2016. https://www.soasta.com/performance-monitoring/
12. Resource Timing, July 2016. https://www.w3.org/TR/resource-timing/
13. Third-party content could be slowing Britain's retail websites, March 2016. https://goo.gl/1gi1Li
14. WebPageTest Framework, July 2016. http://www.webpagetest.org/
15. Alstad, K.: Can third-party scripts take down your entire site? June 2014. https://goo.gl/V0iLfa

16. Belshe, M., Peon, R., and E. M. Thomson. Hypertext Transfer Protocol Version 2 (HTTP/2), RFC 7540, May 2015
17. Bermes, B.: Third Party Footprint: Evaluating the Performance of External Scripts, September 2014. https://goo.gl/Cqhafq
18. Bishop, M., Thomson, M.: Secondary Certificate Authentication in HTTP/2, May 2016. http://www.ietf.org/internet-drafts/draft-bishop-httpbis-http2-additional-certs-01.txt
19. Chen, F., Sitaraman, R.K., Torres, M.: End-user mapping: next generation request routing for content delivery. In: ACM SIGCOMM, August 2015
20. Enaganti, R.C.: Merge Overlapping Intervals, August 2015. http://www.geeksforgeeks.org/merging-intervals/
21. Goel, U., Steiner, M., Na, W., Wittie, M.P., Flack, M., Ludin, S.: Are 3rd parties slowing down the mobile web? In: ACM S3 Workshop, October 2016
22. Goel, U., Steiner, M., Wittie, M.P., Flack, M., Ludin, S.: A case for faster mobile web in cellular IPv6 networks. In: ACM MobiCom, October 2016
23. Goel, U., Steiner, M., Wittie, M.P., Flack, M., Ludin, S.: Detecting cellular middle-boxes using passive measurement techniques. In: Karagiannis, T., Dimitropoulos, X. (eds.) PAM 2016. LNCS, vol. 9631, pp. 95–107. Springer, Heidelberg (2016). doi:10.1007/978-3-319-30505-9_8
24. Goel, U., Steiner, M., Wittie, M.P., Flack, M., Ludin, S.: HTTP/2 performance in cellular networks. In: ACM MobiCom (Poster), October 2016
25. Nygren, E., Sitaraman, R.K., Sun, J.: The Akamai network: a platform for high-performance internet applications. In: ACM SIGOPS, July 2010
26. Rula, J.P., Bustamante, F.E.: Behind the curtain: cellular dns and content replica selection. In: ACM IMC, November 2014
27. Wang, X.S., Balasubramanian, A., Krishnamurthy, A., Wetherall, D.: Demystify page load performance with WProf. In: USENIX NSDI, April 2013

The Utility Argument – Making a Case for Broadband SLAs

Zachary S. Bischof[1(✉)], Fabián E. Bustamante[1], and Rade Stanojevic[2]

[1] Northwestern University, Evanston, USA
zbischof@eecs.northwestern.edu
[2] Qatar Computing Research Institute, Al-Rayyan, Qatar

Abstract. Most residential broadband services are described in terms of their maximum potential throughput rate, often advertised as having speeds "up to X Mbps". Though such promises are often met, they are fairly limited in scope and, unfortunately, there is no basis for an appeal if a customer were to receive compromised quality of service. While this 'best effort' model was sufficient in the early days, we argue that as broadband customers and their devices become more dependent on Internet connectivity, we will see an increased demand for more encompassing Service Level Agreements (SLA).

In this paper, we study the design space of broadband SLAs and explore some of the trade-offs between the level of strictness of SLAs and the cost of delivering them. We argue that certain SLAs could be offered almost immediately with minimal impact on retail prices, and that ISPs (or third parties) could accurately infer the risk of offering SLA to individual customers – with accuracy comparable to that in the car or credit insurance industry – and price the SLA service accordingly.

1 Introduction

In today's broadband markets, service plans are typically described in terms of their maximum download throughput rate, often advertised as "up to X Mbps". This advertised capacity, along with the associated monthly cost, are the two primary, and many times only, pieces of information available to consumers when comparing service providers. Such "constrained" service agreements place services using technologies as diverse as fiber, DSL, WiMAX or satellite on nearly equal grounds, and leave consumers without clear expectations given that, strictly speaking, any speed less than X would meet such a guarantee.

We argue that as Internet users and their devices become more dependent on connectivity and consistency, broadband will move from a loosely regulated luxury to a key utility. This in turn will usher in a growing demand for more encompassing, well-defined SLAs similar to those of other utilities, such as electricity and water.

We believe that the adoption of SLAs could benefit all players in the broadband market – service providers, customers, and regulators. From the ISP's perspective, contracts with SLAs could allow them to better differentiate their

M.A. Kaafar et al. (Eds.): PAM 2017, LNCS 10176, pp. 156–169, 2017.
DOI: 10.1007/978-3-319-54328-4_12

retail services and fine-tune their contracts to the needs of particular classes of customers (e.g., a service for gamers or business users).[1] For customers, SLAs could significantly simplify the process of comparing services offered by different providers, allowing customers to make more informed decisions. This could improve competition and potentially lower prices. Similarly, for regulators and policymakers, SLAs would provide a better way to gauge broadband infrastructure across communities and justify investments.

Despite these potential benefits, there are several challenges in defining SLAs for broadband services that range from identifying metrics and defining the appropriate SLA structures to engineering compliance monitoring.

SLAs must be designed so that they can be accurately and efficiently monitored and that they add value to providers and consumers, while limiting the risk of non-compliance. We expect broadband SLAs to be specified, as other network SLAs, in terms of transport-level performance assurances using Quality of Service metrics such as bandwidth, packet loss, delay and availability. While the relationship between such QoS metrics and users' experience with different applications is a topic of ongoing research, existing approaches rely on such QoS metrics as input to application specific models of QoE estimation (e.g., [5, 15]).

An SLA could be seen as an insurance policy against the risk of not receiving the contracted level of service. Consequently, SLA-enhanced services would come with a price-tag for providers that depends on the structure of the SLA and degree of risk involved in the delivering the desired levels of service. Using four-years of data from the largest, publicly available dataset of broadband performance [10], we study the design space of broadband SLAs and demonstrate that certain SLAs could be offered almost immediately with minimal impact on retail prices and network investment.

In this paper, we make a case for broadband SLAs and follow a data-driven approach to explore some of these key challenges. We makes the following contributions:

- We analyze different QoS metrics for use in SLA and define a set of broadband SLAs (Sect. 2). We find that, across all ISPs and access technologies, bandwidth is the most consistent of the studied performance metrics.
- We evaluate the relationship between SLA structure and the cost of supporting them with different access technologies (Sect. 3). We show that many of the studied ISPs could offer moderate SLAs with minimal impact on their existing business, but that SLAs with stringent constraints are much harder to deliver across the whole user-base.
- We show that ISPs (or third parties) could accurately infer the risk of offering SLA to individual customers – with accuracy comparable to that in the car or credit insurance industry – and price the SLA service accordingly (Sect. 4).

We conclude the paper (Sects. 5 and 6) with a discussion of some of the key open issues and potential future directions for this work.

---

[1] Some ISPs already try this if in coarser terms; e.g., Comcast's "What type of Internet connection is right for you?" http://www.xfinity.com/resources/internet-connections.html.

Table 1. Three examples of possible broadband SLAs.

SLA	Throughput (% of service)	Latency	Packet loss	Description
A	>90%	<50 ms	<1%	Demanding applications (e.g., real-time gaming)
B	>50%	<150 ms	<5%	Video streaming, telephony
C	>10%	<250 ms	<10%	Web browsing, email

2   Metrics for a Broadband SLA

An SLA is a contract between a service provider and its customers that specifies what services the provider will support and what penalties it will pay upon
violations. A meaningful SLA should (*i*) capture the needs of consumers, (*ii*) be
feasible to support by most service providers today and (*iii*) be expressed in measurable terms that can be validated by both consumers and services providers.

To understand the need of broadband consumers, we must consider the
requirements of commonly used network applications. Clearly, one would not
expect that "broadband consumers" would be a homogeneous class in either
the type of applications they value most or their expectations. For some consumers, being able to browse the web or read their email may be sufficient,
and paying for a higher guaranteed throughput would not be a priority. Others
may have higher performance requirements, wanting a connection that reliably
allows them to stream HD video content or play online games with strict timing
requirements.

Driven by these observations, current literature on the needs of different
application classes (e.g., [6,7,27]) and our dataset [10], we drafted three potential broadband SLAs that cover a wide range of user requirements. Note that
these are mere examples of possible SLAs, focused on the points relevant to our
argument, and ignoring the specifics of a practical SLA, such as the form of
reporting quality of service violations, the procedure to be invoked in case of
violations or the exact cost model of violations.

Our basic SLAs (see Table 1) are stated in terms of throughput, latency
and packet loss. Considering that subscription capacity is already advertised
by ISPa and varies across users, we structure SLAs in terms of the percentage
of subscription speed available. For latency and packet loss, we adopt a simple
"below-threshold" model. *SLA A* represents a service that should be able to fit
the demands of users with very strict performance requirements for applications
such as real time gaming. *SLA C* characterizes a service that could support
simple applications, such as browsing the web or email. Finally, *SLA B* matches
the middle-of-the-road services, capable of supporting most applications, such
as video chat or video streaming, but with less than perfect performance for
network-intensive applications.

Although they are somewhat arbitrary, the thresholds we use for our sample
SLAs – from fractions of throughput to latency and loss rate – are based on
existing literature and earlier studies of broadband services.

For service capacity, we selected 10% of capacity as a bottom threshold
(*SLA C*) since the vast majority of users in our dataset had a connection much

faster than 1 Mbps and that 100 kbps can support basic browsing and email requirements. We opted for 50% as a threshold for *SLA B* following a 2010 report from the UK Office of Communication (Ofcom) reporting that surveyed users received, on average, nearly half (46%) of the their advertised speed [16]. Finally, for our highest SLA we opted for 90% as a threshold to highlight providers that consistently deliver capacities close to their subscription speeds.

In terms of packet loss, previous work has shown that rates above 1% can have a negative impact on users' QoE while using gaming applications [7]. High loss rates can also affect other common services such as audio and video calls [6]. Xu et al. [27], for instance, shows that loss rates above 4% can significantly degrade iChat video calls and rates larger than 10% result in a sharp increase in packet retransmissions.

We selected thresholds for latency in a similar manner. Our least demanding SLA, *SLA C*, has a latency threshold of 250 ms, since larger latencies can significantly increase page loading time [3] and would likely have a negative impact on QoE. End-to-end latencies below approximately 150 ms, the threshold for *SLA B*, should be sufficient for Skype calls [21]. Last, our low threshold for *SLA A* is based on previous work showing that an increase of just 10 ms can yield an increase in page loading delays by hundreds of milliseconds [25].

3   Supporting SLA Today

Building on these SLAs that would be meaningful to end-users, we now explore what sort of service guarantees it would be feasible for ISPs to provide to subscribers. We do this by looking at the performance and consistency of broadband services offered by US-based ISPs. We first describe the dataset on broadband services used throughout our analysis.

3.1   Dataset

We leverage the largest, publicly available dataset of broadband performance collected through the FCC's Measuring Broadband America effort [10]. Since 2011, the US FCC has been working with SamKnows to distribute home gateways ("whiteboxes") to broadband customers that conduct and report network measurements. These devices have collected increasingly rich data, including metrics such as latency, throughput and page loading time for a number of popular websites. A full description of all the tests performed and data collected is available in the FCC's technical appendix [9]. This data has been mostly used by the FCC to create periodic reports on the state of broadband access in the United States.

We employ the full four years of measurements made available in order to quantify network performance in terms of latency, packet loss, and download/upload throughput. For this, we used three different measurement tables (out of eleven present) from the dataset for our analysis: (1) UDP pings, (2)

HTTP GETs, which measure download throughput, and (3) HTTP POSTs, which measure upload throughput.

The UDP pings run continuously, measuring round-trip time to two or three measurement servers. These servers are hosted by either M-Lab or within the user's provider's network. Over the course of each hour, the gateway will send up to 600 probes to each measurement server at regular intervals, less if the link is under heavy use for part of the hour. Each gateway reports hourly statistical summaries of the latency measurements (mean, min, max, and standard deviation) as well as the number of missing responses. We use the average latency to the nearest server (in terms of latency) to summarize the latency during that hour. We also use the number of missing responses to calculate the packet loss rate over the course of each hour.

As mentioned above, the HTTP GET and POST tables record the measured download and upload throughput rate, respectively. Similar to the latency measurements, throughput measurements are typically done to two different target servers. However, throughput measurements are run once every other hour, alternating between measuring upload and download throughput rates.

We combined these performance measurements with user metadata, which includes the user's provider, service tier (i.e., subscription speed), service technology (e.g., cable or DSL), and geographic region. This allows us to group measurements by ISP, compare the achieved throughput as a fraction of the subscription capacity and differentiate between subscribers of the same ISP with different access technologies (e.g., Verizon customers with DSL or fiber).

3.2 Throughput

We first analyze ISPs' download and upload throughput. A challenge in comparing performance across providers and services, is that users do not have the same subscription speeds; individual ISPs typically offer a number of service capacities and the stated capacities of such offerings vary from one ISP to another. In order to directly compare the consistency of performance, we first normalize throughput measurements by the speed that each user should be receiving.

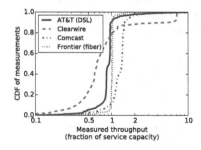

Fig. 1. CDF of measured download throughput rates as a fraction of the subscriber's service capacity.

For this, we use the reported download and upload subscription rate included as part of the FCC dataset, as described in Sect. 3.1.

Throughput distribution. Figure 1 shows a CDF of each normalized download throughput measurement from subscribers of four services: AT&T's DSL service, Clearwire, Comcast, and Frontier's fiber service. Of the services we studied, Frontier's fiber had the most consistent throughput rates, both in terms of the fraction of probes that measured at least 90% of the subscription speed and the variations between measurements. Although measurements were unlikely to achieve download rates significantly higher than their subscription speed, 96% of measurements were above 90% of the subscription speed.

For Comcast (cable), measurements were slightly less likely to reach 90% of the subscription speed (about 91%). However, download throughput measurements were often much higher than the user's subscription speed – the median measurement on Comcast's network was 135% of the subscription speed. We observed a similar trend for most cable broadband providers, as well as Verizon's fiber service.

Download throughput measurements from subscribers of AT&T's DSL service were fairly consistent (i.e., showing little variation). However, in contrast to cable and fiber services, they rarely exceeded the subscription speed, with less than 10% of measurements at or above the subscription speed. Nearly half (48%) of measurements were below 90% of the subscription speed. Other DSL providers showed a similar trend. Of the ISPs in our study, Clearwire had the largest fraction of measurements (73%) below 90% of the subscription speed.

Variation over time. Looking only at Fig. 1, it is still unclear how much performance can vary for an individual subscriber over the course of a month. To capture this, we aggregated all measurements that were conducted from the same vantage point and run during the same month, which we refer to as a "user-month". For each user-month, we calculate the fraction of measurements that were below a threshold of 10%, 25%, 50%, 75%, and 90% of the subscription speed.

Figure 2 shows, for AT&T, Comcast and Frontier fiber subscribers, how frequently measurements during the same month measured below a particular threshold. The vertical gray lines represent a particular frequency of throughput measurements being below a given threshold (from left to right): once a month, once a week, once a day, and once every other hour.

In the case of AT&T, shown in Fig. 2a, during 47% of the user-months, subscribers got less than 90% of their service capacity at least once every other hour (the right-most vertical line). In contrast, for Comcast subscribers, shown in Fig. 2b, only about 9% of user-months measured less than 90% of the subscription speed at the same frequency. Comcast users were also less likely to receive less than 50% of their subscription speed. Frontier's fiber was even less likely to have degradations in download throughput every other hour; less than 3% of months of Frontier measurements saw throughput rates below 90% of the subscription speed.

In general, the distributions of upload (Fig. 3) and download throughput measurements shown similar trends. The most obvious difference was that upload measurements from Clearwire subscribers were noticeably higher, more consistent, and much closer to the subscription speed. For each ISP in Fig. 3, the median measurement was at least 90% of the subscription speed.

3.3 Latency

As mentioned in Sect. 3.1, we use the average latency (measured over an hour) to the nearest measurement server as an estimate of the subscriber's latency. Figure 4 shows a CDF of the hourly average latency for five ISPs. Cablevision, with 96% of hourly averages below 20 ms, showed the lowest latencies of all ISPs in our dataset and appeared to consistently meet even the most demanding SLA. Other fiber, DSL, and cable ISPs had slightly higher latencies, but were fairly consistent, with at least 90% of average latency reports for each provider being less than 70 ms. AT&T, with 95% of measurements below 57 ms had the lowest latencies of all DSL providers, but the overall distribution was higher than most cable providers.

Latency measurements from Clearwire subscribers were noticeably higher, with a median of approximately 90 ms. Satellite providers had the highest latency

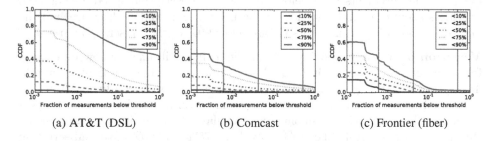

(a) AT&T (DSL)   (b) Comcast   (c) Frontier (fiber)

Fig. 2. CCDF of the fraction of a user's download throughput measurements per month that are below a percentage of the subscription capacity. Each gray vertical line represents a frequency of (from left to right) once a month, once a week, once a day, and once every other hour.

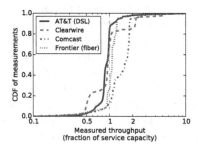

Fig. 3. CDF of upload throughput rates as a fraction of the subscriber's service capacity.

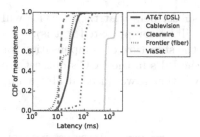

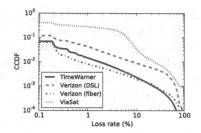

Fig. 4. CDF of latency measurements to servers.

Fig. 5. CCDF of hourly loss rates to servers.

measurements, consistently above 600 ms, as a result of the fundamental limitations of the technology.

3.4 Packet Loss

Using the number of UDP pings that succeeded and failed to the target measurement server, we calculated the percentage of packets lost over each hour. Figure 5 shows the CCDF of the hourly packet loss rates for four ISPs. On average, fiber providers tended to have lower loss rates and had the lowest frequency of high loss. More specifically, Verizon had the lowest frequency of loss rates above 1%, occurring during only 0.82% of hours. Comcast (not in the figure) and TimeWarner had the lowest frequency for cable providers, with loss rates above 1% occurring in approximately 1.5% of hours. Satellite providers had the highest frequency of loss rates above 1%, occurring during over 26% of hours.

3.5 Applying an SLA

In Sect. 2, we defined SLAs in measurable terms with thresholds that would be meaningful to users' Quality of Experience. Building on our characterization, we now explore how effectively today's ISPs could meet our proposed set of SLAs.

There are a number of ways that a broadband SLA could be structured in terms of how users are compensated for periods of poor performance. As an example, we looked at how some broadband ISPs structure the agreements that they offered to businesses. In the case of Comcast [8], business class subscribes are compensated once the network become unavailable for more than four hours in a single month. For each hour of downtime after the first four, customers are reimbursed 1/30 of the monthly subscription price.[2] We believe that general broadband service plans could have a similar structure. For example, the SLA could state that the network may be unavailable for up to two hours per day (or about 8.33% of hours in a month). This would allow ISPs to schedule downtime

---

[2] This effectively means that if the service was 'unavailable' for 34 h in a month (approximately 5% of the month) the user gets the monthly subscription for free.

for maintenance and provide a guarantee for subscribers that their service will not be down for days at a time (or that they will be compensated if it is).

However, our focus in this paper is not on the structure of compensation for SLA violations. Instead, we look at how well the ISPs in the FCC's dataset are able to meet the SLAs defined in Sect. 2, and whether it would be at all feasible to provide guarantees of service.

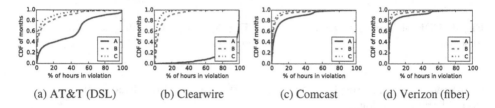

(a) AT&T (DSL)   (b) Clearwire   (c) Comcast   (d) Verizon (fiber)

Fig. 6. CDF of the percent of hours per month in violation of each SLA for four providers.

Figure 6 summarizes the total number of SLA violations per month for four example ISPs. AT&T, shown in Fig. 6a struggles to meet the requirements of *SLA A* but is able to meet *SLA B* during 90% of hours per month for 73% of users and meets *SLA C* during 90% of hours for 82% of users.

The wireless provider in our dataset, Clearwire (Fig. 6b), face difficulties in meeting *SLA A*, as the average latencies were almost always higher than 50 ms. This appears to be a result of the underlying technology and many cellular providers are unable to meet this latency requirement [18]. Interestingly, Clearwire actually did a better job of meeting *SLA C* than AT&T, with 94% of users meeting *SLA C* performance during at least 90% of hours in a month.

Both Comcast and Verizon's fiber service did a relatively good job of meeting the requirements of all three SLAs. Comcast was able to meet *SLA A* during 90% of hours in a month for 75% of users while Verizon was able to do the same for 83% of fiber subscribers. Both were able to provide both *SLA B* and *C* during 90% of hours for at least 90% of users.

To summarize our findings in this section, moderate SLAs (those which require SLA compliance up to 90% of time) are feasible nowadays and could be offered by many ISPs with minimal effect on their current business. However, stricter SLAs (those which require SLA compliance 99% of the time or more) would be much more challenging to offer across the whole user base. In the following section, we examine how difficult it would be to assess the individual risk of breaking and SLA, a central challenge in personalized SLA offerings.

4   Personalized SLAs

As we noted in a previous section, SLA can be seen as an insurance policy against poor broadband experience, which may in turn have financial consequences in case of broken SLA. In this section we study if SLAs could be tailored for each end-user individually.

The key question we try to answer is whether the provider could infer the likelihood of delivering the SLA. For instance, it is possible that certain user characteristics are correlated with the quality of service the user receives and hence the SLA provider may choose to price the service (premium in insurance terms) according to the risk of not delivering promised SLA to this set of users. With a good understanding of how likely it is to break the SLA the insurer (either a third party or the broadband provider itself) can fine tune the SLA parameters and the premium[3] (in \$ per month) in order to improve user satisfaction with the service and ensure the profitability of the SLA service.

We train a simple model to examine the predictability of the service of individual subscribers complying to an SLA based on several simple user features available to us: (1) access technology, (2) base latency (to the nearest measurement server), (3) aggregate usage (in bytes per month) and (4) city population (a proxy of urban/rural residence). More advanced models, using a range of additional demographic and technological features, would likely improve the prediction accuracy, yet such analysis is out of scope of this short study and is left for future work.

We use supervised learning for estimating the likelihood of breaking the SLA, for the three SLA types described in Table 1 with 95% time threshold (i.e., the users' performance complies with the SLA 95% of the time). This is basically a binary classification task, where we use four user features described above to predict whether the user complies with SLA or not. The features are extracted on 4038 active users in October and November 2014. The categorical feature describing access technology is projected to a binary vector (of length 4) encoding the access technology of every user.

We experimented with several classification methods including L2-regularized logistic regression, gradient boosting trees and random forests. We report the results from random forests which showed slightly better performance although the performance of all methods were comparable. The hyper-parameters were optimized using a grid-search over a validation set extracted from the training set. We use fourfold cross validation to predict the chance of breaking SLA. The features are extracted in October 2014 and the (binary) SLA compliance is extracted for November 2014.

We use *Area Under Curve Receiver Operating Characteristic (AUCROC)*, a standard metric for measuring the performance of the binary classifiers [13]. The ROC curve as well as the AUCROC are reported in Fig. 7 for the three SLAs from Table 1.

The AUCROC for all three SLAs: A, B and C, is similar and is around 0.8. Such AUCROC is comparable to the precision of classifiers build from demographic user information in other insurance products such as cars and credit ratings [17].

---

[3] The key cost for the ISP selling an SLA is the loss of revenue when the SLA is broken. Hence the stricter SLA the higher expected cost for the ISP which may be passed down to the end-user in the form of higher premium/monthly subscription.

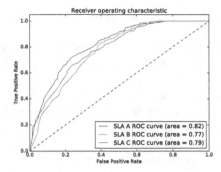

Fig. 7. Area under ROC for Random Forest classifiers.

This accuracy of prediction for SLA compliance suggests that it would be possible to offer personalized SLAs with a price which accurately matches the likelihood of breaking the SLA.

City population and population density are loosely correlated with last-mile performance, especially in the context of DSL [1]. However, city population appears to have minor predictive power for inferring the likelihood of SLA violations in our dataset.

5   Discussion

Recent efforts [4,19,20,24] have attempted to address the lack of detailed evaluations of ISPs. Annual reports published by the FCC in the US and Ofcom in the UK have studied whether or not ISPs are providing the capacities promised to users. The recent Net Neutrality ruling from the FCC [11,12] discussed the issue of how service plans are described to subscribers. One part of the ruling states that ISPs must disclose reasonable estimates of performance metrics, including both latency and packet loss. Unfortunately, what exactly is a "reasonable" estimate of these metrics is somewhat unclear. Additionally, providing the estimates alone does not offer any protection for consumers that may experience seriously degraded performance.

This work points to a number of interesting research directions that are crucial for implementing broadband SLAs. For example, perhaps the largest roadblock to adoption of broadband SLAs is the lack of infrastructure for monitoring performance and reporting SLA violations. One potential avenue to explore would be the deployment of a system, such as SLAM [23], on home gateways or modems that could monitor SLA compliance. These devices could be distributed by the SLA provider (either the ISP or a third party). The design of a reliable processes for the automatic generation and filing of SLA violation reports and reporting, to both the subscriber and the ISP, is another interesting research direction.

There is also a need to consider factors beyond throughput, latency, and packet loss. For example, high packet delay variations could impact user quality of experience. Furthermore, recent peering disputes between content providers and broadband access providers [14,22] highlight the importance of measuring congestion on a provider's peering links and its potential impact on performance. Poor quality of experience while streaming via Netflix or making Skype calls would not be captured by the measurements used in this paper if this is caused by congestion at the edge of the provider's network.

Another aspect we have not explored is the design of SLAs that both fit what a user's needs and what they can afford, an area we have explored in past work [2]. For example, an SLA that promises to provide lower latency, from 25 ms to 15 ms, could come at a hefty price for the ISP and yet provide little value to subscribers. Additionally, the availability of other services that are typically hosted by the ISP, such as DNS or email, may be more important to some users than a guaranteed throughput rate.

Previous work has suggest that consumers could benefit from improvements in how service offerings are described to customers [26] and shown that the relationship between QoS metrics (as those we used in our definitions of SLA) and users' experience with different applications is an open research problem. Nevertheless, all existing approaches we are aware of rely on such QoS metrics as input to application specific models of QoE estimation (e.g., [5,15]).

6   Conclusion

This work is partially motivated by the FCC's recent classification of broadband as a utility. We believe that this is a natural course for broadband Internet, as it progresses from a luxury to a key utility and, in some countries, considered a basic human right. The growing understanding of broadband connectivity as a utility will, in turn, usher in a demand for more encompassing, well-defined SLAs. The introduction of SLAs could enable broadband operators to personalize the service offerings down to the individual customer and improve their efficiency and overall user satisfaction. Broadband SLAs could also facilitate transparent competition, ultimately benefiting both consumers and service providers. In this paper, we explored the possibility of implementing broadband SLAs and demonstrated that certain SLAs could be offered almost immediately with small impact on the retail prices and network investment. We showed that ISPs (or third parties) could accurately infer the risk of offering SLA to individual customers, with accuracy comparable to that in other insurance markets, and price SLA services accordingly.

Acknowledgments. We thank our shepherd Monia Ghobadi and the anonymous reviewers for their invaluable feedback. This work was supported in part by the National Science Foundation through Award CNS 1218287.

References

1. Bischof, Z., Bustamante, F., Feamster, N.: (The Importance of) Being connected: on the reliability of broadband internet access. Technical report NU-EECS-16-01, Northwestern University (2016)

2. Bischof, Z.S., Bustamante, F.E., Stanojevic, R.: Need, want, can afford - broadband markets and the behavior of users. In: Proceedings of IMC, November 2014
3. Bischof, Z.S., Otto, J.S., Bustamante, F.E.: Up, down and around the stack: ISP characterization from network intensive applications. In: Proceedings of W-MUST (2012)
4. Bischof, Z.S., Otto, J.S., Sánchez, M.A., Rula, J.P., Choffnes, D.R., Bustamante, F.E.: Crowdsourcing ISP characterization to the network edge. In: Proceedings of W-MUST (2011)
5. Casas, P., Gardlo, B., Schatz, R., Melia, M.: An educated guess on QoE in operational networks through large-scale measurements. In: Proceedings of SIGCOMM Workshop Internet-QoE, August 2016
6. Chen, K.-T., Huang, C.-Y., Huang, P., Lei, C.-L.: Quantifying Skype user satisfaction. In: Proceedings of ACM SIGCOMM (2006)
7. Chen, K.-T., Huang, P., Lei, C.-L.: How sensitive are online gamers to network quality? Commun. ACM **49**(11), 34–38 (2006)
8. Comcast Business Class: Service level agreement. http://business.comcast.com/pdfs/cbc-trunks-sla-110922.pdf
9. FCC: 2013 measuring broadband America February report. http://data.fcc.gov/download/measuring-broadband-america/2013/Technical-Appendix-feb-2013.pdf
10. FCC: Measuring Broadband America. http://www.fcc.gov/measuring-broadband-america
11. FCC: In the matter of preserving the Open Internet broadband industry practices, December 2010
12. FCC: In the matter of protecting and promoting the Open Internet, February 2015
13. Green, W.: Econometric Analysis. Prentince Hall, Upper Saddle River (2003)
14. Higginbotham, S.: Why the consumer is still held hostage in peering disputes. http://bit.ly/1KbBBhl
15. Nikravesh, A., Hong, D.K., Chen, Q.A., Madhyastha, H.V., Mao, Z.M.: QoE inference without application control. In: Proceedings of SIGCOMM Workshop Internet-QoE, August 2016
16. Office of Communication (Ofcom). UK fixed broadband speeds, November/December 2010. Technical report, London, UK, March 2011
17. Pedro, J.S., Proserpio, D., Oliver, N.: Mobiscore: towards universal credit scoring from mobile phone data (2015)
18. Rula, J.P., Bustamante, F.E.: Behind the curtain: cellular DNS and content replica selection. In: Proceedings of IMC (2014)
19. SamKnows.: Samknows & the FCC American broadband performance measurement. http://www.samknows.com/broadband/fcc_and_samknows, June 2011
20. Sánchez, M.A., Otto, J.S., Bischof, Z.S., Choffnes, D.R., Bustamante, F.E., Krishnamurthy, B., Willinger, W.: Dasu: pushing experiments to the Internet's edge. In: Proceedings of USENIX NSDI (2013)
21. Skype.: Plan network requirements for skype for business. https://technet.microsoft.com/en-us/library/Gg425841.aspx
22. Solsman, J.E.: Cogent: Comcast forced netflix with clever traffic clogging. http://cnet.co/1l3aDw1, May 2014
23. Sommers, J., Barford, P., Duffield, N., Ron, A.: Accurate and efficient SLA compliance monitoring. In: Proceedings of ACM SIGCOMM (2007)
24. Sundaresan, S., de Donato, W., Feamster, N., Teixeira, R., Crawford, S., Pescapè, A.: Broadband internet performance: a view from the gateway. In: Proceedings of ACM SIGCOMM (2011)

25. Sundaresan, S., Feamster, N., Teixeira, R., Magharei, N.: Measuring and mitigating web performance bottlenecks in broadband access networks. In: Proceedings of IMC, October 2013
26. Sundaresan, S., Feamster, N., Teixeira, R., Tang, A., Edwards, W.K., Grinter, R.E., Chetty, M., de Donato, W.: Helping users shop for ISPs with internet nutrition labels. In: Proceedings of HomeNets (2011)
27. Xu, Y., Yu, C., Li, J., Liu, Y.: Video telephony for end-consumers: measurement study of Google+, iChat, and Skype. In: Proceedings of IMC (2012)

Latency

Why Is the Internet so Slow?!

Ilker Nadi Bozkurt[1]([✉]), Anthony Aguirre[4], Balakrishnan Chandrasekaran[2],
P. Brighten Godfrey[3], Gregory Laughlin[5], Bruce Maggs[1,6], and Ankit Singla[7]

[1] Duke University, Durham, USA
{ilker,bmm}@cs.duke.edu
[2] TU Berlin, Berlin, Germany
balac@inet.tu-berlin.de
[3] UIUC, Champaign, USA
pbg@illinois.edu
[4] UC Santa Cruz, Santa Cruz, USA
aguirre@scipp.ucsc.edu
[5] Yale University, New Haven, USA
greg.laughlin@yale.edu
[6] Akamai, Cambridge, USA
[7] ETH Zürich, Zürich, Switzerland
ankit.singla@inf.ethz.ch

Abstract. In principle, a network can transfer data at nearly the speed of light. Today's Internet, however, is much slower: our measurements show that latencies are typically more than one, and often more than two orders of magnitude larger than the lower bound implied by the speed of light. Closing this gap would not only add value to today's Internet applications, but might also open the door to exciting new applications. Thus, we propose a grand challenge for the networking research community: building a speed-of-light Internet. To help inform research towards this goal, we investigate, through large-scale measurements, the causes of latency inflation in the Internet across the network stack. Our analysis reveals an under-explored problem: the Internet's infrastructural inefficiencies. We find that while protocol overheads, which have dominated the community's attention, are indeed important, reducing latency inflation at the lowest layers will be critical for building a speed-of-light Internet. In fact, eliminating this infrastructural latency inflation, without any other changes in the protocol stack, could speed up small object fetches by more than a factor of three.

1 Introduction

Measurements and analysis by Internet giants have shown that shaving a few hundred milliseconds from the time per transaction can translate into millions of dollars. For Amazon, a 100 ms latency penalty implies a 1% sales loss [18]; for Google, an additional delay of 400 ms in search responses reduces search

---

B. Chandrasekaran—This work was done when the author was a graduate student at Duke University.

© Springer International Publishing AG 2017
M.A. Kaafar et al. (Eds.): PAM 2017, LNCS 10176, pp. 173–187, 2017.
DOI: 10.1007/978-3-319-54328-4_13

volume by 0.74%; and for Bing, 500 ms of delay decreases revenue per user by 1.2% [10,13]. The gaming industry, where latencies larger than even 80 ms can hurt gameplay [19], has even tougher latency requirements. These numbers underscore that latency is a key determinant of user experience.

We take the position that the networking community should pursue an ambitious goal: cutting Internet latencies to close to the limiting physical constraint, the speed of light, roughly one to two orders of magnitude faster than today. Beyond the obvious gains in performance and value for today's applications, such a technological leap may help realize the full potential of certain applications that have so far been confined to the laboratory, such as tele-immersion. For some applications, such as massive multi-player online games, the size of the user community reachable within a latency bound plays an important role in user interest and adoption, and linear decreases in communication latency result in super-linear growth in community size [25]. Low latencies on the order of a few tens of milliseconds also open up the possibility of *instant response*, where users are unable to perceive any lag between requesting a page and seeing it rendered in their browsers. Such an elimination of wait time would be an important threshold in user experience.

But the Internet's speed is quite far from the speed of light. As we show later, the time to fetch just the HTML document of the index pages of popular Web sites from a set of generally well-connected clients is, in the median, 37 times the round-trip speed-of-light latency. In the 80th percentile it is more than 100 times slower. Given the promise a speed-of-light Internet holds, *why are we so far from the speed of light?*

While ISPs compete primarily on the basis of peak bandwidth offered, bandwidth is no longer the bottleneck for a significant fraction of the population: for instance, the average Internet connection speed in the US is 15.3 Mbps [9], while the effect of increasing bandwidth on page load time is small beyond as little as 5 Mbps [17]. If bandwidth isn't the culprit, then what is? In our short workshop paper [25], we staked out our vision of a speed-of-light Internet, discussed why it is a worthy goal to pursue, and, provided a preliminary analysis of latency inflation across the network stack. In this work, we present a more thorough analysis of latency inflation using three new data sets. Our contributions are as follows:

1. We quantify the factors that contribute to large latencies today using four sets of measurements: from PlanetLab nodes to Web servers[1]; between a large CDN's servers and end hosts; from volunteer end-user systems[2] to Web servers; and between RIPE Atlas nodes. Our analysis breaks down Internet latency inflation across the network stack, from the physical network infrastructure to the transport layer (including, in some instances, TLS).

---

[1] Data sets (gathered in 2016) and code are available at https://cgi.cs.duke.edu/~ilker/cspeed/pam2017-data/.

[2] Explicit volunteer consent was obtained, listing precisely what tests would be run. We have a letter from the IRB stating that our tests did not require IRB approval.

2. This work places in perspective the importance of latency inflation at the lowest layers. While in line with the community's understanding that DNS, TCP handshake, and TCP slow-start are all important factors in latency inflation, the Internet's infrastructural inefficiencies are also important. We consider this an under-appreciated piece of the latency puzzle.
3. We find that removing latency inflation in the physical infrastructure and routing without *any* changes at layers above, could improve latencies for fetching small objects by more than 3 times.

2   The Internet Is Too Slow

We pooled the top 500 Web sites from each of 138 countries listed by Alexa [7]. We followed redirects on each URL, and recorded the final URL for use in our measurements; the resulting data set contains 22,800 URLs. We fetched just the HTML at these URLs from 102 PlanetLab locations using cURL [1], and 25% of all fetches in our experiments were over HTTPS[3].

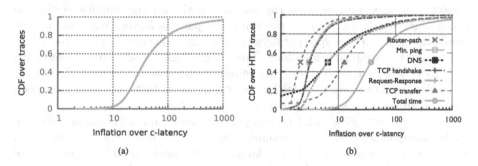

Fig. 1. (a) Inflation in fetch time, and (b) its breakdown across various components of HTTP fetches of just the HTML of the landing pages of popular Web sites.

For each connection (or fetch), we geolocated the Web server using six commercial geolocation services, and (since we do not have any basis for deciding which service is better than another) used the location identified by their majority vote (MV). We computed the time it would take for light to travel round-trip along the shortest path between the same end-points, *i.e.*, the c-latency. Finally, we calculated the Internet's latency inflation as the ratio of the fetch time to c-latency. Figure 1(a) shows the CDF of inflation over 1.9 million connections. The HTML fetch time is, in the median, 36.5 times the c-latency, while the 80th percentile exceeds 100 times. We note that PlanetLab nodes are generally well-connected, and latency can be expected to be poorer from the network's *true* edge. We verify that this is indeed the case with measurements from end users in Sect. 3.7.

---

[3] We do not claim this is the percentage of Web sites supporting HTTPS.

3   Why Is the Internet so Slow?

To identify the causes of Internet latency inflation, we break down the fetch time across layers, from inflation in the physical path followed by packets to the TCP transfer time.

3.1   Methodology

We use cURL to obtain the time for DNS resolution, TCP handshake, TCP data transfer, and total fetch time for each connection. For HTTPS connections, we also record the time for TLS handshake. TCP handshake is measured as the time between cURL sending the SYN and receiving the SYN-ACK. The TCP transfer time is measured as the time from cURL's receipt of the first byte of data to the receipt of the last byte. We separately account for the time between cURL sending the data request and the receipt of the first byte as 'request-response' time; this typically comprises one RTT and any server processing time. For each connection, we also run a traceroute from the client PlanetLab node to the Web server. We then geolocate each router in the traceroute path, and connect successive routers with the shortest paths on the Earth's surface as an optimistic approximation for the route the packets follow. We compute the round-trip latency at the speed of light in fiber along this approximate path, and refer to it as the 'router-path latency'. From each client, we also run 30 successive pings to each server, and record the minimum and median across these ping times. We normalize each of these latency components by the c-latency between the respective connection's end-points.

Our experiments yielded 2.1 million page fetches with HTTP status code 200, which corresponds to 94% of all fetches. We also filtered out connections which showed obvious anomalies such as c-latency being larger than TCP handshake time or minimum ping time (probably due to errors in geolocation), leaving us with 1.9 million fetches.

3.2   Overview of Results

Figure 1(b) shows the results for all connections over HTTP. DNS resolutions are shown to be faster than c-latency 14% of the time. This is an artifact of the baseline we use—in these cases, the Web server happens to be farther than the DNS resolver, and we always use the c-latency to the Web server as the baseline. (The DNS curve is clipped at the left to more clearly display the other results.) In the median, DNS resolutions are 6.6× inflated over c-latency.

The TCP transfer time shows significant inflation—12.6 times in the median. With most pages being at most tens of KB (median page size is 73 KB), bandwidth is not the problem, but TCP's slow start causes even small data transfers to require several RTTs. 6% of all pages have transfer times less than the c-latency—this is due to all the data being received in the first TCP window. The TCP handshake (counting only the SYN and SYN-ACK) and the minimum ping time are 3.2 times and 3.1 times inflated in the median. The request-response

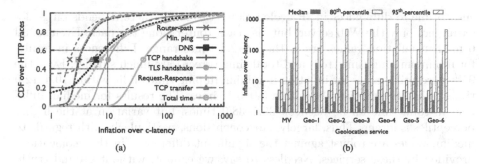

(a)   (b)

Fig. 2. (a) Various components of latency inflation over HTTPS connections, and (b) the median, $80^{th}\%$ *and* $95^{th}\%$ of inflation in min. ping (red), router-path (blue) and total (green) latency using 6 different geolocation databases as well as their majority vote. (Color figure online)

time is 6.5 times inflated in the median, *i.e.*, roughly twice the median RTT. However, 24% of the connections use less than 10 ms of server processing time (estimated by subtracting one RTT from the request-response time). The median c-latency, in comparison, is 47 ms. The medians of inflation in DNS time, TCP handshake time, request-response time, and TCP transfer time add up to 28.8 times, lower than the *measured* median total time of 36.5 times, since the distributions are heavy-tailed.

Figure 2(a) shows the results for fetches over HTTPS. The inflations in DNS resolution and TCP handshake are similar to those for HTTP (6.3 times and 3.1 times in the median respectively). The largest contributor to the latency inflation is the TLS handshake, which is 10.2 times inflated in the median, roughly corresponding to 3 RTTs. Inflation in TCP transfer time, being 5.2 times in the median, is significantly lower than for HTTP connections. This difference is partly explained by the smaller size of pages fetched over HTTPS, with the median fetch size being 43 KB. The median inflation in request-response times increases from 6.5 times for HTTP to 7.7 times for HTTPS.

3.3   Impact of IP Geolocation Errors

The correctness of our latency inflation analysis crucially depends on geolocation. While we cull data with obvious anomalies, such as when the min. ping time is smaller than c-latency, arising from geolocation errors (some of which may be due to Anycast), less obvious errors could impact our results. For PlanetLab node locations, we have ground truth data and our tests did not indicate any erroneous location. Retrieving similar ground truth data for the large IP space under consideration appears infeasible. Thus, we focused our efforts on comparing the results we obtained by using 6 different commercial IP geolocation services, as well as a location computed as their majority vote. We computed latency inflation in router-path, minimum ping, and total time using each of these 7 sets of IP geolocations (Fig. 2(b)). As we might expect, router-path latency (blue) is most susceptible to differences in IP geolocation—the result there depends on geolocating not only the Web server, but also each router along the path. Even so, all 6 median inflation values are in the 1.9–2.4 times range. Differences in results for minimum ping time (red) and total time (green) are much smaller. Even the 95th-percentile values for inflation in minimum ping time all lie within 10.4–12.0 times, while the medians lie within 3.0–3.1 times. The results for median inflation in total time all lie between 35.5–38.0 times, but variation at the higher percentiles is larger. Thus, largely, our conclusions, particularly with regards to median values are robust against the significant differences in the geolocations provided by these services. Needless to say, we cannot, without ground truth, account for systematic errors that may impact all geolocation services. Except in Fig. 2(b), we use the majority vote geolocation throughout.

On a related note, small client-server distances can cause a small absolute latency increase to translate into a large inflation over c-latency; effect of geolocation errors can also be more pronounced at short distances. When we restricted our analysis to connections with client-server distances above 100 km, 500 km and 1000 km, we found that the median inflations are relatively close to each other, being 35.5, 33.7 and 31.9 respectively. So, large inflations are not just caused by short distances, and even after limiting ourselves to connections at long distances we observe significant inflation. Section 3.5 (and Fig. 3(a)) discusses in more detail on the relationship between latency inflation and client-server distances (equivalently, c-latency) and locations.

3.4 Results Across Page Sizes

While we fetch only the HTML for the landing pages of Web sites in our experiments, some of these are still larger than 1 MB. Most pages, however, are much smaller, with the median being 67 KB. To analyze variations in our results across page sizes, we binned pages into 1 KB buckets, and computed the median inflation for each latency component across each bucket. While the median inflation in minimum ping time shows little variation, inflation in TCP transfer time increases over page sizes in an expected linear fashion, also causing an increase in total fetch time.

We also examine latency inflation in a narrow range of Web page sizes around the median, using pages within 10% of the median size of 67 KB. These pages comprise roughly 7% of our data set. The results of this analysis are similar to the overall results in Fig. 1(b), with expected differences in the transfer time (8% smaller) and total time (5% smaller). The request-response time is 10% larger. Other components of inflation are within 1% of the corresponding values in Fig. 1(b).

3.5 Results Across Geographies

We fetch pages in 138 countries from 81 unique PlanetLab locations, leading to a wide spread in the pairwise c-latencies observed across these connections. The median c-latency is 47 ms, with 5th and 95th percentiles being 2 ms and

101 ms respectively. In a manner similar to our analysis across page sizes, we also analyzed latency inflation in router-path latency, minimum ping time, and total time across c-latencies (Fig. 3(a)).

An interesting feature of these results is the inflation bump around a c-latency of 30 ms. It turns out that some countries connectivity to which may be more circuitous than average, are over-represented at these distances in our data. For instance, c-latencies from the Eastern US to Portugal are in the 30 ms vicinity, but all transatlantic connectivity hits Northern Europe, from where routes may go through the ocean or land southward to Portugal, thus incurring significant path 'stretch'. That the differences are largely due to inflation at the lowest layers is also borne out by the inflation in minimum ping and total time following the inflation in the router-path latency.

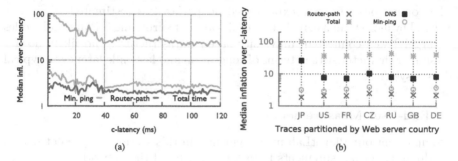

Fig. 3. Inflation in router-path latency, minimum ping time, and total time: (a) as a function of c-latency; and (b) as a function of Web server country.

An encouraging observation from Fig. 3(a) is that the inflation in minimum ping and total time follows the inflation in the router-path latency. Thus, despite the router-path latency estimation containing multiple approximations (omitting routers that did not respond to traceroutes or we could not geolocate, as well as paths between successive routers themselves potentially being circuitous), it is a useful quantity to measure.

To compare measurements from a geographically balanced set of client locations, we selected 20 PlanetLab hosts such that no two were within 5° of longitude of each other. Then we looked at requests from these PlanetLab clients to Web servers in each country. Figure 3(b) shows the median inflation in router-path latency, minimum ping time, DNS, and total time across each of the 7 countries for which we had 5, 000+ connections. The median c-latencies from these selected PlanetLab hosts to each of these 7 countries all lie in the 48–55 ms range, with the exception of Japan (12 ms). Most of the latencies are fairly consistent across geographies, with the exception of DNS and total time for Japan. We observed that roughly half of the requests to Web servers in Japan come from two PlanetLab nodes in Japan, and it is likely that DNS resolvers are further away than the Web servers causing the larger inflation.

3.6   The Role of Congestion

Figure 1(b) shows that TCP transfer time is more than 10 times inflated over
c-latency. It is worth considering whether packet losses or large packet delays
and delay variations are to blame for poor TCP performance. Oversized and
congested router buffers on the path may exacerbate such conditions—a situation
referred to as *bufferbloat*.

In addition to fetching the HTML for the landing page, for each connection,
we also sent 30 pings from the client to the server's address. We found that
variation in ping times is small: the 2nd-longest ping time is only 1.1% larger
than the minimum ping time in the median. While pings (using ICMP) might use
queues separate from Web traffic, even the TCP handshake time is only 1.6%
larger than the minimum ping time in the median. We also used `tcpdump` at
PlanetLab clients to analyze the inter-arrival times of packets. More than 92%
of the connections we made experienced no packet loss (estimated as packets
reordered by more than 3 ms). These results are not surprising—PlanetLab nodes
are (largely) well-connected, university-based infrastructure, and likely do not
have similar characteristics in terms of congestion and last-mile latency to typical
end-user systems.

3.7   End-User Measurements

To complement our PlanetLab measurements, in this section we present results
from three sets of measurements from the *real edge* of the network.

Client Connections to a CDN. For a closer look at congestion, we examined
RTTs in a sample of TCP connection handshakes between the servers of a large
CDN and clients (end users) over a 24-hour time period, passively logged at the
CDN. (Most routes to popular prefixes are unlikely to change at this time-scale
in the Internet [24].) We exclude server-client pairs with minimum latencies of
less than 3 ms—'clients' in this latency range are often proxy servers in a data
center or colocation facility rather than our intended end users.

To evaluate the impact of congestion, we examine our data for both variations
across time-of-day (perhaps latencies are, as a whole, significantly larger in peak
traffic hours), and within short periods of time for the same server-client pairs
(perhaps transient congestion for individual connections is a significant problem). Thus, we discard server-client pairs that do not have repeat measurements.
We only look at server-client pairs in the same timezone to simplify the time-
of-day analysis. Server locations were provided to us by the CDN, and clients
were geolocated using a commercial geolocation service. We include results for
a few geographies that have a large number of measurements after these restrictions. We bin all RTT measurements into 12 2-hour periods, separately for each
country, and produce results aggregated over these bins.

Time-of-Day Latency Variations Across Bins. We selected server-client
pairs that have at least one RTT measurement in each of the twelve bins. For

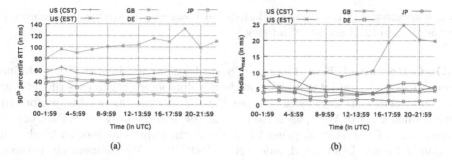

Fig. 4. Variations in latencies of client-server pairs grouped into 2-hr windows in different geographic regions: (a) 90th percentile of RTTs of client-server pairs with measurements in each 2-hr window; and (b) medians of maximum change in RTTs (max - min) in repeat measurements within each time window.

pairs with multiple RTTs within a bin, we use the median RTT as representative, discarding other measurements. This leaves us with the same number of samples between the same host-pairs in all bins. Figure 4(a) shows the 90th percentile of RTTs in each 2-hour bin for each of 5 timezones. For the United States (US), we show only data for the central (CST) and eastern (EST) timezones, but the results are similar for the rest. The timezone classification is based on the location of the client; servers can be anywhere in the US and not necessarily restricted to the same timezone as that of the clients. Median latency across our aggregate (not shown) varies little across the day, most timezones seeing no more than 3 ms of variation. The 90th percentile in each bin (Fig. 4(a)) shows similar trends, although with larger variations. In Great Britain, RTTs are higher in the evening (and results for a different 24-hour period look similar.) It is thus possible that congestion is in play there, affecting network-wide latencies. But across other timezones, we see no such effect.

Transient Latency Variations Within Bins. To investigate transient congestion, we do not limit ourselves to measurements across the same set of host-pairs across all bins. However, within each bin, only data from host-pairs with multiple measurements inside that time period is included. For each host-pair in each bin, we calculate the maximum change in RTT (Δ_{max})—the difference between the maximum and minimum RTT between the host-pair in that time period. We then compute the median Δ_{max} across host-pairs within each bin. The variation within bins (in Fig. 4(b)) is a bit larger than variations across median latencies across the day, e.g., for US (CST), the median Δ_{max} is as large as 9 ms in the peak hours. That Δ_{max} also shows broadly similar time-of-day trends to median latency is not surprising. Great Britain continues to show exceptionally large latency variations, with a $\Delta_{max} \simeq 25$ ms at the peak, and also large variations across the day. In summary, in end-user environments, network-wide latency increases in peak hours were largely limited in our data set to one geography (GB). However, individual flows may sometimes experience a few additional milliseconds of latency.

MOOC-Recruited End Users. 678 students in a Massive Open Online Course (MOOC) run by two of the authors volunteered to run experiments for us. The experiments are identical to our PlanetLab experiments, but performed with a smaller list of Web pages. Each volunteer fetched (only the HTML of) 50 pages, with a fixed set of 25 pages for all the participants and another 25 chosen randomly from a handpicked, safe, set of 100 URLs. We deliberately chose a small number of Web sites so that each volunteer could look at the provided descriptions, and make an informed decision to participate. We also asked each volunteer to provide their location and various characteristics of their Internet service such as download speed and connection type.

A total of 24,784 pages were fetched in these experiments. The latency inflation measured in these experiments was much larger than in our PlanetLab data set—even after filtering out connections between clients and servers within a 100 km distance of each other, we found that total fetch time is 66 times inflated in the median. One reason for this significantly larger latency inflation is the over-representation of shopping and news Web sites in the handpicked URLs, resulting in larger HTML pages, with the median fetch size being 148 KB. To investigate further, we also computed results over the same set of pages by fetching them from PlanetLab. Over this set, with the same filtering (client-server distances of at least 100 km), median inflation in total fetch time is 49.4 times. This is still smaller than the measurements from the volunteer systems.

Another factor causing this difference is the larger latency inflation in minimum ping time: 4.1 times in the median over the volunteer-runs, compared to 3 times over PlanetLab (over this set of URLs). Of course, if each RTT is longer in this way, the total fetch time will also be longer. In fact, both numbers differ by roughly a factor of 4/3.

One possible reason of larger inflation in minimum ping time in the end-user experiments is the connection type of the user, affecting the last mile latency. Even though our data is small, we get a glimpse of the situation when we compare different user provided connection types in terms of inflation of minimum ping time over c-latency. The lowest median inflation (3.76) is observed over connections users described as Company/University network, whereas the worst median inflations are observed for mobile and DSL connections, for which minimum ping time is inflated 5.4× and 5.2× respectively in the median.

RIPE Atlas. So far, we have limited ourselves to client-server connections, where the server belongs to a popular Web service. In this section, we describe our measurements between RIPE Atlas platform [6] *probes*, which are small network devices that are typically deployed in end-user networks. The locations of the RIPE Atlas probes are known within 1 km resolution, obviating the need for IP geolocation.

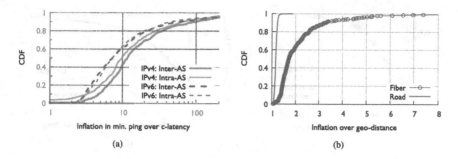

Fig. 5. (a) Minimum pings between RIPE Atlas nodes are highly inflated regardless of IPv4 or IPv6, inter- or intra-AS connections; (b) comparison of fiber lengths of the Internet2 network to road distances.

We collected ICMP pings over IPv4 (IPv6) between 935 (1012) sources in 26 (34) countries and 72 (97) destinations in 29 (40) countries every 30 min for 24 h. The data set contains ping measurements between 288,425 (63,884) unique IPv4 (IPv6) endpoint (or source-destination) pairs; 85% (78%) of the IPv4 (IPv6) endpoint pairs are inter-AS pairs with the source and destination belonging to different ASes. To account for the skew in inter-AS and intra-AS pairs, we compute the round-trip distance between the endpoints and bin them into 5 km wide buckets. From each bucket, we uniformly sample an equal number of inter-AS and intra-AS pairs and compute the inflation of the min. pings (minimum across the entire day of measurements) of these endpoint pairs. Figure 5(a) shows that the median inflation in minimum ping times (ranging from 7.2–11.6 times) is significantly larger than that in our PlanetLab measurements, where median inflation in minimum ping latency was 3.1 times. That the latencies between Atlas probes (typically attached to home networks) are larger than that between PlanetLab nodes and Web servers should not be suprising—home networks surely add more latency than servers in a university cluster or a data center. Perhaps paths from clients to Web servers are also much shorter than between arbitrary pairs of end-points on the Internet, since Web servers are deliberately deployed for fast access, and the Internet's semi-hierarchical nature can make paths between arbitrary end-points long. Interference from concurrent measurements may also be a contributing factor [16], albeit the effect on inflation might be marginal.

4   Infrastructural Latency

In line with the community's understanding, our measurements affirm that TCP transfer and DNS resolution are important factors causing latency inflation. However, as we shall detail in this section, our measurements also reveal that the Internet's infrastructural inefficiencies are an equally, if not more important culprit.

In Fig. 1(b), the router-path is only 2.1 times inflated in the median. The long tail is, in part, explained by 'hairpinning', *i.e.*, packets between nearby end

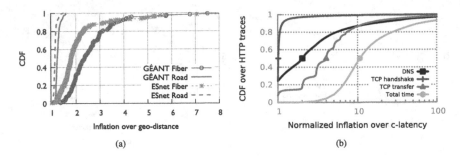

Fig. 6. (a) Comparison of fiber lengths of the ESnet and GÉANT network to road distances; (b) various components of latency inflation normalized by minimum ping time.

points traversing circuitous routes across the globe. Note that 1.5 times inflation would occur even along the shortest path along the Earth's surface because the speed of light in fiber is roughly $2/3^{rd}$ the speed of light in vacuum. In that light, the router-path inflation of 2.1× (which already includes the 1.5× factor) may appear small, but this estimate is optimistic.

The gap between minimum ping time and the router-path latency may be explained by two factors: (a) we perhaps see artificially shorter paths, since traceroute often does not yield responses from all the routers on the path; and (b) even between successive routers, the physical path may be longer than the shortest arc along the Earth's surface. We investigate the latter aspect using data from 3 research networks: Internet2 [5], ESnet [2], and GÉANT [3]. We obtained point-to-point fiber lengths for these networks and calculated end-to-end fiber distances between all pairs of end points in each network. We also computed the shortest distance along the Earth's surface between each pair of end points, and obtained the road distances for comparison using the Google Maps API [4]. In Fig. 6(a), road distances are close to shortest distances (i.e., smaller inflations), while fiber lengths are significantly larger and have a long tail. The median inflation in the three networks, after accounting for the lower speed of light in fiber is 2.6× (Internet2), 2.7× (ESnet), and 3.6× (GÉANT). A recent analysis of US long-haul fiber infrastructure [12] found results that support ours: even for cities directly connected by fiber conduits, the mean conduit's latency was in the median more than 2× worse than the line-of-sight latency. Of course, we expect end-to-end inflation between cities not connected directly to be higher. Thus, infrastructural inflation (which includes routing sub-optimalities and inflation of end-to-end fiber-distances over geodistance) is likely to be larger than the optimistic estimate from router-path latency (2.1 times), bringing it closer to the inflation in minimum ping latency (3.1 times).

As Fig. 1(b) shows, DNS resolution (6.6× inflated over c-latency), TCP handshake (3.2×), request-response time (6.5×), and TCP transfer (12.6×), all contribute to a total time inflation of 36.5×. With these numbers, it may be tempting to dismiss the 3.1× inflation in the minimum ping time. But this would be incorrect because lower-layer inflation, embodied in RTT, has a *multiplicative* effect on each of DNS, TCP handshake, request-response, and TCP transfer time. The total time for a page fetch (without TLS) can be broken down roughly (ignoring minor factors like the client stack) as: $T_{total} = T_{DNS} + T_{handshake} + T_{request} + T_{serverproc} + T_{response} + T_{transfer}$. If we changed the network's RTTs as a whole by a factor of x, everything on the RHS except the server processing time (which can be made quite small in practice) changes by a factor of x (to an approximation; TCP transfer time's dependence on RTTs is a bit more complex), thus changing T_{total} by approximately a factor of x as well.

What if there was no inflation in the lower layers, *i.e.*, RTTs were the same as c-latencies? For an approximate answer, we can normalize DNS, TCP handshake, request-response (excluding the server processing time, *i.e.*, only the RTT) and TCP transfer time by the minimum ping time instead of c-latency, as shown in Fig. 6(b).

The medians are 2 times (DNS), 1.02 times (TCP handshake), 4 times (TCP transfer), and 10.7 times (Total time) respectively. (Request-response is excluded because processing time at the server does not depend on the RTT.) When the 3.1 times inflation in minimum ping time is compared to these numbers, instead of the medians without such normalization, it appears much more significant. Also consider that if, for example, TCP transfer could be optimized such that it happens within an RTT, the Internet would still be more than ~25 times slower than the c-latency in the median, but if we could cut inflation at the lower layers from 3.1 times to close to 1, even if we made no transport protocol improvements, we would get to around ~10.7 times.

5   Related Work

There is a large body of work on reducing Internet latency. However, this work has been limited in its scope, its scale, and most crucially, its ambition. Several efforts have focused on particular pieces; for example, [23,31] focus on TCP handshakes; [11] on TCP's initial congestion window; [28] on DNS resolution; [14, 20] on routing inflation due to BGP policy. Other work has discussed results from small scale experiments; for example, [26] presents performance measurements for 9 popular Web sites; [15] presents DNS and TCP measurements for the most popular 100 Web sites. The WProf [29] project profiles 350 pages and produces a break down of time spent in various browser activities. Wang [30] investigate latency on mobile browsers, but focus on the compute aspects rather than networking.

The central question we have not seen answered, or even posed before, is *'Why are we so far from the speed of light?'*. Even the ramifications of a speed-of-light Internet have not been explored in any depth. The 2013 Workshop on Reducing Internet Latency [8] focused on potential mitigation techniques, with bufferbloat and active queue management being among the centerpieces. The goal of achieving latencies imperceptible to humans was also articulated [27]. Our measurements and analysis put the focus on an aspect of the latency problem that has been largely ignored so far: infrastructural inefficiencies. We hope that our work urges greater consideration for latency in efforts for expanding Internet's reach to under-served populations. However, so far, infrastructural latency has only garnered attention in niche scenarios, such as the financial markets, and isolated submarine cable projects aimed at shortening specific routes [21,22].

6 Discussion and Conclusion

Speed-of-light Internet connectivity would be a technological leap with the potential for new applications, instant response, and radical changes in the interactions between people and computing. To shed light on what's keeping us from this vision, in this work, we quantify the latency gaps introduced by the Internet's physical infrastructure and its network protocols. Our analysis suggests that the networking community should, in addition to continuing efforts for protocol improvements, also explore methods of reducing latency at the lowest layers.

Acknowledgments. Dhruv Diddi helped process the ESnet data. Data on fiber mileages from GÉANT, the high-speed pan-European research and education network, was obtained through personal communication with Xavier Martins-Rivas, DANTE. DANTE is the project coordinator and operator of GÉANT.

References

1. cURL. http://curl.haxx.se/
2. ESnet. http://www.es.net/
3. GÉANT. http://www.geant.net/
4. Google Maps API. http://goo.gl/I4ypU
5. Internet2. http://www.internet2.edu/
6. RIPE Atlas. https://atlas.ripe.net
7. Top 500 sites in each country or territory, Alexa. http://goo.gl/R8HuN6
8. Workshop on reducing internet latency (2013). http://goo.gl/kQpBCt
9. Akamai: State of the Internet, Q1 (2016). https://goo.gl/XQt324
10. Brutlag, J.: Speed matters for Google Web search (2009). http://goo.gl/t7qGN8
11. Dukkipati, N., Refice, T., Cheng, Y., Chu, J., Herbert, T., Agarwal, A., Jain, A., Sutin, N.: An argument for increasing TCP's initial congestion window. In: SIGCOMM CCR (2010)
12. Durairajan, R., Barford, P., Sommers, J., Willinger, W.: Intertubes: a study of the US long-haul fiber-optic infrastructure. In: ACM SIGCOMM (2015)
13. Schurman, E., (Bing), Brutlag, J., (Google): Performance related changes and their user impact. http://goo.gl/hAUENq
14. Gao, L., Wang, F.: The extent of AS path inflation by routing policies. In: GLOBE-COM (2002)
15. Habib, M.A., Abrams, M.: Analysis of sources of latency in downloading web pages. In: WEBNET (2000)

16. Holterbach, T., Pelsser, C., Bush, R., Vanbever, L.: Quantifying interference between measurements on the RIPE Atlas platform (2015)
17. Grigorik, I., (Google): Latency: the new web performance bottleneck. http://goo.gl/djXp3
18. Liddle, J.: Amazon Found Every 100ms of Latency Cost Them 1% in Sales. http://goo.gl/BUJgV
19. Maynard-Koran, P.: Fixing the Internet for real time applications: Part II. http://goo.gl/46EiDC
20. Mühlbauer, W., Uhlig, S., Feldmann, A., Maennel, O., Quoitin, B., Fu, B.: Impact of routing parameters on route diversity and path inflation. Comput. Netw. **54**(14), 2506–2518 (2010)
21. NEC: SEA-US: Global Consortium to Build Cable System Connecting Indonesia, the Philippines, and the United States. http://goo.gl/ZOV3qa
22. Nordrum, A.: Fiber optics for the far North [News]. IEEE Spectr. **52**(1), 11–13 (2015)
23. Radhakrishnan, S., Cheng, Y., Chu, J., Jain, A., Raghavan, B.: TCP fast open. In: CoNEXT (2011)
24. Rexford, J., Wang, J., Xiao, Z., Zhang, Y.: BGP routing stability of popular destinations. In: ACM SIGCOMM Workshop on Internet Measurment (2002)
25. Singla, A., Chandrasekaran, B., Godfrey, P.B., Maggs, B.: The Internet at the speed of light. In: HotNets. ACM (2014)
26. Sundaresan, S., Magharei, N., Feamster, N., Teixeira, R.: Measuring and mitigating web performance bottlenecks in broadband access networks. In: IMC (2013)
27. Täht, D.: On reducing latencies below the perceptible. In: Workshop on Reducing Internet Latency (2013)
28. Vulimiri, A., Godfrey, P.B., Mittal, R., Sherry, J., Ratnasamy, S., Shenker, S.: Low latency via redundancy. In: CoNEXT (2013)
29. Wang, X.S., Balasubramanian, A., Krishnamurthy, A., Wetherall, D.: Demystify page load performance with WProf. In: NSDI (2013)
30. Wang, Z.: Speeding up mobile browsers without infrastructure support. Master's thesis, Duke University (2012)
31. Zhou, W., Li, Q., Caesar, M., Godfrey, P.B.: ASAP: a low-latency transport layer. In: CoNEXT (2011)

Anycast Latency: How Many Sites Are Enough?

Ricardo de Oliveira Schmidt[1]([✉]), John Heidemann[2], and Jan Harm Kuipers[1]

[1] University of Twente, Enschede, The Netherlands
r.schmidt@utwente.nl, j.h.kuipers@student.utwente.nl
[2] USC/Information Sciences Institute, Marina Del Rey, USA
johnh@isi.edu

Abstract. Anycast is widely used today to provide important services such as DNS and Content Delivery Networks (CDNs). An anycast service uses multiple *sites* to provide high availability, capacity and redundancy. BGP routing associates users to sites, defining the *catchment* that each site serves. Although prior work has studied how users associate with anycast services informally, in this paper we examine the key question *how many anycast sites are needed* to provide good latency, and the worst case latencies that specific deployments see. To answer this question, we first define the *optimal performance* that is possible, then explore how routing, specific anycast policies, and site location affect performance. We develop a new method capable of determining optimal performance and use it to study four real-world anycast services operated by different organizations: C-, F-, K-, and L-Root, each part of the Root DNS service. We measure their performance from more than 7,900 vantage points (VPs) worldwide using RIPE Atlas. (Given the VPs uneven geographic distribution, we evaluate and control for potential bias.) Our key results show that a few sites can provide performance nearly as good as many, and that geographic location and good connectivity have a far stronger effect on latency than having many sites. We show how often users see the closest anycast site, and how strongly routing policy affects site selection.

1 Introduction

Internet content providers want to provide their customers with good service, guaranteeing high reliability and fast performance. These goals can be limited by underlying resources at servers (load) and in the network (throughput, latency, and reliability). Replicating instances of the service at different *sites* around the Internet can improve all of these factors by increasing the number of available servers, moving them closer to the users, and diversifying the network in between.

Service replication is widely used for naming (DNS) and web and media Content Delivery Networks (CDNs). Two different mechanisms associate users with particular service instances: DNS-based redirection [12] and IP anycast [1, 30], and they can be combined [13,28]). When the service is DNS, IP anycast is the primary mechanism, used by many operators, including most root servers, top-level domains, many large companies, and public resolvers [22,38]. IP anycast is also used by several web CDNs (Bing, CloudFlare, Edgecast), while others use

© Springer International Publishing AG 2017
M.A. Kaafar et al. (Eds.): PAM 2017, LNCS 10176, pp. 188–200, 2017.
DOI: 10.1007/978-3-319-54328-4_14

DNS-based redirection (Akamai, Google, and Microsoft), or their combination (LinkedIn). This paper, however, focuses only on IP anycast.

In IP anycast, service is provided on a specific *service IP address*, and that address is announced from many physical locations (*anycast sites*), each with one or multiple servers[1]. BGP routing policies then associate each user with one site, defining that site's *catchment*. Optimally users are associated with the nearest site, minimizing latency. BGP provides considerable robustness, adapting to changes in service or network availability, and allowing for some policy control. However, user-to-site mapping is determined by BGP routing, a distributed computation based on input of many network operators policies. Although mapping generally follows geography [27], studies of routing have shown that actual network topology can vary [36], and recent observations have shown that the mapping can be unexpectedly chaotic [6,23].

Anycast has been widely studied, typically with measurement studies that assess anycast coverage and latency [5,8,9,17,21,25,26,29,34], and also to enumerate anycast sites [19]. Latency studies using server-side traces show that anycast behaves roughly as expected—many geographically distributed sites reduce latency. These studies also show surprising complexity in how users are assigned to anycast sites. While prior studies cover what *does* happen, no prior work defines what *could* and *should* happen—that is, what latency is *possible*, and the reasons actual latency may differ from this ideal.

The **main contribution** of this paper is to develop a *new measurement methodology that identifies optimal latency* in IP anycast systems (Sect. 2), enabling a first evaluation of how close actual latencies are to their potential. Our insight is that we can determine optimal anycast latency by measuring unicast latency to *all* anycast sites of a system, providing a comparison to the assigned site by BGP. Thus, while prior work reports only latency for the selected anycast site, we can see when catchments differ from optimal and then study why. Our dataset from this study is publicly available at http://traces.simpleweb.org/.

Our **second contribution** is to carry out a *measurement study of four IP anycast deployments:* the C-, F-, K- and L-Root DNS services, consisting of more than 240 sites together. These services have different architectures and deployment strategies, that we study from around 7,900 RIPE Atlas probes worldwide, creating a rich dataset to inform our understanding of anycast latency.

The **final contribution** of this work is what we learn from this first comparison of actual and optimal anycast latency. Our central question is: *How many anycast sites are "enough" to get "good" latency?* To answer this question, we must first answer several related questions: Does anycast give good absolute performance (Sect. 3.1)? Do users get the closest anycast site (Sect. 3.2)? How much does the location of each anycast site affect the latency it provides overall (Sect. 3.3)? How much do local routing policies affect performance (Sect. 3.5)? With these questions resolved, we return to our key contribution and show that a modest number of well-placed anycast sites—**as few as twelve**—can provide

---

[1] The term anycast *instance* can refer to a site or to specific servers at a site. Because of this ambiguity we avoid that term in this paper.

nearly as good performance as many (Sect. 3.6). We also show that more sites improve the tail of the performance distribution (Sect. 3.4).

This paper focuses on anycast *latency*. We consider latency because it motivates huge investments, such as Google's 2013 expansion to thousands of locations [12], gradual expansion of Root DNS anycast to more than 500 sites [18], and CDN design in multiple companies. We recognize that anycast serves other purposes as well, including distributing load, improving resilience to Denial-of-Service attacks, and to support policy choices. These are, however, out of the scope of this paper. Our population of vantage points is European-centric (Sect. 3.3); while this skew affects our specific results, it does not change our qualitative conclusions. Broader exploration of CDNs, other metrics, and other sets of vantage points are future work (some in-progress).

2   Measurement Methodology

Our approach to observe anycast latency is straightforward: from as many locations (*vantage points*, or VPs) as we can, we measure *latency to all anycast sites* of each *service* that we study. These measurements approximate the *catchment* of VPs that each site serves. We use RIPE Atlas probes as VPs, and we study the C-, F-, K- and L-Root DNS services as our targets. We measure latency with pings (ICMP echo requests), and identify sites with DNS CHAOS queries. Prior studies [6,19] have used both of these mechanisms, but only to preferred site; to our knowledge, we are the first to measure latency to *all anycast sites* from all VPs, the key that allows us to study optimal latency (not just actual), and to explore policy questions (Sect. 3).

Measurement sources: We use more than 7,900 VPs (probes) in the RIPE Atlas framework [32]. Figure 1 shows the locations of all VPs: these cover 174 countries and 2927 ASes. We maximize coverage by using all probes that are available at each measurement time. The exact number, shown in Table 1, varies slightly as VPs come and go over measurements taken in 2015 and 2016. While RIPE VPs are global, their geographic distribution does not exactly match that of the overall Internet population. We show in Sect. 3 that this skew strongly affects the specific *quantitative* latencies we observe, favoring sites and VPs in Europe. But it *does not* affect our *qualitative* results about the number of anycast sites and the effects of routing policies.

Measurement targets: We study four operational anycast services: the C-, F-, K- and L-Root DNS services [18] (Fig. 2). Each service is run by a different operator and is optimized to meet their goals. They are diverse in both number of sites (with C small, F and K mid-sized, and L numerous), and in routing policy: all C and L sites are global (available to all), while many K and most F sites are local (service limited to specific AS). To identify optimal possible latency (Sect. 3), we chose these services because they all make public the *unicast* IP address of each site. We measure K Root both in 2015 (K), and again

Fig. 1. Locations of more than 7,900 vantage points we use from RIPE Atlas.

Fig. 2. Locations of sites for each service (each site is identified by its letter).

Table 1. Summary of each root service, its size in sites, and their routing policy; measurement date and number of VPs then available; how many hits are optimal, latency for each type of hit, and the cost of mishits (Sect. 3.2). We measure K-Root both before (K) and after (NK) its change in routing policy (Sect. 3.5).

letter	sites (local)	date	VPs	hit type		median RTT (ms)				mishit penalty(ms)		
				optimal	*mishit*	all	optimal	*mishit*	*(pref.)*	25%ile	50%ile	75%ile
C	8 (0)	2015-09	5766	84%	*16%*	32	28	*61*	*55*	*2*	*5*	*10*
F	58 (53)	2015-12	6280	44%	*56%*	25	12	*39*	*20*	*8*	*15*	*51*
K	33 (14)	2015-11	6464	*41%*	*59%*	32	14	*43*	*23*	*8*	*18*	*42*
NK	36 (1)	2016-04	5557	*40%*	*60%*	30	12	*41*	*19*	*9*	*18*	*48*
L	144 (0)	2015-12	5351	24%	*76%*	30	11	*47*	*16*	*10*	*24*	*82*

in 2016 (NK—*New K*) after major changes on its anycast policies, discussing implications in Sect. 3.5.

Measuring anycast catchments: We map the catchments of each anycast service by observing DNS CHAOS queries [39] (with name `hostname.bind` and type `TXT`) from each VP. The reply to each VP's CHAOS query indicates its anycast site, as determined by BGP routing. The exact contents of the reply are service-specific, but several root operators (including C, F, K and L) reply with the unicast hostname of the reached site. For example, a reply for C Root is `lax1b.c.root-servers.org`, where `lax` gives the geographic location of the replying site and `1b` identifies the replying server within the site. The resolution of this name gives the unicast IP address of that server. Sites sometimes have multiple servers, but we treat all servers at a site as equivalent.

Measuring latency: We use ICMP ECHO requests (pings) to measure *latency* from VPs to both the public anycast service address (BGP-assigned site), and the unicast address of all sites for each service. To suppress noise in individual pings, we use multiple pings and report the 10th-percentile value as the measured latency. On average VPs send 30 pings to each anycast site, but the exact number varies due to dynamics on the RIPE Atlas framework, limitations on availability of probes, and measurement scheduling.

3   Observation and Findings

3.1   Does Anycast Give Good Absolute Performance?

We first look at absolute latency seen from VPs for each anycast service. The solid lines in Fig. 3 show the distribution of latency seen from each VP to the service of the four measured letters. It reports the *actual* RTT to each VP's BGP-assigned site. We see that *all letters provide low latency to most users*: median RTT for C and K Root is 32 ms, L's median is 30 ms and F's is 25 ms.

Is 30 ms latency "good"? For DNS during web browsing (DNS on www. example.com), every millisecond matters. However, names at the root (like com) are easily cachable: there are only around 1000 names and they allow caching for two days, so shared caches at recursive resolvers are *very* effective. But we consider 30 ms great, and somewhat arbitrarily define 100 ms as high latency (matching ideal network latencies from New York to California or Sydney).

More study is needed to understand the relationship between Root DNS performance and user-perceived latency to provide definitive thresholds.

This data shows that *median latency does not strictly follow anycast size—* while F and L have better latency than C and K, corresponding with their larger number of anycast sites (58 and 144 vs. 8 and 33), the improvement is somewhat modest. Actual latency is no more than 30 ms different between any letter in most of the distribution. (At the tail of the distribution however, this difference increases up to 135 ms.) This result is quite surprising since there is a huge difference on the sizes of the anycast deployments of the measured letters. For services with many sites, *careful route engineering can also make a large difference in latency.* F's median latency is lower than L's (25 ms vs. 30 ms), even though it has about half the sites (58 vs. 144). This difference may be from route engineering by F, explicitly using RIPE Atlas for debugging [6].

3.2   Do Users Get the Closest Anycast Site?

While we showed a few sites can provide good latency, do they provide *optimal* latency? Anycast relies on BGP to map users to sites, but BGP only approximates shortest-path routing. The dotted lines in Fig. 3 show the *optimal possible* performance based on unicast routing to each individual site of all measured letters, ignoring anycast routing policies and catchments. We see that C-Root's actual service is very close to optimal (solid and dotted lines nearly overlap). We believe that this is because C has only a few, geographically distributed sites, and all sites are global—that is, C's sites are all visible across the Internet.

By contrast, larger anycast deployments show a larger difference between actual and optimal latency. These differences arise because more sub-optimal choices are available, and because these services have some or many local nodes that might place policy limitations on routing (Sect. 3.5). Looking at optimal possible performance in Fig. 3 we see that routing freedom would improve median latency for F-, K- and L-Root by 16 ms, 19 ms and 14 ms, which represents an improvement of 36%, 40% and 53% respectively. (We recognize that constraints

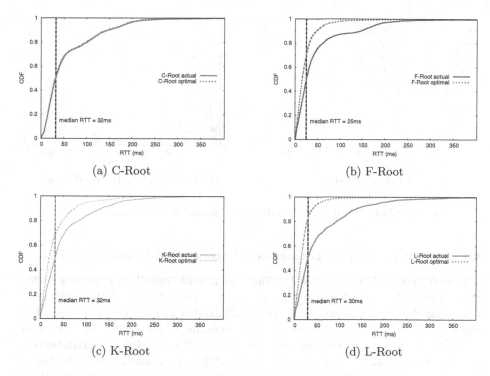

Fig. 3. Distribution of RTT to all four measured letters: *optimal* RTT ignoring BGP assignment (dotted line) compared to all *actual* RTT (solid line).

on routing may be a condition of site deployment, but we wish to understand the *potential* optimal absent such constraints.)

We define *mishits* as the cases when VPs are sent to sites other than the lowest latency. Table 1 shows how often mishits occur for each measured letter. Missing the nearest site often has a serious cost: the median RTT for VPs that mishit is 40 ms or higher for all letters. These large latencies are reflected in large penalties: the difference between latency cost of the mishit relative to the best possible choice (*i.e.,* optimal hit ignoring BGP). Table 1 shows the 25, 50 and 75th percentiles of the distribution of mishit penalties to all four letters.

Surprisingly, C-Root's few sites also have the lowest penalty of mishitting (median of 5 ms). We believe that this low penalty is because C's site are well connected and relatively close to each other (in the U.S. or Europe), so missing the closest often results in finding another site on the same continent, incurring little additional delay. In fact, 70% of all mishits for C-Root reached a site in the same continent as their optimal hit. The opposite is seen for L-Root, which shows the highest mishit penalty (median of 24 ms). L's many sites give many opportunities for mishit, and mishits incur much greater latency, often being served by a distant site with a global routing policy. (Consequences of mishits and differences in the distribution tail are discussed in Sect. 3.4.)

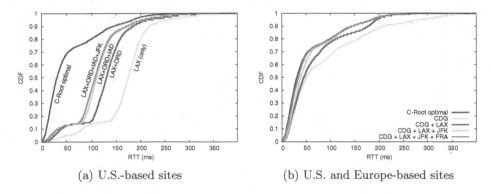

(a) U.S.-based sites   (b) U.S. and Europe-based sites

Fig. 4. Distribution of RTT to two different anycast services with 1 to 4 sites.

3.3 Effects of Anycast Location on Latency and Observation Bias

It is well known that *no single location can provide equally low latency to the global Internet*, one motivation for the use of anycast by root letters. We next show that the latency of anycast service is affected more by site *location* than the absolute *number* of sites, and consider how to manage bias due to the location of our VPs. For this study we draw locations from C Root to simulate artificial services of different sizes. We then estimate client latency assuming all VPs choose their closest site (an optimistic assumption, but close, as shown in Sect. 3.2).

Effects of Site Location: Figure 4a compares the RTT distribution of four subsets of C-Root's U.S.-based sites to C-Root's optimal. The subsets begin on the right using a single location in Los Angeles (LAX), then sites are added going eastward until New York (JFK). As each site is added, the distribution shifts to the left, improving performance. In all configurations, 80% of VPs see relatively large latencies: from 150 ms for LAX-only down to 75 ms for the four-site configuration. This trend reflects speed-of-light from European VPs to the U.S., with latency improving as sites closer to Europe are added.

Effects of VP Location: The analysis in Fig. 4a shows our measurements are dominated by the many RIPE VPs in Europe (Fig. 1), characterizing a bias that weights our quantitative results to services with sites in Europe. However, this *bias in VP location does not change our qualitative conclusion that site location dominates latency.* In addition, this bias is reflected in measurement tools based on RIPE Atlas, such as DNSMON [31], and others have recognized that RIPE Atlas does not represent all global traffic [33].

Low latency with geographically distributed locations: While Fig. 4a shows a pessimal selection of locations, we can minimize latency by selecting geographically distant sites. Figure 4b again compares the RTT distribution of four subsets of C-Root's sites, but now mixing sites located in U.S. and in Europe. We start with a site in Paris (CDG), close to the majority of our VPs in Europe, and with a tail elsewhere in the world—this configuration is within 20% of opti-

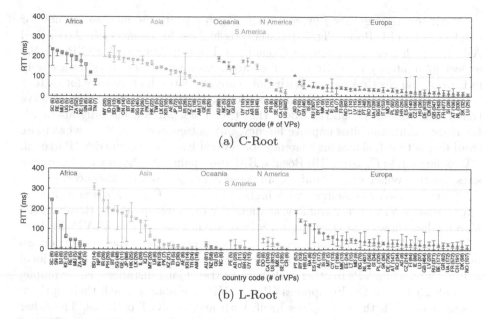

(a) C-Root

(b) L-Root

Fig. 5. Median RTT (quartiles as error bars) for countries with at least 5 VPs (number of VPs per country is given between parenthesis). Letters at top indicate continents.

mal (as defined by C's 8 sites). We then add U.S. west (LAX) and east (JFK) coasts, and then Frankfurt (FRA), each pulling the distribution closer to optimal, particularly in the tail. With the four-site combination, we virtually reach C's optimal possible performance. This data shows that *geographically distributed anycast sites can improve latency for the most distant users.* Wide geographic distribution helps because mature networks become well-connected, with latency converging down to the speed-of-light (in fiber) limit.

Although both network topology and routing policies mean network and geographic proximity may diverge [36], dispersion in geography correlates with network dispersion.

Finally, comparing these figures shows that *site location matters more than number of sites.* Four ideally positioned sites do well (the CDG, LAX, JFK, and FRA line in Fig. 4b is leftmost), while four poorly chose sites are far from optimal (compare the LAX, ORD, IAD, JFK line against optimal in Fig. 4a).

3.4 How Much Do "Many Sites" Help?

A key result of Fig. 3 is that the four letters provide roughly similar latency across most VPs, in spite of an 18× more sites (C- and L-Root show similar median latencies, 32 ms vs. 30 ms). While many sites does not affect median latency, *more sites help the tail of the distribution,* from 70th to 90th percentiles. To evaluate this tail, we next examine each country with at least 5 VPs. (We omit countries with fewer to avoid potential bias from bad "last miles" [3].)

With countries grouped by continent, Fig. 5 reports the median latency for C- (Fig. 5a) and L-Root (Fig. 5b). Latency is highest for countries in Africa and Asia for both roots, and also in Oceania and South America for C-Root. We expect high latency for C-Root in these areas because its anycast sites are only in Europe and North America. With global anycast sites, high latency for L-Root is surprising. Using our 100 ms threshold for high latency (Sect. 3.1), we observe that C has about 38 countries above that threshold, while L has only about 21. L's many additional sites improve latency, but not everywhere. Somewhat more troubling is that L shows high latency for several European countries (Portugal, PT; Belarus, BY; Croatia, HR; Bosnia, BA; and Spain, ES). Even with European sites, routing policies send traffic from these countries to long distances.

When we look at countries with highest latency in Fig. 5, L's many sites do improve *some* VPs in each country, as shown by the lower quartiles. However, the high median shows that these improvements are not even across all VPs in these countries. This wide variation suggests interconnection inside these countries can be poor, resulting in good performance for those VPs in ISPs that have a local anycast site, while VPs in other ISPs have to travel long distances. For example, from all 20 VPs in the Philippines (PH), 7 VPs are able to reach their optimal L sites located in the Philippines itself, with average RTT of 18 ms. The other 13 VPs, however, reach L sites in U.S. and Australia, seeing average RTT of 56 ms. None of the "unlucky" 13 VPs are within the same ASes than the other 7 "lucky" ones. We therefore conclude that *routing policies can drastically reduce the benefits of many sites*.

3.5   Do Local Anycast Policies Hurt Performance?

Anycast sites are often deployed with a *local* routing policy, where the site is only available to the hosting AS, or perhaps also directly adjacent ASes. An important question in anycast deployments is how much these policies impact on performance. The anycast deployments we studied allow us to answer if policy routing matters. The similar distributions of latency among the four letters we study (Fig. 3) show that policy does not matter much. C- and L-Root place no restriction on routing, while about half of F- and most of K-Root sites are local in our initial study (Table 1). We also observe K after they changed almost all sites to global (NK in Table 1).

We study *mishits* to get a more detailed look into this question. In Table 1, mishits are VPs that do not hit the optimal site. We have examined mishits based on those that go to local or global sites in detail in our technical report [35]. Due to space, we summarize those findings here and refer that report for the detailed analysis. We see that a fair number of VPs are prevented from accessing their nearest site because they instead go to a global site: this case accounts for about 58% of F-root VPs that mishit, and 42% of K-Root mishits. Thus, restrictive local routing does add latency; and relaxing this policy could improve median latency from 37 ms to 19 ms in F-Root, and from 43 ms to 25 ms in K-root.

K-Root provided a natural experiment to evaluate if relaxing routing helps. After our initial measurements of K-Root in 2015-11, K changed all but one site to global routing; our NK dataset re-examines K-Root in 2016-04, after this policy change. Comparing K and NK in Table 1, we see only modest changes in latency: 2 ms drop in median latency, and no real change in the fraction of mishits. From discussion with the K-Root operators, we learned that local routing policies were inconsistently applied (routing limits were often ignored by peers), thus routing policies can be dominated by routing bugs.

Our main conclusion is that *careful examination and debugging routing polices of local sites* can make a large difference in performance. Bellis' tuning of F-Root anycast routing showed that debugging can improve performance [6].

3.6 How Many Sites?

Given this analysis, how many sites are needed for reasonable latency? Section 3.1 shows minimal difference for median latency from 8 to 144 sites, suggesting 8 sites are reasonable based on C-Root measurements from RIPE Atlas. If we consider two sites per six continents for some redundancy, and account for under-representation of VPs in some areas, we suggest **twelve sites can provide reasonable latency**. We caution that this number is only a rough suggestion— by no means do we suggest that 12 is perfect but 11 or 13 is horrible. This count considers only latency; we recognize more sites may be needed for many other reasons (for example, DDoS-defense and many dimensions of diversity), and it applies to an individual IP anycast service, not DNS or a CDN, which often employ multiple, independent IP anycast services. It assumes geographic distribution (Sect. 3.3) and that routing problems allow use of geographically close sites (Sects. 3.4 and 3.5), and effective DNS caching (Sect. 3.1).

4 Related Work

The DNS Root has been extensively studied in the past. CAIDA's measurement infrastructure `skitter` [11] has enabled several early studies on DNS performance [8,9,21,25]. In 2004, Pang *et al.* [29] combined probing and log analysis to show that only few DNS servers were being used by a large fraction of users. Following works studied the performance of DNS, focusing on latency between clients and servers [5,17,34]. DNS CHAOS has been used to study client-server affinity [7,34]. Liu *et al.* [27] used clients geolocation to estimate RTT, and others evaluated the effect of route changes on the anycast service [4,10]. Liang *et al.* [26] used open resolvers to measure RTT from the DNS Root and major gTLDs. Bellis [6] carried out a comprehensive assessment of latency in F Root's anycast, fixing faulty route announcements to improve performance. Other work [14,24] used large and long-term datasets to show that the expansion of the anycast infrastructure improved overall performance of the Root DNS. Finally, Calder *et al.* [13] studied the choice of anycast or LDNS for redirection to CDN services.

Our work differs from these prior studies in methodology and analysis. We build on prior studies, but define *optimal* possible performance and measure it with probes to unicast addresses of all sites. This new methodology allows our analysis to go beyond measurements of what happens to statements about what *could* happen, allowing the first answers about effects of routing policy. In addition, this methodology allows us to estimate performance of alternate anycast infrastructures that are subsets of current deployments, enabling strong conclusions about the effect of numbers of sites on latency.

Furthermore, complementing our work are studies that enumerate and characterize content delivery services that use IP anycast. To exemplify some, Calder *et al.* [12] used EDNS client subnet (ECS) and latency measurements to characterize Google's serving infrastructure. Streibelt *et al.* [37] also used ECS to study Google's, Edgecast's and CacheFly's ancyast user to server mapping. Fan *et al.* [19] combined DNS queries and traceroutes to study the anycast at TLDs. Cicalese *et al.* [16] used latency measurements to geolocate anycast services, and later characterize IPv4 anycast adoption [15]. Fan *et al.* [20] combined ECS and open resolvers to measure Google's and Akamai's front-ends. Finally, Akhtar *et al.* [2] proposed a statistical approach for comparing CDNs performance.

5   Conclusions

We studied four real-world anycast deployments (the C-, F-, K- and L-Root DNS nameservers) with 7,900 VPs (RIPE Atlas probes) to systematically explore the relationship between IP anycast and latency. Unique to our collection is the combination of latency to each VP's current site, and to *all* sites, allowing evaluation of optimal possible latency. We collected new data for each of the measured services in 2015 and revisited K-Root in 2016 to evaluate changes in its routing policies. Our methodology opens up future directions, including assessment of anycast for resilience to Denial-of-Service and load balancing in addition to latency reduction.

Our new ability to compare actual to optimal latency allows us untangle several aspects of our central question: *how many anycast sites are "enough"*. Our data shows similar median performance (about 30 ms) from 8 to 144 sites, suggesting that **as few as twelve sites can provide reasonable latency**, provided they are geographically distributed, have good local interconnectivity, and DNS caching is effective.

Acknowledgments. We thank Geoff Huston (APNIC), George Michaelson (APNIC), Ray Bellis (ISC),Cristian Hesselman (SIDN Labs), Benno Overeinder (NLnet Labs) and Jaap Akkerhuis (NLnet Labs), Duane Wessels (Verisign), Paul Vixie (Farsight), Romeo Zwart (RIPE NCC), Anand Buddhdev (RIPE NCC), and operators from C Root for their technical feedback.

This research uses measurements from RIPE Atlas, operated by RIPE NCC.

Ricardo Schmidt's work is in the context of SAND (Self-managing Anycast Networks for the DNS: http://www.sand-project.nl) and DAS (DNS Anycast Security: http://www.das-project.nl) projects, sponsored by SIDN, NLnet Labs and SURFnet.

John Heidemann's work is partially sponsored by the U.S. Dept. of Homeland Security (DHS) Science and Technology Directorate, HSARPA, Cyber Security Division, via SPAWAR Systems Center Pacific under Contract No. N66001-13-C-3001, and via BAA 11-01-RIKA and Air Force Research Laboratory, Information Directorate under agreement numbers FA8750-12-2-0344 and FA8750-15-2-0224. The U.S. Government is authorized to make reprints for Governmental purposes notwithstanding any copyright. The views contained herein are those of the authors and do not necessarily represent those of DHS or the U.S. Government.

References

1. Abley, J., Lindqvist, K.E.: Operation of Anycast Services. RFC 4786 (2006)
2. Akhtar, Z., Hussain, A., Katz-Bassett, E., Govindan, R.: DBit: assessing statistically significant differences in CDN performance. In: IFIP TMA (2016)
3. Bajpai, V., Eravuchira, S.J., Schönwälder, J.: Lessons learned from using the RIPE atlas platform for measurement research. ACM CCR **45**(3), 35–42 (2015)
4. Ballani, H., Francis, P.: Towards a global IP anycast service. In: ACM SIGCOMM, pp. 301–312 (2005)
5. Ballani, H., Francis, P., Ratnasamy, S.: A measurement-based deployment proposal for IP anycast. In: ACM IMC, pp. 231–244 (2006)
6. Bellis, R.: Researching F-root Anycast Placement Using RIPE Atlas (2015). https://labs.ripe.net/
7. Boothe, P., Bush, R.: Anycast Measurements Used to Highlight Routing Instabilities. NANOG 34 (2005)
8. Brownlee, N., Claffy, K.C., Nemeth, E.: DNS Root/gTLD performance measurement. In: USENIX LISA, pp. 241–255 (2001)
9. Brownlee, N., Ziedins, I.: Response time distributions for global name servers. In: PAM (2002)
10. Bush, R.: DNS anycast stability: some initial results. In: CAIDA/WIDE Workshop (2005)
11. CAIDA. Skitter. http://www.caida.org/tools/measurement/skitter/
12. Calder, M., Fan, X., Hu, Z., Katz-Bassett, E., Heidemann, J., Govindan, R.: Mapping the expansion of Google's serving infrastructure. In: ACM IMC, pp. 313–326 (2013)
13. Calder, M., Flavel, A., Katz-Bassett, E., Mahajan, R., Padhye, J.: Analyzing the performance of an anycast CDN. In: ACM IMC, pp. 531–537 (2015)
14. Castro, S., Wessels, D., Fomenkov, M., Claffy, K.: A day at the root of the internet. ACM CCR **38**(5), 41–46 (2008)
15. Cicalese, D., Augé, J., Joumblatt, D., Friedman, T., Rossi, D.: Characterizing IPv4 anycast adoption and deployment. In: ACM CoNEXT (2015)
16. Cicalese, D., Joumblatt, D., Rossi, D., Buob, M.-O., Augé, J., Friedman, T.: A fistful of pings: accurate and lightweight anycast enummeration and geolocation. In: IEEE INFOCOM, pp. 2776–2784 (2015)
17. Colitti, L.: Effect of anycast on K-root. In: 1st DNS-OARC Workshop (2005)
18. DNS Root Servers. http://www.root-servers.org/
19. Fan, X., Heidemann, J., Govindan, R.: Evaluating anycast in the domain name system. In: IEEE INFOCOM, pp. 1681–1689 (2013)
20. Fan, X., Katz-Bassett, E., Heidemann, J.: Assessing affinity between users and CDN sites. In: Steiner, M., Barlet-Ros, P., Bonaventure, O. (eds.) TMA 2015. LNCS, vol. 9053, pp. 95–110. Springer, Heidelberg (2015). doi:10.1007/978-3-319-17172-2_7

21. Fomenkov, M., Claffy, K.C., Huffaker, B., Moore, D.: Macroscopic internet topology and performance measurements from the DNS root name servers. In: USENIX LISA, pp. 231–240 (2001)
22. Google Public DNS. https://developers.google.com/speed/public-dns/
23. Kuipers, J.H.: Analysing the K-root anycast infrastructure (2015). https://labs.ripe.net/
24. Lee, B.-S., Tan, Y.S., Sekiya, Y., Narishige, A., Date, S.: Availability and effectiveness of root DNS servers: a long term study. In: IFIP/IEEE NOMS, pp. 862–865 (2010)
25. Lee, T., Huffaker, B., Fomenkov, M., Claffy, K.C.: On the problem of optimization of DNS root servers' placement. In: PAM (2003)
26. Liang, J., Jiang, J., Duan, H., Li, K., Wu, J.: Measuring query latency of top level DNS servers. In: Roughan, M., Chang, R. (eds.) PAM 2013. LNCS, vol. 7799, pp. 145–154. Springer, Heidelberg (2013). doi:10.1007/978-3-642-36516-4_15
27. Liu, Z., Huffaker, B., Fomenkov, M., Brownlee, N., Claffy, K.C.: Two days in the life of the DNS anycast root servers. In: Uhlig, S., Papagiannaki, K., Bonaventure, O. (eds.) PAM 2007. LNCS, vol. 4427, pp. 125–134. Springer, Heidelberg (2007). doi:10.1007/978-3-540-71617-4_13
28. Palsson, B., Kumar, P., Jafferalli, S., Kahn, Z.A.: TCP over IP anycast - pipe dream or reality? (2015). https://engineering.linkedin.com/
29. Pang, J., Hendricks, J., Akella, A., Prisco, R.D., Maggs, B., Seshan, S.: Availability, usage, and deployment characteristics of the domain name server. In: ACM IMC, pp. 1–14 (2004)
30. Partridge, C., Mendez, T., Milliken, W.: Host Anycasting Service. RFC 1546 (1993)
31. RIPE NCC. Dnsmon (2015). https://atlas.ripe.net/dnsmon/
32. RIPE NCC Staff: RIPE Atlas: a global Internet measurement network. Internet Protocol J. 18(3), 2–26 (2015)
33. Rootops. Events of 2015–11–30. Technical report, Root Server Operators (2015)
34. Sarat, S., Pappas, V., Terzis, A.: On the use of anycast in DNS. In: ICCCN, pp. 71–78 (2006)
35. Schmidt, R.d.O., Heidemann, J., Kuipers, J.H.: Anycast latency: how many sites are enough? Technical report ISI-TR-2016-708, USC-ISI, May 2016
36. Spring, N., Mahajan, R., Anderson, T.: Quantifying the causes of path inflation. In: ACM SIGCOMM, pp. 113–124 (2003)
37. Streibelt, F., Böttger, J., Chatzis, N., Smaragdakis, G., Feldman, A.: Exploring EDNS-client-subnet adopters in your free time. In: ACM IMC, pp. 305–312 (2013)
38. Toonk, A.: How OpenDNS achieves high availability with anycast routing (2013). https://labs.opendns.com/
39. Woolf, S., Conrad, D.: Requirements for a Mechanism Identifying a Name Server Instance. RFC 4892 (2007)

Where Has My Time Gone?

Noa Zilberman[✉], Matthew Grosvenor, Diana Andreea Popescu,
Neelakandan Manihatty-Bojan, Gianni Antichi,
Marcin Wójcik, and Andrew W. Moore

Computer Laboratory, University of Cambridge, Cambridge, UK
{noa.zilberman,matthew.grosvenor,diana.popescu,
neelakandan.manihatty-bojan,gianni.antichi,
marcin.wojcik,andrew.moore}@cl.cam.ac.uk

Abstract. Time matters. In a networked world, we would like mobile
devices to provide a crisp user experience and applications to instan-
taneously return results. Unfortunately, application performance does
not depend solely on processing time, but also on a number of different
components that are commonly counted in the overall system latency.
Latency is more than just a nuisance to the user, poorly accounted-for, it
degrades application performance. In fields such as high frequency trading, as well as in many data centers, latency translates easily to financial
losses. Research to date has focused on specific contributions to latency:
from improving latency within the network to latency control on the
application level. This paper takes an holistic approach to latency, and
aims to provide a break-down of end-to-end latency from the application level to the wire. Using a set of crafted experiments, we explore the
many contributors to latency. We assert that more attention should be
paid to the latency within the host, and show that there is no silver bul-
let to solve the end-to-end latency challenge in data centers. We believe
that a better understanding of the key elements influencing data center
latency can trigger a more focused research, improving the user's quality
of experience.

1 Introduction

Time plays a major role in computing, as it translates directly to financial
losses [6,13]. User demands for a highly interactive experience (e.g., online shopping, web search, online gaming etc.) has put stringent demands on applications
to consistently meet tight deadlines. Nowadays, the question *Can the application
(job) meet a deadline?* is replaced by *Will the application get the consistent, low
latency, guarantees needed to meet user demands?*

In the past, large propagation delays and unoptimized hardware have eclipsed
inefficiencies in end-system hardware and software: operating systems and applications. Yet decades ago, latency was identified as a fundamental challenge [2,11].
The emergence of data centers increased the importance of the long tail of latency
problem: due to the scaling effect within a data center, every small latency issue
is having an increasing effect on the performance [1]. Only 5 years ago a switch

© Springer International Publishing AG 2017
M.A. Kaafar et al. (Eds.): PAM 2017, LNCS 10176, pp. 201–214, 2017.
DOI: 10.1007/978-3-319-54328-4_15

latency of 10 μs and an OS stack latency of 15 μs were considered the norm [12], however, since then, a significant improvement has been achieved [3,5]. To fully understand this latency improvement, this paper takes an end-to-end approach, focusing upon the latency between the time a request is issued by an application to the time a reply has returned to that application. This approach has the advantage of maximizing the throughput of a system, which is the main goal of a user, rather than optimizing discrete parts of the system. We consider the best-possible configurations, which may not be identical to the most realistic configuration, and further focus on the Ethernet-based systems common in data centers.

In this paper we use bespoke experiments (described in Sect. 2) to derive a breakdown to the end-to-end latency of modules in commodity end-host systems (discussed in Sect. 3). We identify the latency components that require the most focus for improvement and propose trajectories for such work. Finally, we contribute a taxonomy of latency contributors: low-latency/low-variability: the "Good", high-latency/high-variability: the "Bad", and heavy-tailed or otherwise peculiar latency: the "Ugly", while also noting the challenge of profiling application network performance.

1.1   Motivation

The contribution of latency affects a user-experience in a significant, sometimes subtle, manner. More than a simple, additive, increase in run-time, application performance can be dramatically decreased with an increase in latency. Figure 1 illustrates the impact of latency upon performance for several common data center applications.

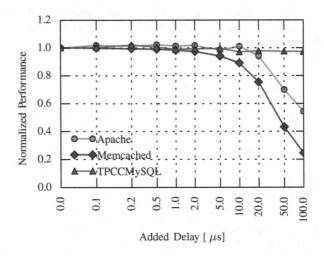

Fig. 1. Delay effect on application performance.

Using an experimental configuration described in Sect. 2, Fig. 1 illustrates experimental results for three application-benchmarks. Each benchmark reports results for an application-specific performance metric. These application-specific benchmarks are normalized to allow comparisons to be made among the applications.

The three benchmarks we use are Apache benchmark[1] reporting mean requests per second, Memcached benchmark[2] reporting throughput, and TPC-C MySQL benchmark[3] reporting New-Order transactions per minute, (where New-Order is one of the database's tables).

Between the two hosts of the experimental configuration described in Sect. 2, we insert a bespoke hardware device to inject controlled latency. We implemented a latency-injection appliance[4] that allows us to add arbitrary latency into the system. Past latency injection has been done with approaches such as NetEm [4], yet this proved inappropriate for our work. Alongside limited granularity, such approaches may not reliably introduce latency of less than several tens of microseconds [8]. In contrast, our latency gadget adds 700 ns of base latency and permits further additional latency, at 5 ns granularity, up to a maximum[5] determined by the rate of operation.

Each test begins by measuring a baseline, which is the performance of each benchmark under the default setup conditions, taking into account the base latency introduced by the latency-injection appliance. Latency is then artificially inserted by the appliance, and the application-specific performance is measured. We can derive the impact on experiments of the artificially inserted latency by removing the baseline measurement. For the three benchmarks, Fig. 1 shows the effect of added latency. Each benchmark was run 100 times for the baseline and for each added latency value. The graph plots the average values, and standard errors are omitted for clarity, as they are below 0.005. In one run, the Apache benchmark sends 100000 requests and the Memcached benchmark sends 10 million requests. The TPC-C benchmark runs continuously for 1000 s, with an additional time of 6 minutes of warm-up, resulting in 100 measurements over 10 s periods. The application most sensitive to latency is Memcached: the addition of 20 μs latency leads to a performance drop of 25%, while adding 100 μs will reduce its throughput to 25% of the baseline. The TPC-C benchmark is the least sensitive to latency, although still exhibits some performance loss: 3% reduction in performance with an additional 100 μs. Finally, the Apache benchmark observes a drop in performance that starts when 20 μs are added, while adding 100 μs leads to a 46% performance loss.

---

[1] https://httpd.apache.org/docs/2.4/programs/ab.html.

[2] http://docs.libmemcached.org/bin/memaslap.html.

[3] https://github.com/Percona-Lab/tpcc-mysql.

[4] Our latency-injection appliance is an open-source contributed project as part of NetFPGA SUME since release 1.4.0.

[5] The maximum latency introduced is a function of the configured line-rate. The appliance can add up to 700 μs of latency at full 10 Gb/s rate, and up to 7 s at 100 Mbps.

While the results above are obtained under optimal setup conditions, within an operational data center worse-still results would be expected as latency is further increased under congestion conditions and as services compete for common resources. The results of Fig. 1 show clearly that even a small increase in latency, of the scale shown in this paper, can significantly affect an application's performance.

2   Experiments

This section presents experiments we used to provide a decomposition of the latency between the application and the physical-wire of the host. Full results of these experiments are given in Sect. 3 with the outcome of successive tests presented in Table 1. Each experiment in this section is annotated with the corresponding entry number in Table 1.

2.1   Tests Setup

For our tests setup we use two identical hosts running Ubuntu server 14.04 LTS, kernel version 4.4.0-42-generic. The host hardware is a single 3.5 GHz Intel Xeon E5-2637 v4 on a SuperMicro X10-DRG-Q motherboard. All CPU power-saving, hyper-threading and frequency scaling are disabled throughout our tests. Host adapter evaluation uses commodity network interface cards (NICs), Solarflare SFN8522, and Exablaze X10, using either standard driver or a kernel bypass mode (test dependent). For minimum latency, interrupt hold-off time is set to zero. Each host uses identical NICs for that particular NIC experiment and we only consider Ethernet-based communication. As illustrated in Fig. 3, an Endace 9.2SX2 DAG card (7.5 ns time-stamping resolution) and a NetOptics passive-optical tap are used to intercept client-server traffic and permit independent measurement of client & server latency. The experiments are reproducible using the procedures documented at http://www.cl.cam.ac.uk/research/srg/netos/projects/latency/pam2017/.

2.2   In-Host Latency

Figure 2 illustrates the various elements contributing to the experienced latency within the host.

Timestamp Counter Latency (1). To accurately measure latency, we set an accuracy baseline for our methods. Our latency measurements are based on the CPU's Time Stamp Counter (TSC). TSC is a 64-bit register, present on the processor, it counts the number of cycles since reset and thus provides a resolution of approximately 288 ps-per-cycle although realistically there is tens of cycles resolution due to CPU pipeline effects. Access to TSC is done using *rdtsc* x86 assembly instruction. In order to understand hidden latency effects, and following the Intel recommendations for TSC access [10], we conduct two read

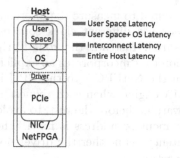

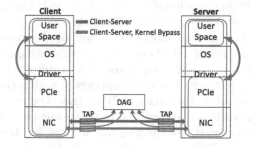

Fig. 2. End host tests setup.   **Fig. 3.** Client-server tests setup.

operations consecutively. We repeat this simple TSC read operation a large number of times (order of 10^{10} events), and study the time gaps measured between every pair of consecutive reads. Results are saved into previously allocated and initialized buffers, and access to the buffers is outside the measurement mainline.

This test is conducted in three different modes: firstly, *Kernel Cold Start* (1a) which serves as our approximation of a bare metal test. Kernel Cold Start measures very early within the kernel boot process, before the scheduler, multiprocessing and multicore support have been started. The second test, *Kernel Test* (1b), runs from within the kernel, and represents an enhanced version of the recommended test described in [10]. The third test, *User Space Test* (1c), provides high-accuracy time stamping measurement from within a user-space application. The application is pinned to a single CPU core and all other tasks and interrupts are moved to other cores. This is representative of real-time application operation. In contrast to the Kernel Test, interrupts, such as scheduling pre-emption, are not disabled so as to represent the runtime conditions of real applications.

User Space + OS Latency (2). This experiment investigates the combined latency of the (user-space) application and the operating system. The test sets up two processes and opens a datagram socket between them, measuring the round trip time (RTT) for a message sent from a source process to the destination process, and back. TSC is used to measure the latency and the time is measured by reading TSC before and after the message reply is received. While this does not fully exercise the network stack, it does provide useful insight into the kernel overhead.

Virtualized Environment (1d). The contribution of a virtualized environment is examined by repeating the TSC tests from within a Virtual Machine (VM). We used VirtualBox [9] version 4.3.36 as the hypervisor, with an Ubuntu VM (same version as the base OS). The VM was configured to run the guest OS on a single dedicated CPU core with no co-located native operating system activities.

Host Interconnect (3). To evaluate the latency of the host interconnect (e.g., PCI-Express), we used the NetFPGA SUME platform [16], which implements x8

PCIe Gen3 interface. The DMA design is instrumented to measure the interconnect latency. As the hardware and the processor use different clock sources, the one-way latency can not be directly measured. Instead, the round trip latency of a read operation (a non-posted operation that incorporates an explicit reply) is measured. Every read transaction from the NetFPGA to the CPU is timestamped at 6.25 ns accuracy within the DMA engine when each request is issued and when its reply returns. The cache is warmed before the test, to avoid additional latency due to cache misses, and the memory address is fixed. The measured latency does not account for driver latency, as neither the driver nor the CPU core participate in the PCIe read transaction.

Host Latency (4). To measure the latency of an entire host we use a bespoke request-reply test to measure the latency through the NIC, PCIe Interconnect, Kernel and network stack, the application level, and back to the NIC. Contrast to the *User Space + OS Latency* experiment, here packets traverse the networks stack only once in each direction. Packets are injected by a second host, and using the DAG card we isolate the host latency, measuring the latency from the packet's entrance to the NIC and until it returns from the NIC.

Kernel Bypass Influence (5). Kernel bypass is promoted as a useful methodology and we consider the latency contribution of the operating-system kernel alone and the impact of kernel-bypass upon latency. Using tests comparable to those of *Host Latency* experiment we can then measure latency using the kernel bypass supported by our NICs (X10, SFN8522). Our performance comparison contrasts the kernel with bypass enabled and disabled.

2.3   Client-Server Latency (6)

Experiments are extended from single-host (and, where appropriate, hardware request-reply server) to a pair of network-hosts as shown in Fig. 3. The two servers are directly connected to each other. Using a test method based upon that described in the *Host Latency* experiment, we add support for request-reply at both hosts. This allows us to measure latency between the user-space application of both machines. We further extend this experiment to measure the latency of queries (both get and set) under the Memcached benchmark, indicative of realistic user-space application latency.

2.4   Network Latency

We measure three components that contribute to network latency: networking devices within the network, cabling (e.g., fiber, copper), and networking devices at the edge. The network device at the edge is represented in this study by the NIC. For networking devices within the network we focus on electrical packet switches (EPS) as the most commonly used networking devices within data center today. Networking devices such as routers will inherently have a latency that is the same or larger than a switch, thus we do not study them specifically.

Our focus in this work is on the minimum latency components within a system. We therefore do not evaluate latency components of networking devices such as queueing and buffering or congestion. We consider these out of scope in our attempt to understand the most-ideal latency situation.

Cabling. The propagation delay over a fiber is 4.9 ns per meter, and the delay over a copper cable varies between 4.3 ns and 4.4 ns per meter, depending on the cable's thickness and material used. We corroborate these numbers by sending packet trains over varying lengths of cable and measuring using DAG the latency between transmit and receive[6]. In our reported tests we use fiber exclusively.

NIC Latency (7). Measuring NIC-latency is a subtle art. At least three components contribute to a typical NIC latency figure: the NIC's hardware, the Host Bus Adapter (a PCI-Express interconnect in our case) and the NIC's driver. There are two ways to measure the latency of a NIC: the first is injecting packets from outside the host to the NIC, looping the packets at the driver and capturing them at the NIC's output port. The second is injecting packets from the driver to the NIC, using a (physical or logical) loopback at the NIC's ports and capturing the returning packet at the driver. Neither of these ways allows us to separate the hardware-latency contribution from the rest of its latency components or to measure one way latency. Acknowledging these limitations, we opt for the second method, injecting packets from the driver to the NIC. We use a loopback test provided by Exablaze with the X10 NIC[7]. The test writes a packet to the driver's buffer, and then measures the latency between when the packet starts to be written to PCIe and when the packet returns. This test does not involve the kernel. A similar open-source test provided by Solarflare as part of Onload (eflatency), which measures RTT between two nodes, is used to evaluate SFN8522 NIC. The propagation delay on the fiber is measured and excluded from the NIC latency results.

Switch Latency (8). We measure switch latency using a single DAG card to timestamp the entry and departure time of a packet from a switch under test. The switch under test is statically configured to send packets from one input port to another output port. No other ports are being utilized on the switch during the test, so there is no crosstalk traffic. We vary the size of the packets sent from 64B to 1514B.

We evaluate two classes of switches, both of them cut-through switches: an Arista DCS-7124FX layer 2 switch, and an ExaLINK50 layer 1 switch. The latency reported is one way, end of packet to end of packet.

Caveats: Latest generation cut through switching devices, such as Mellanox Spectrum and Broadcom Tomahawk, opt for lower latency than we measure, on the order of 330 ns. We were not able to obtain these devices. As a result, later discussion of these, as well as of large store-and-forward spine switches (e.g., Arista 7500R) relies on results taken from vendors' datasheet and industry analysis [15].

---

[6] We note that the resolution of the DAG of 7.5 ns puts short fiber measurements within this range of error.

[7] The source code for the test is provided with the NIC, but is not open source.

3   Latency Results

The results of the experiments described in Sect. 2 are presented in Table 1. The accuracy of time-measurements in kernel space, user space, or within a VM is on the order of tens of CPU clock cycles (approximately 10 ns in our system). Any operation beyond that is on the order of between hundreds of nanoseconds and microseconds. To better understand this, Fig. 4 shows the relative latency contribution of each component. The figure makes it clear that there is no single component that contributes overwhelmingly to end-host latency: while the kernel (including the network stack) is certainly important, the application level also makes significant contribution to latency as, even in our straightforward evaluation example, applications incur overheads due to user-space/kernel-space context switches.

Deriving the latency of different components within the network is not as straightforward as within the host, and depends on the network topology.

To illustrate this impact we use four typical networking topologies, depicted in Fig. 6, combined with the median latency results reported in Table 1. Representing the store-and-forward spine switch we use the latency of Arista-7500R switch. Figure 5 shows the relative latency contribution within each network topology.

While differences in latency contribution here are enormous, just as in the end-host case single huge contributor to network latency. Furthermore, the

Table 1. Summary of latency results.

	Experiment	Minimum	Median	99.9th	Tail	Observation period
1a	TSC - Kernel Cold Start	7 ns	7 ns	7 ns	11 ns	1 h
1b	TSC - Kernel	9 ns	9 ns	9 ns	6.9 μs	1 h
1c	TSC - From User Space	9 ns	10 ns	11 ns	49 μs	1 h
1d	TSC - From VM User Space	12 ns	12 ns	13 ns	64 ms	1 h
2a	User Space + OS (same core)	2 μs	2 μs	2 μs	68 μs	10 M messages
2b	User Space + OS (other core)	4 μs	5 μs	5 μs	31 μs	10 M messages
3a	Interconnect (64B)	552 ns	572 ns	592 ns	608 ns	1 M transactions
3b	Interconnect (1536B)	976 ns	988 ns	1020 ns	1028 ns	1 M transactions
4	Host	3.9 μs	4.5 μs	21 μs	45 μs	1 M packets
5	Kernel Bypass	895 ns	946 ns	1096 ns	5.4 μs	1 M packets
6a	Client-Server (UDP)	7 μs	9 μs	107 μs	203 μs	1 M packets
6b	Client-Server (Memcached)	10 μs	13 μs	240 μs	20.3 ms	1 M queries
7a	NIC - X10 (64B)	804 ns	834 ns	834 ns	10 μs	100 K packets
7b	NIC - SFN8522 (64B)	960 ns	985 ns	1047 ns	3.3 μs	100 K packets
8a	Switch - ExaLINK50 (64B)	0[a]	2.7 ns[a]	17.7 ns[a]	17.7 ns[a]	1000 packets
8b	Switch - ExaLINK50 (1514B)	0[a]	2.7 ns[a]	17.7 ns[a]	17.7 ns[a]	1000 packets
8c	Switch - 7124FX (64B)	512 ns	534 ns	550 ns	557 ns	1000 packets
8d	Switch - 7124FX (1514B)	512 ns	535 ns	557 ns	557 ns	1000 packets

Entries marked [a] return results that are within DAG measurement error-range.

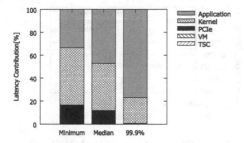
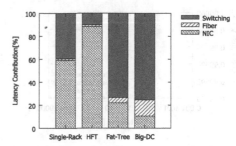

Fig. 4. End host latency contribution.   **Fig. 5.** Network latency contribution.

latency of the fibers, which is often disregarded, has a magnitude of microseconds in big data centers and becomes a significant component of the overall latency. However, unlike any other component, propagation delay is one aspect that can not be improved, hinting that minimizing the length of the traversal path through data centers needs to become a future direction of research.

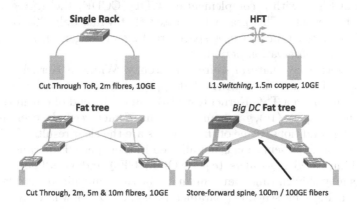

Fig. 6. Different network topologies.

4   Tail Latency Results

Results in the previous section range between their stated minimum and the 99.9th percentile. However, our experiments also provide insight into heavy-tail properties of the measured latency. Such results, which are not caused by network congestion or other oft-stated causes of tail-latency, are briefly discussed in this section.

The relative scale of these tail latency cases is usefully illustrated by considering the TSC (1). The tail latency values are clearly illustrated when using the TSC experiment (Sect. 2.2) and all subsequent experiments using the TSC measurement.

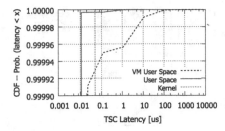

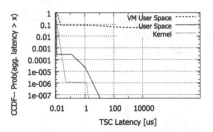

Fig. 7. CDF of TSC tail latency.

Fig. 8. CCDF of aggregated TSC tail latency.

While up to 99th percentile for the typical TSC measurements, the latency is in the order of 10 ns, in both kernel and user space, TSC latencies can be in the order of microseconds or hundreds of microseconds. VMs show even greater sensitivity with higher-still outlier values. The CDF of these results is shown in Fig. 7. While long latency events may be infrequent, even a single outlier event can overshadow hundreds to thousands of other operations. This is keenly illustrated in Fig. 8 with a complementary CDF (CCDF) the aggregated time wasted on tail events. This graph illustrates that while only 364 out of 22G events of TSC latency in VM user space are 1 ms or longer, these events take almost 5% of the observation period.

The OS kernel is a natural source of latency. While in Kernel Cold Start tests (1a) we did not find any outliers that approach a microsecond, microsecond-long gaps do occur in a TSC Kernel test (1b) run at the end of our initialization sequence. In user space (1c), gaps can reach tens of microseconds, even under our best operating conditions. Some of these events are the clear results of scheduling events, as disabling pre-emption is not allowed in user space. Experimenting with different (Linux) OS schedulers (e.g., NOOP, CFQ and Deadline) show that such events may shift in time, but remain at the same magnitude and frequency. Further, changing some scheduler parameters, e.g. CFQ's "low latency" and "Idle slice", does not reduce the frequency of microsecond-long gaps.

The most prominent cause of long time-gaps is not running an application in real time or pinned to a core. While the frequency of gaps greater than 1 μs does not change significantly, the latency does increase. When pinned in isolation on a CPU, 99.9[th] percentile of the 1 μs-or-more gaps are less than 10 μs. Without pinning and running in real time, over 10% of the gaps are 10 μs or longer, and several hundreds-of-microsecond long gaps occur every second. A pinned application sharing a core with other processes exhibits latency in-between the aforementioned results - which makes clear VMs are more prone to long latencies, especially when the VM is running on a single core.

A different source of latency is coding practice: Listings 1.1 and 1.2 show two ways to conduct the TSC user-space test. While Listing 1.1 measures the exact gap between two consecutive reads, it potentially misses longer events occurring between loops. Listing 1.2 overcomes this problem, but also captures

```
1    while (!done) {
2        //Read TSC twice, one immedately after the other
3        do_rdtscp(tsc, cpu);
4        do_rdtscp(tsc2,cpu2);
5        //If the gap between the two reads is above a threshold, save
             it
6        if ((tsc2 - tsc > threshold) && (cpu == cpu2))
7            buffer[samples++] = tsc2-tsc; }
```

Listing 1.1. Reading and Comparing TSC - Code 1.

```
1    while (!done) {
2        //Read TSC once
3        do_rdtscp(tsc, cpu);
4        //If the gap between the current and the previous reads is
             above a threshold, save it
5        if ((tsc - last > threshold) && (cpu == lastcpu))
6            buffer[samples++] = tsc-last;
7        last = tsc;
8        lastcpu = cpu; }
```

Listing 1.2. Reading and Comparing TSC - Code 2.

gaps caused by the code itself. Consequently, Listing 1.2's minimal gap grows from 9 ns to 14 ns, while the maximal gap is about twofold longer. In addition, page faults lead to hundreds of microseconds latencies that can be avoided using e.g. *mlock*.

5 Discussion

This paper contributes a decomposition of the latency-inducing components between an application to the *wire*. We hope that other researchers can make use of this work to calibrate their design goals and results, and provide a better understanding of the key components of overall latency. The results are generalizable also to other platforms and other Linux kernel versions[8].

Four observations summarize the lessons learned. First, there is no single source of latency: using ultra low latency switches or NICs alone are insufficient even when using sophisticated kernel bypass options. It is only the combination of each of these efforts which may satisfactorily reduce latency experienced in a network system. Second, tail events are no longer negligible and result in two side effects: (1) latency-sensitive transactions may experience delays far worse than any performance guarantee or design for resilience (e.g. if the event is longer than retransmission timeout (RTO)) and (2) the "noise" – events well beyond the 99.9th percentile – potentially consume far more than 0.01% of the time. This calls for a change of paradigm: instead of qualifying a system by its 99.9th percentile, it may be that a new evaluation is called for; for example a system might need to meet a certain signal-to-noise ratio (SNR) (i.e. events below 99.9th percentile divided by events above it), as in other aspects of engineered systems.

---

[8] Based on evaluation on Xeon E5-2637 v3, i7-6700K and i7-4770 based platforms, and Linux kernels ranging from 3.18.42 to 4.4.0-42.

Finally, in large scale distributed systems (e.g., hyper data center) the impact of the speed of light increases. When a data center uses hundreds of meters long fibers [14] and the RTT on every 100 m is 1 μs, the aggregated latency is of the order 10 μs to 20 μs. Consequently, the topology used in the network and the locality of the data become important, leading to approaches that increase networking locality, e.g. rack-scale computing. While hundred-meter long fibers can not be completely avoided within hyper-data center, such traversals should be minimized.

5.1 The Good, the Bad and the Ugly

The obtained results can be categorized into three groups: the "Good", the "Bad", and the "Ugly".

The Good are the latency contributors whose 99.9th percentile is below 1 μs. This group includes the simple operations in kernel and user space, PCIe and a single switch latency.

The Bad are the latency contributors whose 99.9th percentile is above 1 μs, but less than 100 μs. This includes the latency of sending packets over user space+OS, entire host latency, client-server latency, RTT over 100 m fibers and multi-stage network topology.

The Ugly are the large latency contributors at the far end of the tail, i.e. the "noise", contributing more than 100 μs. These happen mostly on the user space and within a VM. "Ugly" events will increasingly overshadow all other events, thereby reducing the SNR. Some events outside the scope of this paper, such as network congestion, also fall within this category [7].

5.2 Limitations

This paper focuses upon the **unavoidable** latency components within a system. It thus does not take into account aspects such as congestion, queueing or scheduling effects. No attempt is made to consider the impact of protocols, such as TCP, and their effect on latency and resource contention within the host is also outside the scope.

This work has focused on commodity hardware and standard networking practices and on PCIe interconnect and Ethernet-based networking, rather than, e.g., RDMA and RCoE, reserved for future work.

6 Conclusion

Computer users hate to wait – this paper reports on some of the reasons for latency in a network-based computer system. Using a decompositional analysis, the contribution of the different components to the overall latency is quantified, and we show that there is no single overwhelming contributor to saving the end-to-end latency challenge in data centers. Further we conclude that more and more latency components, such as the interconnect and cabling, will become significant as the latency of other components continues to improve. We also conclude that the long tail of events, beyond the 99.9^{th} percentile, is far more significant than its frequency might suggest and we go some way to quantify this contribution.

"Good", "Bad", and "Ugly" classes are applied to a range of latency-contributors. While many of the "Bad" latency contributors are the focus of existing effort, the "Ugly" require new attention, otherwise performance cannot be reasonably guaranteed. Giving the "Ugly" latencies attention will require concerted effort to improve the state of instrumentation, ultimately permitting end-to-end understanding.

Acknowledgments. We would like to thank the many people who contributed to this paper. We would like to thank Salvator Galea and Robert N Watson, who contributed to early work on this paper. This work has received funding from the EPSRC grant EP/K034723/1, Leverhulme Trust Early Career Fellowship ECF-2016-289, European Union's Horizon 2020 research and innovation programme 2014-2018 under the SSI-CLOPS (grant agreement No. 644866), ENDEAVOUR (grant agreement No. 644960) and EU FP7 Marie Curie ITN METRICS (grant agreement No. 607728).

Dataset. A reproduction environment of the experiments, and the experimental results, are both available at http://www.cl.cam.ac.uk/research/srg/netos/projects/latency/pam2017/ and https://doi.org/10.17863/CAM.7418.

References

1. Barroso, L.A.: Landheld Computing. In: IEEE International Solid State Circuits Conference (ISSCC) (2014). Keynote
2. Cheshire, S.: It's the latency, stupid. http://www.stuartcheshire.org/rants/Latency.html. Accessed July 2016
3. Guo, C., et al.: RDMA over commodity ethernet at scale. In: SIGCOMM 2016 (2016)
4. Hemminger, S.: NetEm - Network Emulator. http://man7.org/linux/man-pages/man8/tc-netem.8.html. Accessed July 2016
5. Kalia, A., et al.: Design guidelines for high performance RDMA systems. In: USENIX ATC, vol. 16, pp. 437–450 (2016)
6. Mayer, M.: What Google knows. In: Web 2.0 Summit (2006)
7. Mittal, R., et al.: TIMELY: RTT-based congestion control for the datacenter. SIG-COMM Comput. Commun. Rev. **45**, 537–550 (2015). ACM
8. Nussbaum, L., Richard, O.: A comparative study of network link emulators. In: SpringSim 2009, pp. 85:1–85:8 (2009)
9. Oracle: Oracle VM VirtualBox. https://www.virtualbox.org/. Accessed Oct 2016
10. Paoloni, G.: How to benchmark code execution times on Intel IA-32 and IA-64 instruction set architectures. Technical report 324264–001, Intel (2010)
11. Patterson, D.A.: Latency lags bandwidth. Commun. ACM **47**(10), 71–75 (2004)
12. Rumble, S.M., et al.: It's time for low latency. In: HotOS 2013, p. 11. USENIX Association (2011)
13. SAP: Big data and smart trading (2012)

14. Singh, A., et al.: Jupiter rising: a decade of clos topologies and centralized control in Google's datacenter network. SIGCOMM Comput. Commun. Rev. **45**(4), 183–197 (2015)
15. Tolly Enterprises: Mellanox spectrum vs. broadcom StrataXGS Tomahawk 25GbE & 100GbE performance evaluation - evaluating consistency & predictability. Technical report 216112 (2016)
16. Zilberman, N., et al.: NetFPGA SUME: toward 100 Gbps as research commodity. IEEE Micro **34**(5), 32–41 (2014)

Characterization and Troubleshooting

Mind the Gap Between HTTP and HTTPS in Mobile Networks

Alessandro Finamore$^{(\boxtimes)}$, Matteo Varvello, and Kostantina Papagiannaki

Telefonica Research, Barcelona, Spain
{alessandro.finamore,matteo.varvello,
kostantina.papagiannaki}@telefonica.com

Abstract. Fueled by a plethora of applications and Internet services, mobile data consumption is on the rise. Over the years, mobile operators deployed webproxies to optimize HTTP content delivery. Webproxies also produce HTTP-logs which are a fundamental data source to understand network/services performance and user behavior. The recent surge of HTTPS is progressively reducing such wealth of information, to the point that it is unclear whether HTTP-logs are still representative of the overall traffic. Unfortunately, HTTPS monitoring is challenging and adds some extra cost which refrains operators from "turning on the switch". In this work, we study the "gap" between HTTP and HTTPS both quantifying their intrinsic traffic characteristics, and investigating the usability of the information that can be logged from their transactions. We leverage a 24-hours dataset collected from a webproxy operated by a European mobile carrier with more than 10M subscribers. Our quantification of this gap suggests that its importance is strictly related to the target analysis.

1 Introduction

Mobile operators are facing an explosion of demand for data access services. Recent estimates forecast an eight-fold increase of demand between 2015 and 2020, a rate three times higher than for fixed access networks [15]. This explosion is driven both by the constant evolution of the mobile apps and Internet services ecosystem, and the roll out of 4G technologies.

In this dynamic and demanding scenario, traffic monitoring is paramount. Accurate understanding of both user behavior and service quality are key to drive network investments. To study data services, mobile operators rely on *Usage Data Records (UDRs)* and *HTTP-logs*. UDRs aggregate users data activity over periods of time lasting from minutes up to multiple hours. They are collected for billing purposes and do not detail the apps/services used [8,9].

Differently from UDRs, HTTP-logs contain detailed information on individual HTTP transactions. They are usually collected by *webproxies*, middle-boxes that aim at optimizing HTTP delivery through in-network caching and content modification (e.g., image resolution reduction) [4,13]. HTTP-logs have been extensively used both by operators and academia to characterize mobile network traffic [2,3,6,11,12,16].

© Springer International Publishing AG 2017
M.A. Kaafar et al. (Eds.): PAM 2017, LNCS 10176, pp. 217–228, 2017.
DOI: 10.1007/978-3-319-54328-4_16

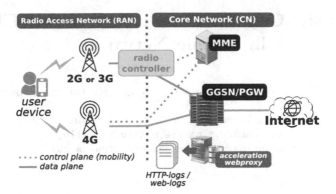

Fig. 1. Sketch of a mobile network architecture where a web acceleration proxy is deployed.

With the rise of HTTPS, this scenario is however rapidly changing. For instance, between June 2015 and June 2016,[1] Google reported a +13% increase of requests served over HTTPS. Sandvine also reports that more than 60% of mobile traffic worldwide is currently encrypted [10]. While this calls for instrumenting webproxies to also log HTTPS transactions, it is unclear whether the additional cost is justified. In fact, HTTPS exposes little information about the service and content users access. In addition, network performance indexes (e.g., throughput and latency) can only be computed on the whole TLS connection and not on individual transactions, as commonly done for HTTP.

In this work we present the first comparative study between HTTP and HTTPS traffic for mobile networks. Our goal is to quantify the "gap" between HTTP and HTTPS both in term of their macroscopic qualities and of their accuracy when singularly used to perform common analysis such as data consumption, user mobility, etc. The input of our study is a unique dataset spanning HTTP and HTTPS traffic, radio-layer information, and device information from a 10M-subscriber European mobile operator.

Our quantification of this gap suggests that its importance is strictly related to the target analysis. When focusing on volume, neither HTTP nor HTTPS alone are enough to characterize users activity. This is because of a combination of factors including type of device and usage pattern across time. Conversely, both traffic types are capable to capture human-driven behaviors like user mobility, which in turn drives analysis like traffic consumption in space and cell towers utilization.

2   Background

This section overviews the classic mobile network architecture while emphasizing the role of webproxies in it (Fig. 1). The Radio Access Network (RAN), commonly called "last mile", is composed of thousands of elements such as cell

---

[1] https://www.google.com/transparencyreport/https/?hl=en.

sectors, towers, and radio controllers. The Core Network (CN) bridges the RAN with the Internet by mean of packet data gateways (GGSN and PGW) which allow mobile users to access data services. The Mobility Management Entity (MME) servers handle *network events* related to handovers, paging, and access control to radio channels, each carrying the device id and the sector from which the event was triggered. The MME is the *control plane* of a mobile network.

Figure 1 also shows an *acceleration webproxy*; this is a transparent (or explicit) HTTP proxy that operators deploy to speed up content delivery at the RAN while reducing traffic volume at the CN. Common webproxy services are: (i) content caching, (ii) content compression (e.g., reducing image size/resolution or video format re-encoding), and (iii) dynamic traffic policies enforcement (e.g., bandwidth throttling for users that reach their monthly data cap, protection from malware and third party tracking services). Webproxies log each HTTP transaction into HTTP-logs, but some vendors provide monitoring solutions that also log the remaining TCP activity [10]. We call such "extended" logs *web-logs* .

3   Dataset

We consider web-logs collected for 24 consecutive hours (April 27th, 2016) by the acceleration webproxy of a major European mobile operator serving more than 10M subscribers. The considered webproxy usually logs HTTP traffic only, but it can be sporadically instrumented to report on other TCP traffic like HTTPS.

We call *transaction* an entry in the web-logs. Each transaction contains at least the following fields: IPs/ports tuple (source and destination), timestamp, duration, user-id, and bytes delivered. Additional fields can be provided based on the transaction type. Specifically, an "HTTP transaction" corresponds to an HTTP request/response exchange for which the webproxy further logs HTTP meta-data such as hostname, URL, user-agent, and content-type. User privacy is guaranteed by hashing sensible information like user-id, requested URL, etc. For the remainder of the traffic, a transaction corresponds to a TCP connection. If the `ClientHello` message from a TLS handshake is detected, the webproxy also logs the Service Name Identification (SNI), when provided.

We combine the webproxy dataset with two additional data sources.

Radio-layers enrichment: We process MME network events (see Sect. 2) to create *mobility radio-layers, i.e.,* per user timelines detailing to which sectors each user's device connects to over time. It follows that given the tuple (user-id, timestamp, duration) of a web-log transaction we can identify the list of sectors the transaction relates to. This enables us to investigate how content is consumed by users while moving across the network (see Sect. 5) at a finer granularity with respect to the literature [12,16].

TAC enrichment: The Type Allocation Code (TAC) database is an internal resource of the considered operator, and it is based on the GSMA TAC database,[2]

---

[2] https://imeidb.gsma.com/imei/login.jsp.

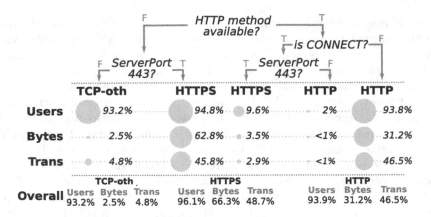

Fig. 2. Dataset overview.

i.e., the standardized allocation of TAC among vendors.[3] The TAC database is a static table mapping vendor and device model to a user-id. This mapping is more robust than the classic approach based on HTTP user-agent string, and it works also in presence of HTTPS.

3.1   Dataset Curation

Following the logic described in Fig. 2, we split web-log transactions into three classes: HTTP, HTTPS, and TCP-oth (*i.e.*, the TCP traffic that is neither HTTP nor HTTPS). Since the webproxy does not explicitly label web-log entries originated by TLS traffic, we identify HTTPS based on the destination port (443). The webproxy logs the HTTP METHOD for each HTTP transaction which eases the identification of HTTP traffic. In presence of a CONNECT, *i.e.*, for clients explicitly connecting through a proxy, we still use the destination port to distinguish between HTTP and HTTPS.

The middle of Fig. 2 reports the percentage of users, bytes, and transactions of each classification tree leaf, while aggregated statistics are reported at the bottom. Overall, HTTPS dominates the volume of bytes (66.3%) but we also find a non negligible 2.5% of TCP-oth volume. When we focus on transactions, we notice that they are equally distributed between HTTPS (48.7%) and HTTP (46.5%), which is counter-intuitive due to the bytes difference observed above. This is due to the presence of *persistent connections* that go undetected in HTTPS. We further analyze this issue in the following.

Content consumed in mobile networks is usually "small", e.g., the average object size is in the order of tens of kB [5,16]. To reduce the TCP handshake overhead, HTTP 1.1 introduced the concept of persistent connections which allow devices to use a single TCP connection to send multiple requests. Such technique is common to both HTTP and HTTPS, but it is a

---

[3] The TAC is part of the IMEI, *i.e.*, the unique identifier of a mobile device.

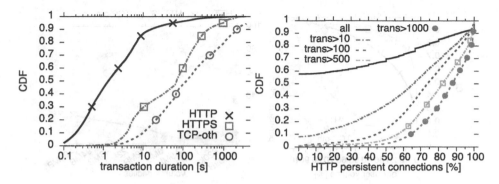

Fig. 3. Impact of persistent connections: transaction duration (left) and percentage of HTTP persistent connections (right).

hassle only when monitoring HTTPS. In fact, encryption does not allow to identify request/response pairs over the same TLS connection, resulting in a coarser view over HTTPS traffic if compared to HTTP.

To visualize the impact of the latter limitation, Fig. 3 (left) shows the Cumulative Distribution Function (CDF) of the transaction duration for HTTP, HTTPS, and TCP-oth. If on the one hand the three traffic classes are subject to different dynamics due to how different services use them, on the other hand such huge differences hint to the presence of persistent connections.

We further corroborate on this by counting the percentage of TCP connections having more than one HTTP transaction for each user. Figure 3 (right) shows the CDF of the fraction of persistent HTTP connections during one peek hour (results hold for different hours). The figure shows that the usage of persistent connections is indeed extremely common and proportional to user activity, e.g., 90% of the very active users (trans > 1,000 in the plot) have more than 65% of their HTTP connections being persistent.

To the best of our knowledge, no previous study has quantified the adoption of persistent connections in the wild. Our results indicate that their high popularity can introduce substantial errors when comparing HTTP with HTTPS traffic. Accordingly, to enable a meaningful comparison among the considered traffic classes, we have opted for pre-processing HTTP traffic to aggregate different transactions belonging to the same individual TCP connections.

4   Overall Volumes

We start our analysis with a top-down characterization of how traffic volume (bytes) is split between traffic types.

Daily aggregate breakdown: Figure 4 (left) shows the CDF of the percentage of HTTP, HTTPS, and TCP-oth volume, per user. As expected, HTTPS is the dominant traffic type: 50% of users have more than 77.6% of their volume carried

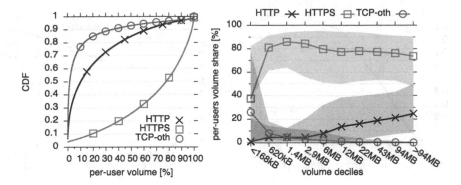

Fig. 4. Comparing traffic volume: on the left, overall percentage of per user HTTP, HTTPS, and TCP-oth; on the right, further breakdown with respect to absolute consumption (lines reflect the 50th percentile of each volume decile, while shaded areas indicate 25th–75th).

over encrypted connections. The figure also shows that TCP-oth volume is far from being negligible: 5.6% of users have more than 70% of TCP-oth traffic.

We further dig into the TCP-oth traffic using the destination port to classify the specific service being used. We find that 84% of volume is associated to email (e.g., 995/IMAP-SSL, 993/POP3-SSL, 110/POP3) and push notification services (5223 for Apple, 5228 for Android). We also find a few thousands users with "suspicious" behaviors: they contact 227 k IP addresses using 49 k ports (in a peak hour) and do not transfer any data on the opened TCP connection. For these 227 k IP addresses, we further retrieve the Autonomous System Number (ASN) using Team Cymru[4] and its classification using PeeringDB[5] and CAIDA AS ranking [1]. Such analysis reveals that 97% of these IPs belong to fixed and mobile ISPs, and are not linked to classic services. We conjecture the presence of malware, of which we also find evidences,[6] or some form of P2P communication.

We further divide users into ten groups based on the deciles of the distribution of their volume consumption. For each group we then extract the 25th, 50th, and 75th percentiles of the share of HTTP, HTTPS, and TCP-oth. Figure 4 (right) reports the results (the x-axis details the used deciles). Beside noticing that HTTPS dominates indistinctly within each bin, we observe that TCP-oth shares are inversely proportional to the overall volume consumed, while the opposite is true for HTTP. Results reported in Fig. 4 hold also when considering the number of transactions (we avoid reporting them for brevity). Those differences are possibly due to the combination of apps/services used, but to the best of our knowledge, there are not robust techniques available to classify mobile traffic. Hence we leave a detailed characterization for the future.

---

[4] http://www.team-cymru.org/IP-ASN-mapping.html#dns.

[5] www.peeringdb.com.

[6] http://bit.ly/1Uv9hNF.

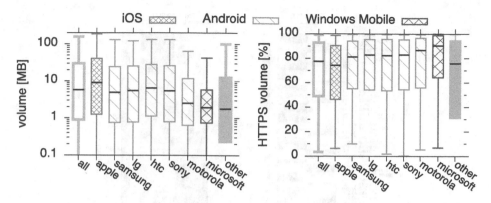

Fig. 5. Comparing OS per-device volume: daily aggregate (left) and related percentage of HTTPS (right).

Device type: We here investigate the relationship between device type and consumed volume. Figure 5 (left) shows the boxplots (5th, 25th, 50th, 75th, 95th percentiles) of the users absolute volume consumption per vendor. Notice the y-axis in logscale. For the sake of visibility, we only report on vendors with at least 1% of users and we group the remaining vendors as "other". The figure shows that Apple devices consume 3.6× and 1.6× (median values) more traffic than Microsoft and Android devices, respectively. If we focus on the fraction of HTTPS traffic (Fig. 4, right), we notice that the share of HTTPS is inversely proportional to the absolute volume, e.g., 50% of the Microsoft devices only consume about 2 MB, out of which 90% is HTTPS.

We further investigate the HTTPS traffic generated by Microsoft devices and find that, on average, 60% of their traffic is addressed to Windows services like *.bing.* and *.live.*. A similar result holds for Motorola devices as well (having Google instead of Microsoft services). This suggests that most of this HTTPS traffic consists of "background noise", *i.e.*, communications generated by the operating system and apps but not strictly triggered by users activity. However, corroborating this belief with numbers is hard based on the available data.

Second Level Domain: Finally, we process the transaction hostnames to understand if they offer visibility on the HTTPS services. Recall that for HTTPS the hostname corresponds to the SNI communicated in the TLS handshake.

From each hostname, we remove the Top Level Domain (TLD) using the Mozilla Public Suffix list [7]. Then, for each Second Level Domain (SLD) found we compute the total number of bytes, and the associated share of HTTP and HTTPS. Overall, we find 1.6M SLDs, out of which 92% and 15% are used in HTTP and HTTPS transactions respectively. The heatmaps in Fig. 6 show the top-50 (left) and top-1000 (right) SLDs which account for 79.5% and 93.8% of volume in the whole day. SLDs mostly coincide with CDN providers; however, in some cases they accurately identify actual services (e.g., *streaming* – googlevideo, spotify; *social network* – facebook, instagram, twitter, snapchat, whatsapp; *gaming* – applifier, etc.).

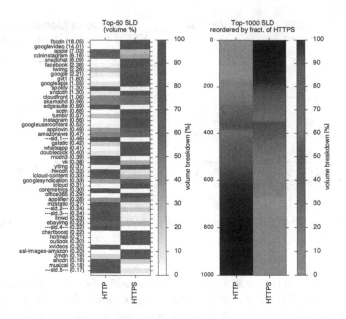

Fig. 6. Top Second Level Domain (SLD) volume breakdown.

Takeaways: We observed and quantified a "traffic gap" between HTTP and HTTPS. This gap originates from the different mix of services behind each protocol as well as OS (and device vendors). It follows that focusing on either one of the two protocols only for traffic-based analysis introduces a substantial bias not only on the overall volume, but also to capture device type diversity, and accessed services. A proper characterization of these aspects is key for mobile operators.

5   Spatial and Temporal Analysis

Mobile operators are extremely interested in understanding *where/how/when* their customers consume data when moving across the network. This is crucial to drive investments (e.g., where to deploy/upgrade towers) and to support novel services such as geofencing and SON (Self Organizing Networks). In the literature, Call Data Records (CDRs) have been largely exploited to study human mobility [14]. However, a recent study [9] shows that UDRs (see Sect. 1) offer a richer vision on user mobility. We argue that web-logs enable an even finer grained spatial-temporal analysis than UDRs. This is because UDRs aggregate activities in (large) time windows, and associate them with coarse spatial information. Unfortunately, our dataset does not include UDRs and we thus cannot further quantify this intuition.

We here explore to which extent HTTP traffic is representative of how users consume content across time and space when compared with HTTPS. As done in the literature [9], we approximate a user location with the position of the

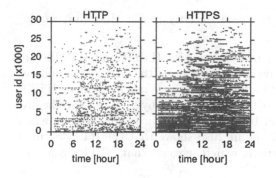

Fig. 7. HTTP and HTTPS activity over time (30 k random users).

Fig. 8. Number of towers used (all users).

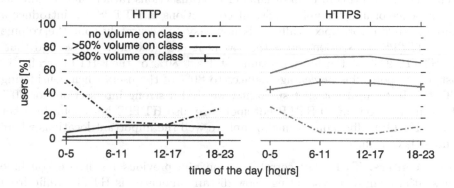

Fig. 9. Percentage of users consuming HTTP, HTTPS, and TCP-oth traffic with respect to time of the day.

cell *towers* she is connected to. Note also that HTTP(S) transactions can be associated to different towers during their lifetime due to user mobility and/or load balancing at the radio layer. Our enrichment process (see Sect. 3) allows to identify all the towers associated to a transaction.

Traffic discontinuity: For each user we group HTTP and HTTPS transactions in 10 min bins. Each bin has a binary value depending if at least 1 transaction has been found or not. Figure 7 shows the obtained bitmaps for 30,000 random users (results hold for other users). Notice how HTTP traffic (left plot) is more "discontinued" than HTTPS (right plot), *i.e.*, HTTP activity is more occasional and sparse across the day.

Figure 9 shows a more detailed quantification of traffic variation across the day. We partition the day in 6 h bins starting from midnight. Within each bin, we compute the percentage of users having 0%, >50%, or >80% of volume over HTTP(S). Notice how HTTP better captures users activity during daily hours; instead, at night time (00:00–05:00) 50% of the users do not generate any HTTP traffic. As also observed for the device analysis (see Sect. 4), this suggests that HTTP traffic better captures real user activity rather than (automatic) background services.

Cell tower perspective: We here investigate how HTTP and HTTPS are consumed from a cell tower perspective. Figure 8 reports the CDF of the number of distinct towers each device connect to during the day. When focusing on HTTP traffic only, we underestimate the set of towers contacted by a device. Specifically, only 6% of devices contact more than 10 towers, while such value doubles when focusing on HTTPS traffic only. The figure also shows that the HTTPS curve matches quite well the "all traffic" curve, which suggests that HTTPS is a very good "proxy" of the overall activity.

Next, we quantify how traffic is distributed among towers with the goal to identify per user "hot spots", *i.e.*, which towers carry most of the traffic for each user. We do this in term of number of transactions rather than volume as the presence of undetectable persistent connections in HTTPS can introduce a non-negligible error. Specifically, it is not easy to accurately split the volume of an HTTPS transaction across the towers it uses (see Sect. 3). We find that, for HTTP, 93% of the users consume at least 80% of their HTTP traffic in just 5 hot spots; this percentage reduces to 80% of the users when considering HTTPS. In term of hot spot similarity, we find a strong intersection: for 70% of the users, 7 out of 10 HTTP hot spots are also HTTPS hot spots. In other words, HTTP traffic alone seems to capture well the important locations where content is consumed.

Mass centers: To further corroborate on the previous result, we conclude our spatial analysis investigating "how distant in space" is HTTP traffic from HTTPS, and vice-versa. For each user, we compute a mass center [9] representing where HTTP, HTTPS, and the whole traffic is consumed. A mass center is computed as the average of towers coordinates weighted by their number of transactions. Let us call those points *mass-HTTP*, *mass-HTTPS*, and *mass-ALL* respectively. We then compute the Euclidean distance between (*mass-ALL*, *mass-HTTP*) and (*mass-ALL*, *mass-HTTPS*) for each user. Figure 10 (left) shows the CDF of the obtained distances. Results show that HTTP content tends to be consumed further away than the majority of the traffic. This result is independent from users activity, e.g., the plot obtained for very active HTTP users (trans > 1,000) is not significantly different from the plot obtained for the whole set of users.

To further quantify the "spatial gap" between HTTP and HTTPS, we normalize the euclidean distances with respect to the user *radius of gyration* computed considering the whole traffic activity. The gyration radius is a well established metric to characterize user mobility [9,14]; it captures the average distance between a point (the mass center) and another set of points (all towers locations). For each user, we normalize the Euclidean distance between (*mass-ALL*, *mass-HTTP*) and (*mass-ALL*, *mass-HTTPS*) with the gyration obtained considering the whole traffic. Figure 10 reports the CDFs of the normalized Euclidean distances. The figure shows that HTTPS captures very well user mobility, e.g., 97% of users have a normalized Euclidean distance <0.5. The mobility observed from

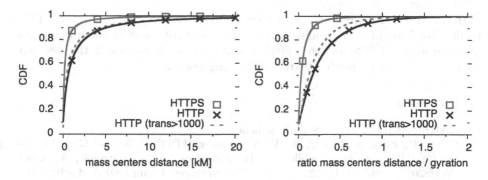

Fig. 10. Euclidean distance between mass centers (left) and normalized distance with respect to overall gyration (right).

HTTP is very close to the overall one, and the normalized Euclidean distance tends to decrease for heavy HTTP users.

We conjecture that the latter result derives from the human component of the mobility problem. Users do not explicitly choose to use HTTP or HTTPS; the presence of a traffic type is an "artifact" of the device and applications used. However, a user chooses the location to visit and, as far as some traffic is consumed, this is enough to characterize her mobility pattern.

Takeaways: The "time gap" between HTTP and HTTPS is substantial, with each protocol being respectively the most popular one at different points in time. Conversely, the "spatial gap" between HTTP and HTTPS is limited and both protocol are quite good in approximating user mobility.

6 Conclusions

In this work we presented the first comparative study between HTTP and HTTPS traffic for mobile networks. The input of our study was a unique dataset including HTTP and HTTPS traffic, radio-layer information, and device information from a 10M-subscriber European mobile operator. Our analysis highlighted three different "gaps" between HTTP and HTTPS. First, a "traffic gap" related to how different services and OS/vendors use HTTP and HTTPS. Second, a "time gap" due to protocols being more used at different time of the day. Third a surprisingly small "spatial gap", probably motivated by the human component of mobility.

From an operator perspective, logging non-HTTP traffic implies additional investments. Based on the available dataset, we estimate that for a mid/large mobile operator such logging requires few additional TB of storage each day. This is an affordable investment compared to the potential need to upgrade the processing cluster along with the monitoring solution. Similarly, the extensive adoption of persistent connections represent a hassle for monitoring network metrics that accurately reflect service performance. Overall, we argue that state of the art monitoring solutions are not yet ready to properly characterize HTTPS traffic. We hope that the results provided in this work quantify the importance of monitoring HTTPS, and they further stimulate the discussion in the research community towards creating better monitoring systems.

References

1. CAIDA: As rank. http://as-rank.caida.org
2. Casas, P., Fiadino, P., Bär, A.: Understanding HTTP traffic and CDN behavior from the eyes of a mobile ISP. In: Faloutsos, M., Kuzmanovic, A. (eds.) PAM 2014. LNCS, vol. 8362, pp. 268–271. Springer, Cham (2014). doi:10.1007/978-3-319-04918-2_28
3. Erman, J., Ramakrishnan, K.: Understanding the super-sized traffic of the super bowl. In: Proceedings of the ACM Internet Measurement Conference (IMC), October 2013
4. Erman, J.E., Gerber, A., Hajiaghayi, M., Pei, D.: To cache or not to cache: The 3G case. IEEE Internet Comput. 15(2), 27–34 (2011)
5. Falaki, H., Lymberopoulos, D., Mahajan, R., Kandula, S., Estrin, D.: A first look at traffic on smartphones. In: Proceedings of the ACM Internet Measurement Conference (IMC), November 2010
6. Keralapura, R., Nucci, A., Zhang, Z.L., Gao, L.: Profiling users in a 3G network using hourglass co-clustering. In: Proceedings of the ACM MobiCom, September 2010
7. Mozilla: Public suffix list. http://publicsuffix.org/
8. Mucelli, E., Oliveira, R., Carneiro, A.V., Naveen, K.P., Sarraute, C.: Measurement-driven mobile data traffic modeling in a large metropolitan area. In: Proceedings of the IEEE Conference on Pervasive Computing and Communications (PerCom), St. Luis, March 2015
9. Ranjan, G., Zang, H., Zhang, Z.L., Bolot, J.: Are call detail records biased for sampling human mobility? ACM SIGCOMM Mob. Comput. Commun. Rev. 16(3), 33–44 (2012)
10. Sandvine, Global Internet Phenomena: Spotlight: encrypted internet traffic. https://www.sandvine.com/trends/encryption.html
11. Shafiq, M.Z., Ji, L., Liu, A.X., Pang, J., Venkataraman, S., Wang, J.: A first look at cellular network performance during crowded events. In: Proceedings of the ACM SIGMETRICS, June 2013
12. Trestian, I., Ranjan, S., Kuzmanovic, A., Nucci, A.: Measuring serendipity: connecting people, locations and interests in a mobile 3G network. In: Proceedings of the ACM Internet Measurement Conference (IMC), November 2009
13. Vallina-Rodriguez, N., Sundaresan, S., Kreibich, C., Weaver, N., Paxson, V.: Beyond the radio: illuminating the higher layers of mobile networks. In: Proceedings of the ACM MobiSys, November 2015
14. Blondel, V.D., Adeline Decuyper, G.K.: A survey of results on mobile phone datasets analysis. CoRR arXiv arXiv:1502.03406 (2015)
15. Vni, C.: The Zettabyte Era: Trends and analysis. http://www.cisco.com/c/en/us/solutions/collateral/service-provider/visual-networking-index-vni/vni-hyperconnectivity-wp.html
16. Xu, Q., Erman, J., Gerber, A., Mao, Z., Pang, J., Venkataraman, S.: Identifying diverse usage behaviors of smartphone apps. In: Proceedings of the ACM Internet Measurement Conference (IMC), November 2011

Using Loops Observed in Traceroute
to Infer the Ability to Spoof

Qasim Lone[1(✉)], Matthew Luckie[2], Maciej Korczyński[1], and Michel van Eeten[1]

[1] Delft University of Technology, Delft, The Netherlands
{Q.B.Lone,Maciej.Korczynski,M.J.G.vanEeten}@tudelft.nl
[2] University of Waikato, Hamilton, New Zealand
mjl@wand.net.nz

Abstract. Despite source IP address spoofing being a known vulnerability for at least 25 years, and despite many efforts to shed light on the problem, spoofing remains a popular attack method for redirection, amplification, and anonymity. To defeat these attacks requires operators to ensure their networks filter packets with spoofed source IP addresses, known as source address validation (SAV), best deployed at the edge of the network where traffic originates. In this paper, we present a new method using routing loops appearing in traceroute data to infer inadequate SAV at the transit provider edge, where a provider does not filter traffic that should not have come from the customer. Our method does not require a vantage point within the customer network. We present and validate an algorithm that identifies at Internet scale which loops imply a lack of ingress filtering by providers. We found 703 provider ASes that do not implement ingress filtering on at least one of their links for 1,780 customer ASes. Most of these observations are unique compared to the existing methods of the Spoofer and Open Resolver projects. By increasing the visibility of the networks that allow spoofing, we aim to strengthen the incentives for the adoption of SAV.

1 Introduction

Despite source IP address spoofing being a known vulnerability for at least 25 years [6], and despite many efforts to shed light on the problem (e.g. [7–9]), spoofing remains a viable attack method for redirection, amplification, and anonymity, as evidenced in February 2014 during a 400 Gbps DDoS attack against Cloudfare [19]. That particular attack used an amplification vector in some implementations of NTP [19]; a previous attack against Spamhaus [10] in March 2013 achieved 300+ Gbps using an amplification vector in DNS. While some application-layer patches can mitigate these attacks [20], attackers continuously search for new vectors.

Defeating amplification attacks, and other threats based on IP spoofing, requires providers to filter incoming packets with spoofed source IP addresses [11] – in other words, to implement BCP 38, a Best Current Practice also known as source address validation (SAV). SAV suffers from misaligned incentives: a network that adopts SAV incurs the cost of deployment, while the security benefits

© Springer International Publishing AG 2017
M.A. Kaafar et al. (Eds.): PAM 2017, LNCS 10176, pp. 229–241, 2017.
DOI: 10.1007/978-3-319-54328-4_17

diffuse to all other networks. That being said, SAV is a widely supported norm in the community. Increasing the visibility of which networks have or have not adopted SAV reduces the incentive problem by leveraging reputation effects and the pressure of other providers and stakeholders. These factors put a premium on our ability to measure SAV adoption.

In this paper, we report on the efficacy of a new measurement technique that is based on an idea of Jared Mauch. It allows an external observer to use traceroute to infer the absence of filtering by a provider AS at a provider-customer interconnect. This study makes the following five contributions: (1) We show that it is generally feasible for providers to deploy static ingress ACLs, as their customers rarely change address space. (2) We describe a scalable algorithm for accurately inferring the absence of ingress filtering from specific patterns in traceroute data. (3) We validate the algorithm's correctness using ground truth from 7 network operators. (4) We demonstrate the utility of the algorithm by analyzing Internet-scale inferences we made. (5) We build a public website showing the provider-customer edges that we inferred to imply the absence of filtering, combined with actionable data that operators can use to deploy filtering.

2   Background on Ingress Filtering

The canonical documents describing the use of ingress filtering methods for SAV are RFCs 2827 [11] and 3704 [5], known in the network operations and research communities as BCPs 38 and 84. BCP 38 describes the basic idea: the source address of packets should be checked at the periphery of the Internet against a set of permitted addresses. For an access network, this check could be at the point of interconnection with a single customer; for an enterprise, this could be on their edge routers to their neighbors; and for a transit provider, this could be on the provider-edge router where a customer connects. For single-homed customers, a transit provider can discard packets that have a source address outside the set of prefixes the customer announces to the transit provider, using Strict or Feasible Reverse Path Forwarding (RPF). A router using Strict RPF will drop a packet if it arrived on a different interface than the router would choose when forwarding a packet to the packet's source address; a router using Feasible RPF will consider all paths it could use to reach the source address, not just the best path.

BCP 84 discusses challenges in deploying ingress filtering on multi-homed networks. Both Strict and Feasible RPF are not always feasible if a customer is multi-homed and does not announce all of its prefixes to each neighbor router, as it might do for traffic engineering purposes. Instead, an operator might define a set of prefixes covering source addresses in packets the router will forward, known as an Ingress Access List, or Ingress ACL. BCP 84 states that while ingress ACLs require manual maintenance if a neighbor acquires additional address space, they are "the most bulletproof solution when done properly", and the "best fit ... when the configuration is not too dynamic, .. if the number of used prefixes is low."

3 Related Work

Testing a network's SAV compliance requires a measurement vantage point inside (or adjacent to) the network, because the origin network of arbitrary spoofed packets cannot be determined [5]. The approach of the Spoofer project [7] is to allow volunteers to test their network's SAV compliance with a custom client-server system, where the client sends spoofed packets in coordination with the server, and the server infers that the client can spoof if the server receives these spoofed packets. However, the Spoofer project requires volunteer support to run the client to obtain a view from a given network. In May 2016, CAIDA released an updated client [1] that operates in the background, automatically testing attached networks once per week, and whenever the system attaches to a network it has not tested in the previous week. The number of prefixes tested per month has increased from ≈400 in May 2016 to ≈6000 in December 2016 [1].

Jared Mauch deployed the first technique to infer if a network had inadequate SAV without requiring a custom client-server system. As a product of the Open Resolver Project [3], he observed DNS resolvers embedded in home routers forwarding DNS queries from his system with IP_X to other resolvers, without rewriting the source IP address of the packet. These other resolvers returned the subsequent answer directly to IP_X, rather than to the DNS resolver in the home router as they should have.

We emphasize that these methods are complementary, and that no one technique is able to test deployment of SAV for all networks.

4 Motivation of Ingress ACLs

As described in Sect. 2, the best place to deploy filtering is at the edge. However, not all edge networks have the technical ability or motivation to filter their own traffic. A transit provider, however, is often managed by skilled network operators who may already deploy defenses to prevent their customers from announcing inappropriate routes. The provider-customer interconnect for an edge network represents the other straightforward place to deploy ingress filtering.

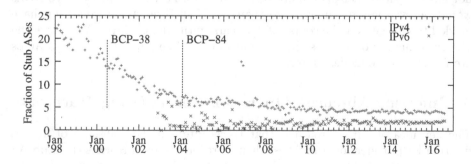

Fig. 1. Fraction of ASes whose prefix announcements changed month-to-month.

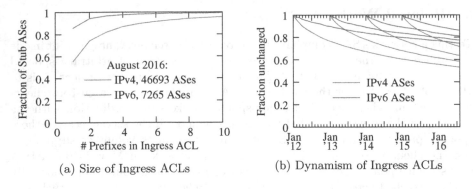

(a) Size of Ingress ACLs   (b) Dynamism of Ingress ACLs

Fig. 2. Size and dynamism of ACLs to filter traffic from stub ASes.

Figure 1 quantifies the dynamism of address space announced by stub ASes over time. Using BGP data collected by Routeviews and RIPE RIS with the method described in Sect. 5.1, we aggregated the prefixes each stub AS originated in BGP into the minimum prefix set, and examined month-to-month changes in the set. Perhaps a consequence of IPv4 address exhaustion, we see a trend toward stable announcement patterns. This trend may improve the practicality of static ingress ACLs: in May 2000, ≈15% of stub ASes would have required deployment of a different IPv4 ingress ACL month-to-month, but in 2015, less than 5% of ASes would have required the same.

As BCP 84 states that because ingress ACLs require manual maintenance they are best suited "when the configuration is not too dynamic" and "if the number of used prefixes is low", Fig. 2 examines the size and dynamism of ingress ACLs required for stub ASes in August 2016. Figure 2a shows that 88.9% of stub ASes would require an IPv4 ACL of no more than 4 prefixes, and 85.6% of stub ASes would require an IPv6 ACL of a single prefix. Figure 2b shows the dynamism of these ACLs over time, based on ACLs that could have been defined for all stub ASes in January 2012, 2013, 2014, and 2015. For stub ASes for these times, at least 77.4% of IPv4 ACLs would not have had to change over the course of one year; for those defined in January 2012, 54.4% of the inferred ACLs would not have required change even up to August 2016. Further, required IPv6 ACLs would be even less dynamic: more than 74.6% of IPv6 ACLs would not have needed to change over the course of 4.5 years until August 2016. We believe the observed number of prefixes and dynamism over time imply that ingress ACLs are feasible in the modern Internet.

5   Inferring Absence of Ingress Filtering Using Traceroute

The key idea of our approach is that traceroute can show absence of ingress filtering by providers of stub ASes when a traceroute path reaches the stub AS and then exits out of the stub, as the traceroute packets contain a source address belonging to the vantage point (VP) launching the traceroute. If the provider's border router is performing SAV, it should filter the traceroute packet when it arrives from the stub AS, as the packet has a source address not belonging to the stub AS. If the provider's router does not perform SAV, it will forward the packet, and the traceroute will show an apparent IP-level forwarding loop as the provider's router returns subsequent packets to the stub AS.

Xia *et al.* found that 50% of persistent loops were caused by a border router missing a "pull-up route" covering address space not internally routed by the customer [21]. However, a forwarding loop does not imply absence of SAV at the edge: a loop resulting from a transient misconfiguration or routing update can occur anywhere in the network. The key challenge in this work is inferring the provider-customer boundary in traceroute [16,18]. In this paper, we superimpose millions of traceroutes towards random IP addresses in /24 prefixes to build a topology graph, and use a small set of heuristics to infer provider-customer edges for stub ASes in the graph. Sect. 5.1 describes the Internet topology datasets that we used, and Sect. 5.3 describes the algorithm we used to filter the loops that imply the absence of ingress filtering by the provider – in other words, the lack of compliance with BCP 38.

5.1 Input Data

CAIDA IPv4 routed /24 topology datasets: We used CAIDA's ongoing traceroute measurements towards every routed /24 prefix in the Internet. CAIDA's probing of all routed /24s is especially useful here, as the goal is to find unrouted space that can result in a forwarding loop. CAIDA's traceroute data is collected with scamper [15] using Paris traceroute which avoids spurious loops by keeping the ICMP checksum value the same for any given traceroute [4]. As of August 2016, CAIDA probes every routed /24 using 138 Vantage Points (VPs) organized into three teams; each team probes the address space independently. Each team takes roughly 1.5 days to probe every routed /24.

CAIDA IPv4 AS relationships: We used CAIDA's ongoing BGP-based AS relationship inferences [17] to identify customer-provider interconnections in traceroute paths. The relationship files were inferred by CAIDA using public BGP data collected by Routeviews and RIPE RIS, using RIB files recorded on the 1–5 of each month. We also used the same BGP data to identify the origin AS announcing each prefix measured with traceroute.

CAIDA Sibling Inferences: We used CAIDA's ongoing WHOIS-based AS-to-organization inference file [13] to identify ASes that belong to the same underlying organization (are siblings). The sibling files were inferred by CAIDA using textual analysis on WHOIS databases obtained from Regional Internet Registries (RIRs) at 3-month intervals. We used sibling inferences to avoid mis-classifying a loop that occurs within a single organization using multiple ASes as one that occurs between distinct provider and customer ASes.

5.2   Construction of Topology

Our first goal is to correctly identify the provider-customer boundaries towards stub ASes with high precision. Because the customer usually uses address space provided by the provider to number their interface on their router involved in the interconnection, the customer-edge router usually appears in traceroute using an IP address routed by the provider. Therefore, one of our goals is to accurately identify customer routers using provider address space without incorrectly inferring that a provider's backbone router belongs to a customer.

We assemble all traceroutes collected for a single cycle by a single team that do not contain loops, and label each interface with (1) the origin AS of the longest matching prefix for the interface address, and (2) the set of destination ASes the interface address is in the path towards. If an address is in the path towards multiple ASes, the address could not be configured on a customer router of a stub AS.

5.3   Algorithm to Infer Absence of Ingress Filtering from Loops

Our algorithm considers two different ways a traceroute path may enter a stub AS and exit through a provider AS: (1) a simple point-to-point loop between a single provider-edge router and a single customer-edge router, (2) a loop from a customer-edge router that exits using a different provider.

Simple point-to-point loops: Figure 3 illustrates the first case, where R_3 is a customer-edge router belonging to AS B configured with a default route via R_2. If the operator of B announces address space in BGP but does not have an internal route for a portion of that address space, and does not have a "pull-up route" covering the unused portion on R_3, then R_3 forwards the packet back to R_2 using the default route [21]. R_2 will then forward the packet back to R_3,

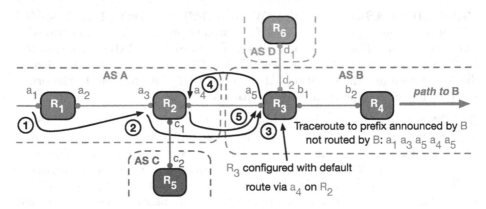

Fig. 3. A simple loop between AS A and its customer B implying absence of filtering by A at R_2. R_2 should discard packet 4 because it arrives with a source address outside of B's network, rather than send it back to B (5).

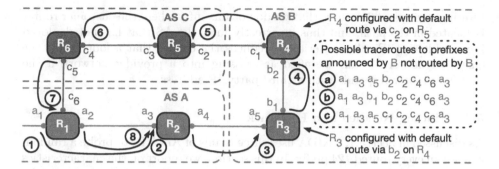

Fig. 4. A two-provider loop between ASes A and C and their customer B implying absence of filtering by C at R_5. R_5 should discard packet 5 because it arrives with a source address outside of B, rather than forward the packet to R_6.

the loop sequence will likely be a_5 (customer-edge router), a_4 (provider-edge router), and a_5 (customer-edge router), with a_4 and a_5 assigned from the same IPv4 /30 or /31 prefix the routers use to form the point-to-point link. Therefore, our criteria are: (1) that the addresses in the loop are assigned from a single /30 or /31 prefix, (2) that the AS originating the longest matching prefix is an inferred provider of the stub AS and not a sibling of the stub AS, (3) that the assumed customer router only appears in traceroute paths towards the stub AS, (4) that there is at least one other address originated by the provider in the traceroute path towards the stub. Criteria #3 avoids incorrectly inferring a provider-operated router as a customer-edge router when a loop occurs before the stub AS (e.g. a_1 a_3 a_2 a_3) as a_3 appears in traceroute paths towards both B and C. Criteria #4 avoids incorrectly inferring which router in a traceroute path is the customer-edge router when the customer-edge router is multi-homed and the traceroute path enters via a second provider AS D (e.g., d_2 a_4 a_5 a_4).

Two-provider loops: Figure 4 illustrates the second case, where R_3 and R_4 are customer-edge routers belonging to AS B, with default routes configured on R_3 and R_4. The underlying routing configuration issues are the same as a point-to-point loop, except the default route is via a different AS than the AS the traceroute entered the network. Figure 4 shows the traceroute visiting two routers operated by AS B; however, it is possible that the traceroute will never contain an IP address mapped to B, depending on how many routers in B the traceroute visits, and how the routers respond to traceroute probes. Therefore, our criteria are: (1) that the assumed customer router where the traceroute exits appears only in paths towards the stub AS, (2) that both the ingress and egress AS in the traceroute path are inferred providers of the stub AS and not a sibling of the stub AS, (3) that there is no unresponsive traceroute hop in the traceroute path where a customer router could be located, (4) that at least two consecutive IP addresses mapped to the same egress AS appear in the loop. Criteria #2 does not require different provider ASes: if the stub AS is multi-homed to the same provider with different routers, our method will still infer an absence of filtering. Criteria #3 ensures that we do not mis-infer where the customer router is located in the path, and thus incorrectly infer the AS that has not deployed ingress filtering. Finally, criteria #4 reduces the chance that a loop inside the customer network is mis-classified as crossing into a provider network if the customer router responds with a third-party IP address.

5.4   Finding Needles in a Haystack

As discussed in Sect. 5.1, CAIDA uses three teams of Ark VPs to probe a random address in every routed /24 prefix. In this section, we report on the characteristics of cycle 4947 conducted by team 3. The characteristics of data conducted by other teams and for other cycles is quantitatively similar. In total, cycle 4947 contains 10,711,132 traceroutes, and 163,916 (1.5%) of these contain a loop. 105,685 (64.5%) of the traceroutes with loops were not towards a stub network.

Of the remaining 58,231 traceroutes with loops towards stub ASes, we inferred 31,023 (53.3%) had a loop within the stub network, i.e. the addresses in the loop were announced in BGP by the stub, or involved the customer-edge router. A further 11,352 traceroutes (19.5%) contained a loop with an unresponsive IP address, and 1,373 traceroutes (2.4%) contained an unrouted IP address that prevented us from inferring if the loop occurred at a provider-customer interconnect. 610 traceroutes (1.0%) had a loop that we disqualified as occurring at a customer-provider boundary, as the loop occurred at a router that also appeared in paths towards multiple destination ASes, and 494 traceroutes (0.8%) contained an IP address that could have been a third party address on a customer router, rather than a router operated by a provider. In total, only 2,530 traceroutes with loops (4.3%) contained simple point-to-point loops, and only 93 (0.2%) contained more complex two-provider loops.

5.5   Persistence of Loops

Given that we are looking for needles in haystacks, how reliably can we find them? Ideally, we would be able to consistently reproduce the loops that imply absence of ingress filtering, and discard observations caused by transient events. Unfortunately, there is currently no straightforward way of doing so.

The data we used was collected by CAIDA using traceroutes conducted by a distributed set of VPs towards a random IP address in each routed /24 prefix. This approach adds efficiency by reducing the number of probes, at the cost of potentially missing loops that occur for smaller prefixes. It also means that when such a loop is in fact discovered, the next probe might miss it again by selecting a random address outside the smaller prefix. In other words, the traceroute data itself does not tell us much about the persistence of loops.

To better understand the impact of random address selection and the persistence of loops, we collected traceroutes towards the same addresses that revealed the loops. We first applied the algorithm outlined in Sect. 5.3 to the traceroute data for August 2016 and found 2,500 unique loops between 703 provider and 1,780 customer ASes. In October 2016, we collected traceroutes towards the same IP addresses that revealed the loops, using two different vantage points. We were able to reproduce 1,240 of the loops between 461 provider and 1,026 customer ASes. Next, we repeated this procedure for over a year of traceroute data: August 2015–August 2016. We found 7,784 unique loops between 1,286 provider and 3,993 customer ASes. In October 2016, we were able to reproduce 1,542 unique loops between 505 provider and 1,176 customer ASes. In other words, the additional data identified 342 loops that persisted.

A significant portion of all loops could not be reproduced and the longer the time lag, the higher the odds of failure, for four reasons. First, the loop might have been transient, i.e., it only occurred during routing protocol convergence [12] or temporary misconfiguration [21]. Second, it might depend on the vantage point of the probe, e.g., because of multi-homed routers. Third, the provider might have fixed the routing issue that caused the loop. Fourth, and most relevant, the provider has implemented ingress filtering.

Future work is needed to untangle these causes. We know from our validation effort (Sect. 6) that even loops that appeared only once can correctly signal absence of ingress filtering. Some of the loops that we could not reproduce had already been validated by the provider as true positives. In the remainder of the paper, we will work with the full set of loops as identified by our algorithm.

6   Validation by Network Providers

In order to validate our results and obtain ground truth, we contacted providers in two rounds: September 2015 and September 2016. We got feedback from one hosting provider, one data center provider, one ISP, two national research and education networks, and two Tier 1 networks. We contacted some providers only in one round, some in both, depending on whether we inferred absence of ingress filtering for links involving their network at both times, and our ability to reach the right specialist in the organization. We gave all providers a formal assurance that their names would not be included in the paper.

Feedback from the providers during the first round resulted in improvements in our methodology. We applied the final methodology to both the August 2015 and August 2016 data. We then compared the final results to the feedback that we received from the providers in both rounds. We talked to 6 providers in round 1 and 4 in round 2, and 3 providers participated in both rounds.

We defined a result as a true positive if we identified a provider-to-customer link where the provider does not perform ingress filtering and an operator at the provider confirms this. That is, we correctly inferred the absence of SAV as well as the boundary between provider and customer. A false positive occured when we either incorrectly detected the boundary or the provider is actually performing SAV at the boundary. Our methodology correctly identified the absence of ingress filtering on the provider boundary in 94 out of 98 IP links between provider and customer ASes (45 of 49 links in round 1, and 49 of 49 links in round 2).

The four false positives had different causes. Three of them occurred because of route aggregation. Providers perform route aggregation by consolidating multiple routes in a single, more general route. This practice can lead to problems with our border router detection. Imagine this scenario: a provider is assigned a /16 prefix X by the Regional Internet Registry (RIR). The provider allocates a /24 subnet Y from prefix X to a customer, and the customer assigns addresses from Y to its routers. The customer also has its own prefix Z allocated by an RIR. If the provider aggregates Y into a single /16 advertisement for X, we would infer that customer routers with addresses in Y belong to the provider AS. Our methodology would then categorize a loop between provider prefix X and customer prefix Z as signaling the absence of SAV, when the loop was actually within the customer network.

For the fourth false positive, the provider informed us that the traceroute data suggested that the loop had occurred inside their network rather than on the boundary. However, they could not reproduce it anymore and blamed it on a transient event. Note that in the second round, we found 3 loops for the same provider and they were all true positives.

One additional piece of feedback that we received was that some of the providers, while confirming the validity of our inference that they were not doing ingress filtering on their boundary, objected to the implication that they *should* be filtering. They saw their services as offering transit and contracted them as such, which meant no filtering on the provider's side. In the view of these providers, the downstream customer AS should perform SAV at their border router. The customer ASes were business entities like ISPs, hosting providers or large enterprises. Evaluating whether this interpretation of BCP 38 [11] is merited falls outside the scope of this paper and is for the community to address. For this paper, the key point is that the proposed method performed accurately.

7   Results

We first summarize the results in terms of the number of networks that do not implement SAV. We then compare our method to the two alternatives: the Spoofer and the Open Resolver projects. Like those methods, our approach only observes a subset of the networks without SAV. In the absence of loops, we cannot tell anything about the presence of ingress filtering.

Using one month of CAIDA's traceroute data from August 2016, our approach identified 2,500 unique loops involving 703 provider ASes as lacking SAV on one or more of their customer-facing links and 1,780 customer ASes. These represent approximately 1.3% and 3.2% of all advertised ASes, respectively. Moreover, when compared to all advertised stub ASes and their providers [17], we found 9.0% of provider ASes without ingress filtering involving 3.8% of all stub ASes.

As discussed in Sect. 6, some providers argued that customer ASes should be responsible for SAV within their networks or at their borders. However, we found that about 63% of the involved customer ASes advertise /20 or smaller prefix lengths. It is unlikely that such small entities have the resources and incentives to implement SAV in their networks. On the other hand, such small prefixes should allow the providers to implement static ACLs.

We now compare our results to the data from the Spoofer and Open Resolver projects (see Sect. 3 for details). Our method only detects the lack of ingress filtering for provider networks, which means that their customer ASes might be able to spoof. We compared those customer ASes with the Spoofer data from February to August 2016 [1]. Of 54 overlapping ASes, 38 of the Spoofer tests were only conducted from behind a Network Address Translation (NAT) device that likely prevented spoofing. Of the systems not behind a NAT, 10 of the 16 stub ASes allowed spoofing, i.e., more than half of these ASes had not deployed SAV, suggesting the provider's expectation for their customers to deploy filtering is not being met, and supporting the case for transit providers to filter their customers. This means that the connected provider ASes do not implement ingress filtering, which is consistent with our results. Packets with spoofed source addresses from Spoofer tests in the 6 remaining customer ASes were not received, suggesting that filtering took place in the customer AS. The overlap between both methods contains only a small sample, but it does indicate that the majority of the overlapping customer networks were not doing SAV – a finding that reinforces the point that providers should not expect their customer ASes to be willing and able do SAV, even if they are not that small.

Kührer et al. used the Open Resolver data in 2014 by to identify 2,692 unique ASes from within which spoofing was possible [14]. Following the same approach, we analyzed the August 2016 data from the Open Resolver project, generously provided to us by Jared Mauch, and found a total of 3,015 unique ASes that were able to spoof. We compared these to the customer ASes that our method identified as allowing spoofing – i.e., those connected to the providers which lack ingress filtering. We found only a modest overlap: 244 ASes.

In sum: these findings show that our method can add unique data points to both existing methods, and improve visibility of networks lacking SAV. In terms of the volume of observations, it resides between Spoofer and Open Resolver. The three methods are complementary and provide views into the problem, contributing to improved overall visibility of SAV adoption.

8   Conclusion

In this paper we implemented and validated an algorithm that uses traceroute data to infer a lack of SAV between a stub and provider network. We inferred 703 providers that do not implement ingress filtering on at least one of their links facing 1,780 customer ASes. We also built a public website showing the provider-customer edges that we inferred as lacking ingress filtering: https://spoofer.caida.org/. Providers can use the data to deploy filtering, which would not only stop attackers from sending packets with spoofed addresses from the customer's network, but also block attempts to attack the provider-customer link by sending packets to addresses that enter the forwarding loop [21].

To improve the reliability of the method, future work is needed on border detection and on untangling the different factors that prevent loops from being reproduced, to separate the implementation of ingress filtering from the other causes. A completely different direction for future work is to experimentally test the strength of reputation effects among providers and network operators. The networks that allow spoofing could be made public in varying ways, to see which mechanism best incentivizes providers into taking action.

For the community of network operators, the results support efforts such as the Routing Resilience Manifesto [2] and other community initiatives to improve network security. By complementing the Spoofer and Open Resolver data, our method increases visibility into the adoption of SAV. Public visibility of spoofing-enabled networks is a critical step in incentivizing providers to deploy ingress filtering in their networks. The dataset is also useful for the national CERTs who want to push BCP 38 compliance in their countries. The problems caused by IP spoofing have been recognized for years [6], and the task to reduce its role in attacks is becoming increasingly urgent.

Acknowledgments. The technique in this paper is based on an idea from Jared Mauch. Christian Keil (DFN-CERT) provided informative feedback. This work was partly funded by the EU Advanced Cyber Defence Centre (ACDC) project CIP-ICT-PSP.2012.5.1 #325188. This material is based on research sponsored by the Department of Homeland Security (DHS) Science and Technology Directorate, Homeland Security Advanced Research Projects Agency, Cyber Security Division BAA HSHQDC-14-R-B0005, and the Government of United Kingdom of Great Britain and Northern Ireland via contract number D15PC00188.

References

1. CAIDA spoofer project. https://spoofer.caida.org/
2. Mutually Agreed Norms for Routing Security (MANRS). https://www.routingmanifesto.org/manrs/
3. Open Resolver Project. http://openresolverproject.org/
4. Augustin, B., Cuvellier, X., Orgogozo, B., Viger, F., Friedman, T., Latapy, M., Magnien, C., Teixeira, R.: Avoiding traceroute anomalies with Paris traceroute. In: IMC, pp. 153–158, October 2006
5. Baker, F., Savola, P.: Ingress filtering for multihomed networks. RFC 3704, IETF BCP84, March 2004
6. Bellovin, S.: Security problems in the TCP/IP protocol suite. CCR **19**(2), 32–48 (1989)
7. Beverly, R., Bauer, S.: The spoofer project: inferring the extent of source address filtering on the Internet. In: Proceedings of USENIX SRUTI, July 2005
8. Beverly, R., Berger, A., Hyun, Y., claffy, k.: Understanding the efficacy of deployed Internet source address validation. In: IMC, pp. 356–369, November 2009
9. Beverly, R., Koga, R., claffy, kc.: Initial longitudinal analysis of IP source spoofing capability on the Internet, July 2013. http://www.internetsociety.org/
10. Bright, P.: Spamhaus DDoS grows to Internet-threatening size, March 2013
11. Ferguson, P., Senie, D.: Network ingress filtering: defeating denial of service attacks which employ IP source address spoofing. RFC 2827, IETF BCP38, May 2000
12. Francois, P., Bonaventure, O.: Avoiding transient loops during IGP convergence in IP networks. In: INFOCOM, pp. 237–247, March 2005
13. Huffaker, B., Keys, K., Koga, R., claffy, kc.: CAIDA inferred AS to organization mapping dataset. https://www.caida.org/data/as-organizations/

14. Kührer, M., Hupperich, T., Rossow, C., Holz, T.: Exit from hell? Reducing the impact of amplication DDoS attacks. In: USENIX Security, August 2014
15. Luckie, M.: Scamper: a scalable and extensible packet prober for active measurement of the Internet. In: IMC, pp. 239–245, November 2010
16. Luckie, M., Dhamdhere, A., Huffaker, B., Clark, D., claffy, k.: bdrmap: inference of borders between IP networks. In: IMC, pp. 381–396, November 2016
17. Luckie, M., Huffaker, B., Dhamdhere, A., Giotsas, V., claffy, k.: AS relationships, customer cones, and validation. In: IMC, pp. 243–256, October 2013
18. Marder, A., Smith, J.M.: MAP-IT: multipass accurate passive inferences from traceroute. In: IMC, November 2016
19. Prince, M.: Technical details behind a 400 Gbps NTP amplification DDoS attack. http://blog.cloudflare.com/
20. Vixie, P.: Rate-limiting state: the edge of the Internet is an unruly place. ACM Queue 12(2), 1–5 (2014)
21. Xia, J., Gao, L., Fei, T.: A measurement study of persistent forwarding loops on the Internet. Comput. Netw. 51(17), 4780–4796 (2007)

A Characterization of Load Balancing on the IPv6 Internet

Rafael Almeida[1(✉)], Osvaldo Fonseca[1], Elverton Fazzion[1,2], Dorgival Guedes[1],
Wagner Meira Jr.[1], and Ítalo Cunha[1]

[1] Department of Computer Science,
Universidade Federal de Minas Gerais, Belo Horizonte, Brazil
{rlca,osvaldo.morais,elverton,dorgival,meira,cunha}@dcc.ufmg.br
[2] Department of Computer Science,
Universidade Federal de São João del-Rei, São João del-Rei, Brazil

Abstract. As IPv6 deployment grows, it is important to develop new
measurement techniques that allow us to study the IPv6 Internet. We
implement an IPv6 version of the Multipath Detection Algorithm and
use it from 12 geographically-distributed vantage points on two different platforms to characterize IPv6 routers that perform load balancing.
Overall, we find that 74% of IPv6 routes traverse at least one router
that performs load balancing. Similar to previous reports for IPv4, we
find per-destination is the most prevalent type of load balancing; surprisingly, we find a significantly higher prevalence of per-packet load
balancing for IPv6 traffic than previously reported for IPv4. We investigate which header fields are used for load balancing, and find that 4% of
IPv6 routers that perform load balancing consider IPv6's Traffic Class
or Flow Label fields. Finally, we quantify how often routers modify the
Traffic Class and Flow Label IPv6 header fields and their impact on load
balancing.

Keywords: IPv6 · Traceroute · Measurement · Load balancing ·
Topology

1   Introduction

The growing deployment of IPv6 [7] increases its relevance for application performance and reliability. As a result, the networking community has developed new
(and adapted existing IPv4) measurement tools to collect datasets and study the
IPv6 Internet (e.g., [4,12]).

Topology measurements collected with traceroute serve a number of purposes in Internet studies [17]. The introduction of Paris traceroute in 2006 [1]
showed that load balancing is widely used in the Internet and causes several
measurement artifacts in traceroute measurements. Since then, most traceroute
implementations—including those used in Ark, iPlane, and RIPE Atlas—were
updated to keep probe flow identifiers fixed to prevent load balancing and avoid

© Springer International Publishing AG 2017
M.A. Kaafar et al. (Eds.): PAM 2017, LNCS 10176, pp. 242–254, 2017.
DOI: 10.1007/978-3-319-54328-4_18

measurement artifacts. This approach is adequate for ongoing measurement campaigns, as it prevents artifacts without increasing measurement cost; unfortunately, it does not identify if routers perform load balancing.

Studying load balancing properties, like the number of simultaneous routes between two networks, helps us understand the impact of load balancing on performance (e.g., due to out-of-order packet delivery) and robustness (e.g., against failures and congestion). Studying load balancing also provides insight into traffic engineering practices.

In this paper we implemented an IPv6 version of the Multipath Detection Algorithm (MDA) [16].[1] Our implementation identifies routers that perform load balancing and classifies load balancing behavior by systematically varying four different fields in the IPv6 and TCP headers.

We analyze IPv6 route measurements from 12 vantage points distributed across 7 countries in 3 continents. We characterize the prevalence of load balancing in the IPv6 Internet, different load balancing behaviors, and load balancing properties such as asymmetry. We also study whether routers overwrite the IPv6 traffic class and flow label fields, which might impact load balancing. Whenever possible, we compare our results against previous observations for IPv4 load balancing by Augustin et al. [1]. Our main findings are:

- IPv6 load balancing is widespread, although less so than previously observed for IPv4. We find 74% of IPv6 routes traverse at least one load balancer.
- Similar to IPv4, IPv6 per-destination is the most common class of load balancing. However, we find that IPv6 per-packet load balancing is significantly more common than previously reported for IPv4.
- A non-negligible fraction (4%) of IPv6 routers performing load balancing consider the traffic class and flow label header fields.

Our results further our understanding of the IPv6 Internet; as far as we are aware, this is the first study of IPv6 load balancing. Although IPv6 and IPv4 load balancing have many similarities, we identify differences. In particular, the higher prevalence of per-packet load balancing for IPv6 might negatively impact TCP performance as a result of higher risk of packet reordering.

2   Load Balancing

Load balancing is traffic engineering and can be configured manually or automatically by mechanisms such as ECMP and EIGRP. Motivations for load balancing include increasing bandwidth and reducing maximum link utilization. Figure 1 shows a route traversing four routers that perform load balancing (*load balancers*) measured from a vantage point in the Linode cloud hosting service.

Load balancers choose the next hop of a packet based on a *flow identifier* computed from the packet's headers. Augustin et al. [1] defined three classes of load balancers depending on what header fields are used as flow identifiers. In decreasing order of load balancing granularity, the three classes are:

---

[1] Code available at https://www.github.com/TopologyMapping/mda6.

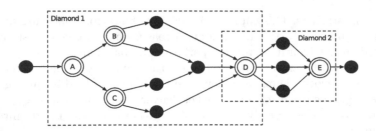

Fig. 1. Real route measurement with four load balancers (A, B, C, and D) and two diamonds (A-D and D-E).

- *Per-destination* load balancers use a packet's source and destination IP addresses as the packet's flow identifier. This behavior ensures all packets exchanged between a source and a destination traverse the same sequence of interfaces and experience similar performance.
- *Per-flow* load balancers use a 5-tuple—source and destination addresses, source and destination ports, and protocol number—as the flow identifier. This guarantees that all packets belonging to the same connection will follow the same sequence of interfaces and experience similar performance. Different connections between the same source and destination pair might traverse different sequences of interfaces and experience different performance.
- *Per-packet* load balancers send packets to a random next hop regardless of header field values. Per-packet load balancing may result in packets from the same connection traversing different sequences of interfaces and experiencing different performance. This incurs higher risk of packet reordering, which might negatively impact traffic, e.g., decreasing TCP performance [5].

To detect load balancing, the Multipath Detection Algorithm (MDA) [16] systematically varies the flow identifier in traceroute probes to detect different next hops after a load balancer. MDA proceeds hop-by-hop. MDA assumes each load balancer b in hop h has $N_b + 1$ next hops, where N_b is the number of next hops of b detected so far. MDA then computes the number of probes necessary to identify $N_b + 1$ next hops with a given confidence α, usually set to 0.95.[2] This computation assumes load balancer b distributes flow identifiers uniformly among its next hops. If the number of computed probes is larger than the number of probes already sent to b's next hops, MDA sends additional probes to cover the difference. If the additional probes detect no new next hop, then MDA proceeds to the next load balancer or hop. If the additional probes detect new next hops, then MDA updates N_b and repeats the process.

Augustin et al. [1] characterize load balancer *diamonds*, defined as a subgraph containing all hops between a divergence hop (a load balancer) and a convergence hop, with the condition that all flow identifiers traverse both divergence and convergence hops. Figure 1 shows two diamonds. Augustin et al. [1]

---

[2] More precisely, MDA computes the number of probes required to bound the probability of not detecting a next hop, across all load balancers, to $1 - \alpha$.

defined the *length* of a diamond as the number of edges in the longest sequence of interfaces across the diamond; the *min-width* of a diamond as the number of edge-disjoint sequences of interfaces across the diamond; the *max-width* as the maximum number of reachable interfaces at any given hop; and *asymmetry* as the maximum length difference between any sequence of interfaces across the diamond (a diamond with asymmetry zero is said to be symmetric). In Fig. 1, diamond 1 has asymmetry 1, length 4, min-width 2, and max-width 4; while diamond 2 is symmetric, has length 2, min-width 3, and max-width 3.

3 IPv6 Load Balancing and Measurement Methodology

The IPv6 header, shown in Fig. 2, is simpler than the IPv4 header. To identify load balancing, we vary the IPv6-specific traffic class and flow label fields. The traffic class field serves a purpose similar to the TOS field in IPv4. RFC2460 says that routers may modify the traffic class field. Other routers or the destination should not expect the traffic class field to have the same value of when the packet was first created. The flow label field allows IPv6 routers to efficiently identify flows.[3] RFC6437 recommends that source hosts set one flow label value for all IPv6 packets belonging to the same connection or application. RFC6437 also specifies that a router may initialize the flow label when it is zero, but should not modify a nonzero flow label.

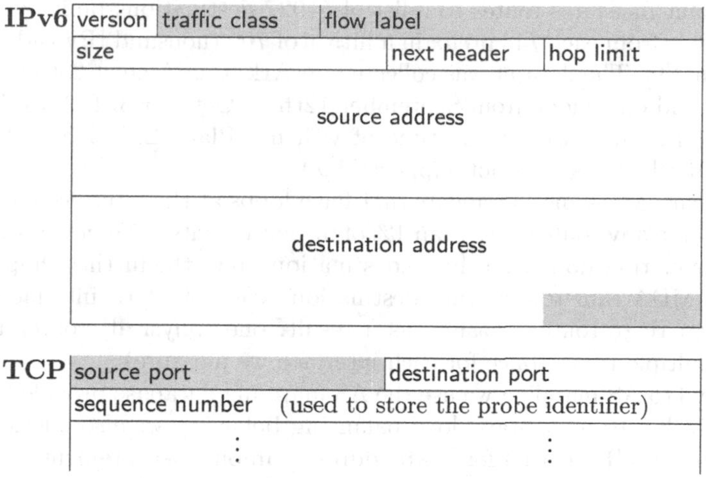

IPv6	version	traffic class	flow label		
	size			next header	hop limit
	source address				
	destination address				

TCP	source port		destination port	
	sequence number	(used to store the probe identifier)		
	⋮		⋮	

Fig. 2. IPv6 header and first 8 bytes of the TCP header. We systematically vary gray bits to identify IPv6 load balancing.

---

[3] The usual 5-tuple flow definition used in IPv4 is unsuitable in IPv6 as routers need to follow the variable-length chain of IPv6 extension headers (starting at the next header field) until the end to find the TCP header.

We also vary the last 8 bits of the destination address to identify per-destination load balancers. Current IPv6 prefixes routed in the Internet are less specific than /48s [2]; packets with differences in the last 8 bits of the destination address will take the same route up to the destination's network. Finally, we also vary the TCP source port to check whether IPv6 routers also consider port numbers for per-flow load balancing, as in IPv4. We choose source port numbers starting from 33435, as typically done in traceroute implementations. We use TCP packets to destination port 80 to improve reachability [13] and avoid complaints. We store probe identifiers in the TCP sequence number field.

We execute MDA between each source and destination pair. Each execution varies the four gray fields in Fig. 2. This lets us identify load balancers and which header fields they use when computing a probe's flow identifier. At each hop, we probe with up to 256 different flow identifiers, a limitation imposed by the 8 bits available in the traffic class field and in the destination address. Having 256 different flow identifiers lets MDA identify up to 39 distinct next hops at the chosen $\alpha = 0.95$ confidence level; 256 probes were enough for 99.99% of the hops measured.

4   Dataset

We collect IPv6 route measurements[4] from 7 vantage points on CAIDA's Ark platform and from 5 vantage points on the Linode cloud hosting service, as shown on Table 1. The vantage points are spread across 7 countries in 3 continents. Each vantage point measures routes to a list of 51927 destinations built by sampling two addresses from each /48 prefix in a hitlist of 700 thousand IPv6 addresses by Gasser et al. [9]. The dataset was collected on Ark from August 29th to October 3rd, 2016; and on Linode from September 12th to October 3rd, 2016. We chose these platforms because, at the time of writing, PlanetLab does not support IPv6 and RIPE Atlas does not support MDA.

We discard MDA measurements that have loops at the interface level or that do not observe any router (less than 1% of measurements). We *do* consider MDA measurements that do not reach the destination up to the furthest hop common to all four MDA runs toward that destination. We look at IP interfaces and do not perform IP-to-router aliasing; as a result, one (physical) router might be counted multiple times (once for each interface we measure).

For IPv6 to AS mapping we use the AS mapping database provided by Team Cymru.[5] To better understand load balancing behavior, we also queried reverse DNS entries (PTR records) for IPv6 addresses in our measurements.

5   Results

In this section we characterize the prevalence of IPv6 load balancing (Sect. 5.1), the behavior of IPv6 routers performing load balancing (Sect. 5.2), and diamond

---

[4] Dataset available at http://www.dcc.ufmg.br/~cunha/datasets.

[5] Available at http://www.team-cymru.org/IP-ASN-mapping.html.

Table 1. Vantage point locations and prevalence of load balancing

Platform	Location	Routes with load balancing (Sect. 5)	
		Overall	Filtered
Ark	Ballerup, DK (AS59469)	58%	31% ⋆
	Berkeley, CA, US (AS25)	100%	22% ⋆
	Quezon City, PH (AS6360)	16%	16%
	Los Angeles, US/CA (AS2152)	25%	25%
	San Diego, US/CA (AS1909)	23%	23%
	Singapore, SG (AS37989)	99%	27% ⋆
	Barrie, CA (AS19764)	84%	38% ⋆
Linode	Fremont, US/CA	100%	28% ⋆
	London, UK	99%	37% ⋆
	Frankfurt, DE	100%	31% ⋆
	Newark, US/NJ	97%	35% ⋆
	Singapore, SG	98%	38% ⋆

properties (Sect. 5.3). Finally, we discuss some IPv6-specific confounding factors (Sect. 5.4). Our results mostly match previous reports on the IPv4 Internet, but we discuss a few punctual differences.

5.1   Load Balancing Prevalence

Table 1 shows the fraction of routes from each vantage point that traverse a load balancer ('Overall' column). We find load balancing is prevalent in IPv6 routes. The heterogeneity among vantage points can be explained by load balancers one or two hops upstream of some of the vantage points (marked with a ⋆). In the case of Linode, these load balancers are inside Linode's own network (as identified by IP-to-AS mapping). These load balancers appear on most routes and significantly impact observations. To remove the impact of these load balancers, we also show the fraction of routes traversing a load balancer when we ignore load balancers two IP hops upstream of vantage points if they are on the same (origin) AS ('Filtered' column). After filtering we observe more homogeneous prevalence of load balancing across vantage points. The filtered results give a better picture of load balancing on IPv6 transit networks and might be representative of other vantage points. We find that of the 45% of routes that traverse a Tier-1 AS, as identified by CAIDA's AS-relationship inference algorithm [10], 29% traverse a load balancer inside the Tier-1.

Figure 3 shows the distribution of the number of load balancers over all routes in our dataset for each platform. We find routes traverse multiple load balancers. (Note that one hop can have multiple load balancers, e.g., hop 2 in Fig. 1.) In particular, 76% of Linode routes traverse three or more load balancers. This is because routes often traverse three load balancers in Linode's network (see

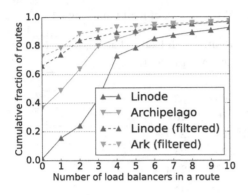
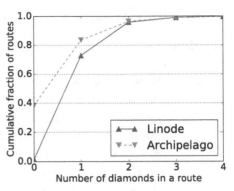

Fig. 3. Load balancers   **Fig. 4.** Number of diamonds

'Diamond 1' in Fig. 1). Figure 3 also shows the number of load balancers traversed when we ignore load balancers two IP hops upstream of vantage points if they are on the same (origin) AS (dotted lines). After filtering, we observe similar load balancing from Ark and Linode vantage points.

Figure 4 shows the distribution of the number of diamonds over all routes in our dataset. As diamonds start and end on interfaces that all packets traverse, the number of diamonds on a route gives a lower bound of the number of load balancers that packets traverse to reach the destination. Although Fig. 3 shows routes can traverse many load balancers, these are grouped into a small number of diamonds. As we will show later (Sect. 5.3), diamonds are complex and contain many load balancers. This result is similar to previous results for IPv4 load balancing [1].

5.2   Classes of Load Balancing Behavior

We now investigate what IPv6 header fields load balancers use to compute flow identifiers to choose next hops. We identify load balancers by their IPv6 addresses. Table 2 shows the fraction of load balancers in each class and the percentage of routes that traverse at least one load balancer in each class. We also report results from Augustin et al. [1] for IPv4 load balancers. (Note that Augustin's results are from 2011, so the differences we discuss might also be due to network evolution and not only IP version).

We find per-destination, per-flow, and per-packet load balancers are not only the most common load balancer classes, but also the most prevalent across route measurements. This is expected, as these classes were used for IPv4 load balancing. Despite this similarity, we observe a significantly higher fraction of IPv6 routes traverse per-packet load balancers. We discuss this further in Sect. 5.4.

We also find other classes of load balancers. We find 3.2% of load balancers perform per-flow load balancing considering the traffic class field (in addition to the destination address and source port). This behavior is the default in at least JunOS 15.1. We could not find any reports on how many IPv4 load balancers

Table 2. Classes of load balancing behavior

	Overall			Filtered	
	Fraction of Balancers	% Routes		Fraction of Balancers	% Routes
		IPv6	IPv4 [1]		IPv6
Per-destination	29.3%	43.5%	78.0%	29.2%	11.1%
Per-flow	50.0%	30.0%	54.8%	50.1%	17.7%
Per-packet	10.7%	30.1%	1.0%	10.6%	7.7%
Per-flow with TC	3.2%	14.8%	—	3.2%	3.3%
Per-application	6.0%	5.1%	—	6.0%	3.3%
Others	0.8%	1.2%	—	0.9%	0.6%
Total	**100%**	**74%**	**92%**	**100%**	**29%**

consider the TOS field to compare. Interestingly, we find 6% of load balancers that use only the TCP ports for load balancing. We manually investigated these load balancers and found this behavior can be configured in RouterOS under the name of "per-application load balancing." Perhaps surprisingly, we find only 0.8% of load balancers that consider IPv6's flow label (with or without other fields). Overall, 4% of the load balancers consider either IPv6's traffic class or flow label fields.

5.3 Diamond Characteristics

We now characterize diamonds on routes with load balancing using the same methodology and metrics as Augustin et al. [1] and compare the observations.

Diamond length. Figure 5 shows the distribution of diamond lengths. We find diamonds are usually short, and that load balancers one or two hops upstream of vantage points have longer diamonds than average. If we ignore these load balancers (dashed lines), then both datasets observe very similar distributions of diamond length, with 93% of diamonds of length 5 or less.

Diamond asymmetry. Figure 6 shows the distribution of diamond asymmetry in our dataset. Linode has asymmetric diamonds in its network that show up on many routes (solid blue line). If we ignore load balancers one or two hops upstream of the vantage point (dashed lines), these diamonds are not considered and we observe that 96% of diamonds are symmetric. The few asymmetric diamonds usually have asymmetry less than or equal to 2. We find that 71% of asymmetric diamonds are instances of inter-domain load balancing, i.e., when the diamond starts and ends in different ASes.[6] This illustrates that more complex inter-domain traffic engineering leads to more complex load balancing

---

[6] This can happen as a result of traffic engineering or, for example, when a BGP router with ECMP enabled receives and installs multiple routes to a prefix (e.g., at an IXP) or when multiple BGP routers redistribute different routes to the same prefix into an IGP (e.g., OSPF) with ECMP enabled.

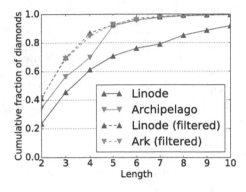

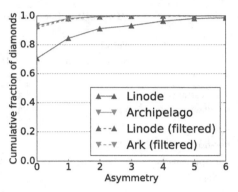

Fig. 5. Diamond length

Fig. 6. Diamond asymmetry (Color figure online)

configurations. Conversely, only 26% of symmetric load balancers are instances of inter-domain load balancing. Different inter-domain routes might have different performance, fortunately, we find that 70% of asymmetric diamonds start at per-destination load balancers, which will send all packets from the same source and destination pair on the same inter-domain route.

Diamond max-width. Figure 7 shows the distribution of max-width for all diamonds in our dataset. By definition, the minimum max-width for a diamond is 2. We find most diamonds are narrow, in particular around 81% of diamonds across both platforms have max-width equal or less than 5. By varying the last 8 bits of the destination address, probe packets will follow the same route since IPv6 prefixes in global routing tables are usually shorter than /48 [2]. However, when reaching the destination network, packets may be directed to different hosts whose addresses share a /116 prefix with the destination. (We found this to be common in Microsoft's datacenters.) Figure 7 includes these measurements as diamonds with very large max-width, and shows that such errors are rare and do not impact the overall findings.

Diamond min-width. Figure 8 shows the distribution of min-width over all diamonds in our dataset. By definition, the minimum min-width is 2 and is bounded by the max-width. We find most diamonds have a min-width of 2.

Comparison to IPv4 diamonds. Our findings for diamond lengths, asymmetry, max-widths, and min-widths are similar but not quantitatively close to findings on IPv4 load balancers by Augustin et al. [1]. For example, they found that load balancers are often short and narrow, and reported that 55% of routes with load balancing traverse a diamond of length 2 and max-width less than or equal to 3; in our dataset, we find 24% diamonds of this kind. Augustin et al. also found that long and wide diamonds are rare; in our dataset, only 14% of diamonds have both length and max-width larger than 3. Similar to our results, Augustin et al. also found that most IPv4 load balancers are symmetric.

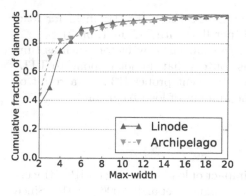

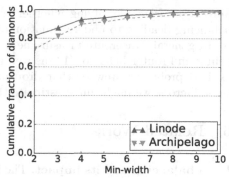

Fig. 7. Max-width   **Fig. 8.** Min-width

5.4   Confounding Factors

Routers may override the traffic class or flow label fields for traffic engineering or other reasons. Such routers may interfere with our identification of load balancers by modifying a probe's traffic class or flow label fields with a variable value when we try to keep the values fixed, and by overwriting fields with a fixed value when we try to vary them.

ICMPv6 time-exceeded messages encapsulate the header of the expired TTL-limited probe. We use the encapsulated header to identify the values of the traffic class and flow label fields on all probes received by each router in a route. If we identify a router that received a probe with a traffic class or flow label field different from the expected value we infer that the previous router has overwritten it. If the field is overwritten, we identify whether it is overwritten with a fixed or variable value. Note that the 'expected' values for the traffic class and flow label fields change along the route as routers overwrite them. We identify router behavior proceeding hop-by-hop starting from the vantage point.

Table 3. Fraction of routers that overwrite the traffic class and flow label fields.

Overwriting behavior	Field	
	Traffic class	Flow label
Variable value	0.7%	0.0%
Fixed value	4.7%	0.0%

We find that a small (but not negligible) portion of the routers overwrite the traffic class field. Table 3 summarizes router behavior. The few routers (0.7%) that overwrite the traffic class field with a variable value might lead to the (incorrect) identification of per-packet load balancers. Routers that overwrite the traffic class field with a fixed value do not impact the identification of load balancing, but prevent us from identifying whether routers use the traffic class field for load balancing (leading to underestimation of 'per-flow with TC' in Table 2).

In general, traceroute measurements are challenged by factors such as tunneling and router behavior [14] as well as routers that do not respond to TTL-expired probes or firewalls that drop measurement probes [13]. As a result of these factors, we might underestimate the amount of load balancing.

6   Related Work

Load balancing and its impact. The impact of load balancing on IPv4 traceroute measurements was first reported on by Augustin et al. in 2006 (see [1]). Since then, MDA has been proposed to bound load balancer identification errors [16] and an extensive characterization of IPv4 load balancing was published [1]. Paris traceroute was the first, but today most traceroute tools and measurement platforms keep flow identifiers fixed to avoid load balancing. Besides impacting traceroute measurements, load balancing has also been reported to impact latency measurements [15] and observed routing dynamics [6].

IPv6 measurement tools and characterization studies. As far as we are aware, Scamper [11] is the only other implementation of MDA that supports IPv6. Also, we are not aware of any other characterization of IPv6 load balancers. Other work have developed techniques to measure IPv6 routers, including IPv6 alias resolution [3,12] and router availability [4]; while others have quantified IPv6 deployment and performance [7,8].

7   Conclusions and Future Work

We implemented an IPv6 version of the MDA to identify routers that perform load balancing and classify their behavior. We collected measurements from 12 nodes in 7 countries to 51927 destinations. We find that IPv6 load balancing shares many similarities with IPv4 load balancing, with a few differences. First, although IPv6 load balancing is widespread, it is less so than IPv4 load balancing. Second, IPv6 routes have significantly higher probability of traversing per-packet load balancers than IPv4 routes, which may negatively impact TCP performance. Although we cannot explain the causes behind the higher prevalence of per-packet load balancers, this is partially explained by routers that overwrite the traffic class field in IPv6 headers with variable values. Other possible explanations include less mature IPv6 load balancing implementations or less established best practices when compared to IPv4.

The prevalence of per-packet load balancers we observe motivate investigation of the impact of IPv6 load balancing on IPv6 traffic. As future work, we plan to correlate performance metrics with load balancing behavior. We also plan to extend our MDA implementation to allow more fine-grained classification of load balancers. In particular, we plan to add support for IPv6 extension headers and to allow measurements varying a combination of fields in probe headers.

Acknowledgements. We thank Young Hyun for the support in setting up and running our measurements on the Ark platform. This work is supported by Comcast and Brazilian research funding agencies (CAPES, CNPq, and FAPEMIG).

References

1. Augustin, B., Friedman, T., Teixeira, R.: Measuring multipath routing in the internet. IEEE/ACM Trans. Netw. **19**(3), 830–840 (2011)
2. Bayer, D.: Visibility of Prefix Lengths in IPv4 and IPv6 (2010). https://labs.ripe.net/Members/dbayer/visibility-of-prefix-lengths
3. Beverly, R., Brinkmeyer, W., Luckie, M., Rohrer, J.P.: IPv6 alias resolution via induced fragmentation. In: Roughan, M., Chang, R. (eds.) PAM 2013. LNCS, vol. 7799, pp. 155–165. Springer, Heidelberg (2013). doi:10.1007/978-3-642-36516-4_16
4. Beverly, R., Luckie, M., Mosley, L., Claffy, K.: Measuring and characterizing IPv6 router availability. In: Mirkovic, J., Liu, Y. (eds.) PAM 2015. LNCS, vol. 8995, pp. 123–135. Springer, Heidelberg (2015). doi:10.1007/978-3-319-15509-8_10
5. Blanton, E., Allman, M.: On making TCP more robust to packet reordering. ACM SIGCOMM Comput. Commun. Rev. **32**(1), 20–30 (2002)
6. Cunha, Í., Teixeira, R., Diot, C.: Measuring and characterizing end-to-end route dynamics in the presence of load balancing. In: Spring, N., Riley, G.F. (eds.) PAM 2011. LNCS, vol. 6579, pp. 235–244. Springer, Heidelberg (2011). doi:10.1007/978-3-642-19260-9_24
7. Czyz, J., Allman, M., Zhang, J., Iekel-Johnson, S., Osterweil, E., Bailey, M.: Measuring IPv6 adoption. In: Proceedings of SIGCOMM (2014)
8. Dhamdhere, A., Luckie, M., Huffaker, B., Claffy, K., Elmokashfi, A., Aben, E.: Measuring the deployment of IPv6: topology, routing and performance. In: Proceedings of the ACM Internet Measurement Conference (IMC) (2012)
9. Gasser, O., Scheitle, Q., Gebhard, S., Carle, G.: Scanning the IPv6 internet: towards a comprehensive hitlist. In: Proceedings of the Traffic Monitoring and Analysis Workshop (TMA) (2016)
10. Luckie, M., Huffaker, B., Claffy, K., Dhamdhere, A., Giotsas, V.: AS relationships, customer cones, and validation. In: Proceedings of the ACM Internet Measurement Conference (IMC) (2013)
11. Luckie, M.: Scamper: a scalable and extensible packet prober for active measurement of the internet. In: Proceedings of the ACM Internet Measurement Conference (IMC) (2010)
12. Luckie, M., Beverly, R., Brinkmeyer, W., Claffy, K.: Speedtrap: internet-scale IPv6 alias resolution. In: Proceedings of the ACM Internet Measurement Conference (IMC) (2013)
13. Luckie, M., Hyun, Y., Huffaker, B.: Traceroute probe method and forward IP path inference. In: ACM Internet Measurement Conference (IMC) (2008)
14. Marchetta, P., Montieri, A., Persico, V., Pescape, A., Cunha, I., Katz-Bassett, E.: How and how much traceroute confuses our understanding of network paths. In: Proceedings of the International Symposium on Local and Metropolitan Area Networks (LANMAN) (2016)

15. Pelsser, C., Cittadini, L., Vissicchio, S., Bush, R.: From paris to tokyo: on the suitability of ping to measure latency. In: Proceedings of the ACM Internet Measurement Conference (IMC) (2013)
16. Veitch, D., Augustin, B., Friedman, T., Teixeira, R.: Failure control in multipath route tracing. In: Proceedings of the IEEE International Conference on Computer Communications (INFOCOM) (2009)
17. Willinger, W., Roughan, M.: Internet topology research redux. In: Recent Advances in Networking, ACM SIGCOMM eBook, vol. 1 (2013)

Wireless

Enhancing WiFi Throughput with PLC Extenders: A Measurement Study

Kittipat Apicharttrisorn[1]([✉]), Ahmed Osama Fathy Atya[1], Jiasi Chen[1],
Karthikeyan Sundaresan[2], and Srikanth V. Krishnamurthy[1]

[1] University of California, Riverside, Riverside, CA, USA
kapic001@ucr.edu
[2] NEC Labs, Princeton, NJ, USA

Abstract. Today, power line communications (PLC) based WiFi extenders are emerging in the market. By simply plugging an extender to a power outlet, a user can create a second access point which connects to a master AP/router using the power line infrastructure. The underlying belief is that this can enhance the throughput that a user can achieve at certain locations (closer to the extender) and potentially increase wireless capacity. In this paper, we conduct an in-depth measurement study to first see if this belief always holds true, and if it does, the extent to which the end-to-end throughput improves. Our measurement study covers both homes and enterprise settings, as well as single and multi-user (or multi-device) settings. Surprisingly, we find that in 46% of cases in an office environment, using a PLC extender does not result in an increase in throughput, even when a single client accesses the network and is located close to the extender. This is because unlike in the case of an Ethernet backhaul, the PLC backhaul could consist of poor quality links (49% of the time in an office environment). We also find that the further away the extender is from the master router, the more likely this possibility becomes. We find that sharing of the PLC backhaul across devices could also be undesirable in some cases, and certain users should connect directly to the master AP in order to improve total throughput. Our study sheds light on when these effects manifest themselves, and discusses challenges that will need to be overcome if PLC extenders can be effectively used to enhance wireless capacity.

1 Introduction

Today there are a number of power line communications (PLC) based WiFi extenders from different vendors on the market (e.g., TP-Link, Netgear, Zyxel, Linksys, and Amped). A user can plug in these extenders (we call them PLC extenders or EXT) into power outlets and they interface with an access point (AP) or router that has access to the Internet (we call this the master router or MRT) using power lines, to essentially act as (additional) APs. By using these plug-and-play extenders in homes or enterprises, users can conceivably improve the quality of their wireless links; this is because clients can now potentially

© Springer International Publishing AG 2017
M.A. Kaafar et al. (Eds.): PAM 2017, LNCS 10176, pp. 257–269, 2017.
DOI: 10.1007/978-3-319-54328-4_19

connect to an extender which is closer and clear of obstructions than to an AP that is obstructed or far away.

Objectives: In this paper, we conduct an in-depth measurement study to see if the better quality wireless links translate to real throughput gains with PLC extenders. We also seek to quantify these gains (or losses if they occur) and determine the root causes for these. We perform this measurement study despite the common belief that these extenders are beneficial because of two motivating observations. First, the throughputs achievable on power lines are not deterministic; in other words, the throughputs achievable between the master router and different PLC extenders could be different. Second, if multiple client devices (or users) share the PLC backhaul, there could be contention on the backhaul that results in degraded performance.

Take aways: In brief, the key take aways of our measurement study are as follows: (**1**) While using a PLC extender does provide throughput benefits in majority of the cases, it does not always do so. In some cases, even with a single client, a throughput degradation is observed compared to connecting to the master router, even if the client is much closer to the extender. (**2**) The sharing of the PLC backhaul among multiple connections (to a plurality of clients) could hurt the overall performance of the network. The overall performance could improve if some of the clients connect directly to the master router as opposed to the closest PLC extender (which provides the strongest WiFi signal). In addition to the above key take aways, our study provides an understanding of how many other factors such as the distance and the number of walls between the extender and the master router, as well as the configuration of the electrical distribution circuits, influence performance.

Our work in perspective: To the best of our knowledge, our work is the first study on the effectiveness of PLC extenders in providing enhanced throughputs in homes and offices. The work also sheds light on the factors that influence whether or not throughput gains can be realized and can thus influence future work on configuration solutions for integrated PLC/WiFi networks. Unlike in traditional WiFi networks wherein the performance on an underlying backhaul (such as Ethernet) is assumed to be commensurate with that of the WiFi links, care must be taken in terms of accounting for PLC idiosyncrasies.

2   PLC Background and Related Work

The PLC Channel: In the US, broadband PLC operates in the 1.7–80 MHz band. It is similar to wireless communications in that the PLC signal is attenuated with distance due to cable branching/losses. While a wireless signal is obstructed by walls and floors, a PLC signal is degraded by (a) noise generated by electrical apparatuses sharing the cables and (b) electrical components, e.g. transformers, that sit between end points. At the MAC layer, although both PLC and WiFi standards (IEEE 1901 and 802.11) use CSMA/CA to avoid collisions when multiple stations share the same channel, IEEE 1901 uses deferral counters to prevent collisions from happening so that congestion windows of the stations do not grow rapidly.

PLC-based WiFi Extenders: PLC extenders on the market couple PLC's AV2 and WiFi's 802.11 to take advantage of existing power lines and enhance WiFi performance and coverage to end users. Recent products typically support HomePlug AV2 and 802.11ac (which operates in the 5 GHz band). However, according to a recent survey [3], 2.4 GHz WiFi access points are still dominant in homes and offices. As a result, in this paper, we focus on networks using 2.4 GHz 802.11n for front-end access and AV2 as a backhaul.

Related work: To the best of our knowledge, we are the first to do an in-depth measurement study on the use of PLC extenders towards improving WiFi coverage or performance. Below, we briefly summarize related work.

Hybrid networks: In [6,9], the authors consider a network where clients have two interfaces viz., a PLC interface and a WiFi interface. They propose metrics for comparing the performance on the two interfaces and consider methods to use them jointly as parallel links. They do not perform measurements on commercial PLC extenders, which concatenate PLC and WiFi links, as we do.

PLC vs WiFi: There has been work to compare the WiFi MAC and the IEEE 1901 MAC that is used with PLC [7]. However, this does not yield any insights on why PLC extenders may be useful (or not) in enhancing WiFi throughputs.

PLC studies: There are also a number of studies on PLC. For example, [2,5] provide insights on current PLC standards (AV2). However, they do not consider the use of PLC in building extenders to improve WiFi coverage or throughput. There have also been efforts to enhance PLC performance either by tuning MAC parameters [8] or by using an application level learning based framework [1]. However, again these efforts do not consider interactions between PLC and WiFi.

3 The Influence of Power Line Configurations

Measurement Setup: Our equipment consists of a commercial WiFi router (Netgear Nighthawk AC1900), six commercial PLC extenders (TP-Link TL-WPA8630), and four clients (Lenovo Ideapad 300S). We perform measurements

Table 1. Properties of the four testbeds

Name	Description	Area (m^2)	Walls	Floors	Client locations	PLC extenders
ENT1	Multi-room office	350	14	1	87 (hallways)	6
ENT2	Single-room lab	213	0	1	20 (room)	4
HNW1	Two-story house	245	10	2	8 (bedrooms)	3
HNW2	One-story apartment	170	6	1	6 (bedrooms)	4

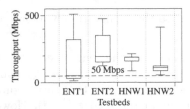 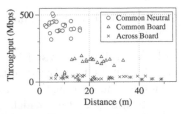

(a) Throughput Ranges of the Four Testbeds

(b) Impact of Power Distribution on PLC Throughput (ENT1)

Fig. 1. PLC-only throughputs in typical home and work environments.

in four environments: a 10-room office space (ENT1), a large single-room laboratory (ENT2), a two-story home (HNW1), and a one-story apartment (HNW2); further details are omitted due to space limitations. Clients are placed roughly uniformly in each environment, and by default choose a WiFi access point with the highest RSSI. Further details of the measurement environments are provided in Table 1. We perform 10-minute `iperf3` tests between the PLC extenders or clients, and the master router, to measure the total achievable (saturation) TCP throughputs between each pair. We also experiment with web browsing and video streaming applications to showcase application performance. On all four testbeds, we measure the pairwise throughput between unoccupied power outlets.

We classify connections based on the achieved throughput into two classes viz., good and bad PLC connections (Table 2). Since the maximum throughputs achievable over WiFi to nearby extenders is 50 Mbps, we set this as the threshold to delineate good and bad PLC connections.

Table 2. Network conditions

PLC condition	Throughput (Mbps)
Good	≥ 50
Bad	<50

Results and analysis: Our results are shown in Fig. 1(a). We find that in all but the ENT1 testbed, the achievable saturation throughputs are higher than the threshold. We then look at the power circuit diagrams of ENT1 to determine when the saturation throughputs are lower than the threshold. We find that if two power outlets connect to circuits that use a common neutral line, they have very high throughput (around 400 Mbps). If two power outlets connect to the circuits that belong to the same distribution board but different neutral lines, the throughput between them drops to less than 200 Mbps. Most importantly, if two power outlets connect to circuits that belong to different distribution boards, the throughput becomes lower than 50 Mbps, causing the PLC connection to become a bottleneck. The reason for the above is that in order to go between the distribution boards, the connection has to traverse an electrical transformer which attenuates a range of frequencies also used by PLC [10].

Our studies reveal that (Fig. 1(b)) *even if* the distance between two power outlets is relatively small (they are in close proximity), it is still possible that the PLC throughput between them is very low. However, the larger the distance between two power outlets, the more likely it is that they can only sustain a lower PLC throughput between them. Note here that these effects are not seen in the other three testbeds since they use a single distribution board.

4   Single-User Studies

In this section, we investigate whether PLC extenders can improve throughput compared to a WiFi-only scenario, when there is only a single client. We evaluate throughput gains in typical home and enterprise environments, including the impact of distance between routers, extenders, and clients, density of extenders, and attenuation from walls and floors. Our main finding is that PLC can improve average throughput, particularly when there are multiple walls, but careful placement/activation of the extenders is necessary to achieve these gains.

4.1   Throughputs with PLC Extenders

We first examine the improvements in client throughputs in each of our four test environments (Table 1). We measure the end-to-end throughput between the router and the client, when (a) the client associates with the default PLC extender or (b) directly with the master router. We find that the improvements due to PLC extenders depend on the environment, with higher gains in multi-room and multi-story environments (and lesser gains in single large rooms).

When and to what extent do PLC extenders help? The percentage of client locations where the PLC+WiFi throughput exceeds the WiFi-only throughput are plotted in Fig. 2(a). The results suggest that in office, home, and apartment environments, PLC extenders help in the majority of client locations, but not in the laboratory environment. To showcase the gains in these environments, we plot the ratio of the PLC+WiFi (connection via a PLC extender) to WiFi-only (connection to the master router) throughput in Fig. 2(b). In ENT1, which is large and contains many walls obstructing the WiFi signal from the main router, the PLC extenders can potentially provide very high throughput gains of up to 30x. In contrast, in ENT2 where there are no walls, the

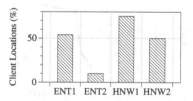 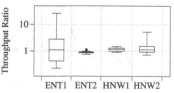

(a) % of Client Locations Where PLC+WiFi > WiFi-only

(b) Ratio of PLC+WiFi to WiFi-only throughput

Fig. 2. Throughput gains from PLC extenders over WiFi-only.

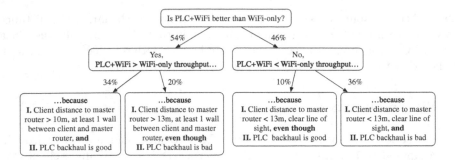

Fig. 3. Reasons why PLC extenders help (or not) compared to WiFi-only (ENT1).

throughput gains are negligible, since the WiFi signal from the master router is strong. The HNW1 and HNW2 environments contain a mix of walls and floors, and can thus benefit from PLC extenders, but not to the extent as in the ENT1 case. Interestingly, we note that in HNW1, despite the master router and PLC extenders being spread over two floors, the throughput gains are minor. This is because the master router WiFi signal can easily penetrate a single floor, suggesting that PLC extenders may be more beneficial in the multiple-wall rather than multiple-floor scenarios.

Reasons for throughput gains from PLC extenders. To delve further into the office environment (ENT1) where PLC can be most helpful, we analyze the reasons for the throughput gains. Specifically we ask the following questions. Can PLC extenders help even when the PLC backhaul quality is poor? Are there cases where good PLC backhaul is not helpful, because the WiFi-only throughput is very high?

For each client location, in addition to the end-to-end throughput, we measure the throughput of the PLC backhaul, and classify it as good or bad according to Table 2. Figure 3 summarizes our results. In 34% of cases, we have the expected scenario where throughput gain results from a poor (direct) master WiFi and a good PLC backhaul connection. However, in 20% of cases, even a poor-quality PLC backhaul connection can help if the WiFi link to the master

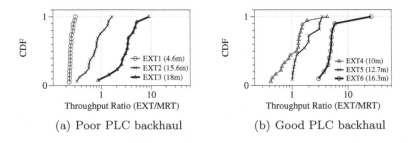

Fig. 4. Impact of PLC extender backhaul and router distance on throughput gain.

router is poor (due to at least one obstructing wall). We also see the opposite scenario where in 10% of locations, a good-quality PLC backhaul link does not help because the WiFi link to the master router is still very good (due to the clear line of sight).

4.2 Impact of Distance

In reality, users who purchase off-the-shelf PLC devices may not have access to electrical diagrams and thus may be unable to infer which PLC connections are good or bad as we did in Sect. 3. Therefore, we next examine benefits from PLC extenders given easy-to-estimate quantities such as physical distance. We conduct an in-depth study in the office environment (ENT1). Our main findings are that (1) throughput gains improve with distance between the router and the extender, especially when the extender has a good PLC connection to the router, (2) the location of the extender must be chosen based on both the PLC backhaul throughput and the PLC extender's WiFi throughput, in order to ensure that neither hop becomes the bottleneck for end-to-end throughput.

Throughput changes with distance from the master router: We first examine the impact of distance of the PLC extender from the master router. If the extender is close to the router, we expect the throughput gains for the client to be minimal, because the master router's WiFi signal will be already strong. However, as the distance between the extender and the router increases, the master router's WiFi quality will degrade, and the PLC extenders should help, especially when the PLC backhaul is good. In Fig. 4, we plot the CDF of throughput gains of each client when they associate with their default extender (highest received signal strength or RSS) in lieu of the master router. Figure 4(a) indicates that even a poor-quality PLC backhaul yields throughput gains if (and only if) the extender is quite far (18 m or further) from the router. When the PLC backhaul is good however, we see a throughput gain when the extender is as close as 12.7 m away from the router (Fig. 4(b)).

Since the default association of the client is to a nearby extender, we expect that the impact of distance on throughput gains enjoyed by clients to be similar to that in our aforementioned study with just the extenders. In Fig. 5(a), we

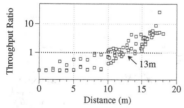

(a) Client Distance from Router vs.   (b) Client Distance from Extender
Throughput Ratios (EXT/MRT)

Fig. 5. Impact of distance from the master router on throughput.

plot the relationship between client distance from the master router and the throughput gain. We observe that the client begins to see a throughput gain at distances that are greater than ~13 m, across all extenders (with good or bad PLC backhaul connections).

Impact of distance between a client and its extender: In this set of experiments, we seek to answer the question: Given a client that is located very far from the master router, where should the extender be placed to maximize throughput? Placing the extender close to the client will result in good WiFi signal quality but may result in a poor PLC backhaul quality, especially if the outlet is on a different distribution board than the master router. On the other hand, placing the extender close to the router to ensure good PLC backhaul quality may result in a poor quality WiFi link between the client and the extender (low signal strength). We place a client 35 m from the master router and examine cases where it associates with three possible power outlets. We plot the PLC backhaul throughput, the extender WiFi throughput, and the end-to-end throughput in Fig. 5(b). The closest power outlet to the client (PO-3) is suboptimal because a poor PLC backhaul bottlenecks the end-to-end throughput. On the other hand, the power outlet (PO-1) with the best PLC backhaul quality is also suboptimal, because it has a poor WiFi connection to the client. The extender that maximizes end-to-end throughput is PO-2, which has both good (but not best) PLC backhaul and extender WiFi throughputs. In summary, the PLC extender must be carefully placed between the client and router to balance PLC and WiFi throughput bottlenecks. Since it may be difficult for a casual user to measure and optimize extender placement, a reasonable approach may be to provide simple guidelines for extender placement, and focus on the appropriate client association strategy. A simple strategy might be to consider the end-to-end throughput as a metric for association instead of the WiFi signal strength.

4.3   Can More Extenders Help?

Next we ask: Are more extenders always helpful, or is there decreasing marginal utility? To measure this, we activate each of the six extenders one-by-one in decreasing order of throughput gain. For each client location, the client associates with either the master router or the activated PLC extenders based on the default

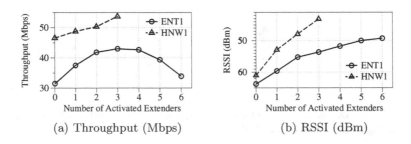

(a) Throughput (Mbps)   (b) RSSI (dBm)

Fig. 6. Single client: Impact of number of PLC extenders on throughput.

association policy (highest RSSI). We plot the average throughput across all client locations versus the number of activated PLC extenders in Fig. 6(a). In the house environment (HNW1), as expected, increasing the number of extenders improves the client throughput, due to better spatial coverage of WiFi signal throughout the home. However, in the office environment of ENT1, adding too many extenders actually decreases average throughput. This is because some outlets in the office environment have poor PLC backhaul quality. Clients see higher RSSI values (Fig. 6(b)) and associate with the new extenders, but since the last three extenders have poor PLC backhaul, the clients inadvertently associate with an extender with poor end-to-end throughput. Therefore, before adding PLC extenders, it is important to consider both the PLC backhaul quality and the WiFi signal strength in the deployment environment; otherwise, poor PLC connectivity may result in reduced network throughput.

5   Multi-user Studies

Building on our studies in Sect. 4, we next examine if the benefits of using PLC extenders carry over when there are multiple clients or users present. Our main findings are: (1) to relieve PLC backhaul contention and improve throughput for clients far from the master router, some clients close to the master router should connect directly to it, possibly at the expense of their own throughputs; and (2) in an office setting (ENT1), adding new PLC extenders may decrease average client throughput because the extenders choose the same WiFi frequency to avoid contention with existing WiFi APs.

5.1   Sharing PLC Backhaul

In the single-user scenario, we found that in 54% of locations in the office environment (ENT1), a client can benefit by connecting to a PLC extender. However, in the multi-user scenario, the client's benefit from connecting to a PLC extender may be reduced due to increased PLC backhaul contention. Should clients close to the master router connect to it, relieving contention on the PLC backhaul for the remaining clients on PLC? If this causes a reduction in the switching client's throughput, does the resulting gain of the other clients provide a net benefit?

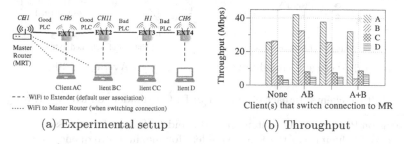

(a) Experimental setup   (b) Throughput

Fig. 7. Clients switch connection to master router.

To investigate this, we consider four clients in the office environment (ENT1) which can potentially associate with four PLC extenders, as shown in Fig. 7(a).[1] In the single-user case, a client far away from the master router (client D) received 12 Mbps when connecting to a PLC extender, but in the multi-user case when three other clients also connect via PLC extenders (clients A, B, C), its throughput drops to 2.98 Mbps. What if the client closest to the master router (client A) switches? If that case, we see that all clients increase their throughputs, as shown in Fig. 7(b). However, if a client slightly further away from the master router switches (client B), it slightly sacrifices its own throughput to benefit the other clients.

If switching one client helps, does switching both clients help? We find that switching both clients (A, B) to the master router lowers total throughput due to increased contention on the master router's WiFi. This suggests that when multiple clients are present, a few clients close to the master router should connect to it in order to reduce PLC backhaul contention and improve throughput for distant users; however, switching too many clients[2] causes contention between the master router's clients and lowers total throughput. We envision that an iterative approach where clients closest to the master router are sequentially switched could help effectively identify the optimal set that should be switched.

5.2 Can More Extenders Help?

In the single-user case, increasing the number of PLC extenders sometimes resulted in suboptimal throughput, due to clients associating with extenders with poor PLC backhaul. We investigate whether this holds in the multi-user case, and what additional complexities arise from inter-client interference. We expect that the benefits of additional extenders depends on the spatial configuration of the clients, and so we setup clients in two configurations: *distributed*, where a client is placed at each of the four corners of the office (ENT1), and *clustered*, where all the four clients are situated in the middle of the office area. We activate each of the six extenders one-by-one in decreasing order of average RSSI.

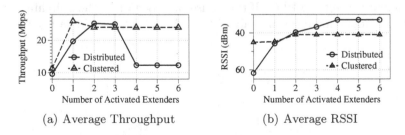

(a) Average Throughput   (b) Average RSSI

Fig. 8. Multiple clients: Impact of number of PLC extenders on average throughput.

---

[1] To focus on PLC backhaul contention and avoid WiFi interference issues, we configure the WiFi channels of the PLC extenders for maximum frequency reuse.

[2] In our testbed, one switching client is optimal.

In Fig. 8(a), we plot the average client throughput versus the number of PLC extenders. Initially, we see that the first 1–2 extenders increases average throughput, because clients experience higher RSSI (Fig. 8(b)) and the PLC backhaul is good. However, in *distributed* configurations, further adding PLC extenders can result in decreased average throughput (e.g., from 25 Mbps to 12 Mbps when a fourth extender is added). This is because in addition to poor user association policies discussed previously, the additional extenders choose the same WiFi frequency band to avoid interfering with existing office WiFi networks, causing inter-client interference.[3] In the *clustered* configuration, adding more PLC extenders is unhelpful because clients associate with the first 1–2 extenders with higher RSSI and ignore later extenders.

In conclusion, although more PLC extenders results in higher client RSSI, it does not necessarily lead to higher throughput. Two main factors directly impact the performance of PLC+WiFi: frequency reuse and user association. PLC extenders may not be helpful in environments with multiple existing WiFi networks, as the PLC extenders try to avoid interfering with external APs, choosing the same frequency band and decreasing the throughput of their own clients. For client association, as in the single-user case, clients may need to consider the quality of the PLC extender's backhaul connection when deciding which extender to associate with.

6   Applications

In the previous sections, we studied saturation throughput of PLC+WiFi networks. In this section, we wish to understand how PLC extenders impact application performance. To do this, we conduct experiments with two popular applications viz., video streaming and web browsing (hosted on local machines).

Video Streaming: Dynamic adaptive streaming over HTTP (DASH) is one of the most common video streaming protocols in use today. However, previous studies have shown that multiple clients sharing a bottleneck link unfairly choose

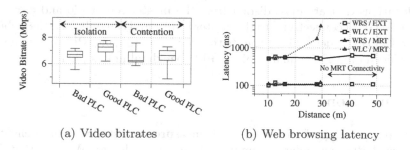

(a) Video bitrates   (b) Web browsing latency

Fig. 9. Video and web browsing performance

---

[3] For example, in our setup, existing WiFi networks use channel 1 and 6, so all PLC extenders choose channel 11.

video bitrates that allow some clients to monopolize the link, and also experience a high degree of instability [4]. In our study, we find that not only does this issue manifest over PLC links, but in addition the magnitude of the video bitrate and frequency of bitrate switches depends on the quality of the PLC backhaul.

In our setup, we stream an 8-minute 1080p DASH video[4] encoded at four different bitrates (1.6, 2.4 4.8, 8 Mbps) to two clients[5]. To see the impact of the PLC backhaul, one client is associated with a good PLC extender, and the other with a bad PLC extender. The video bitrates are plotted in Fig. 9(a) across ten trials. In the multi-user case, both clients are negatively impacted by PLC contention, decreasing the average video bitrate and increasing the average number of switches compared to the single-user case. Moreover, both metrics have higher variance. In particular, the good-PLC client suffers a higher variance despite enjoying a higher video bitrate on average, than the bad-PLC client. This is because it occasionally suffers from very low bitrates due to contention on the PLC backhaul. Similarly, the good-PLC client enjoys a fewer number of bitrate switches on average but occasionally sees a large number of bitrate switches (not shown due to space limitations).

Web Browsing: How does good and bad PLC impact page load time? In contrast to video streaming applications, which suffer from reduced video bitrates when the PLC backhaul is poor, we find that web-browsing clients can still enjoy low page load times even when they are located far from the master router.

To show this, we load the Top 100 Alexa websites on a client and record two metrics: (a) web response start (WRS), the latency between when the browser requests the page and when it receives the first web object, (b) web load complete (WLC), the latency between when the browser requests the page and when it receives the last web object. We evaluate this in the office environment (ENT1), and place the client close to each extender to focus on impact due to PLC backhaul quality. In Fig. 9(b), we plot the WRS and WLC as a function of the client's distance from the master router. If the client connects to the PLC extenders we can see that no matter the client's distance from the master router, the WRS and WLC are nearly constant. However, if the client connects to the master router, it experiences relatively high WLC after 29 m. Notably, at the two user locations that are most distant from the master router (40 and 48 m), the client loses WiFi connectivity to the master router and can only load the webpage via the PLC extenders. This suggests that for web browsing, PLC extenders can be beneficial even if the quality of the PLC backhaul link is poor.

7   Conclusions

In this paper, we perform an in-depth measurement study of the benefits of commercial PLC extenders to improve WiFi throughputs. We find that PLC extenders can be most beneficial in multi-room environments (e.g., office spaces),

---

[4] https://peach.blender.org/.
[5] http://dashif.org/reference/players/javascript/.

but can also suffer from degraded throughput due to more complex power line configurations resulting in poor-quality PLC backhaul. Our results suggest that more sophisticated client association policies (instead of highest RSSI by default) and frequency planning around existing WiFi APs, taking into account the quality of the PLC backhaul, could potentially help realize maximum benefits from PLC+WiFi. We intend to investigate these avenues as future work.

Acknowledgments. This work was partially supported by the NSF NeTS grant 1528095.

References

1. Atya, A.O.F., Sundaresan, K., Krishnamurthy, S.V., Khojastepour, M.A., Rangarajan, S.: Bolt: realizing high throughput power line communication networks. In: ACM CoNEXT (2015)
2. Cano, C., Pittolo, A., Malone, D., Lampe, L., Tonello, A.M., Dabak, A.G.: State of the art in power line communications: from the applications to the medium. IEEE JSAC **34**(7), 1935–1952 (2016)
3. Fukuda, K., Asai, H., Nagami, K.: Tracking the evolution and diversity in network usage of smartphones. In: ACM IMC (2015)
4. Jiang, J., Sekar, V., Zhang, H.: Improving fairness, efficiency, and stability in HTTP-based adaptive video streaming. In: ACM CoNEXT (2012)
5. Yonge, L., Abad, J., Afkhamie, K., et al.: An overview of the homeplug AV2 technology. J. Electr. Comput. Eng. **2013**(Article ID 892628), 20 (2013). doi:10.1155/2013/892628
6. Lin, Y.J., Latchman, H.A., Newman, R.E., Katar, S.: A comparative performance study of wireless and power line networks. IEEE Commun. Mag. **41**(4), 54–63 (2003)
7. Vlachou, C., Herzen, J., Thiran, P.: Fairness of MAC protocols: IEEE 1901 vs. 802.11. In: IEEE International Symposium on Power Line Communications and Its Applications (2013)
8. Vlachou, C., Banchs, A., Herzen, J., Thiran, P.: Analyzing and boosting the performance of power-line communication networks. In: ACM CoNEXT (2014)
9. Vlachou, C., Henri, S., Thiran, P.: Electri-fi your data: measuring and combining power-line communications with WiFi. In: ACM IMC (2015)
10. Yenamandra, V., Srinivasan, K.: Vidyut: exploiting power line infrastructure for enterprise wireless networks. ACM SIGCOMM **44**(4), 595–606 (2014)

Cutting Internet Access Costs Through HTTPS Caching: A Measurement Study

Prerna Gupta, Mohammedsalman Patel, and Kameswari Chebrolu[✉]

Department of Computer Science and Engineering, IIT Bombay, Mumbai, India
chebrolu@cse.iitb.ac.in

Abstract. In this paper, we look at web caching as a means to cut Internet access costs. We specifically look at caching of HTTPS traffic which has thus far not received much attention. We first look at client side caching on smartphones in mobile web scenarios to evaluate the potential for bandwidth savings. Our analysis based on user logs reveals that app traffic dominates browser traffic at 82.7% and HTTPS traffic dominates HTTP traffic at 82.3%. There is around 15% redundancy in this traffic, however much of this redundancy does not lend itself to practical savings since app logic or server cache configurations cannot be controlled.

Given the negative result of above approach, we shifted our attention to infrastructure side caching (wired) in an organizational setting. Analysis of our logs indicate that HTTPS accounts for 91.6% of all considered traffic and YouTube accounts for 82% of this HTTPS traffic. We found that there is some amount of redundancy in this traffic and hence potential for bandwidth savings. However proxying HTTPS traffic is challenging given that the proxy has to act as a man in the middle of a secure transaction. To circumvent this problem, we propose a new architecture that serves only insensitive HTTPS traffic from the proxy. We validate the feasibility of this approach via an implementation. A trace driven simulation shows that one can realize bandwidth savings of between 13–17% with our architecture.

1   Introduction

Web browsing is a popular activity and web caching both at client and infrastructure side is often employed to eliminate redundant transfers. This helps not only to improve user experience but can also cut Internet access costs. HTTP is the protocol behind web browsing but with increasing concern over security and privacy, there has been a drastic rise in the use of HTTPS, a secure version of HTTP that runs on top of TLS/SSL. All of the prior work we are aware of has focused exclusively on HTTP based caching. In this paper, we delve into HTTPS traffic with an aim to understand the scope for caching and the resulting bandwidth savings one can achieve.

© Springer International Publishing AG 2017
M.A. Kaafar et al. (Eds.): PAM 2017, LNCS 10176, pp. 270–282, 2017.
DOI: 10.1007/978-3-319-54328-4_20

We first look at client side caching on smartphones to cut down Internet access costs. Compared to network/infrastructure side caching, client-side caching alone can eliminate redundancy over the last mile (cellular link). To aid this analysis, we collected HTTP as well as HTTPS logs over 25 days across 27 smartphone users. We analyzed the logs to (A) quantify the extent of HTTPS traffic; (B) validate if scope for HTTPS caching is similar to HTTP caching as carried out in various other studies, notably [2] and (C) quantify how effective current solutions are in realizing savings in practice.

Our logs revealed that smartphone apps account for 82.7% of overall traffic while the rest is due to the browser. HTTPS traffic is significant and accounts for 82.3% of overall traffic. Within HTTPS, there is only 13.9% redundancy, while in HTTP, there is 23.2% redundancy. Our analysis also showed that 15.8% of browser and 15.4% of app traffic is redundant. These percentages are basically an upper bound and may not be realizable in practice since we have no control over app cache logic or server-side cache configurations. The overall savings that we could practically realize is a meagre 2.4%. So, client-side mobile web caching is not very promising.

Given the not so encouraging results with client-side caching in mobile web scenarios, we shifted our attention to infrastructure side caching (via a proxy) in an organization. To analyze the potential for bandwidth savings, we collected browser based user-logs across 29 laptop/desktop users for 75 days. Even here, HTTPS dominates and accounts for 91.6% of all considered traffic with YouTube accounting for 82% of this HTTPS traffic. A preliminary analysis revealed that there is good scope for caching at the proxy since we can leverage redundancy across users. However realizing the same is difficult since to cache, the proxy has to act as a man-in-the-middle of a secure transaction. Further YouTube traffic does not lend itself to URL based caching after its migration to adaptive streaming. We found that many parameters vary from URL to URL and there is no easy way to determine if they refer to the same video.

To solve this problem, we propose a new architecture, where a browser separates out URLs corresponding to insensitive HTTPS traffic (e.g. public YouTube videos where the same video is served irrespective of user login credentials) from sensitive traffic such as bank transactions. The browser then relies on the proxy to serve insensitive content. To show the feasibility of this approach, we used the dominant YouTube traffic as a case study. We implemented the concept by building a Chrome browser extension and modifying Squid proxy since the default URL based caching does not work for YouTube. We tested this implementation and observed that the YouTube player accepted our cached responses across a variety of videos. To quantify the bandwidth savings that can be realized in practice, we also ran trace based simulations. We found that 13.4% of YouTube traffic can be served from cache. This can be extended upto 22% if we can prevent videos repeating with different resolutions. In terms of overall savings across all traffic (both HTTP and HTTPS) upto 17% savings is feasible.

Our solution shows some promise but our data set is small. One has to evaluate whether these savings translate to an organizational level. Further, whether the savings are worth the implementation hassles of client side browser changes which are not user friendly and easy to implement. The rest of the paper is organized as follows. Section 2 covers related work. Section 3 describes measurements related to client side caching on smartphones while Sect. 4 covers infrastructure side caching in an organization. We conclude the paper in Sect. 5.

2   Related Work

There are two solutions commonly employed when caching: client-side and infrastructure-side. We cover related work specific to the two.

In the recent past, client side solutions [3–5] have predominantly focused on improving latency in mobile web scenarios and have exclusively focused on HTTP traffic. In contrast, our goal is cutting Internet access costs and our analysis extends to both HTTP and HTTPS traffic. In [3], user's instant browsing experience is improved by prefetching dynamic web content using a machine learning model. Such solutions can cut down on delay but can increase Internet access costs which goes against our main focus. In [4] three client-only solutions to improve mobile browser speed were evaluated: caching, speculative loading and prefetching. They concluded that caching and prefetching are ineffective while speculative loading shows promise. They attribute reason for ineffectiveness of caching to expired timers and large percentage of revalidations increasing RTT. Our focus is again not on delay. The authors in [2] carried out an extensive study of smartphone traffic and found that 17–20% of smartphone traffic is redundant due to imperfect web caching implementation of HTTP libraries and developers not utilizing the library caching support. Our client-side caching analysis is a revalidation of this work but extended to HTTPS traffic. Flaws in imperfect web caching are also cited in [5], further, to solve the problem they propose a novel system wide caching architecture that can cache content across apps. However this does not work with HTTPS traffic since apps have to reveal employed security keys to cache.

In the wired domain, use of infrastructure-side web caching to reduce bandwidth costs and improve user experience is a well known technique. However, with the dominance of HTTPS traffic, caching is often disabled in many organization settings to avoid the proxy acting as a man-in-the-middle. In [6], authors propose outsourcing middlebox functionality to a trusted cloud, but these allow decryption of traffic at the middlebox and raise security concerns. There is also effort in the security domain [7] involving homomorphic and other encryption schemes to support middlebox functionality over encrypted traffic. These are still at an early stage of research and do not currently support all web caching primitives, neither are they compatible with current HTTPS standard.

As part of our analysis, we also analysed YouTube architecture. Prior work [8–10] have looked at efficiency of caching YouTube content at campus networks and ISPs. However, all of these approaches are applicable to a previous version of YouTube that employed HTTP based progressive download. Our study in contrast focuses on the latest version of YouTube which employs HTTPS based adaptive streaming.

3   Client-Side Web Caching on Smartphones

Modern web is witnessing a shift from HTTP to HTTPS traffic due to most web-sites adopting SSL/TLS encryption in order to provide privacy and security. In this section, we evaluate the efficacy of client side solutions to web caching. Specifically we provide answers to these three questions: (A) The extent of HTTPS traffic in current smartphone traffic; (B) Validate if scope for HTTPS caching is similar to HTTP caching as carried out in various other studies, notably in [2]; (C) Quantify how effective current solutions are in realizing bandwidth savings.

3.1   Data Collection and Properties

Our dataset consists of HTTP(S)records collected across 27 smartphone users for a period of 25 days amounting to 9.6 GB of data. All the users are students from the same department at IIT Bombay and used local WiFi to access Internet. Since we are interested in HTTPS traffic specifically, we used Charles web proxy [1] as a man-in-the-middle to record all transactions between users and servers. To handle user security concerns, we also logged only HTTP(S) headers with the payload hashed. In the user's smartphone, we configured the proxy settings to redirect all network traffic to our proxy running Charles. In the process, we had to install Charles root certificate in each user's phone. Since one of our requirements is to segregate smartphone app traffic from browser traffic, we modified firefox browser's 'User-Agent' string in each user's phone so that we can easily segregate the traffic. Given the ethical considerations involved, we recruited only volunteers and took an informed consent from them all after explaining and demonstrating the entire process.

The collected dataset can be viewed as a series of HTTP(S) records (request/response pair) of all users. From this data set, we rejected records corresponding to POST (34% of the total records but only 3.1% in bytes) since they cannot be cached. The remaining data is divided into 2 categories based on user-agent string: (1) Browser and (2) App traffic. The browser traffic accounted for 17.3(34)% of bytes (records) on average per user, while app traffic accounted for 82.7(66)% of bytes (records) on average per user. We further categorized the records into 6 categories to know the potential for caching in the dataset. 'Normally Cacheable' refers to records with valid expiration time and cache-control headers; 'Non Storable' refers to records with cache directive set to no-store; 'No Cache' refers to records with cache directive set to no-cache or max-age-value set to 0 or expiration time set to some old time (these can be cached but require revalidation); 'Heuristically Cacheable' refer to records with no cache control directive (in this case browsers typically assign heuristic expiration times); 'Always Expired' is similar to 'No Cache' but with no Last-Modified and ETag fields (we cannot revalidate these requests i.e. use conditional GET) and 'Others' corresponds to records with status code such as 204, 304, 404 etc. Table 1 shows the properties of the data (ignore columns starting with Repeat).

Table 1. Percentage is relative to total data in that category post cleanup.

Tags	Browser			App			
	[Records, Bytes]	Repeat: Same-URL	Repeat: Diff-URL	[Records, Bytes]	Repeat: Same-URL	Repeat: Diff-URL	Support Cache
Normally Cacheable	[37.1%, 75%]	8.60%	2.2%	[24%, 56%]	5.80%	4.00%	Yes
Non-Storable	[15.6%, 3%]	0.20%	0.07%	[11%, 2%]	0.00%	0.14%	No
No-Cache	[7.1%, 7%]	0.48%	0.08%	[13%, 19%]	1.02%	0.50%	Yes
Heuristically Cacheable	[9.2%, 13%]	3.78%	0.18%	[20%, 14%]	2.89%	0.07%	Yes
Always Expired	[9%, 2%]	0.20%	0.01%	[10%, 9%]	0.62%	0.33%	No
Others	[22%, ~0%]	0.00%	0%	[22%, ~0%]	0.00%	0.00%	No

Out of the above six categories, 'Non-Storable', 'Always Expired' and 'Others' do not lead to any caching benefit. The percentage of traffic in bytes that can leverage caching is large; 95% and 89% for browser and app categories respectively. The percentage of No-Cache is higher in case of app traffic. This shows that the application developers likely want requests to hit their server. The percentage of 'Heuristically-Cacheable' content is also not very small. This means that the mobile content developers are negligent towards caching.

3.2 Dataset Analysis

We now answer the 3 questions we set out to answer. The first being, what is the extent of HTTPS traffic in current smartphone traffic?

Our analysis reveals that HTTPS traffic does indeed dominate accounting for 82.3(61)% of overall bytes (records). Within browser traffic, HTTPS accounts for 79.3(67)% in bytes (records), while within app traffic, HTTPS accounts for 83.0(59)% in bytes (records). While the above results are aggregated across users, this trend prevails at the individual user level in most cases. In [11], the authors showed that the HTTPS traffic has nearly doubled in just 2 years and stood at 50% in 2014, albeit over a dataset captured in a residential ADSL network. Two years hence, our results show a further increase in dominance of HTTPS traffic which stands at around 82% in 2016, albeit over smartphone traffic.

Our second question was on validating if scope for HTTPS caching is similar to HTTP caching? Since caching is client-based, we analyzed the percentage of redundant data in our traces on a **per user** basis. Any downloaded content is redundant if it should have been served from cache of the user but is actually downloaded from Internet. This we check by comparing the hash of the payloads. Note that our definition of redundancy is based on content not URL since the same content can be served from multiple URLs due to use of CDNs.

Table 1 shows the results of this analysis both for 'Repeated-Content-Same-URLs' and 'Repeated-Content-Different-URLs'. The results are averaged across users. Overall 15.8% of the browser and 15.4% of the app traffic in bytes is redundant (summation of all cells corresponding to repeat). The same if analyzed over protocol type, 23.2% of HTTP and 13.9% of HTTPS traffic is redundant. Though HTTPS is merely the addition of transport layer security (TLS), the scope for HTTPS caching is not similar to HTTP based on our dataset.

Redundant transfer could arise in the case of 'Repeated-Content-Different-URLs' due to the URL having changed but in case of 'Repeated-Content-Same-URLs', this could be due to two reasons. One, the validation mechanism (conditional GET) is not being used due to improper implementation of cache libraries on the client handset. Two, content developers are not configuring caching semantics or configuring very strict expiration time. From the table, the categories 'Non-Cacheable' and 'Heuristically-Cacheable' contribute to most of this redundancy. Redundancy due to content repeated with different URLs is lesser than the content repeated with same URL, though this difference is less in case of app traffic. This shows improper implementation of HTTP caching libraries in browsers/apps is the leading cause for redundancy in smartphone traffic.

It is important to note that redundant data transfer specifies the upper bound on the savings we can achieve for a given user. Actual savings will depend on the techniques that can be implemented in practice. We answer this question next.

3.3   Bandwidth Savings

Our original goal was to design a framework which when implemented on the smartphone cuts redundancy and hence Internet access costs or alternatively gets more bytes out of a given data plan. The apps/browser already may be implementing some caching framework, our framework is supposed to handle redundancy missed by them (due to say improper implementation; this redundancy is what is captured in Sect. 3.2). We make the following two assumptions going forward. (1) We ignore revalidation requests in calculating bandwidth savings. No doubt they increase delay but in terms of bytes which is our main focus their contribution is minimal. (2) We assume we have no control over apps or web content when it comes to implementing novel ideas. It is unreasonable to expect app or website developers (whose number is many) to follow caching semantics or other mechanisms to facilitate caching. Note also that the redundancy as captured in Sect. 3.2 is redundancy arising on top of whatever caching framework the apps/browser our framework

We begin our answer by observing that app traffic accounts for a high 82.7% of overall traffic. Further HTTPS traffic also dominates and accounts for 82.3% of overall traffic in bytes. Given the dominance of app traffic and the fact that we have very little control over apps, the only way redundancy can be cut is via system wide caching as proposed in [5]. Unfortunately system wide caching required un-encrypted data and does not work with HTTPS traffic unless the apps share security keys with the cache. So, there is really no easy way to cut redundancy in app traffic. Browser traffic on the other hand can be handled by the design of a new browser that follows caching semantics and which can implement newer techniques. Even with browser traffic, if we could achieve the upper

bound of 15.8% savings as calculated in the previous section, the overall savings
we get is a mere 2.7% since browser traffic accounts to just 17.3% of overall
traffic. Nonetheless, to take this thread to its logical conclusion, we evaluated
the savings that can be achieved by a browser in practice.

Since a browser cannot control server side cache configurations, the best it
can do is (1) implement proper cache validation mechanism (note that this also
handles heuristically cacheable content since, even with improperly set expiration timers, the revalidation will avoid unnecessary download of repeat content)
and (2) employ prefix-based web caching [12] to eliminate redundancy due to
'Repeated-Content-Different-URLs'. In prefix-based web caching, in case of a
cache miss, hash of the N-byte prefix from the downloaded response along with
content length is compared with hashed objects in cache. If there is a match,
downloading stops and the leftover is delivered from the cache instead.

The above two mechanisms basically take care of all the repeated content
resulting from same URL/different URL corresponding to categories "Normally-
Cacheable", "No-cache", "Heuristically-cacheable". This amounts to 14% savings on average per user for browser content (this does not exactly match the
values from the table due to the initial prefix download in case of prefix-based
caching). But since the browser portion is 17.3% of overall considered traffic, the
overall savings realized is a mere 14% * 17.3% = 2.4% in practice.

4   Infrastructure-Side Web Caching

Given the low potential for practical bandwidth savings in the smartphone scenario, we shifted our attention to see if savings are feasible in a proxy-based
organizational settings. In this setting we could leverage redundancy across users
and further browser traffic dominates giving us better control to implement novel
ideas. The challenge in this setting is however the need for the proxy to act as
a man-in-the-middle which is problematic in case of HTTPS traffic since it vio-
lates confidentiality and privacy concerns. Nonetheless we examine the nature
of HTTPS traffic and the scope for bandwidth savings before deciding on a
mechanism that can trade-off savings with security considerations.

We collected web logs (both http and HTTPS) from 29 laptops/desktops
users for a duration of around 2.5 months amounting to 480 GB. Users are
all students from the same department at IIT Bombay whose informed consent was again taken. Unlike the earlier approach, where we collected logs at
Charles proxy, in this case, we instrumented a Chrome extension to intercept
every request/response and log HTTP headers (not payload) to a file in the local
system which in turn is pushed to our logging server via rsync. The reason for
this change of approach was that that desktop version of Chrome did not autho-
rize third party certificates (like Charles) for websites like Facebook, Google,
YouTube etc.

4.1   Dataset Analysis

Before starting the analysis of logs, we cleaned them up to remove all transaction that have no potential for caching at the proxy. This includes removing transactions which can be served from user's client cache, records corresponding to POST/no-store/non-200-ok responses. We also removed entries with no 'Content-Length' field set since we cannot measure bandwidth savings for them. Among the removed content, user's client cache and no-store dominate at 14.7% and 23.5% respectively. Post clean-up, we were left with 288 GB of traffic, which is 60% of total traffic.

Table 2. Dataset properties

	Records (Million)	Bytes (GB)	Repeat-records (Million)	Repeat-bytes (GB)
All	3.1	288	0.8	24
HTTP	0.6	24	0.3	5
HTTPS	2.5	264	0.5	19

Table 2 shows the results of the analysis. Repeated Records/Bytes were calculated based on **URL based** caching at the proxy, which is typical in real life. The percentage of repeated bytes within HTTP is 20.8% (5/24) and for HTTPS this number is 7.2% (19/264). Across all traffic, the overall repeated content is 8.3% since HTTPS traffic dominates (91.6%) here as well and has less repetition. We found this low repeated content in HTTPS in absolute terms as well as in comparison with HTTP a bit surprising. To understand the reasons behind this, we split the HTTPS traffic (Bytes) based on content type as shown in Table 3. Repeated bytes specifies the percentage of bytes that repeated within that content type. Cumulatively audio and video traffic contribute to 85.4% of total HTTPS traffic in bytes, yet the repeated content in the individual categories is negligible. YouTube turns out to be the dominant player here accounting for 96.4% of the HTTPS video and 99.94% of HTTPS audio.

Table 3. HTTPS Byte distribution and redundancy

Content-type	Video	Audio	Images	Other
Distribution	72.1%	13.3%	6.2%	8.4%
Repeated bytes	0.01%	0.03%	16.6%	74.0%

Given the popularity of YouTube, which accounts for 75% of all considered traffic (216 GB/288 GB), we set to understand the cause for low repetition in this traffic. Normally a user accesses YouTube videos via https://www.YouTube.com/watch?v=videoid, where video-id is a unique 11 character string. Based on this, an analysis of the logs showed that 73% of all distinct videos never repeated but 27% videos repeated at-least once, some as many as 25 times. Then why the low percentage of repetition? To understand this it is important to understand how YouTube which a few years back shifted to adaptive streaming loads videos in the browser. These steps listed below have been identified after performing downloads of a variety of videos both with and without Google login.

1. In response to a video request (of the form https://www.YouTube.com/watch?v=videoid), rather than a complete video download, YouTube front-end server responds with the name of the content server to be contacted in order to download the video.
2. The actual video is downloaded from the content server in chunks i.e. as separate requests (which we will refer to as video-playback requests). Note video and audio are downloaded independently and synced locally.
3. The video-playback requests contain very long URLs that apart from specifying the byte range of the chunk, also includes other parameters such as mime-type (audio/video), resolution etc.
4. YouTube dynamically adapts the video resolution based on Internet speed of the user; hence resolution parameter can vary from request to request.
5. Further the video-id which is part of the very first main request is nowhere mentioned as part of the video-playback URLs.

The above operation explains why our analysis based on URL caching yielded poor results. When a user watches the same video the main URL repeats but videoplayback URLs do not[1]. A simple idealized analysis based on the video ids observed in our logs, assuming unlimited cache size and user always watching the video in full at same resolution as 1st video download, revealed that 29.5% of YouTube traffic can potentially be served from the cache. Since YouTube accounts for 75% of all considered traffic, this can give 22.1% bandwidth savings. This is worth further exploration. But a URL based caching is not adequate due to nature of YouTube traffic. We need to device a new mechanism and validate the same via implementation.

4.2   Caching HTTPS Traffic: YouTube as a Case Study

Above analysis of HTTP(S) traffic shows good potential for caching and hence bandwidth savings for an organization. However caching HTTPS traffic and serving it from a proxy raises security as well as privacy concerns. Most organizations by default disable HTTPS caching. This tradeoff between savings and security/privacy is a difficult one to handle. As a first step towards solving this tradeoff, we begin with an observation. As far as confidentiality is concerned, there is considerable traffic like YouTube videos where the same content is served

---

[1] In the smartphone logs, the redundancy in HTTPS was also less than HTTP, but the analysis there was based on content not URL. That was the nature of HTTPS traffic in smartphone logs, which seems to differ from desktop logs.

to different users. There isn't anything secret about such content (we can view it as being open) but HTTPS is likely used to address privacy/integrity. In contrast, URLs of banks or e-commerce sites carry sensitive password or account details and it is important that this information (private) not be exposed at a proxy. If one could devise rules at a browser to separate out such open vs private content and use the proxy to serve open content, we could have it both ways. Integrity is less of a concern in an organizational setting where the proxy can be trusted to not modify content. Privacy i.e. who is accessing which URLs can still be a concern if the proxy directly handles the user's requests. So our solution as explained below works if we make the assumption that an organization is unwilling to compromise on confidentiality but would like to place its bandwidth savings ahead of privacy/integrity concerns. This we believe may work in many organizations since after all the organization is the one paying for user traffic.

In our solution, end users in an organization need to install a browser extension that examines URLs and matches them against a preconfigured list (henceforth referred to as white list). The proxy then redirects these URLs to the proxy which then serves the content from cache if there is a hit. The white list can be generated after suitable analysis of an organization's encrypted HTTPS traffic (IP addresses can be manually mapped to specific URLs). The list should naturally include URLs who are heavy consumers of bandwidth and yet whose content is open and static. Based on our analysis, having just YouTube on this white list may suffice in most settings. This approach however requires users in the organization to install the extension, which many may not without some form of enforcement. For this, the firewall within the organization could be configured to drop packets from users (not proxy) destined to domains corresponding to the preconfigured URLs. While a user can access all websites outside the preconfigured list, she can access the preconfigured list URLs (hopefully a very small set), only if she installs the extension. We emphasize that the solution above is only a first step, a complete and comprehensive security vs bandwidth savings tradeoffs require more detailed study.

As a proof of concept of above proposal, we implemented the idea and use the dominant YouTube traffic as a case study and the only URL in our white list. We built a browser extension for Chrome to process URLs and redirect only YouTube **video** related requests to our HTTPS proxy which is based on Squid. Note user login requests for YouTube are not directed to our proxy since they map to a different URL. We installed the proxy certificate in the browser and used HTTPS as the means of communication between proxy and browser. Since YouTube employs adaptive streaming, URL based caching will not work. To fix this, rather than use a plain URL as a hash key for caching at the proxy, we use a 4 tuple of [video-id, range, mime-type, resolution] which uniquely identifies each video-playback request. Since the video-id information is not part of the playback URL, the browser extension tracks this information across requests and appends relevant video-id to video-playback requests sent to the proxy. Note that caching at the proxy is chunk based not video based. If a user fetches only two chunks and then stops watching the video, another user requesting the same video will get a hit only for the first two chunks. We tested our implementation for a variety of YouTube videos including ones whose HTTP cache timers expired and observed that in all cases YouTube player accepted our cached responses from the proxy.

4.3   Evaluation of Bandwidth Savings

Given the success of our implementation, we ran a trace driven simulation on YouTube traffic extracted from our logs to determine the bandwidth savings that can be achieved in practice. Note that in this analysis we assumed that the video content corresponding to a given video id does not change for the duration of our logs, which is true in practice. Table 4 shows the results of our analysis for varying cache sizes based on Least-Recently-Used caching policy. Even with a small cache size, the savings are close to the infinite cache size.

Table 4. % Bandwidth savings of YouTube traffic

Cache size (GB)	infinite	216	100	50	25
Savings	13.4%	13.4%	12.7%	11.5%	10.2%

The achieved savings which is around 10–13% is much lower than the projected ideal savings of 29.5% as discussed in Sect. 4.1. The reasons for this are mainly due to (1) videos repeating with different resolutions; (2) users not watching the full video and (3) mismatch in downloaded chunk ranges when the video is repeated with same resolution.

Out of total repeated videos, 69% videos repeat in same resolution while 23% in different resolution and remaining 8% repeated in multiple resolutions due to the autoplay feature of YouTube. These $(23 + 8)\%$ cannot contribute to bandwidth savings in our current cache model and responsible for a loss of 9.6% savings from the ideal case. However, in our current logs, the content is accessed directly from YouTube servers over a WAN link. But with a proxy in place, the content will be accessed over a high speed LAN and it is possible that the video resolution may not vary during play-out and across users. Given this, it is possible to boost our bandwidth savings from 13% upto 22.6%.

With respect to the second cause of loss in savings, if a user stops watching the video in the middle, there is not much that can be done. We find that approximately 70% of the videos were downloaded fully while the rest downloaded in varying amounts. This aspect contributes to a loss of 6.1% bandwidth savings from the ideal case. With respect to the third cause, if ranges do not overlap for the same resolution video, then according to our model it will be a miss and the chunk has to be downloaded from the YouTube server. We found that when we download the same video multiple times, most of the time the range URLs coincide. In our logs, range mismatch is mainly due to user jumping forward and backward within video. This was found to be a very small percentage and not a major factor for loss of bandwidth savings.

To put the overall savings in perspective, the total HTTP(S) logs accounted for 480 GB. From this we do need to exclude content that can be served from a user's browser cache, this left us with 408 GB. YouTube traffic accounted for 216 GB (216/408 = 53%). Of this traffic we can potentially save 29 to 47 GB (13.5%–22% of YouTube traffic) depending on how effective we are at preventing videos repeating with different resolutions. This accounts for an overall savings of 7.1–11.5% (29/408 to 47/408) if only YouTube traffic was cached. If one were to include potential savings from the remaining 47% of overall traffic (HTTP as well as non YouTube HTTPS traffic; see last column of Table 2), we can potentially save a total of 53–71 GB provided all of the HTTPS traffic URLs are in the white list. So, in practice the savings will range from 13–17.4% (53/408 to 71/408).

Our design shows promise, however our data set is small. One has to evaluate if these savings translate to a much larger data set at the organization level. In a larger data set, the number of users will increase leading to more redundancy but at the same time number of requests will also increase. One has also to evaluate whether the savings are worth the client side browser changes which are not user friendly and easy to implement (transparent proxies will not work with HTTPS traffic; a certificate has to be installed at the client).

5   Conclusion

With the dominance of HTTPS traffic, we re-evaluated the effectiveness of web caching as a means to cut Internet access costs. An analysis of user collected logs showed that client side caching on smartphones are not very effective in saving bandwidth due to lack of control over app logic and server side cache configurations. The total realized savings is a meagre 2.4%. Infrastructure side proxy based caching in an organization on the other hand show more promise but this needs an altogether different architecture to handle security concerns of HTTPS traffic. Our proposed architecture and its implementation using YouTube as a case study show that HTTPS caching is realizable in practice. The savings realized currently over our data set can go upto 17% and are worthy of further exploration at an organization level.

References

1. Charles Proxy. http://www.charlesproxy.com
2. Qian, F., et al.: Web caching on smartphones: ideal vs. reality. In: MobiSys 2012 (2012)
3. Lymberopoulos, D., et al.: PocketWeb: instant web browsing for mobile devices. In: ASPLOS 2012 (2012)
4. Wang, Z., et al.: How far can client-only solutions go for mobile browser speed? In: WWW 2012 (2012)
5. Zhang, Y., Tan, C., Qun, L.: CacheKeeper: a system-wide web caching service for smartphones. In: UbiComp 2013 (2013)

6. Sherry, J., et al.: Making middleboxes someone else's problem: network processing as a cloud service. In: SIGCOMM 2012 (2012)
7. Lan, C., et al.: Embark: securely outsourcing middleboxes to the cloud. In: NSDI 2016 (2016)
8. Zink, M., et al.: Characteristics of YouTube network traffic at a campus network measurements, models, and implications. Comput. Netw. **53**(4), 501–514 (2009)
9. Guillemin, F., et al.: Experimental analysis of caching efficiency for YouTube traffic in an ISP network. In: Teletraffic Congress (ITC) (2013)
10. Lothar, B., et al.: Analyzing caching benefits for YouTube traffic in edge networks—a measurement-based evaluation. In: NOMS (2012)
11. Naylor, D., et al.: The Cost of the "S" in HTTPS. In: CONEXT 2014 (2014)
12. Woo, S., et al.: Comparison of caching strategies in modern cellular backhaul networks. In: MobiSys 2013 (2013)

Author Index

Printed in the United States
By Bookmasters